THE DEEDS OF
FREDERICK BARBAROSSA

D1245302

RECORDS OF WESTERN CIVILIZATION

RECORDS OF WESTERN CIVILIZATION

The Art of Courtly Love, by Andreas Capellanus.
Translated with an introduction and notes by John Jay Parry.

The Correspondence of Pope Gregory VII: Selected Letters from the Registrum.
Translated with an introduction by Ephraim Emerton.

Medieval Handbooks of Penance: The Principal Libri Poenitentiales and Selections from Related Documents. Translated by John T. McNeill and Helena M. Gamer.

Macrobius: Commentary on The Dream of Scipio.
Translated with an introduction by William Harris Stahl.

Medieval Trade in the Mediterranean World: Illustrative Documents. Translated with introductions and notes by Robert S. Lopez and Irving W. Raymond, with a foreword and bibliography by Olivia Remie Constable.

The Cosmographia *of Bernardus Silvestris.*
Translated with an introduction by Winthrop Wetherbee.

Heresies of the High Middle Ages.
Translated and annotated by Walker L. Wakefield and Austin P. Evans.

The Didascalicon *of Hugh of Saint Victor: A Medieval Guide to the Arts.*
Translated with an introduction by Jerome Taylor.

Martianus Capella and the Seven Liberal Arts.
Vol. I: *The Quadrivium of Martianus Capella: Latin Traditions in the Mathematical Sciences*, by William Harris Stahl with Richard Johnson and E. L. Burge.
Vol. II: *The Marriage of Philology and Mercury*, by Martianus Capella. Translated by William Harris Stahl and Richard Johnson with E. L. Burge.

The See of Peter, by James T. Shotwell and Louise Ropes Loomis.

Two Renaissance Book Hunters: The Letters of Poggius Bracciolini to Nicolaus de Niccolis. Translated and annotated by Phyllis Walter Goodhart Gordan.

Guillaume d'Orange: Four Twelfth-Century Epics.
Translated with an introduction by Joan M. Ferrante.

Columbia University Press
Publishers Since 1893
New York   Chichester, West Sussex

Library of Congress Cataloging-in-Publication Data
Otto I, Bishop of Freising, d. 1158.
[Gesta Friderici I imperatoris. English]
The deeds of Frederick Barbarossa / by Otto of Freising and his
continuator, Rahewin ; translated and annotated with an introduction by
Charles Christopher Mierow ; with the collaboration of Richard Emery.
p.   cm.—(Records of Western civilization)
Includes bibliographical references and index.
ISBN 0–231–13418–5 (cloth : alk. paper)—ISBN 0–231–13419–3 (pbk. : alk. paper)
1. Frederick I, Holy Roman Emperor, ca. 1123–1190.
2. Germany—History—Frederick I, 1152–1190—Sources. I. Rahewin, d. ca. 1177.
II. Mierow, Charles Christopher, b. 1883. III. Title. IV. Series.
DD149.O78413 2004
943′.024′092—dc22
2004045583

Columbia University Press books are printed on permanent and durable acid-free paper.
Printed in the United States of America
c 10 9 8 7 6 5 4 3 2 1
p 10 9 8 7 6 5 4 3 2 1

THE DEEDS OF
FREDERICK BARBAROSSA

BY

OTTO OF FREISING

AND HIS CONTINUATOR, RAHEWIN

TRANSLATED AND ANNOTATED WITH AN INTRODUCTION BY

Charles Christopher Mierow

With the collaboration of Richard Emery

COLUMBIA UNIVERSITY PRESS

NEW YORK

RECORDS OF WESTERN CIVILIZATION is a series published under the auspices of the Interdepartmental Committee on Medieval and Renaissance Studies of the Columbia University Graduate School. The Western Records are, in fact, a new incarnation of a venerable series, the Columbia Records of Civilization, which, for more than half a century, published sources and studies concerning great literary and historical landmarks. Many of the volumes of that series retain value, especially for their translations into English of primary sources, and the Medieval and Renaissance Studies Committee is pleased to cooperate with Columbia University Press in reissuing a selection of those works in paperback editions, especially suited for classroom use, and in limited clothbound editions.

Committee for the Records of Western Civilization

Caroline Walker Bynum

Joan M. Ferrante

Carmela Vircillo Franklin

Robert Hanning

Robert Somerville, editor

In Loving Memory of my Wife,

BERNADINE BEECHER MIEROW,

and our forty-one years
of happy married life

CONTENTS

THE DEEDS OF
FREDERICK BARBAROSSA

INTRODUCTION

Tantillum hoc, quod in Romano orbe per quinquennium fecimus, paucis perstringere curamus.

FREDERICK BARBAROSSA'S
LETTER TO OTTO OF FREISING
END OF FIRST PARAGRAPH

Durum siquidem est scriptoris animum tamquam proprii extorrem examinis ad alienum pendere arbitrium.

OTTO, BOOK II, 41

Sepius autem lectorem admonitum esse cupimus, ut in hoc facto ad disquirendam rerum veritatem non nostra dicta consulat, sed litteris et scriptis, quae ad manus nostras venerunt et huic operi inserendae visae sunt, innitatur, suo servans arbitrio.

RAHEWIN, BOOK IV, 75

INTRODUCTION

ALMOST a century ago Edward Freeman wrote of Frederick Barbarossa: "He has become, as it were, the patriarch of a nation, and his
memory still lives in the German heart as the impersonation of German unity." [1] We are fortunate in possessing a contemporary account
of the reign of this greatest of German medieval rulers, the *Deeds of
Frederick Barbarossa* (*Gesta Friderici I imperatoris*), begun by his
uncle, Bishop Otto of Freising, and continued by the latter's secretary,
Rahewin. It is this work which is here offered to the reader in English
translation.

Prefaced to this biographical account is a letter of Frederick himself,
written at Otto's request. In this, the monarch outlined for the historian's use what seemed to him the principal events of his reign from his
coronation in 1152 to and including the year 1156. The letter is written
in clear and incisive language, and from it the reader may gather a
lively impression of the quality of mind of the prince, who was thirty-
six years of age when he wrote it.

The work before us is divided into four books, the first two of
which were written by Otto. Book I sketches events from the reign of
Henry IV through that of Conrad III, or, roughly, from 1075 to 1152.
In point of time it thus covers approximately the same period as that
treated in the seventh book of his earlier work, the *Two Cities*. In
subject matter, however, it departs quite widely from the previous
work, as it does also in temper and point of view.

The second book expands the material outlined in Frederick's letter
and thus covers a period of approximately five years. These were critical years in German history, and the work furnishes valuable insight
into the efforts put forth by Frederick to establish and consolidate the
Hohenstaufen empire. It is clear from the closing sentence of this
second book that Otto intended to continue the biography. But death,
which came in 1158, cut short his labors. Rahewin took up the task
where Otto had left off, adding two more books and bringing the narra-

---

[1] Edward Freeman, *Historical Essays* (London, 1875), p. 255.

tive to the year 1160. Thus, except for a few jottings referring to the years 1161 to 1169 and published as an appendix to the printed text, the entire work deals with only the first eight years of Frederick's reign. We leave him with thirty years of rule still ahead of him, studded with major events: his final defeat at the hands of the Lombard League and the pope; his more successful contest in Germany with Henry the Lion; the marriage of his son and heir with the heiress of the Norman rulers of southern Italy; and finally the Third Crusade, on which the emperor was drowned in 1190, to mention only a few.

But it is probably true that it was during these early years of his reign that Frederick's star shone most brightly. Succeeding to a disorganized realm, he restored order at home and prestige abroad; imperial control was reestablished in Burgundy, and an imperial party recreated in Italy. Though these years saw failures and half-successes, they were on the whole better years for Frederick than the thirty that followed.

The reader may find it convenient to have before him a brief sketch of the lives of the two authors of our treatise. The first and senior, Otto of Freising, has already been dealt with at some length in the Introduction to the *Two Cities*, published as Volume IX of this series. No attempt will here be made to repeat any but the more salient points in his life and work, with emphasis upon his contribution in writing the first part of the *Deeds*. Otto was a member of one of the great German princely houses, that of Babenberg. His father, Margrave Leopold III of Austria, had been one of the candidates at the royal election of 1125. His mother, Agnes, was the daughter of Emperor Henry IV; her first husband had been Frederick of Hohenstaufen, duke of Swabia. Otto was thus half brother of Conrad III and maternal uncle of Frederick Barbarossa himself. By accident of birth he was well placed to write the emperor's official biography.

As a younger son, Otto was destined for a clerical career. Born probably around 1110, as a young man he studied some years in Paris, whither he journeyed in 1127 or 1128. Of the great teachers of the day, Abelard, Gilbert de la Porrée, and Hugh of St. Victor seem to have influenced him most, but whether or not he actually attended lectures under any one of them is uncertain.[2] It may be presumed that the inter-

---

[2] See Adolf Hofmeister, "Studien über Otto von Freising," *Neues Archiv*, XXXVII (1911-12), 149-61, especially p. 161. In subsequent pages of a second article (*loc. cit.*, pp. 635-54) the author discusses in more detail the influence upon Otto of the three men mentioned above.

est in philosophy so evident in his writings (and especially in Book I of the present work) dates from this period. Otto probably left Paris in 1133, but on his way home, stopping for the night at the abbey of Morimond in Champagne, he took the important step of entering the young Cistercian Order. He seems to have become abbot of this house, but remained there for only a brief period. In 1137, presumably through family influence, he was chosen bishop of Freising, a position he held until his death in 1158.

Otto's reputation as an historian rests largely upon his major work, the *Two Cities*, a chronicle of world history to 1146, in eight books. Written in the tradition of Augustine and Orosius, it depicts history as the working out in time, upon the world as a stage, of the conflict of the eternal principles of good and evil. On the basis of this work he merits the encomiums bestowed upon him as the leading philosophical historian of the twelfth century, if not of the whole medieval period.[3] In the *Deeds of Frederick*, however, that theme is forgotten. The *Two Cities*, he himself wrote, was composed "in bitterness of spirit . . . in the manner of a tragedy," [4] during the dark days preceding Frederick's accession to the throne. It was in an entirely different spirit that he began the *Deeds;* his theme now was peace, and his attitude is reminiscent of the literature of the Augustan age.[5] This theme is only incidental, however, and there is some truth in Fellner's assertion that in the *Two Cities* Otto "almost rose to the highest point in Catholic philosophy of history," but in the *Deeds* "stepped down to the position of mere chronicler." [6] For this reason the latter, of less interest than the former from the historiographical point of view, is more valuable as a source of factual information.

[3] This judgment is so general that it hardly needs references. See, for example, the following, chosen at random: C. H. Haskins, *Renaissance of the Twelfth Century* (Cambridge [Mass.], 1927), p. 238; Hofmeister, *op. cit.*, p. 767; Max Manitius, *Geschichte der lateinischen Literatur des Mittelalters*, III, 384; J. W. Thompson, *History of Historical Writing*, I (New York, 1942), 195-98; and the authorities cited by Henry Simonsfeld, *Jahrbücher des deutschen Reiches unter Friedrich I* (Leipzig, 1908; only first volume published), pp. 652-53.

[4] *The Two Cities* (New York, 1928), Dedication, p. 89.

[5] Below, Prologue. See also I.xxxiv, II.lvi; cf. Manitius, *op. cit.*, III, 381-82.

[6] Felix Fellner, "The 'Two Cities' of Otto of Freising and Its Influence on the Catholic Philosophy of History," *Catholic Historical Review*, XX (1934-35), 172. The statement of Fellner, though substantially true of the work as a whole, needs qualification in view of the long and important philosophical passages included in the first book.

Otto professed high standards as an historian. "It is a grievous matter," he wrote, "that a writer's mind should depend upon another's judgment, as though lacking the power of personal investigation." [7] Again, "the art of the historian has certain things to clear away and to avoid, and others to select and arrange properly; for it avoids lies and selects the truth." [8] He warned his imperial nephew not to take it amiss if he found his predecessors or ancestors discussed in a frank and critical manner. In controversial matters, where authorities were divided, his ideal was objectivity.[9]

Thus we find Otto refusing to take a stand on the contests between Church and State in his day—though whether from objectivity, from the anomalies of his own dual status, or from caution we cannot say. On the thorny question of the temporal position of the Church, Otto wrote: "I admit that I am absolutely ignorant whether the exaltation of His Church which is so clearly visible today pleases God more than its former humiliation pleased him. Indeed, that former state seems to have been better, this present condition more fortunate." [10] Otto's discussion of Gilbert de la Porrée, whose orthodoxy was, to say the least, suspect, showed some caution, but his sympathy for Gilbert seems clear; it is perhaps noteworthy that on his deathbed, according to Rahewin, Otto had some concern about his remarks on Gilbert.[11]

The caution so evident in Otto's approach to controversial issues is, of course, understandable. And if we recall that the *Deeds of Frederick Barbarossa* was written at the emperor's behest, for the emperor himself and in good part on the basis of an outline furnished by him, omissions and suppressions in the treatment of certain problems may be readily understood. For, like many another historian, Otto found it easier to profess than to practice objectivity.[12] In the footnotes attention is called to a few specific examples of distortion in his text, but some general considerations may be noted here. He omitted entirely a whole series of events in the years 1127–35 not very creditable to the house of Hohenstaufen.[13] At the very end of his first book he gave a wholly

---

[7] See below, II.xli.

[8] The *Two Cities*, Dedication, p. 90.

[9] *Ibid.*, p. 91.

[10] *Ibid.* IV. Prologue (p. 274).

[11] Otto's discussion of Gilbert appears below, I.xlviii, lii–lxi *passim;* Rahewin's comment is in IV.xiv.

[12] See the discussion on this point in Simonsfeld, *op. cit.*, pp. 654–55; Giesebrecht's judgment appears in *Geschichte der deutschen Kaiserzeit*, V, Pt. I, 106.

[13] See below, I.xvii–xxi.

erroneous picture of the state of the German lands at the death of Conrad III (a Hohenstaufen prince and uncle of Frederick).[14] Throughout the second book he consistently overplayed Frederick's successes in Italy and omitted or minimized the failures which led to his ultimate defeat in 1176.

Apart from these quite natural limitations, Otto's half of the *Deeds of Frederick Barbarossa* has well been called "an historical document of immense importance." [15] In addition to the valuable narrative of political events, it furnishes us precious details on the careers of Arnold of Brescia,[16] Gilbert de la Porrée,[17] and Abelard [18] in particular, for Otto's interests were by no means bounded by his main purpose of recounting the deeds of Frederick.

When we turn from Otto to his continuator, Rahewin, we find ourselves dealing with a lesser figure in every respect. In place of the great churchman, closely related to the imperial family, a scholar of some attainments, and an excellent Latinist, we have a relatively obscure cleric, of unknown origin, little scholarly pretense, and inferior style. But Rahewin is the author of two of the four books of the *Deeds of Frederick Barbarossa,* which take up somewhat more than half the total work in length, so he cannot be passed over in silence. What little is known of his life can be briefly stated. He is mentioned in various acts from 1144 to 1170, is called a notary, a canon of Freising, chaplain of Bishop Otto, and finally provost of St. Vitus in Freising. He appears to have died before 1177.[19]

Whether sincerely or from false modesty, Rahewin himself, in his prologue to the third book (his first), professed his complete unworthiness to take up Otto's task. We can only agree with him, despite the fact that he appears to have assisted Otto in the work of compiling the first two books and thus to have been fully familiar with the plan of the work and the materials available for its prosecution. That he had ac-

---

[14] Compare his "all matters in Gaul and Germany satisfactorily arranged" (I.lxiii) with the account of the condition of the realm just prior to Conrad's death given by W. Bernhardi, *Konrad III*, Pt. II (Leipzig, 1883), pp. 927–28: "Das Reich liesz er in einem traurigen Zustande. Während seiner nicht kurzen Regierungszeit hatte er es nicht dahin gebracht, auch nur den Landfrieden herzustellen. Von den grössern Unternehmungen, die er versuchte, ist ihm keine einzige gelungen."

[15] Thompson, *op. cit.,* p. 197.   [16] See below, I.xxviii, II.xxviii.
[17] See above, note 11.   [18] See below I.xlix–li.
[19] The few known facts of his life may be gathered from Manitius, *op. cit.,* III, 388–91.

cess to documents in the imperial chancery seems clear from the number of such pieces which he includes in his text.

And yet Rahewin's very inferiority has some advantages. His style, clumsy and inept to be sure, presents fewer problems to the translator than that of Otto. His diffidence—perhaps even his ignorance—and his reluctance to show partiality in the bitter disputes of his day led him to adopt the device of introducing into the body of his text full copies of letters and official acts stating both positions in a controversial matter, while he carefully avoided any stand himself and repeatedly told his readers to judge for themselves.[20] We may indeed wonder whether the inclusion of much anti-imperial propaganda in the form of papal and other letters had any connection with the cessation of this official biography after Otto's account had been carried only four years further in time.[21] But these documents do lend much interest and value to his work, and the technique itself is striking. Finally, Rahewin did have firsthand knowledge of one matter of much interest to us—the life of Bishop Otto—and we owe to him a good part of our knowledge of Otto's career and person.[22]

Rahewin's most serious defect as an historian was his fondness for borrowed finery. Otto, to be sure, had often embellished his account with quotations from earlier writers, which he felt applicable; this procedure was, of course, typical of medieval writers and is not foreign to the work of some modern historians. But with Rahewin, who must have realized the inadequacy of his own style and often enough the paucity of his information, this was not an occasional but an incessant practice. An attempt has been made (based largely on the care taken by Simson and his predecessors in editing the text) to indicate these borrowings in the footnotes, but we must warn that the record of them is probably incomplete.

This habit of Rahewin obliges us to read his work with great caution. Often whole sentences or even paragraphs were taken by him bodily from some classical treatise (Sallust and Josephus being his favorites). A few examples may show the character and extent of this dependence. His picture of Milan on the eve of Frederick's attack is copied entirely

[20] This comes out most clearly in his handling of the disputed papal election after the death of Hadrian in 1159. See below, IV.lx–lxvi, lxxiv–lxxxiii.

[21] It may be suggested that another reason for breaking the biography at this early date was that Rahewin's inferiority to Otto as an historian was as obvious at Frederick's court as it is to us today.   [22] See below, IV.xiv.

from Sallust—even to the detail of public doles—and is not entitled to much credence as applied to a town of the twelfth century.[23] The speeches Rahewin has put into the mouths of his characters are generally taken verbatim from either Josephus or Sallust and are often fundamentally implausible. At times he is extremely clumsy in piecing together two or more quotations.[24] On other occasions he appears to have deliberately modified the facts to make a chosen quotation applicable.[25] "I admit," Rahewin wrote at the beginning of his work, "that my breath is too slight to suffice for even a tiny flute, to say nothing of filling so magnificent and full-toned a trumpet of writing and of speech as that of the author who preceded me." [26] This modesty loses something of its effect when we realize that the figure of speech is taken bodily from Jordanes, who in turn borrowed it from Rufinus. But most startling of all is Rahewin's description of Frederick in words copied from an epistle of Apollinaris Sidonius depicting Theodoric II, king of the Visigoths, and from the famous life of Charlemagne by Einhard.[27] The resemblance—or rather the identity—extends even to a description of the imperial legs as *honorabilia et bene mascula* and to the statement that Frederick was as dignified standing as sitting. However suitable and well expressed the pictures of other kings by other authors, we should have preferred to have Rahewin tell us in his own words what he thought of his imperial master. Rahewin's tendency toward fulsome praise also detracts from his work; the reader is inclined to place greater credence in Otto's more straightforward account.

It has seemed necessary to point out these deficiencies in Rahewin because of the very favorable impression his portion of the *Deeds of Frederick Barbarossa* is likely to make on the casual reader. Whereas Otto covered five years of Frederick's reign in his relatively brief second book, Rahewin managed only four years in his two longer books. And yet Otto's part furnishes many more valuable and dependable details than does that of Rahewin, which is not only stretched by the inclusion of documentary materials but is also padded by long and often worthless quotations. It is difficult to agree with the statement of Horst Kohl (who translated the *Gesta* into German) that Rahewin "better performed the historian's task than did he whom, with kindly affection,

---

[23] See below, III.xxx.
[25] A case in point is III.xxxiii.
[27] See below, IV.lxxxvi.

[24] See, for example, IV.xxxvii.
[26] See below, III. Prologue.

he termed his lord and master"; [28] the work of Otto seems far superior.

Despite these observations, intended to put the reader on guard against too ready acceptance of the work, especially the part composed by Rahewin, the biography as a whole remains our most important single source for the reign of Frederick Barbarossa and, in point of detailed information and effective interpretation, the most valuable biographical study of the twelfth century. Comparison with the *Gesta Ludovici VI Grossi* by Abbot Suger of St. Denis will support this judgment. Both Otto and Suger were, by association and responsibility, in excellent position to secure the raw materials from which history must be written; in both cases the offices which they held, as churchmen and advisers of their respective monarchs, proved an embarrassment in the writing of objective history. Both acquitted themselves well; but even a hasty reading of their works will convince one of the superiority of Otto as a reflective historian.[29] Thorough study enhances respect for him as a precise and accurate writer.

A second work compiled in Italy by Italians representing the point of view of the growing bourgeois class of the rising north Italian towns parallels closely some portions of the *Deeds* and invites comparison therewith. This is the *Historia Frederici I* which deals with the activities of Frederick Barbarossa in so far as they affected Italy. It was compiled for the years 1153–60 by Otto Morena and was continued to 1168—the first four years by his son, Acerbus, and the last four by an anonymous author. Little is known of the life of Otto Morena beyond the fact that he was a jurist in Lodi and a warm imperial supporter. He appears to have been closely associated with Frederick during his early Italian campaigns, more closely than either Otto or Rahewin; as a chronicler of these campaigns he deserves more credit than is usually accorded him. Otto of Freising reveals firsthand acquaintance with Italy. His description of the Italian city-states shows a quite remarkable grasp of their essential character.[30] The same may not, however, be said of Rahewin. While there is some indication that he accompanied Frederick on at least one of his transalpine journeys, he seems to have

---

[28] Horst Kohl, *Rahewins Fortsetzung der Thaten Friedrichs*, Introd., p. xvii, in "Geschichtschreiber der deutschen Vorzeit."

[29] The most recent and most conveniently accessible edition of the work of Suger is the *Vie de Louis VI le Gros* (Paris, 1929), prepared, with a French translation, by H. Waquet for the Classiques de l'histoire de France (Paris, 1929).

[30] See below, II.xiii–xv.

absorbed little or no accurate information about Italy, and his account of the emperor's campaigns in the peninsula is of relatively little worth. Otto Morena possessed a wider knowledge of Italian affairs than either of our authors, especially those of Lombardy with which he primarily concerned himself. His history is purely factual, with no literary pretensions, and is a more reliable source for the Lombard campaigns of the emperor's early reign than is the work of Otto and Rahewin. A detailed comparison of the overlapping parts of the two works induces much respect for that of Otto Morena, and it is for that reason that its usefulness is here emphasized.[31]

In the translation of the present work the aim has been to give, in so far as possible, a faithful rendering of the text, even at the risk of some clumsiness in phraseology. This entailed occasional difficulty, however. In the philosophical digressions (especially Chapters v and xlviii–lxi of Book 1) some departure from a strictly literal rendering has been made for the sake of clarity, but nowhere has the thought of the author or the sense of the Latin been intentionally violated. In the last two books, also, Rahewin's long-winded and prolix style has been in places compressed, again in the interest of clarity. However, there still remains enough of the original flavor for the reader to be conscious of the author's idiosyncrasies of style and picturesqueness of expression.

Every medieval text presents certain problems of translation, words or phrases being used in a new or unusual meaning which may be clear enough to one familiar with the Latin of the period but which may be puzzling to the more general reader. The present text offers no peculiarities not found in other contemporary writings, and specific points

---

[31] The *Historia Frederici I* was most recently published in a critical edition by Ferdinand Güterbock (*Scriptores rerum Germanicarum* . . . , new series VII [Berlin, 1930]). Earlier editions of the work, notably by Sassi (Muratori, *Scriptores rerum Italicarum* . . . , VI [Milan, 1725], 949–1164), and by Jaffé (*Mon. Germ. hist.: Scriptores*, XVIII [Berlin, 1863], 582–659) appeared, respectively, under the titles *Historia rerum Laudensium* and *De rebus Laudensibus*. For critique of these earlier editions and for appraisal of the work of Otto Morena and his continuators, consult, in addition to his introduction to the text, Güterbock, "Zur Edition des Geschichtswerks Otto Morenas und seiner Fortsetzer," *Neues Archiv*, XLVIII (1929–30), 116–47, XLIX (1930–32), 128–49; idem, "Ottone e Acerbo Morena," *Archivio storico italiano*, series 7, XIII (1930), 61–99. See also Bernhard Schmeidler, *Italienische Geschichtschreiber des XII. und XIII. Jahrhunderts*, Leipzig, 1909. "Leipziger historische Abhandlungen," Vol. XI. Güterbock has no hesitation in characterizing the work as our most important source for the critical events transpiring in Lombardy between the years 1154 and 1168 ("Ottone e Acerbo Morena," *loc. cit.*, p. 67).

are discussed in footnotes to the translation, but a few general observations may serve as a guide to the reader.

Names of people and places have, in general, been rendered in their modern equivalents where these are known. But it is not always easy to follow this rule consistently, and some exceptions had to be made. Both authors, Otto in particular, seem to have had a liking for old forms.[32] For France both authors employ *Gallia, Francia,* and *Francia occidentalis* interchangeably. They also use *Gallia* to include all territories to the west of the Rhine (i.e., the ancient Gaul) or in a more restricted sense to designate an indeterminate strip of land along the left bank of the Rhine. In these latter cases the term "Gaul" has been retained in the translation. In like manner *Francia orientalis* is employed to denote Germany (the old East Francia), or some portion thereof, more particularly the duchy of Franconia.[33] *Alemannia,* Otto is at pains to point out, refers properly only to southwestern Germany, and as such is synonymous with Swabia, and the *Alemanni* are the Swabians.[34] But in one or two instances Otto forgets his own rule, and Rahewin employs the term consistently in the sense of *Germania.*

It may be worth noting, also, that our authors regularly refer to Russia as *Rutenia* and the Russians as *Reuteni* or *Rutheni* (though the Eastern emperor, in a letter to Conrad III, employs the term *Rossia*);[35] that Otto frequently uses *Pyreneus mons* or *Pyreneae alpes* for the Alps, and at least once as synonymous with the Apennines, though Rahewin does not follow this usage;[36] that they employ *miles* not only in the sense of "knight" but more generally as a mounted soldier, who might in the Germany of their day be a member of the dependent class of *ministeriales;*[37] that the term *castrum* is broad enough in their usage

[32] Note especially a term such as *Belgica Gallia* (I.xxx).

[33] For the various uses of the term *Francia* during the Middle Ages consult B. Guérard, "Du nom de France et des différents pays auquel il fut appliqué," *Annuaire historique de la Société de l'histoire de France,* XIII (1849), 152–68. Guérard there lists some fourteen specific uses of *Francia* in addition to a few other scattered meanings found in medieval authors. For our purposes, see especially pp. 157–63.

[34] See below, I.viii.   [35] See below, I.xxv, xxxii; III.i, iii.

[36] In II.xiii. See also I.i, xx; II.xiv, xviii, xx. For a discussion of this, see Heinrich Thomae, *Die Chronik des Otto von St. Blasien* (Leipzig, 1877), pp. 11–13. In I.xxxii, Otto employs *Apenninus* for the Carpathians.

[37] Cf. Philippe Dollinger, *L'Evolution des classes rurales en Bavière depuis la fin de l'époque carolingienne jusqu'au milieu du XIIIe siècle* (Paris, 1949), pp. 286–310, especially pp. 304–8.

to cover the castle, the fortified town or village, or a stronghold that may be either; [38] that *comitatus* may mean the territory ruled by a count, the *contado* of an Italian town, or, as in one case, a part of the regalian rights (along with taxes, tolls, coinage, etc.) which must be relinquished by Milan after its conquest by the emperor in 1158; [39] that *curia* may refer to the royal residence, the emperor's law court, the papal court, or the regal or imperial diet; and that *princeps* is a term sufficiently vague to cover references to the emperor and other nobles down to the most insignificant princeling.

The phrase *divus augustus* or *divus imperator—diva res publica* occurs at least once [40]—is employed by both authors, but chiefly by Rahewin. There is some question regarding the meaning of *divus* as used by a writer of the twelfth century. But it has been rendered, quite literally, "divine" in the thought that this best reflects the growing sense of the sacrosanct character of the person of the emperor. [41] And, finally, the term *coronatus* appears in various combinations—*sub corona incedendo, coronam gestans, coronatus*—in the sense of state appearances of the king or emperor on the occasion of a solemn feast or the holding of a diet, what German scholars characterize as a *Festkrönung*. It is a puzzling phrase to render into understandable English, [42] and in one or two instances there is even uncertainty whether or not an actual coronation is indicated. [43] In connection with the term it may be

---

[38] On the problem of the *castrum* in northern Italy, see Johan Plesner, *L'Emigration de la campagne à la ville libre de Florence au XIIIe siècle*. In Chapter I, " 'Il castello,' la bourgade fortifiée," he shows the difference between the *castrum* in northern Italy and in the states of northern Europe. It is to the former that the authors of our text frequently refer. [39] See below, IV.vii.

[40] II.1. It should be noted that the phrase appears in a letter written by Frederick himself.

[41] See the discussion of this subject by Fritz Kern, *Kingship and Law in the Middle Ages*, Chap. I, especially pp. 61–68, where reference is made to the progress of the theory of divine right under Frederick Barbarossa. But this does not account for *diva res publica*, mentioned above.

[42] For example: Conrad III celebrated Whitsunday, May 7, 1151, at Coblenz, "sub corona incedendo" (I.lxix); "in die sancto pentecostes [Petrus] coronatus, gladium regis sub corona incedentis portavit" (II.v); "rex . . . coronam gestans, duos cardinales . . . secum habuit" (II.ix); "ea ergo die [feast of Peter and Paul, June 29, 1155], missam papa Adriano celebrante, imperator coronatur" (II.xxxiv).

[43] III.1: "Princeps Romanus a Mediolano castra movens aput Modoicum, sedem regni Italici, coronatur" (Sept. [?], 1158). On the question whether this represents an actual coronation, see August Kroener, *Wahl und Krönung der deutschen Kaiser und Könige in Italien* (Freiburg i.B., 1901), who marshals the learned opinion and decides

interesting to note an almost exact parallel from the Peterborough recension of the Anglo-Saxon Chronicle of the eleventh century. In this chronicle, however, the use of the term is restricted to the holding of the royal court at three periods of the year—Easter, Whitsunday, and Christmas.[44]

In the translation of passages quoted from the Bible the King James version has been followed where the quotations are sufficiently close to the Vulgate text to warrant. There are numerous other cases, however, where our authors seem to have quoted from memory or merely paraphrased Biblical passages; in these the translation is our own and is not placed within quotation marks. In every case, where known, the appropriate Scriptural passage is cited.

that it does not. See also Simonsfeld, *op. cit.*, pp. 304–5, n. 83, where the debate over a probable earlier coronation at Pavia (II.xxvii: April 24, 1155) is discussed.

[44] See *The Peterborough Chronicle* (tr. by Harry Rositzke, New York, 1951: "Records of Civilization," No. 44): *sub an.* 1085b [1086], "Here the king wore his crown and held his court"; *sub an.* 1086 [1087], ". . . three times each year he [William] wore his royal crown, as often as he was in England. At Easter he wore it in Winchester, at Pentecost in Westminster, at Christmas in Gloucester . . ."; *sub an.* 1111, "This year King Henry did not wear his crown at Christmas nor at Easter nor at Pentecost . . ."

THE DEEDS OF
FREDERICK BARBAROSSA

HERE BEGINS A LETTER OF THE AUGUST EMPEROR, FREDERICK, TO OTTO, BISHOP OF FREISING [1]

Frederick, by the grace of God emperor of the Romans and august forever, to his beloved uncle Otto, bishop of Freising, sends his regards and every good wish.

We have received with great joy the Chronicle [2]—dispatched to us by your love—which your wisdom compiled, or rather wherein it brought into clear harmony things obscured by neglect.[3] After the sweat of war we ardently desire from time to time to delight ourselves therein and to be instructed in the virtues by the magnificent achievements of the emperors.

But we would gladly commend to your attention an account, briefly compiled in compliance with your request, of the things performed by us since our accession to the throne, save that by comparison with former deeds accomplished by superior men they may be called rather the shadow than the reality of things. However, since your brilliant intellectual powers can exalt what is insignificant and write much from slight materials, we put more confidence in your praises than in our own merits and undertake to outline the little that we have done in the Roman world during the past five years.

After we were anointed at Aachen and received the crown of the German realm, we held a general assembly at Merseburg on Whitsunday. There Peter, king of the Danes, came upon summons to our assembly and, after pledging allegiance and fealty to us, received the crown of his realm from our hand.

Then we transferred Wichmann, bishop of Zeitz, to the archbishopric of Magdeburg; and although many disputes and contro-

---

[1] Frederick's letter was written in 1157 and recounts the events of the five years since his coronation as king (March 9, 1152). These events are covered in greater detail by Otto in Book II of the present work.

[2] Also known, and cited throughout the present work, as the *Two Cities*. It was composed between 1143 and 1147; the reference here is to a second edition sent to the emperor after March, 1157. This work has been translated by Charles C. Mierow: *The Two Cities* (New York, 1928), "Records of Civilization," No. 9.

[3] Cf. Justinian *Institutes*. Prooemium.

versies between us and the Roman Church resulted from this, yet finally
the apostolic authority confirmed our laudable act.

After this we undertook the Roman expedition and entered Lombardy in force. Because this land, on account of the prolonged absence
of the emperors, had become arrogant and, conscious of its strength, had
initiated rebellion, we were wroth and destroyed almost all its strongholds by the just and righteous anger not of our knights but of the
lower ranks.[4]

The proud and cunning people of Milan swore to us falsely and
promised us much money, that by our grant they might exercise lord-
ship over Como and Lodi. But as they could persuade us neither by
prayers nor by price, upon our arrival in their land they forsook their
own fruitful country and guided us for three days in the wilderness
until finally, in opposition to their wishes, we pitched camp about a
German mile [5] from Milan. As we there demanded a market [6] of them
and they refused to furnish it, we caused to be taken and destroyed by
fire their finest fortress, Rosate, which held five hundred armed men.
Thereupon our soldiers advanced as far as the gate of Milan and
wounded many and took many captives. With hostilities ensuing here
and there, we crossed the river Ticino near Novara and took forcible
possession of two bridges defended and fortified with towers. These
bridges we destroyed after the crossing of our entire army. Next we
destroyed three of their strongest fortresses, namely, Momo, Galliate,
and Trecate. After celebrating the Lord's birthday with the greatest
joy, we marched through Vercelli and Turin and crossed the Po.

Next we destroyed Chieri, a very large and well-fortified town. The
city of Asti we laid waste by fire. Then we besieged Tortona, a city excellently fortified by nature and art. After three days we reduced the
outer fortifications and would have captured the citadel itself, had not
night and a severe storm prevented us. Finally, after many assaults,

---

[4] *Non militum, sed servientium.* Like other twelfth-century writers, Otto uses *miles*
in more than one sense. It may mean the army as a unit, or a soldier irrespective of
class. In the present instance, the *miles* is clearly the heavy-armed cavalryman—the
free vassal of noble blood—as opposed to the sergeant (here called *serviens*, but usually
designated by Otto as *strator* or *armiger*), who is also a mounted soldier, but normally
more lightly armed, mounting a smaller horse, and of lower social status. See Oman,
History of the Art of War in the Middle Ages, I, 371–74.

[5] The German mile is almost five English miles.

[6] *Mercatum,* used in the sense of supplies for the imperial army. See below, II.xvii–
xviii.

much bloodshed, the pitiful slaughter of the enemy, and no small loss of our men, the city did capitulate; and we freed a certain leader of the Greeks who had been taken captive by Marchese Malaspina. When Tortona had been destroyed, the people of Pavia invited us to their city that they might afford us a glorious triumph after the victory. There we spent three days, wearing the crown and receiving the greatest acclaim and respect of the citizens. Then we advanced directly through Lombardy, Romagna, and Tuscany and reached Sutri. There the lord pope, with the entire Roman Church, met us joyfully, paternally offered us holy consecration, and complained to us of the injuries which he had suffered at the hands of the Roman populace.

So we reached Rome, advancing together daily, lodging together, and exchanging pleasant converse. The Romans sent their messengers to us and demanded of us a very large sum of money in return for their loyalty and submission, and also three guarantees upon oath. Thereupon we took counsel with the lord pope and cardinals. Since we were not willing to buy the imperial title and were under no obligation to swear to the rabble, in order to evade all their wiles and stratagems the largest part of our army, under the guidance of Cardinal Octavian, gained admission by night through a small gate near St. Peter's, and thus was beforehand in occupying the monastery of St. Peter. When morning came, the lord pope with the entire church preceded us to the Basilica of St. Peter and welcomed us with a magnificent procession at the steps. After celebrating Mass at the altar of the apostles Peter and Paul in honor of the Holy Virgin Mary (for it was the Sabbath), he lavishly bestowed upon my head the benediction of the crown of the Roman empire. After this had been duly performed, while we were all returning to our tents, exhausted by the excessive exertion and by the heat, and were taking food, the Romans dashed forth from the Tiber bridge and attempted to capture the pope in the monastery of St. Peter, killing two of our servants and despoiling the cardinals. But we heard the uproar from without and hurried fully armed in through the walls. All that day we fought the Romans, killing almost a thousand of them and casting them into the Tiber, and leading off captives, until night separated us and them.

When morning dawned, as our food supplies had failed, we withdrew, taking with us the pope and the cardinals and rejoicing in triumph over our victory. After all the strongholds and fortifications around the

City had been surrendered to our control, we came to Albano and remained there for several days with the pope. Thence we went to Spoleto and, because it was defiant and held captive Count Guido Guerra and our other messengers, we made an assault on the city. Marvelous and inscrutable is the judgment of God! Fighting from the third to the ninth hour of the day, we took by storm—that is, by fire and sword—this most strongly fortified city which had almost a hundred towers. After gaining booty beyond measure and burning even more in the fire, we utterly destroyed the city.

Turning from there toward Ancona, we encountered Palaeologus, the most noble prince of the Greeks, and Maroducas, his associate, with other envoys of [the emperor of] Constantinople. They solemnly promised to give us an enormous sum of money to induce us to go into Apulia and undertake by our mighty power the destruction of William, the enemy of both empires. But because our army had been too greatly weakened by its many hardships and campaigns, our leaders decided to return home rather than descend into Apulia.

And as we were thus returning and the Greeks were advancing into Apulia, confident in their numbers and with their rich treasure, Palaeologus died after capturing Bari and destroying its fortifications. William, collecting an army, made a sudden attack on the Greeks, took a few of them captive, killed all the rest, and carried off all the money. But we arrived at Verona with the splendid victory afforded us by God —such a victory as we have never before heard of being won by eighteen hundred soldiers. Now how they laid a trap for us on the precipitous slope of a certain mountain, and how they were slaughtered by us and twelve of them were hanged, you have heard. Moreover, you know in due sequence what accord we effected between your brother, the duke of Austria, and the duke of Bavaria, and how gloriously we elevated Frederick to the office of archbishop of Cologne.

These few incidents, set forth in a few words, we offer to your renowned skill to be amplified and increased.

THE FIRST BOOK

HERE BEGIN THE CHAPTERS OF THE FIRST BOOK [1]

[1] It will be seen that the first book of the *Deeds* covers the years prior to Frederick's reign, and parallels in time the seventh book of the *Two Cities*.

HERE END THE CHAPTERS

HERE BEGINS THE PROLOGUE OF THE WORK THAT FOLLOWS

This, I think, has been the purpose of all who have written history before us: to extol the famous deeds of valiant men in order to incite the hearts of mankind to virtue, but to veil in silence the dark doings of the base or, if they are drawn into the light, by the telling to place them on record to terrify the minds of those same mortals.[2]

Hence I judge those who write at this time to be in a certain measure

[2] While the Christian historian is doubtless reading his own viewpoint into the motives of previous writers, it is interesting to note that of the ancients, Tacitus, at least, professes the same intent: "The chief function of history," he says (*Annals* III.lxv), "is to insure the commemoration of virtuous acts and to set forth before base utterance and deed the fear of the detestation of posterity."

happy. For, after the turbulence of the past, not only has an unprecedented brightness of peace dawned again, but the authority of the Roman empire prevails so greatly by reason of the virtues of our most victorious prince that the people living under his jurisdiction rest in humble quiet, and whatever barbarian or Greek dwells outside his bounds is overawed by the weight of his authority and trembles.[3]

I confess that when, a few years ago, I had finished my previous history and the spirit of the pilgrim God [4] had inspired almost all the western world to take up arms against the peoples that inhabit the East, out of gladness at the peace which then momentarily smiled upon the world, I had intended to put my pen to a new use. I had already begun to write, but—by what impulse I know not—as though my mind foresaw the future and beheld the end, I cast aside the work I had begun.[5]

Thus I believe that the task of bringing to completion my present project was postponed by me, though without intention or knowledge, until a lasting peace (if, in spite of all, we may place some confidence in transitory affairs) is anticipated under the most vigorous prince in the Roman world.

Now as to my saying that at that time the western peoples were inspired by the spirit of the pilgrim God, let no one interpret this to mean that we believe in some pilgrim God, but let him know that we borrowed this term from the document which was read repeatedly in those days in many parts of Gaul. It goes like this: "I say to you, L[ouis], shepherd of bodies, whom the spirit of the time of the pilgrim God has inspired, addressing you by the first letter of the sum total that makes up your name." [6] In the course of this writing, under a certain husk of words concerning the storming of the royal city and also of ancient Babylon, a triumph over the entire Orient, after the manner of Cyrus,

---

[3] Here again we find a point of resemblance with Tacitus; both historians are inclined to look upon the pageant of past history in the light of a tragedy, but each is writing in a happier period that affords hope for brighter days. See *Two Cities* dedication, Prologue, and vi.xxxi; the present work i.xlviii; Tacitus *Agricola* iii and *Histories* i.l.

[4] *Spiritusque peregrini Dei.* The reference is to the Second Crusade, led by Conrad III of Germany and Louis VII of France.

[5] What this projected work may have been is not known.

[6] *Tibi dico L pastor corporum primo elemento materiae silvae tuae, quem inspiravit spiritus diei peregrini Dei.* The prophecy was directed to Louis VII of France. It is from the so-called "Sibylline Books," which had some vogue at the middle of the century. See Giesebrecht, *Geschichte der deutschen Kaiserzeit*, IV, 502.

king of the Persians, or of Hercules, was promised to the aforesaid Louis, king of France.

Hence such words as these are found therein:

"When you have arrived at the side of the eternal seated square and come to the side of the eternal standing squares and to the product of the blessed number and the actual first cube, raise yourself to her whom the angel of your mother promised to visit and did not visit, and you shall extend from her even to the penultimate—when the promiser ascends her first, the promise fails on account of the best goods—then plant your rose-colored standards even as far as the uttermost labors of Hercules, and the gates of the city of B[abylon] will open before you. For the bridegroom has set you up as a mainsail, he whose bark has almost foundered and on whose peak is a triangular sail, that he who preceded you may follow you. Therefore your L[ouis] will be turned into a C[yrus], who diverted the waters of the river,[7] until those who toil to procure sons have crossed the stream."

This document was then considered by the most excellent and pious personages of the Gauls to be of so great authority that it was declared by some to have been found in the Sibylline books, by others to have been divinely revealed to a certain Armenius. But whosoever that prophet or charlatan (*trotannus*) was who spread this abroad, let him determine whether its fulfillment may yet be expected in the future, or if (being scorned as already having failed of fulfillment) the fact that it gained some credence may be attributed to Gallic credulity. Only let him know this, that not without some reasonable analogy was that spirit, which sent practically all westerners on a pilgrimage, called by us—as by him—the spirit of the pilgrim God. For (according to the dictum of certain well-known logicians) although predication or declaration strictly pertains not to separate forms but to subsistent things, yet genus [8] and species are said to be possible of predication by consider-

---

[7] Cyrus diverted the Euphrates and entered Babylon by its dry bed (Herodotus I.cxci). Giesebrecht (IV, 505–6) prints this and another version of the prophecy. According to him (IV, 502), the "side" (*costa*) is Constantinople, and the city Jerusalem. His second text gives the less mystical, but more plausible, *filius* (son) for the *angelus* (angel) of Otto's version.

[8] Otto uses the plural, *genera*. Some such phrase as "though they be not subsistent" is implied after the words "yet genus and species."

ing the predicament as a principle of causality. Or, to use a more familiar example, when we say, "whiteness is brilliant," we mean to say that whiteness is the cause of brilliancy; and when we say "death is pale," we mean to say that death is the cause of paleness. In like manner when we say "the spirit of the pilgrim God," we mean (as though we said "Eurus brings forth rain") that it was because of God that so many and so great men assumed the pilgrim's garb.

Since, therefore, things have changed for the better, and after the time of weeping the time of laughing has now come, and after the time of war, the time of peace,[9] I have thought it unseemly, Frederick, most famous of the Augusti, that having enumerated the achievements of all the other kings and emperors, I should pass over yours in silence. Nay —to speak more truly—I thought it most appropriate to superimpose your virtues upon those of your predecessors like a precious stone upon gold. Because for you almost alone, of all the princes of the Romans, has this privilege been reserved that, although you are known to have exerted yourself since early youth in the duties of war, not yet has Fortune turned upon you her malign aspect. You are known to be so temperate in prosperity, brave in adversity, just in judgment, and prudent and shrewd in courts of law, that these characteristics seem to have taken root within you, not merely from daily habit but as though divinely inspired and granted you by God for the general advantage of the whole world.[10]

Accordingly, I offer this history to Your Nobility, praying and beseeching God, the giver of all good, that your good beginning may be granted an even better ending. But before I touch upon the account of your achievements, I have thought to relate in a brief preface certain deeds of your grandfather, your father, and your uncle,[11] that by this thread of discourse what is to be said of your personality may be revealed as the more illustrious. But if the achievements of some ecclesiastical or secular personage from other realms were incidentally included, this should not be considered foreign to the subject matter of the work, since the story of all realms or peoples returns to the condition of the Roman empire as to its source.

[9] Ecclesiastes 3:4, 8.

[10] Note that Otto attributes to Frederick the four Socratic virtues.

[11] Frederick of Hohenstaufen, duke of Swabia (died 1105); his son Frederick, duke of Swabia and father of Barbarossa (died 1147); his second son Conrad III, king from 1138 to 1152, the uncle of Barbarossa and the half brother of Otto of Freising.

Nor will it be regarded as inconsistent with a work of this sort if the style is exalted, as the opportunity for a digression presents itself, from the simple diction of history to loftier—that is, to philosophic—heights. For this very practice is not at variance with the prerogative of the Roman empire: to intersperse the simpler with loftier affairs. For Lucan and Vergil and all the other writers of the City frequently elevated their style of expression so as to touch certain intimate secrets of philosophy, in recording not only historical events but even fables, whether modestly in the manner of shepherds or peasants or in the more exalted style of princes and lords of the earth. For thus not only those whose pleasure consists in hearing the record of achievements, but also those to whom the refinement of subtle reasoning affords greater delight, are attracted to read and to study such a work.

And thus let the proposed history take its beginning, in the name of God.

HERE ENDS THE PROLOGUE

HERE BEGINS THE CHRONICLE OF BISHOP OTTO OF FREISING AND HIS SECRETARY [12] RAHEWIN: THE FIRST BOOK

i. When, under Emperor Henry, who is found to be fourth of this name among the kings and third among the emperors,[13] the realm had seriously disintegrated and, as the majority of the nobles were in rebellion against their prince, almost the whole extent of the kingdom was being devastated by sword and flame, Gregory VII, who then held the pontificate in the city of Rome,[14] determined to strike this emperor with the sword of excommunication, as one already deserted by his own followers. The novelty of this action aroused all the more indignation in the empire, because it had never before this time known a sentence of this kind to be pronounced against an emperor of the Romans.[15] Therefore the emperor called together many bishops from Italy, Gaul,

---

[12] *Abbreviatoris.* [13] Emperor Henry IV (1065–1106).
[14] Pope Gregory VII (1073–85), or Hildebrand.
[15] Cf. *Two Cities* VI.xxxv. The term which Otto here employs is *princeps*, probably intentionally general because Henry had not been crowned emperor.

and Germany at Brixen, a city of Bavaria situated in the heart of the Pyrenees,[16] not far from the valley of Trent, and held a great council. When all had arrived, he complained bitterly of the injuries inflicted upon him by the Roman Church, namely, that without consulting him (who, as king and patrician, ought to be first at the election of the bishop of his city) the people of Rome had themselves chosen a pontiff, although many had been enthroned there by his father when he was emperor, seemingly without election. By this complaint the feelings of all could the more readily be turned against the Roman Church as not only the laity, inflamed by considerations of secular honor, but also the bishops, instigated by their clerics to whom marriage had recently been forbidden by the same pontiff, acceded to the wishes of the prince. Therefore, as all exclaimed that in their judgment the aforesaid election must be annulled, Guibert, archbishop of Ravenna, called Clement [17] (or rather, Dement!), was elected bishop of the City with the assent of the king, and Gregory VII, termed by them a false monk and a necromancer, was deposed. Whereupon, by common consent, they presumed to direct to the before-mentioned pope a letter full of invectives and slander, saying among other things: "Even as you were hitherto wont to say that no one of us was a bishop, so you may know that to no one of us will you be pope hereafter."

ii. After this, the king collected a large army and invaded Italy. Advancing as far as the City, he ejected Gregory, with the approbation of the Roman people, established Guibert there, and received from him the titles of emperor and Augustus. But the venerable priest, fleeing persecution, betook himself to the safer mountainous regions of Tuscany, to the land of Countess Matilda, who was a relative of the emperor. There he remained for some time, renewing the sentence of excommunication in letters which are extant in many places, and aroused the princes of the realm against their emperor. Then, entering Campania and Apulia, he withdrew to a city of the Normans who under the leadership of Robert Guiscard had recently invaded those provinces

[16] Otto frequently refers to the Alps as the Pyrenees. See the Introduction, p. 12, and below, II.xiii. The "bishops from . . . Gaul" here referred to were presumably from imperial territories west of the Rhine.

[17] The antipope Clement III (1080–1100). The Council of Brixen met in June, 1080. It is perhaps indicative of Otto's attitude that he calls it not a *concilium* but a *curia*, the term he usually applies to a royal assembly.

killing or ejecting or enslaving the natives. There he awaited the day of his death.[18]

iii. This Robert was a man of moderate birth in Normandy, of the type of knights commonly called there *vavasor*, born in a region which the natives call the Cotentin.[19] He left his native land with his brother Roger, in a time of famine (as much out of regard for his father, they say, as because of the barrenness of the region), and he roamed for a long time through many provinces, seeking a more congenial land to live in. Hence he was called in his native tongue (from the extent of his wanderings) Guiscard—which is to say, wanderer or vagabond.[20] Now when he had been, as we have said, a wanderer over many regions for some time, he finally found a refuge in Hither Italy, which is now called Apulia and Calabria. Since he found it in the possession of the Lombards and virtually devoid of proper defense because inhabited by a cowardly folk, he sent back messengers into France, setting forth the desirability of the region and the inactivity of the people, and invited his former associates to share the conquest of those provinces.

To make a long story short, by valor, deceit, and cleverness he became victor over an unwarlike people and finally found himself in possession of Campania, Apulia, Calabria, and Sicily. Now he left to his brother Roger the county of Sicily, to be held subject to him; but he retained for himself the duchy of Apulia, with Calabria. His son, who afterward performed many valiant and glorious deeds both in Greece and in other parts of the East, was Bohemond. But his brother Roger's son was the Roger who afterward assumed the title of king and who was the father of William, the present king.[21] But enough of this.

iv. About the same time the most restless race of the Saxons, rebel-

---

[18] In this paragraph Otto shows some confusion about the events following the Council of Brixen. Gregory's stay in Tuscany occurred in 1077, three years before the council. Henry invaded Italy in 1081, and returned in 1082 and again in 1083; only in this last year did he capture Rome, and even then the pope held out in the castle of St. Angelo until the arrival of his Norman allies forced the emperor to retreat northward. Only in 1084 did Gregory take refuge in Norman territory, where he died, at Salerno, in 1085.

[19] Robert and Roger were two of the twelve sons of Tancred de Hauteville, a minor baron whose lands could not support so large a family. Two of the brothers had reached southern Italy by 1037; others, including Robert and Roger, followed.

[20] It means, rather, "crafty" or "shrewd."

[21] Bohemond was a leader of the First Crusade. His uncle Roger, brother of Robert Guiscard, died in 1111, and Roger II (1113–54) was the real founder of the Norman state in Italy, taking the title of king in 1130. His son, William I, ruled 1154–66.

ling against their prince, as was their custom, completely destroyed a certain stronghold called Harzburg—erected by the emperor, in an extremely well-fortified spot on the borders of the province, for the subjugation of that people—and with it they destroyed the church, in which there was a congregation of canons.[22] However, the occasion for this rebellion had originated not so much from the instability of the aforesaid race as from the arrogance of the sovereign. For when the aforesaid prince, while yet a young man, had entered the land we have mentioned—the whole realm submitting to his rule in silence and humility—he is said to have made the youthful remark that he marveled that throughout the entire extent of his empire no man was to be found on whom he might try his strength; and he attributed this not to loyalty but to cowardice. This statement did not vanish as soon as it had been uttered—as words usually do—but, taking root in the minds of many, germinated so effectively that in a short time the whole province was aroused against him, and, uniting in one body, supplied to countless peoples and tribes death-dealing potions.

Therefore let the princes of the earth, who are set in the highest places, learn to observe moderation by holding before their minds their Creator, who is the highest of all; so that, as Cicero says,[23] the greater they are, the more humbly they may conduct themselves. For we know the excellent saying of the physicians concerning the instability of the human constitution: "Better on the upgrade than at the peak." For since man, born to travail and living but a brief time, and with a nature tending toward dissolution because made up of many elements, can never continue in the same state, if he is at the top, he must soon decline. On this account we may be permitted to philosophize a little, for "Happy is the man who can understand the reasons for things." [24]

v. Whatever is, is either original or created. But as the original must be (1) simple, (2) single—if I may so call it—and (3) separate, so the created must be (1) composite, (2) multiple, and (3) concrete.[25] Let

[22] The Saxon revolt broke out in 1073, and Harzburg, just southeast of Goslar, in the Harz, was destroyed in 1074. It was one of a chain of castles erected by Henry IV after 1066 for the control of the Saxon lands.

[23] *De officiis* I.xxvi; quoted also in *Two Cities* II.xxiv.

[24] Vergil *Georgics* II.490. Otto now proceeds to digress at some length on what he considered to be some basic philosophic considerations.

[25] The author describes the divine attributes by the three words *simplex, singulare,* and *solitarium*. By *simplex* he means uncompounded. In natural things a particle of gold

us now first see what the thing is that is called "original" and what is called "created," so that then the significance of these two words themselves may the more readily be apparent. We call "original" what begets and is not begotten: that is, not subject to generation; we call a thing "created" when it exists as a result of the process of generation and as such is derived from the original. Whence Plato says: "We must, it seems to me, discriminate first of all between that which is eternal and lacking generation, and what is begotten and not eternal."[26] And Boethius says: "Thou orderest time to issue from Eternity." [27]

Now, broadly speaking, we interpret generation as entrance into any property whatsoever or, to speak more clearly, as any transition whatsoever from not being to being. Whence Aristotle's saying, "From opposites generations arise." [28] For in every created thing negation precedes affirmation. The original is therefore without generation, without beginning, such as among us only one thing is found to be, namely, eternity, which can be attributed to divinity alone. For among us there are not to be found the three first principles which Plato assumed, but one only: God the Father, from whom are all things; God the Son, by whom are all things; God the Holy Spirit, in whom are all things.[29] And these three, as they are not three gods, so are they not three first principles nor three eternal beings, but one first principle and one eternal being. Now, that divinity and it alone—in that it is

---

is *simplex*. In God simplicity appears in that His mercy is not distinguishable from His justice, nor His will from His intellect; His will *is* his intellect. The meaning of *singulare* is obvious: there is only *one* God. By *solitarium* Otto consistently indicates that whereas man is made of form and matter, in God there is *no* matter; He is pure form. The human form becomes a subsistent thing (*subsistens*) only in matter. God, on the other hand, subsists by His form; He is subsistent form.

In opposition to these divine attributes, things "created" (used by the translator in a broad sense) are *compositum* (as against the divine *simplex*), *conforme* (as against the divine *singulare*), and *concretum* (as against the divine *solitarium*). The meaning of *compositum* is obvious. *Conforme* means multiple. In the world of nature there are many individuals sharing a given form and called *conformes* (there is not just *one* dog). The word *concretum* indicates, as has been said above, that in natural things we do not have form in separate solitary state, but always "grown into" matter. Not so with God.

[26] *Timaeus*, ed. Stephanus (Henri Estienne), p. 28.

[27] *De consolatione* III.ix*b*.

[28] Otto appears to be citing the *Peri Hermenaias*, in the Latin version of Boethius, II.14.

[29] I Corinthians 8:6; cf. Romans 11:36.

without beginning—is simple can be proved by necessary arguments. For whatever is compounded must of necessity be compounded by some-one else, inasmuch as nothing compounds itself any more than anything generates itself. But that which is compounded by another must have its being from another. Divinity, however, does not have its being from another. Therefore it cannot be compounded by another. Therefore it is simple. Whence Boethius says in the third book of his *De consolatione*,[30] "Suppose now that it [31] is naturally inherent [in God] and yet by reason [is maintained] as distinct. But then, if we realize that we are dealing with God who is the sovereign of the universe, who could be conceived of as having the power of joining these two diverse things?"

Divine essence is proved to be single from the fact that it has none like it either in actual existence or in potentiality. This is more easily shown if we begin by considering natural things.[32] For when we lift our minds to contemplate the heights of divine being, our intellect has no arguments upon which to support itself, and therefore groping in the midst of uncertainties it finds out that we do better by denying than by affirming; that is, by saying what [God] is not rather than by saying what He is. Now, in the sphere of natural things every essence or form which constitutes the entire being of a subsistent thing must have conformity with something else.[33] [And this multiplicity may be] either (1) merely potential, or (2) such that this potentiality has also become an actual fact. The "humanity" of Socrates, for example, both as natural potentiality and as an actuality, has conformity with the "humanity" of Plato, for the reason that in these two men we shall find all the parts of this "humanity" and also every one of its effects. (This is what some people call the form of the substance and the substance of the form.) Hence, although Socrates and Plato are endowed with nu-

---

[30] *De consolatione* III.x.

[31] "It" refers to the highest good. Boethius wants to prove the identity of God with sovereign good. Assuming that they were different, they would have to be conjoined either from the outside or inwardly by nature. He has disproved the first; in the lines that follow he disposes of the second. He then proceeds to demonstrate the singularity of God.

[32] That is, everything other than the Creator. Natural things are accessible to our understanding. Otto next proceeds to deny them the divine attributes in order to establish these as the attributes of the supernatural God.

[33] A man is a subsistent thing; that is, he is made of form and matter, of body, soul, and accidents. For Otto *humanitas* is a form which "informs" the body.

merical individuality from the point of view of dissimilation,[34] so that they are called *two* men, yet on the basis of assimilation they may be called *one* man. For substantial similitude determines in subjects [35] not only conformity but also identity and oneness. This is in accordance with the principle that "because of their participation in species, several men are one," and as we are accustomed to say: "The same wine is drunk here as at Rome."

When I spoke of parts above, I meant those forms which are required to constitute a species, namely, the form of the genus at the top, to which are added the forms of the differentia, to which are finally added the forms of the different accidents.[36] For a definition is one thing, but it is applicable to something else: it is a definition of the form, but it is applicable to the thing itself.[37]

Now from this, I think, what I said is made clear, that the human nature of Socrates in all its parts and in every effect is in conformity with the human nature of Plato, and accordingly Socrates and Plato are usually said to be in a universal sense one and the same. For if one "humanity" was rational and the other mortal, humanity would not in its entirety be either in Plato or in Socrates, for the one "humanity" would consist just of rationality and the other just of mortality.

If we now proceed to consider the effects, we still see that [this man actually exists], made by this human nature rational and mortal, and likewise this other man also, made by it rational and mortal.[38]

[34] Things may be identical in four ways: (*a*) Plato is identical with himself; this is called (after Aristotle) numerical identity; (*b*) Plato and Socrates, numerically different, are one and the same in being men; this is called specific identity (referred to below by Otto as "substantial similitude"); (*c*) Plato has animal identity with a dog; they belong to the same *genus*, animal; (*d*) identity in an *ordo*.

[35] The term *subiectum* has these meanings: (*a*) the matter (subject matter) in contradistinction to the form—e.g., primal matter is the *subiectum* of the elemental forms, and the body is the *subiectum* of the soul; (*b*) a substance as a substratum for accidents (Washington is the *subiectum* of national paternity, Donatus is the *subiectum* of grammar); (*c*) an accident as a substratum of another (superimposed) accident; (*d*) a subject in a political or feudal sense.

[36] To pass over the upper *genera*, we say that Plato is an animal. Animal is the genus of the species man. Plato has therefore in some way that animal form which makes him *conformis* with a cat or a dog. From the genus animal we obtain the species man by applying to the genus the *differentia* of rationality (*rationale*). Plato, therefore, has this form also. Finally, Plato is white and not black, is old, and so forth; he has, in other words, distinguishing accidental forms.

[37] To the subsistent being which is form *and* matter.

[38] The author now passes from conformity to concretion, the third and last attribute.

We may consider that in things of nature concretion exists not only as a result of the conjoining and unifying of the form and the thing that becomes consistent, but by the presence of a multitude of accidents which accompany the substantial being. For example, when "humanity" —which is the total being of man, and which, as has been shown, is made up of many forms—is joined with matter (*subiectum*), which is thus "informed" by it, the resulting individual takes on risibility and the remaining accidents.[39] There are other forms which completely "inform" their subject and which have multiplicity only potentially (*quae naturam tantum conformem habent*). For, as is known, the sun's being has the possibility if not the actuality of conforming [multiplicity]. Accordingly, although there are not many suns, yet there might be without going counter to nature. Now we conclude and, denying these propositions, make affirmations concerning the opposite [of these natural beings, namely, God. Accordingly we may affirm] that the divine essence is not multiple and is not subject to concretion. That is, by transforming terms applicable to natural things into divine categories, we affirm His simplicity, His singleness, His separateness: His simplicity in opposition to [natural] compositeness; His singleness in opposition to [natural] multiplicity; and His separateness in opposition to [natural] concretion. He then is not multiple either actually or by natural potentiality, because there neither was nor is nor can be another God, another Creator, another Omnipotent One. Whence the Psalmist inquires: "O God, who is like unto thee!"[40] Nor does the divine essence admit of concretion, since it has no matter ready to receive a form nor can it possibly be accompanied by accidents. Hence, too, it cannot properly be said to be a substance. For a substance can in a certain measure be called "subject," but form can in no wise be a subject. The divine, according to the philosopher,[41] is not subject to passions or to change; He is not constituted of this or of that. Whatever He is, He is one and therefore can be truly said to be. He is most mighty, in need

---

[39] In addition to his substantial form, man has accidental forms (quality, quantity, and so forth). Of these, one is that of *accidens proprium*, namely, risibility, which every man has and only man can have; the others are common accidents which other beings possess. Having thus covered the case of natural things in which multiplicity of individuals all belonging to the same species is both a potency of nature and a fact, Otto now passes to other alternatives.

[40] Psalms 71 :19.

[41] In this section, Otto leans heavily upon Boethius *De trinitate*.

of no support. [For all these reasons] He can appropriately be called form,[42] for all being proceeds from form. He is not therefore this and again that,[43] but just the one, the mightiest and the most beautiful. If there were another like Him, He could not be called *the* most beautiful. If He had to support Himself on a subject [44] and required a retinue of accidents, He would not be the most mighty. Wherefore He is the most beautiful and the mightiest, depending upon nothing and (as has been excellently stated by the aforesaid philosopher) [45] suited neither to definition nor division, much less to demonstration or resolution. This is true. For, since He has no higher genus from which He may be derived, He does not admit of definition.[46] How could He undergo the cutting or division, since all the species are lacking into which He might be divided? And how could that be open to demonstration which, as the beginning of all things and itself the first, cannot have over itself principles that are prior, truer, and better known? And finally, the very nature of simplicity, of singularity, of separateness, so to speak,[47] necessarily excludes the possibility of resolution so that He alone *is* eternal, invariable, unchangeable, and is naturally believed to be so.

For all the other things—if there are any—which do not admit of variation, like the angels, are shown to have this quality not of their own nature, but of the grace of their Creator, from whose invariableness they themselves are termed invariable, so that accordingly, when I say "God is unchanging, an angel is unchanging," it is not another invariableness that is referred to in the second proposition, but the same as in the first. For example: when I call a workman human and his work human, I am speaking not of one humanity and of another, but what I declare of the workman substantively, I say figuratively of the work; as when I say: "Socrates laughs, the field laughs," I do not speak of one quality of Socrates and another of the field, but I declare of the field improperly or by analogy what I say in all propriety of

[42] Rather than substance, because (as Otto has just said) substance may be called a subject.

[43] Man is body, man is soul, and so forth. This is not the case with God; His being is identical with His essence.

[44] In his literary fervor, Otto here shifts from the metaphysical to the political sense of *subiectum*.

[45] What follows is not found in the *De trinitate.*

[46] A definition must contain the genus and the differentia. Thus, man is a rational animal; animal is the genus and rationality the differentia.

[47] Otto apologizes here and above for the use of this unwonted term, *solitaritas.*

Socrates. In consideration of this fact, Boethius says: "A figure of speech has no quality of its own."

Having shown by the method of negation that the divine essence, since it cannot be called composite, multiple, or concrete,[48] is by all means to be conceived of as simple, singular, and separate, it now remains to be declared that every created thing is to be known as composite, multiple, and concrete. It is granted that everything that is created undoubtedly takes its origin from another. For nothing can be born of itself. But that which is from another is not a first principle; therefore it is this and this, therefore it is not simple, and accordingly it is composite. We are not here venturing to speak of theological and ineffable generation or birth, but have based our argument merely on that which is customarily called by philosophers generation, by us production or creation. But it is to be observed that the composition of forms is one thing, of subsistent things another. Forms are compounded out of forms, subsistent things out of subsistent things. For no form admits of composition with a subsistent thing, nor does any subsistent thing admit of composition with form. For the diversity existing between "that which is" and "being" is so great that neither does "that which is" admit of composition with its "being," nor does "being" admit of composition with "that which is" because of it.[49] And yet, although they unite under no genus and, as has been said, the one does not admit of composition with the other, nevertheless the one cannot exist without the other. And this sort of putting together (if we may call it so) of these most diverse elements is called rather a concretion of opposites than the combination of things that are alike. The combination of forms then, as we have said, is one thing; that of subsistent things is another. Now some forms are composite, others are simple: simple, as for example "whiteness"; composite, as for example "humanity." Simple forms, however, though they may be joined to a composite

[48] "Concrete" means that it is constituted of matter and form.

[49] That is, being. Any given thing that exists *is* in so far as it has being. Something is as a body because it has being from corporality (*corporalitas*), its form. Plato is a man by virtue of manness (*humanitas*), his form. Otto maintains that *humanitas* and Plato do not admit of composition, in that they cannot be brought under one category. This is explained by Gilbert de la Porrée, in his commentary on Boethius' third theological treatise, *Quomodo substantiae* (PL, LXIV, 1318) in these words: "He says 'being,' that is subsistence which is in a subsistent thing, and 'that which is,' that is the subsistent thing itself in which substance is, are diverse, as, e.g., corporality (*corporalitas*) is different from body and *humanitas* is different from *homo*. And this is true."

form, cannot, in the sphere of natural things, "inform" [that is, give form to] a subject matter.[50] From this it follows that every form by which a fully subsistent thing has been "informed" must be composite, must be this and that. There can be no doubt that subsistent things themselves are made up of subsistent things: a body is made up of several bodies.[51] Nor do philosophers go amiss when they assume that just as quantity can be subdivided beyond the point where measuring becomes impossible, so a body may be cut up into an infinite number of bodies.[52] Neither the form which is the whole being nor the matter to which this form gives subsistence can ever be anything but composite.[53]

But you must know that certain subsistent things admit of a conjunction of parts, while others do not. The body admits of it, the spirit does not. Wherefore, then, it might seem as though the spirit were simple. In this connection, however, we must be careful sometimes to discriminate merely between the simple and the composite, sometimes between the simple and what is both composite and concrete. Hence Boethius says, in the eighth rule of the Hebdomadal Book:[54] "In every composite thing the essence is one thing, the thing itself is another." For this rule does not deal with the difference between that which is and that whereby it is (which is given in the second rule, which states that "being and that which is are two different things"[55]), but rather the difference of forms whereby the subject is because of something, and is something because of something else. For example, a body is said "to be" by virtue of its corporeality, but "to be something" by virtue of its color. So then a created spirit—since "it is" because of something, and because of

---

[50] That is, the simple form "whiteness" does not make anything a subsistent thing, but appears after the composite form "corporality" has appeared. A thing has to be a body in order to be white.

[51] The body is made up of bones, flesh, sinews—all subsistent things, all bodies; these in turn are made up of the elements.

[52] An infinite number of infinitesimally small bodies. This is anti-atomistic doctrine.

[53] Having concluded that neither the form, which is the whole being, nor the matter, to which this form gives subsistence, can ever be anything but composite, Otto now considers a possible objection. True enough, these produced things are composite; they are made up of form and matter. But what of the spirit that has no body? Is it, too, composite? What follows is Otto's answer to this question.

[54] *Libri ebdomade.* This is the above-mentioned treatise *Quomodo substantiae* of Boethius. Otto's name for it is apparently drawn from its opening phrase: *Postulas, ut ex Hebdomadibus nostris.*

[55] *Ibid.*

something else is wise, although it seems to be simple in that it lacks the combination of parts—can nevertheless not be called entirely simple because it has a form composed of forms, in consequence of the concretion of such a form with the fully subsistent thing. Therefore every created thing is composite.[56] As regards multiplicity and concreteness, it was demonstrated above that multiplicity proceeds from substantial similarity, and that concreteness results when form "informs" matter and draws after itself a multitude of accidents.

But among all created things nothing may be found more composite than man. For he not only has a composite being proceeding from being, and subsists by virtue of many subsisting components, but he also, being constituted of components that are opposite, has within himself the combination of opposite subsistent things [57] as well as the composition of the different subsistences of these same subsistent components. Wherefore it is not surprising if man, being totally compounded and out of many components, is more easily subject to dissolution. Likewise, since in accordance with the ninth rule of Boethius "all diversity is discordant, likeness is to be sought, and that which seeks something else is naturally shown to be such as the very thing that is sought," we tend the more strongly toward dissolution as we consist the more diversely of opposing parts. For example, as the body is made up of the four elements, fire pulling it upward, earth downward, water and air contending on the same plane, and as its parts thus are at variance with each other, what more diverse thing can there be? This we know logically (even if we do not perceive it with our senses) by realizing the composition of the form. Furthermore, not only is the form (which is substantial being) composed of forms, but the very forms which compose it, now coming into existence, now ceasing to be, and never continuing in any fixed and finished condition of existence, do not permit the subject matter to be at rest. Hence, as some depart, others constantly take their places, without intermission. Since the passage of time follows this swift course of forms, time passes so rapidly that its present moment can scarcely, if ever, be perceived. So it has been well said by those who consider the mutability of nature and of time: "Better on the upgrade

---

[56] Otto set out to prove that created things are composite, multiple, and concrete. He has now proved the first, and proceeds to take up multiplicity and concreteness.

[57] Note the distinction between subsistence and a subsistent thing (*subsistentia* and *subsistens*). A thing subsists because of subsistence.

than at the peak," because when one no longer has the means of growth, one must decline.

But as it is the teaching of physicians that good health is dissolved when it reaches a climax, so, not inaptly, proven physicians of the soul advise that the spirit which is wont to be overelated when raised aloft by prosperous events be held in check by the consideration of misfortunes. Whence the saying, "In the day of good fortune be not unmindful of bad fortune." [58]

But let us return to our theme.

vi. So then when the Saxons rebelled against their chief, the prince collected from all corners of his realm a great and brave soldiery to overthrow them and, organizing his army, entered the aforesaid province.[59] There were in his following four great dukes, each with his own force: Vratislav (*Zuerdebaldus*), duke of the Bohemians, Welf, duke of the Bavarians, Rudolf, duke of the Swabians, Godfrey, duke of the Lorrainers, and other princes, counts, and nobles innumerable. So when a pitched battle was fought near the river called Unstrut, the king, after a bloody victory, returned home. No long time afterward the two aforesaid dukes, Welf and Rudolf, rebelling against the prince —on what pretext it is uncertain—joined the Saxons. But Godfrey, duke of Lorraine, undertook a crusade to the Orient and held at Jerusalem the leadership over the people of God. He there died in peace.[60]

vii. But the Roman pontiff Gregory, who, as has been said, was already inciting the princes against the emperor, wrote both secretly and openly to all, instructing them to elect another. Accordingly Rudolf, duke of the Swabians, was made king by them [61] and is said to have received from the Roman Church a diadem with the following inscription: "Rome gave Peter his crown, Peter bestows one on Rudolf."

Berthold, of the stronghold of Zähringen, one of the noblest princes of the realm, took Rudolf's daughter to wife. Shortly afterward Rudolf was slain in public war by those faithful to the emperor and was buried in royal state in the church at Merseburg. It is told of the emperor that when he had come to the aforesaid church at Merseburg (when these seditious uprisings had been quieted a little) and had seen there the

---

[58] Ecclesiasticus 11:25.

[59] See above, I.iv. The Saxon campaign here recorded took place in 1075.

[60] Godfrey of Bouillon, nephew and heir of the Godfrey, duke of Lower Lorraine, just mentioned by Otto. He was a leader of the First Crusade, was chosen ruler of Jerusalem after its capture in 1099, and died July 18, 1100.

[61] Rudolf was elected antiking in 1077, and was killed in 1080.

aforesaid Rudolf buried like a king, he replied to one who asked why he permitted a man who had not been a king to lie buried as though with royal honors, "I would that all my enemies lay as honorably buried." When Rudolf was slain, his son-in-law, Berthold, usurped the duchy of Swabia as if it had been ceded to him by his father-in-law.[62]

viii. At that time a certain count named Frederick, who traced his descent from the most noble counts of Swabia, had established residence in a fortress called Staufen. Since this man was prudent in counsel and vigorous in war,[63] he had been summoned to the emperor's court and had rendered military service there for many days, playing the part of a zealous and noble soldier.[64] In every peril he had manfully stood by his emperor. Now the prince, in view of the precarious state of the government, secretly called to him the aforesaid count and addressed him thus:

"Best of men, whom of all my subjects I have found most faithful in peace and most valiant in war, see you how the Roman world, veiled in darkness and devoid of loyalty, according to the line,

Last of the heavenly host, Astrea leaves the earth,[65]

is enticed to wicked strivings and shameful deeds. Neither respect for parents nor due subjection to overlords is observed. Oaths of fealty, which by divine as well as by human law are customarily sworn publicly by the warrior to his prince, are held in despite, and seditious oaths, made in secret places at the instigation of the devil and in opposition to divine and human law, are held as sacrosanct. No honor is paid to the laws and none to divine ordinances. Now, since all authority is from God, he who resists authority resists the ordinance of God.[66] Arise, therefore, against this pestilential scourge and gird yourself like a man to overthrow the enemies of the empire. I am not unmindful of your former merits, nor shall I be ungrateful for future services. I will give you in marriage my only daughter [67] and will grant you the duchy of Swabia which Berthold has invaded."

---

[62] Rudolf was succeeded by his son Berthold; only after the latter's death in 1091 did Berthold of Zähringen claim the duchy. Otto may have been confused by the identity of name between the son and son-in-law of Rudolf.

[63] Otto uses almost the same words to describe Conrad II in *Two Cities* VI.xxviii.

[64] Cf. *Two Cities* IV.xii and Sallust *Catiline* lx.4.

[65] Ovid *Met.* I.150.   [66] Romans 13:2.

[67] Agnes, betrothed to Frederick in 1079. By him she had two sons, Frederick (born 1090) and Conrad (born 1093). After the death of her husband in 1105, Agnes mar-

So then the aforesaid Frederick, becoming at once duke of the Swabians and son-in-law of the king, returned to his own home and (not to make a long story of it) finally forced Berthold to seek peace. Yet some relate that this befell under his son, Frederick.[68] Now the condition of peace was as follows: that Berthold should relinquish the duchy, yet in such wise that Zurich, the finest town of Swabia, should remain his to be held directly from the emperor. This town, situated in the mountain passes facing Italy and on a lake from which the river Limmat flows, was once a colony of emperors and kings and, according to the account handed down by our ancestors, was of so great authority that the people of Milan, when summoned by the emperor to the assizes across the Alps, must have their cases heard and adjudicated there. Whence, in consequence of its abundance of treasures as well as of honors, the city is said to have inscribed upon its gate, "Zurich, the noble city abounding in many possessions." Moreover, after the aforesaid stream, the Limmat (whence Lucan: "They have deserted the tents erected by hollow Lemannus"), that whole province is called *Alemannia*.[69] Therefore, some believe that the entire land of Germany was called *Alemannia*, and are accustomed to call all the Germans *Alemanni*, whereas only that province, namely, Swabia, is called *Alemannia*, after the river Lemannus, and only the people who dwell there are properly called *Alemanni*.

Although Berthold was in this affair untrue both to the empire and to justice, he is said nevertheless to have been very vigorous and valiant. Even today older people tell how, whenever a messenger bringing him some bad news hesitated to speak, as often happens, he would say: "Speak up! For I know that joy always precedes sorrow and sorrow precedes joy; therefore it is as acceptable to me first to hear of storm when I am afterward to hear of sunshine as first to hear of sunshine and afterward of storm." A magnificent saying and one worthy of a brave man,[70] who without education instinctively perceived the imperma-

---

ried Leopold, margrave of Austria, by whom she became the mother of Otto of Freising.

[68] This sentence would seem to be a later addition to the text.

[69] Otto is speaking of the river Limmat, Lucan (*Pharsalia* 1.396) of Lake Leman. Otto appears to have borrowed both the derivation and Lucan's quotation from Isidore *Etym.* IX.ii.94. He frequently, but not always, uses the terms *Alemannia* and *Suevia* interchangeably; they are here regularly rendered "Swabia" when it is clear that *Alemannia* refers to the duchy and not to Germany as a whole.

[70] Cf. Cicero *De off.* III.i.

nence of natural events, and was not elated in days of good fortune, forgetting the bad, nor broken in days of disaster through failure to recall the good. But Frederick from this time forth held the duchy of Swabia without opposition and ruled vigorously for many a day.

ix. Frederick's most noble spouse Agnes bore him two sons, Frederick and Conrad. He himself, after many evidences of his virtues, ended his days at a ripe old age and was buried in the monastery at Lorch, erected on his own land. But the aforesaid Berthold, holding from that time forth the empty title of duke, left this as an inheritance to his descendants. For they all, even to the present day, are called dukes, though they have no duchy and participate in the name alone without the substance—unless one were to call a duchy the county that lies between the Jura and the Great St. Bernard [71] which, after the death of Count William, Berthold's son Conrad received from the Emperor Lothar, or maintain that they should be honored by the name of duke from the duchy of Carinthia, which they have never possessed. In other respects, however, they flourish with no small distinction of goods and of honor.[72]

x. On the death of Frederick, duke of the Swabians, his widow Agnes was taken under the protection of her brother Henry, the son of the Emperor Henry, who gave her in marriage to Leopold, margrave of Austria, as we have elsewhere more fully related.[73] Frederick's son Frederick was then fifteen, and his son Conrad twelve years of age. Furthermore, Frederick, as the elder, had succeeded his father as duke. About the same time Emperor Henry died at Liége, a city of Belgic Gaul. His vital organs were buried there, but his body was removed to the city of Speyer in Gaul and was buried there in the church of the Blessed Mother of God and Ever Virgin Mary, in royal

---

[71] *Inter Iurum et montem Iovis;* see below, II.xlviii.

[72] The house of Zähringen was one of the great Swabian noble families of this period, outclassed only by the houses of Welf and Hohenstaufen, and its dukes erected a powerful territorial state largely centering about the Black Forest region and northern Switzerland (see below, II.xlviii). The family became extinct in the male line in 1218, and its lands were split up; much of the Swiss holdings passed to the house of Kyburg and from it, in 1263, to the rising Hapsburg family. For the position of the Zähringer dukes, see the article of Theodor Mayer, "The State of the Dukes of Zähringen," in Geoffrey Barraclough, *Mediaeval Germany, 911–1250: Essays by German Historians* (Oxford, 1938), II, 175–202. Mayer notes (pp. 193–94) that when Otto speaks of the Zähringer ducal title as an empty formality, he is thinking only in terms of the old tribal duchies. [73] *Two Cities* VII.ix.

state beside his father and grandfather, the emperors. This church he had himself constructed—as it is to be seen today—a marvelous and skillful work.

His son Henry—fourth in the line of the emperors, but fifth in that of the kings—succeeded him in the kingdom. He was very energetic in war and subjected the entire empire to his sway in so short a time that all who dwelt within the Roman world bore with humility the yoke of subjection, and the neighboring peoples trembled for fear of his power.

xi. How many and what great and valiant deeds he performed, both at Rome and in Italy, we here omit, as they have been related in our earlier history.[74] It may suffice at present to say only this, that upon his being placed in the position of supreme power, all the people of Gaul were in fear of him. Contrary to the expectation of many, he had taken by assault the fortress of Bar-le-Duc and had led away prisoner Count Reinald, whom he there captured [1113]. Then he pitched camp near Mouzon, a stronghold of the count, which was situated on a lofty mountain and possessed excellent natural fortifications. As he could take it neither by craft nor by violence, he ordered a scaffold to be erected and announced that unless the fortress were speedily surrendered he would hang the count. The townsmen asked for a truce until the next day. That night the countess bore a son. Thereupon the townsmen assembled and swore an oath of fealty to the newborn infant. When morning came and the emperor again summoned the inhabitants to surrender the stronghold and threatened to hang their lord the count, who had been led forth in view of all, they replied that they were not willing to give up the castle under threat of his death, especially since they had a new lord whom his wife had born him that night. Whereupon the sovereign, inflamed with rage, ordered the aforesaid count to be dragged to the gallows. When he was urged by the princes who were present not to do this and yet persisted in his intent, his eyes dark with anger, he is said to have replied to some who held that he should at least desist from his purpose out of regard for divine punishment: "The heaven, even the heavens, are the Lord's; but the earth hath he given to the children of men." [75] At last, however, as his unreasonable passion cooled, the emperor heeded the entreaties

---

[74] *Ibid.* VII.xiv.　　　　　　[75] Psalms 115:16.

of all, revoked the sentence of death, and returned to his own home, taking the aforesaid count with him as his prisoner.

xii. Not long after, while with the participation of many princes he was magnificently celebrating his marriage at Mainz, a city of Gaul, the realm was rent asunder, as we have more fully related elsewhere.[76] The schism at that time was so serious that, except for Duke Frederick and his brother and Godfrey, count palatine of the Rhine, there were scarcely any of the princes who did not rebel against their sovereign. How many and what great deeds worthy of record Frederick, the most noble duke of the Swabians, then performed in the presence of the emperor or while he tarried in Italy, we shall relate in summary fashion, since they are still preserved in the memories of many.

Crossing the Rhine from Swabia into Gaul, he gradually subjected to his will the entire stretch of country from Basel to Mainz, where the principal strength of the realm is known to be. He thus made his way downstream along the bank of the Rhine, now building a fortress in some suitable place and subjecting all the neighborhood to his power, now proceeding again and abandoning the former stronghold to build another, so that it was said of him, "Duke Frederick always hauls a fortress with him at the tail of his horse." Moreover, the aforesaid duke was brave in battle, shrewd in his business dealings, calm in appearance and in spirit, courteous in speech, and so generous of gifts that on this account a great multitude of warriors flocked to him and offered themselves voluntarily for his service.

xiii. Accordingly, when all the country along the Rhine, as has been said above, had been brought under subjection, he declared war on Albert, archbishop of Mainz, the cleverest and richest of all the princes of the realm at that time, because he had been the head and the instigator of the aforesaid rebellion. After devastating all the country round about, he finally besieged the city itself with a countless throng of knights and commoners [1117]. Now, the aforesaid city is great and strong and is situated on the Rhine. On the side where it borders upon the Rhine it is closely built and densely populated, and on the other side it is sparsely settled and bare, merely encircled by a strong wall that has not a few towers. It is much longer than it is wide; thus has

[76] *Two Cities* vii.xv. Henry married Matilda, daughter of Henry I of England, in 1114.

necessity set its mark on the place.[77] For on the side where it borders on Gaul, it is narrowed by a mountain that rises to a moderate height, and on the other side, where it faces Germany, by the Rhine. Consequently, along the Rhine it is adorned with noble temples and other buildings, and toward the mountain it is provided with vineyards and other useful plantations.

The crowd engaged in the siege under the duke wished to take it by storm on the side where the city is thinly populated, in order to plunder it. But the noble duke, fearing that if so great license were given to the thoughtless fury of the rabble the holy places might perhaps be given over to plunder and to flames, strove earnestly that their desire might not be accomplished. But the bishop of the city, rendering no proper return to the piety of the duke, guilefully sent messengers to him from the city and asked for a truce. He asked a time and place of meeting, promised readiness to be reconciled with the emperor, and thus persuaded the duke to disband his army, raise the siege, and so return home with a small following. The bishop, seeing that the siege was raised and the army disbanded, opened the gates, pursued the duke with a great military force, and attacked him unexpectedly. The duke and the men whom he still had left of the great army, then first apprised of the bishop's treachery, were by no means dismayed as usually happens when men must hastily seize their weapons. Instead, all the more inspired to courage by the presence of the enemy, they armed themselves and dashed upon the foe. The Swabians fought manfully, and at last Count Emico,[78] who was the leader of those on the side of the Franks,[79] fell mortally wounded. Thereupon the courage of the Franks broke; they turned their backs and sought safety in flight. The valiant duke pursued them, slaying and capturing many. The rest he drove with their bishop to the very gates of the city and thus won the victory. The hearts of the citizens who had lost relatives and friends in that slaughter were filled with such bitterness that they almost flung

[77] Otto borrows this sentence bodily from Hegesippus *De bello Judaico* III.v; this Latin version of Josephus was a favorite with Otto. See below, II.xxi.

[78] Count of Leiningen. He may have been the Count Emico of Leiningen who had been notorious for his persecution of the Jews of Mainz, Speyer, and Worms at the time of the First Crusade; he had led one group of the crusaders, but returned home after going only as far as Hungary.

[79] By "Franks" (*Francorum*) Otto refers to the natives of the region of Mainz. For Otto's use of *Francia*, see Introduction, p. 12.

themselves upon their own bishop as the one responsible for this defeat.

xiv. Now on another occasion the aforesaid Bishop Albert, with Lothar, duke of the Saxons, and other princes leading a great and powerful company of knights, had laid siege to the stronghold of Limburg, situated in the territory of Speyer [1116]. When he had almost compelled the fortress to surrender because of the hunger and privations of its citizens, this same most illustrious duke gathered an army, marched upon the aforesaid princes, and forced them to raise the siege. It is said that the townsmen mentioned above, under the impulsion of hunger, had taken counsel what to do. When some advised this and others that, a certain Swabian named Ulrich of Horningen, noted for his keenness of wit and great stature, said it would be better to eat the fat monks—for a monastery had been established in that same town—than for the town to be handed over to the enemy for lack of food. The monks, alarmed when the remark became known, surrendered the provisions they had stored up and with this food to the best of their ability fed all the knights that abode there until the town was relieved.

Why say more? The aforesaid duke, to sum up in a few words, was in all things like his father. He was so faithful a knight to his sovereign and so helpful a friend to his uncle that by his valor he supported the tottering honor of the realm, fighting manfully against its foes until the members that were at variance with their head by seeking their sovereign's favor returned again to his affection. Moreover, he took to wife the daughter [80] of Henry, duke of Bavaria. By her he afterward became the father of the most renowned Frederick, who is emperor at the present time, and Judith, who, as all know, was recently united in marriage with Duke Matthew of Lorraine.

xv. Emperor Henry, having reconciled the princes who had opposed him and being now in full possession of the empire, held a diet at Utrecht, a city of Frisia, on Whitsunday [1125]. There he was taken sick and removed from earthly cares. After his vital organs had been buried there, his body was transported along the bank of the Rhine to the upper country and was buried in the city of Speyer beside his fathers.

xvi. But the Empress Mathilda, the daughter of Henry, king of England, had the royal insignia in her possession. The aforesaid

[80] Judith, daughter of Henry the Black and mother of Barbarossa.

Albert, archbishop of Mainz, summoned her to him and by false promises induced her to hand over the regalia to him.

xvii (xvi).   So then Albert—for this is said to be from of old the right of the archbishop of Mainz so long as the throne is vacant—in the autumn called together the princes of the realm to that very city of Mainz. Not unmindful of the reverses he had endured at the hands of Duke Frederick, although the aforesaid duke was demanded by many as successor to the throne, he persuaded all the princes who were present to select Lothar, duke of the Saxons, a man nevertheless worthy of all honor because of his zeal for righteousness. This the archbishop did, in so far as he had the power, more out of regard for his own interests than for the common weal.

This act, however praiseworthy it proved to be, was nevertheless a fresh source of a very serious schism. For on the advice of the same Albert, bishop of Mainz, who had not yet satisfied his hatred for the heirs of Emperor Henry (as it is written: "The leech does not leave the skin until it is filled with blood" [81]), the aforesaid Lothar persecuted Duke Frederick and his brother Conrad. On this account he besieged Nuremberg[1127], where they had established garrisons and which they held as though by hereditary right. He associated with him Ulrich, duke of the Bohemians, and Henry of the Bavarians. [82] But after a time the sovereign permitted the duke of the Bohemians to depart, because the barbarians who had come with him, neither fearing God nor reverencing man, devastated the whole neighborhood and spared not even the churches.

xviii (xvii).   Therefore Duke Frederick and his brother Conrad collected an army and, having agreed with the citizens on a time and a sign, on a certain day approached the town with their soldiery. Seeing this, the inhabitants could not conceal their gladness of heart, and burst forth into loud cheers and songs. The emperor, considering it safer to besiege the aforesaid town at another time than rashly to entrust himself to the faith of faithless fortune, raised the siege and, marching through Bamberg, betook himself to the city of Würzburg. The citizens [of Nuremberg] burst forth, descended with great outcries upon the

---

[81] Horace *Ars poetica* 476.

[82] Ulrich is Soběslav I of Bohemia (1125–40); Henry is Henry the Proud, duke of Bavaria after the death of his father Henry the Black in 1126, and who in 1127 married Gertrude, daughter of the emperor Lothar. This action took place in 1127.

now vacant camp, and plundered whatever had been left there. Receiving their lords with great joy, they escorted them into the fortress. The dukes stocked the town with provisions and other necessities. Then, following after their king, who remained in the city [Würzburg], and engaging with his knights outside the town in military exercise now commonly called a tournament (*turneimentum*),[83] they advanced to the very walls. After this they crossed the Rhine and established a garrison in the city of Speyer, whose inhabitants had received them with due respect because of their loyalty to the emperors who were buried there and because they were descended from the same stock. The emperor, associating with himself Albert of Mainz, besieged this city, but though he spent many days there, he had no success [1128].

xix (xviii). Furthermore Henry, duke of the Bavarians, the son of the aforesaid Duke Henry,[84] out of regard for the sovereign whose daughter Gertrude he had recently taken to wife, declared war on Duke Frederick, unmindful of the relationship between them by virtue of the connection of his sister Judith.[85] After assembling no small army from Bavaria, he entered Swabia and pitched camp not far from the Danube, on a stream named Wernitz. When they heard of this, the aforesaid dukes also collected an armed force and established a camp not far from him. But the duke of the Bavarians, sending out spies, made inquiries as to the strength of the enemy. When they returned and told him what they had seen, he took counsel with his men and asked what was to be done. They judged it inexpedient to await the enemy and advised flight. And so the Bavarians withdrew from before their adversaries with as great haste as if they were already being threatened by them. Distrusting a narrow bridge, they recklessly consigned themselves to the treacherous currents of the stream I have mentioned,

[83] *Tyrocinium, quod vulgo nunc turneimentum dicitur.* Cf. below, I.xxvi and IV.xi.

[84] Otto is under the impression that the Duke Henry mentioned above (I.xvii) was Henry the Black; actually, it was Henry the Proud, the same duke now under consideration. The events of this chapter probably occurred in connection with the campaign just described.

[85]

Henry the Black		
Judith (m. Frederick, duke of Swabia)		Henry the Proud (m. Gertrude, dau. of Emperor Lothar)

which had become swollen to an unusual depth because of frequent heavy rains. They made a perilous crossing, swimming the stream rather than fording it, and returned ignominiously to their homes.

xx (xix). Likewise, at another time the aforesaid Duke Henry entered Swabia and betook himself to his own place of abode there [1129]. For he was Swabian by birth, tracing his lineage from the ancient and very noble family of the Welfs. In consequence, he held by right of inheritance many possessions in that part where Swabia borders on the Pyrenees. He was a man altogether worthy of praise, distinguished by nobility of mind no less than by nobility of birth. It is only for the following deed that he is blameworthy: namely, sending messengers to Frederick, duke of the Swabians, he urged him in friendly fashion as his sister's husband to return to an amicable relationship with the sovereign, saying that it is difficult for anyone, however great and righteous a prince, to sustain alone the burden of the entire empire. And he added further that he himself would be a trustworthy mediator in the matter, if Frederick were willing to be guided by his advice. And so a certain monastery called Zwifalten was selected and a time set for their meeting that they might discuss the matter more intimately, face to face. Duke Frederick, anticipating no treachery, came with a few companions to the aforesaid place. But Henry, not walking uprightly,[86] discovered by secret inquiry where Frederick planned to spend the night. And so, as the sun sank to the hemisphere below, when darkness showed itself opportune to black hearts, the chamber in which the duke slept was surrounded, and it was revealed by word and deed that Henry came not as friend but as enemy. What was Frederick to do? Whither could he turn? Should he take up arms? But he had scarcely anyone to help him. Should he flee? Knowing of no exit from the chamber, he found no help in flight. And so, becoming aware of the treachery, he commended himself solely to the aid of divine grace. By such assistance, through a certain secret passageway from the room, then first providentially revealed to him, he found access to the church and climbed up the tower adjacent to it. His enemies burst into the room and, not finding the duke, even entered the cloistered retreat of the monks, breaking open all their outbuildings with their swords. When Phoebus returned from the world below and began to illumine the upper region of the air, all faithful adherents of the duke in the vicinity,

---

[86] Proverbs 10:9, 28:18.

learning of so foul a deed, hurried in throngs to his assistance. As the enemy were still exploring the inner chambers of the monastery and threatening to burn it, Frederick, now relieved from anxiety as he saw from the tower his friends approaching, called for Duke Henry and addressed him as follows: "It is in defiance of justice that you have acted, good duke; for you summoned me to peace but have shown yourself an enemy rather than a friend, not bearing the tokens of peace. Neither regard for your personal honor nor the blood relationship by which we are united has deterred you from this deed. Yet, lest I appear to render evil for evil,[87] I admonish you in good faith, as a friend, not to await the arrival of my faithful followers, whom I see coming up from all sides." Yet this deed of the duke is excused by some, not only because they were personal enemies at the time, according to the saying,[88]

In an enemy, who distinguishes between guile and valor?

but also from the fact that he did this out of loyalty to the realm and for the sake of peace in the state, desiring to hand him over to the emperor and to restore peace to the empire.

xxi (xx). So the strife between Duke Frederick and Emperor Lothar, dragging on for almost ten years, did not allow the empire to be at peace.[89] But how it was at last quieted, and how many evidences of his great virtues Lothar has left on record has been sufficiently related in my former history.[90]

We are not willing, however, to pass over in silence the fact that the aforesaid emperor experienced excessively adverse fortune at the beginning of his reign. For a certain Count Otto of Moravia, coveting the duchy of Bohemia, approached the emperor and by the promise of

---

[87] I Peter 3:9.   [88] Vergil *Aeneid* II.390.

[89] It is worth noting that Otto, after discussing these early Hohenstaufen successes in the struggle with Lothar and Henry (the relief of Nuremberg in 1127, the occupation of Speyer in 1128, the failure to capture Frederick in 1129), passes over in silence the Hohenstaufen reverses which followed. Conrad was set up as antiking in 1127, and waged an unsuccessful campaign in Italy in 1128–30. Lothar reduced both Speyer and Nuremberg by siege in 1130, and Duke Henry captured Ulm in 1134. In October, 1134, Frederick submitted to the emperor, and Conrad followed suit in September, 1135. None of these occurrences is recorded in the present work; in *Two Cities* (VII.xvii, xix) Otto mentions only the election of Conrad as antiking, the submission to him of Milan in 1128, and the "reconciliation" of the brothers to the emperor. See Giesebrecht, IV, ii, v; *Cambridge Medieval History*, V, 338–41.

[90] *Two Cities* VII.xvii ff.

much money induced him to enter Bohemia with him and there to appoint him its duke. Ulrich,[91] who was then in possession of that duchy and opposed his plan, was unable by any display of devotion to restrain the emperor from his purpose. Thereupon the king proceeded to Saxony, raised an army, and, bringing Otto with him, in the winter entered the forest that separates Bohemia from Saxony.[92] But Duke Ulrich of Bohemia pitched his camp on a certain stream in the most remote part of that same wood, surrounded on all sides by forests. The king and his men became lost because of the deep snow and wandered through the trackless forest; chance brought them to the aforesaid stream. His followers were exhausted by the excessive strain of the march and by lack of food and wished to rest. The barbarians, seeing the muddied water, perceived that an enemy was near. Coming upon them unexpectedly, they attacked the Saxons who were in the vanguard and who were exhausted from tramping through the snow. A few escaped by flight and some were taken captive; all the rest they cruelly slew. The emperor, seeing this and being unable to bring help to his men because the roads were so narrow, was deeply grieved. Nevertheless, inspired by the recollection of the exploits which he had performed since his youth and by the remembrance of his tested valor, as though refreshed with dew from heaven, he retreated to a certain hill with his remaining followers. The aforesaid duke so disposed his men and built barricades of great trees as to make retreat impossible, and thus held him, as it were, surrounded. Finally, through the mediation of Margrave Henry of Saxony,[93] the son of the duke's sister, who had accompanied the king, the duke [Ulrich] cast himself humbly at the emperor's feet, offering him satisfaction and tendering homage and fealty. Then he received the duchy from him and restored the captives. Thus the sovereign, bearing with him the bodies of those who were of distinguished rank, returned with much sorrow.

xxii (xxi). Among others, the most noble Margrave Albert of Saxony had been taken captive.[94] Moreover, such great slaughter of the Saxons, and especially of their noble and illustrious men, had taken

[91] Soběslav I; see above, note 82. These events occurred in 1125–26.

[92] Probably the Erzgebirge.

[93] Henry of Groitsch, son of Soběslav's sister, Judith; he did not become margrave of the East Mark of Saxony until 1131.

[94] Albert the Bear, margrave of the East Mark of Saxony until 1131, and later of the North Mark; see below, II.xlii.

place that the spark of lasting hate between the Saxons and the Bohemians kindled there has not yet been extinguished. Otto, too, who was the instigator of this conflict, there paid the penalty by his death. But, in accordance with the saying,

Better is ever the end that follows a mournful beginning,[95]

a kinder fortune followed this prince. It bore him to such a height that after quieting all the storm of sedition he returned from Italy in triumph and victory and came to the end of his life there in the mountains. Judith died during this time of dissension and Duke Frederick took to wife Agnes, the daughter of Count Frederick of Saarbrücken, a brother of Bishop Albert.[96] By her he had Conrad, who, as is well known, is count palatine of the Rhine at the present time, and Clarissa, now the wife of Count Louis of Thuringia.

xxiii (xxii). Upon the death of Emperor Lothar and his burial in the monastery of Königslutter, which is situated on his own land, the princes of the realm met at Coblenz, a city of Gaul located at the junction of the Moselle and the Rhine, and took counsel regarding the election of a king. Thereupon Conrad, a brother of Duke Frederick, was demanded as their ruler by all who were present, and, being elevated to the throne, he was crowned in the palace at Aachen.[97] This could be done the more easily because hatred of Emperor Henry had now cooled in the hearts of many, and Albert, archbishop of Mainz, had recently departed this life. Conrad's candidacy received additional impetus from the fact that Henry, duke of the Bavarians, had by reason of his arrogance incurred the hatred of almost all who had been on the Italian expedition with Emperor Lothar.

Thereupon Duke Frederick came to Mainz, which was then vacant, being bereft of its shepherd, and prevailed on all—clergy and laity alike—to elect Albert the Younger, the brother of his second wife. The king was called in to add the weight of his influence. As Albert was not unlike his uncle, the elder Albert, he did not show much gratitude for favors, nor was he entirely loyal to his prince. But how Duke Henry of the Bavarians opposed the aforesaid exaltation of the sovereign, what

[95] Ovid *Met.* VII.518.

[96] When Judith died is not known. Frederick's second wife, it will be noted, was the niece of his old opponent, Archbishop Albert of Mainz (see above, I.xiii–xvii).

[97] See *Two Cities* VII.xx, xxii. Lothar died in 1137; Conrad's election followed in 1138.

end he himself met, and also how the prince triumphed over him and many others, has been sufficiently told in our former history.[98]

xxiv (xxiii). About the same time very distinguished delegates of John, emperor of the royal city,[99] came to the prince of the Romans. They sought to renew the bond of union between the two empires, I mean the western and eastern, because of the insolence of Roger of Sicily. And to cement this agreement, they asked that some girl of royal blood be given in marriage to the emperor's son Manuel. The prince selected for him instead a sister of his wife.[100] In confirmation of this arrangement he dispatched to Greece Embrico, the venerable bishop of Würzburg, a prudent and learned man. John was by that time dead, and his son, the aforesaid Manuel, sat upon the throne in the city.[101] Embrico, ordering all things with wisdom and shrewdness, induced them to solemnize the marriage in the week after Epiphany in the royal city, with splendor and regal state. He remained there for many days for the promotion of this and other affairs of the realm. While returning by boat to his native land, honored and onerated with many gifts of the Greeks, he died at Aquileia.

Now as regards these negotiations between the two sovereigns, there are extant the following letters that passed between them. Not to set them down in full, I have abbreviated them.

xxv. "Conrad, by the grace of God august emperor of the Romans, to John, by the same grace emperor at Constantinople, sends greeting and brotherly love.

"As our ancestors, namely, the emperors of the Romans, established friendship, honor, and glory with your predecessors, namely, the realm and the people of the Greeks, so do I establish it, and as they preserved it even so will I preserve it. There is no race, kingdom, or people that knows not that your New Rome is called and shall always be the daughter of the Roman republic. From this root have proceeded its branches and fruits. Therefore we have determined upon the inheritance which is due to the daughter from her mother and desire it to be enduring. And all the more have we done so because we see that

---

[98] *Ibid.* VII.xxii, xxiii.

[99] *Urbs regia* (Constantinople). The emperor in question here is John II Comnenus (1118–43).

[100] Conrad's wife was Gertrude, daughter of Count Berengar of Sulzbach; her sister was Bertha.

[101] Manuel I Comnenus (1143–80).

the daughter desires the mother's due honor: namely, that the mother's authority be preeminent in counsel, but that the love of the daughter may respond in glory and in honor to her aid. Accordingly the affairs of both should be pursued in common; both should have the same friend and the same foe, whether on land or on the sea; and whosoever has not honored the daughter—whether Norman or Sicilian or whosoever else, anywhere—should know and fear the valor and the might of the mother. We have not forgotten, neither I nor the princes of our realm, all incursions and invasions whatsoever affecting the empire and the dignity of Rome. But when divine mercy shall be vouchsafed us, we will repay each of them according to the enormity of their malice. To the furthest ends of the realms all shall see and hear with how little effort the brigands who rebelled against the authority of our two empires will be overthrown. Because, with God's aid, if we extend our wings we shall soon overtake the fleeing enemy and restrain the audacity of his spirit, which is now exalted against the honor and glory of our two empires. For this reason do we preserve just and friendly relations toward you—and you toward us. This we do with the greater zeal as we are the more closely allied by the marriage of the sister of our dearly beloved wife and most noble empress and your son.

"But because we believe that Your Love and Nobility rejoices at our successes, we have deemed it proper to inform you, as our only brother and dearly beloved friend, what, with God's aid, was done (after the departure of your most sagacious delegates) in a general solemn assembly attended at our wish by all the princes of our empire. Know, therefore, that we have, with God's aid, mightily subdued by our imperial power all who had openly assailed our empire. Receiving them with our complete pardon, we have enriched with abundant peace all parts of our empire. Furthermore, France, Spain, England, Denmark, and the other kingdoms adjoining our empire attend upon us with daily embassies of due reverence and respect, declaring by hostages as well as upon oath that they are ready to perform the commands imposed by our authority. Moreover, we would not hide from Your Discretion the fact that the lord pope and all Apulia, Italy, and Lombardy from day to day desire our coming. They importune us with utter devotion to come to their aid with our imperial might.

"On this account we have dispatched to Rome a dearly beloved and sincere prince of our empire, Embrico, the venerable bishop of Würzburg and your friend, to ascertain the will of the lord pope. Having learned his wish concerning us and obtained the counsel of our princes, we make known to Your Nobility the matters that concern the honor of both our empires by our very dear and prudent messengers, namely, Prince Robert of Capua, a particularly illustrious and noble man and faithful to us, and Albert, our chaplain, beloved and firm in the faith. Hear them, then, as you would hear us. Put into effect what they say to you, as befits Your Excellency and as we hope and believe you will. Send back to us without delay your honored and well-qualified delegates, together with our messengers.

"Concerning the Russians,[102] who in contempt of our empire have killed our men and seized our money for themselves, as is fitting in the case of your friend and kinsman, and as you have written us, so do.

"And to the warriors (*militibus*) of our empire, the Germans (*Alemannis*), I mean, who are with you, show yourself kind, as befits Your Magnificence. We beseech you further that you grant to the people of our empire, namely, to the Germans (*Teutonicis*) who sojourn in Constantinople, a place whereon to build a church to the glory of God, both out of regard for the heavenly reward and because of the intercession and petition of our love. Your Discretion must recall that we made the same request of you in previous letters presented to Your Nobility by the aforesaid chaplain, for the love and honor of God. For if He Himself be in our midst, Who giveth salvation to kings,[103] it is sure that our enemies will not rejoice.

"Given on the eighteenth day before the Kalends of March [February 12, 1142], at Regensburg, with joy in Christ. Amen."

(xxiv) "John, a king faithful to God in Christ, born to the purple, exalted, valiant, august, Comnenus and emperor of the Romans, to the most noble brother and friend of our empire.

"Most noble and beloved friend of our empire, O King. The letter of Your Nobility, a token of fraternal affection, delivered to Our Clemency by the most prudent delegate of Your Nobility, has filled us with much joy. For the good will of Your Nobility and the friendly affection and love for a kinsman which you have displayed both by

---

[102] *Reutenis;* see below, in the present chapter, toward the end of John's letter, and also, I.xxxii; III.i, iii; Appendix, *sub an.* 1165. A variant spelling is *Ruthenis*. It seems clear that the reference is to "Russians" rather than "Ruthenians."

[103] Psalms 144:10.

letter and by your very words and deeds toward our empire has in consequence drawn all our affection wholeheartedly to love of you. Accordingly, we have also sent forth to Your Nobility certain of the most trustworthy and most intimate of our followers, desiring through them to communicate again with Your Nobility concerning all the matters about which you have charged and written us. For we wish with God in all matters to be of a friendly, cousinly, and fraternal spirit toward Your Nobility, and to do everything which, to our understanding, is to the honor of Your Nobility.

"Now, because the most prudent doge of Venice, Peter Polani, has been accepted by Your Nobility as mediator in these cases, as a good man and fair to both parties, it has seemed good to us to approve of this also.

"In the matter of Apulia and Lombardy, we have instructed our most perspicacious delegates in what has commended itself to us. For while certain of these have been sent more specifically to receive the most noble lady who is to be, if God wills, the daughter-in-law of our empire, yet the general policy of our empire is known to them also.

"Of the situation which has arisen in Russia (*in Rossia*), even as you have written to our empire, so also have we done as it is proper for our empire to do in the case of a friend and kinsman.

"As regards the knights [104] of Your Nobility: the instructions in your letter about each of them by name, and especially about him who is no longer among the living, our empire has acted in accordance with what you wrote.

"Farewell, most noble friend of our empire, O King." [105]

"Conrad, by the grace of God truly emperor august of the Romans, to his dearest brother Manuel, born to the purple, Comnenus, illustrious and famous king of the Greeks, greeting and brotherly love.

"The letter of Your Nobility, transmitted by so great and so dear a friend of ours to Our Serenity, we have gratefully received, and upon

---

[104] *Caballariis;* see Conrad's letter above, where they are designated as *militibus.*

[105] This letter was written in 1142 or 1143. It is noteworthy that John nowhere in it addresses Conrad as *imperator,* and nowhere speaks of the German realm as an *imperium;* Conrad grants both these titles in his letter preceding this. But in Conrad's letter immediately following this to the Emperor Manuel (written in 1145; Manuel had succeeded John in 1143) the new emperor is called only *rex Grecorum,* though the text of the letter mentions the late John as *imperator.*

learning its contents we rejoiced greatly at your security and your exalted state. But having heard from Nicephorus, the wise delegate of Your Love, beyond the contents of the letter certain harsh words— and, to tell the truth, words unheard in all past time—not only is the mildness of Our Majesty disturbed more than tongue can express, but the length and breadth of our empire is amazed. We have marveled greatly whence or from whom so bitter a word as this has issued, especially since up to the present time the kingdom of the Greeks has flourished among the other kingdoms of this world in all wisdom and discretion. For if that same messenger of yours, Nicephorus, had struck our only son Henry dead before our eyes, he could not have provoked the spirit of Our Majesty to greater anger. And when he had labored in this bitterness of spirit for three days and had been unable by any ingenuity or any cleverness to bend the firmness of our resolution to his will, barely did he on the fourth day cheer Our Excellency with other, friendlier, words. After quieting the fury of our indignation, he revealed to us the will of Your Nobility. And since as matters now stand —and should stand—you, the dearest of all my friends, will receive our most beloved daughter, I mean the sister of our noble consort, as your wife, we desire that there shall be herein an eternal bond of enduring friendship. This friendship we have declared established by word of mouth and in writing, in the presence of your delegate, namely in these terms: that we are to be the friends of your friends and the foes of your foes. Accordingly, let Your Prudence be well assured that if any annoyance or injury shall have been inflicted upon Your Nobility from any source, we consider this, by reason of our love, to have been done not to you only but also to us. For the nobility of your virtue and, above all, the relationship of your noble blood whereby we are united in a pledge of perpetual affection prompt us to embrace you with the arms of all tender affection as our dearest son, and to do gladly all that is pleasing to you. Therefore we think it right that you have the same friendship for us and our empire confirmed, so that, after all has been honorably completed, due honor may redound thence to both empires and peace and Christ's name may thereby be exalted throughout the whole world.

"Further, concerning the five hundred knights whom Your Nobility requests, we reply that we will send you not a mere five hundred but even two or three thousand, should you need them. And, what is still more, sooner than behold you suffer any slight to your honor, we cannot fail you or neglect to come in person, with the united strength of our whole empire, to you, our dearly beloved son and dearest brother.

"Your Nobility has also written that we should send important and valued messengers to Your Sincerity. Herein have we acquiesced in your desire, for we have sent to Your Excellency those whom we held very dear, namely, our most esteemed and greatly beloved Embrico, the venerable bishop of Würzburg, a great and illustrious prince of our realm, who is our very heart and soul; also our dearly beloved Robert, the illustrious and noble prince of Capua. We have sent also as it were our two hands, two blood brothers—I mean brother Berno, a wise and holy man, and his brother Riwin, who is our dear and intimate friend —and that noble and honorable prince of our empire, Roger, the illustrious count of Ariano, whose good faith and trustworthiness we have often tested, and our faithful Walter. To them we have accordingly entrusted matters that are not contained in the letters to be referred to Your Zeal. You may place confidence in their words and believe what they say to you as though spoken by us.

"Concerning the Russians, moreover, about whom we wrote to your father, the Emperor John of blessed memory, by our most faithful chaplain, Albert, and by Count Alexander of Gravina, and concerning the place in which we wish to build for our Germans a church, to the glory of God, and concerning the noble barons of Apulia, namely, Alexander of Claromonte, Philip of Surris, Count Henry, and Sennis Pustellis, that dearly beloved friend of ours, the bishop of Würzburg, and our other confidants will report our will to you. Believe them as you would us. Above all we commend to you very earnestly your faithful delegate Nicephorus, although he did distress us at the outset of his mission. Because he has continued steadfast to the end, we ask that you reward him. Farewell."

So much for that.

xxvi (xxv). Now Frederick,[106] the son of the most redoubtable Duke Frederick, had grown to manhood and had already buckled on the belt of military service, a man destined to be the nobler heir of a noble father. Accordingly, not concealing the virtue of his good inheritance, and trained, as is customary, in military sports, he at length girded himself for the serious business of a soldier's career while his father was still alive and in full possession of his land. For he denounced

---

[106] The future Emperor Frederick Barbarossa.

as his enemy a certain noble named Henry of Wolfrathshausen and invaded Bavaria with a large army. The Bavarians, and particularly the counts and other nobles, betook themselves to the stronghold of the aforesaid count, as though to celebrate a passage at arms which we are now accustomed to call a tournament.[107] And so that most redoubtable youth, coming upon the Bavarians as they stood outside the wall awaiting him under arms, assailed them not as in play but manfully making a serious attack. After both sides had fought long and valiantly, at last he forced his foes to retreat within the stronghold. After the Bavarians had turned in flight and were crowded together because of the narrowness of the gates, a certain Conrad of Dachau, then a noble count and afterward made duke of Croatia and Dalmatia,[108] who had incautiously remained outside, was surrounded by his foes and taken captive. And so the youth returned victorious to his own land, leading with him the aforesaid count. And although many sought to persuade Frederick to extort a large sum of money from Conrad, he rejected this counsel of the ungodly in consequence of his innate fineness of character. For as the count had been valorously captured, so was he nobly released. Frederick permitted him to return to his own country without exacting ransom.

xxvii (xxvi). After this Frederick declared war on Duke Conrad, the son of the aforesaid Berthold.[109] He captured the town of Zurich in Swabia (which I have mentioned before) and placed a garrison there. Then, as certain even of the nobles of Bavaria joined him, he entered the land of the aforesaid duke with a large army. At last, advancing almost to the utmost limits of Swabia, he came to Zähringen, a stronghold of that same duke, with none opposing him or able to resist. Not long afterward he took and possessed himself of a certain fortress of his [Conrad's] which still appears impregnable to all beholders.[110] And, contrary to the expectation of many, he so utterly vanquished that very brave and wealthy duke that he forced him to come to his father and his uncle and sue for peace.

[107] *Tyrocinium . . . quod modo nundinas vocare solemus;* cf. i.xviii, above.

[108] See below, IV.xvii.

[109] Conrad, son of Berthold II of Zähringen (see above, I.vii–viii), and sole ruler of the Zähringer lands after the death in 1122 of his brother, Berthold III.

[110] The reference is presumably to some fortress in the vicinity of Freiburg-im-Breisgau (a town founded by Conrad in 1120), possibly Schlossberg. The Zähringer dukes were major rivals of the Hohenstaufen in Swabia. During the period of Hohenstaufen weakness, the position of the Zähringer had been considerably strengthened.

These and other exploits as arduous he performed even in the years of youth, to the amazement of many, so that not inappropriately it might be said of him, in the words of the Gospel, "What manner of child shall this be?" [111]

xxviii (xxvii). During these days, a certain Arnold,[112] who wore a religious garb but was by no means faithful to it, as was evident from his teaching, entered the city of Rome. Because of his hatred for the honors paid to the Church, and seeking to restore the dignity of the senate and the equestrian order to their ancient status, he aroused almost the entire City, and especially the populace, against his pope. Whence, in corroboration of their rashness, or rather of their folly, there is extant the following document sent by them to their prince:

xxix (xxviii). "To the most excellent and renowned lord of the City and of the whole world, Conrad, by the grace of God king of the Romans, ever august, the senate and Roman people send greeting and wishes for prosperous and glorious administration of the Roman empire.

"We have already zealously set forth to Your Royal Excellency by many letters our deeds and undertakings, declaring how we continue faithful to you and daily strive for the exaltation of your imperial crown and its increase in every way.

"Because Your Royal Industry has not deigned to reply to this, as we requested, we as sons and faithful adherents marvel greatly at our lord and father. For what we are doing we do out of loyalty to you, and to honor you. And since we desire to exalt and to increase the Roman kingdom and empire, vouchsafed by God to your governance, and to restore it to that state in which it was at the time of Constantine and of Justinian, who held the whole world in their hands by the might of the senate and of the Roman people, we have by God's grace reinstated the senate for all these matters and have in large measure trampled under foot those who were always rebels against your sway and who had filched so great honor from the Roman empire. We strive with one accord and labor zealously that you may obtain through all and in all the things that belong to Caesar and the empire.

"And for the accomplishment of this we have made a good beginning and foundation. For we maintain peace and justice toward all wishing

---

[111] Luke 1:66.

[112] Arnold of Brescia (*c.* 1100–1155), who had, by 1147, taken the leadership of the Roman uprising against the pope.

it, and have captured the fortifications, that is, the towers and the palaces of the mighty of the City who, together with the Sicilian and the pope, were preparing to offer resistance to your authority. Some of these we hold in fealty to you and some we have dismantled and leveled to the ground. But for the sake of all these things that we are doing out of loyalty to Your Love, the pope, the Frangipani, and the sons of Pierleone, who are adherents and friends of the Sicilian (except Jordan who as our standard-bearer and our helper is loyal to you),[113] Tolomeus also, and many others, assail us from all sides, that we may not be able freely to place the imperial crown upon the royal head as is fitting. But as no burden is heavy for a lover, we endure gladly for the sake of your love and honor, even though we suffer many injuries thereby. For we know that we shall receive from you as from a father a reward for it, and that you will exact vengeance from them as from enemies of the empire.

"Since, therefore, our loyalty to you is so great and we are enduring so much for you, we pray that our hope may not deceive us, and that Your Royal Dignity will not despise us, who are faithful to you and are your sons. If an unfavorable rumor about the senate and about us should reach the royal ears, let not the king pay heed or regard it, because they who report to Your Highness evil concerning us wish to rejoice over a dissension between you and us—which may Heaven forbid—and (as is their custom) slyly plot to overthrow us both. But may Your Royal Discretion, as is fitting, be concerned and watchful that these things come not to pass. Let Your Perspicacity recall how many great ills the papal curia and our aforesaid one-time fellow citizens have done to the emperors who were before you. Now they have attempted with the Sicilian to do you worse harm. But, by the grace of Christ, we are resisting them manfully, being faithful to you; and we have expelled many of them from the City as the worst enemies of the empire—which they are. Therefore let the Imperial Might speedily approach us, since whatever you wish in the City you will be able to obtain. And, to speak briefly and concisely, you will be able, by dwelling (as is our wish) in the City which is the head of the world and by removing every obstacle of the clergy, to exercise dominion over all Italy and the German realm more freely and better than practically all your predecessors.

"We pray you therefore to come without delay. Meanwhile deign to gladden us by royal letter or messengers concerning these matters in

---

[113] See the reference to this Jordan in *Two Cities* VII.xxxi.

reference to your estate which we ever desire to be sound and prosperous. For we are ready in all things ever to obey your will. Know further that we are making a great effort to restore the Mulvian bridge, not far beyond the City, for so long a time left in ruins as a hindrance to the emperors, in order that your army may be able to cross it and that the sons of Pierleone may not be able to harm you by the castle of St. Angelo, as they have planned with the pope and the Sicilian to do. Within the space of a short time, by God's aid, it will be completed with a very strong wall composed of great stones. Moreover we have learned that the agreement between the Sicilian and the pope is in these terms: the pope has entrusted his staff and ring, his dalmatic, mitre, and sandals to the Sicilian, and he consents to send no legate into his land save him whom the Sicilian requests. And the Sicilian has given him much money for your hurt and to injure the Roman empire, which by God's grace is yours. To all these things, O Excellent King, may Your Prudence give heed.

Strong be the king, obtaining whate'er he desires from the foe;
Reigning as emperor, dwelling at Rome, the world may he sway,
Prince of its lands—thus did Justinian govern before him.
Caesar shall have what is his; the pope what belongs to the pontiff,
Even as Christ gave command, when Peter was paying the tribute.[114]

"For the rest, we pray you receive our ambassadors with kindness and believe what they say to you, because we could not write it all. For they are noble men: Guido the senator, James the son of the procurator Sixtus, and Nicholas their associate." [115]

But the most Christian sovereign refused to give heed to words or fables of this sort. Nay, he even received with honor and honorably dismissed the great and renowned men who came to him on behalf of the Roman Church (one of them was Guido of Pisa, cardinal and chancellor of the same curia) asking for a renewal of their ancient privileges.

xxx (xxix). At that time all over the world the whirlwind of war filled the earth and involved practically the whole empire in seditious uprisings. For in Swabia there raged between the aforesaid youth

[114] Cf. Matthew 17:24 ff. and 22:21.

[115] The Roman uprising had obliged Eugenius III to seek Norman support, and in this letter (1149) the Romans bid for imperial intervention on their behalf. Thus the letter plays upon imperial fears of Norman expansion and presents Roger II ("the Sicilian"), rather than the pope, as the principal enemy of the Roman republic.

Frederick and Duke Conrad (whom I have named) this calamitous strife. In Bavaria a very serious war that had started between Henry,[116] the son of Margrave Leopold, duke of that same land, and Henry, bishop of Regensburg, grew in intensity from day to day. In Belgic Gaul those great and distinguished men, Adalbero, archbishop of Trier, and Henry, count of Namur, were at war, and as they exempted nothing from pillage and fire the greatest loss to the state was anticipated. In Poland, where four brothers fought for the dukedom, three against the fourth,[117] the greatest shedding of blood was impending. Other provinces of the Empire, too, were not free from this evil.[118] Suddenly, by the right hand of the Most High, so great a change was effected that all these tempests of wars were lulled to rest.[119] In a short time you might have beheld the entire world at peace and innumerable hosts from France and Germany, taking the cross and declaring a campaign against the enemies of the Cross.

But before we touch upon the history of so unheard-of a transformation as this, a few words must be said by way of preface concerning the former confusion.

xxxi (xxx). Accordingly, at the time at which the aforesaid Henry, duke of the Bavarians, was carrying on war most actively with Henry, the bishop of Regensburg (whom I have mentioned), the people of the city, and Ottokar, margrave of Styria, certain knights set out from the East Mark and entered Pannonia secretly. They made a surprise attack upon the castle of Bosan (which the Emperor Henry had once besieged) [120] and captured it. Some [of the defenders] they made prisoners, some were slain, others escaped by flight. When Géza, king of Hungary and son of King Béla, heard this, he sent ahead certain of his counts to inquire why and how this had been done, while he him-

---

[116] Henry Jasomirgott, brother of Otto of Freising and half brother of Conrad III, who made him duke of Bavaria.

[117] The four sons of Boleslav III, among whom he had ordered the division of Poland before his death in 1138. The eldest, Vladislav II (husband of Agnes, sister of Otto of Freising and half sister of Conrad III) endeavored to reunite Poland and was opposed by the younger sons, Boleslav IV, Mieszko, and Henry (and later by a still younger son, Casimir, who inherited Henry's share). Vladislav was forced into exile in 1146 despite imperial support. See below, i.lvii and iii.i–iv.

[118] See *Two Cities* VII.xxxiv.

[119] Cf. Psalms 77:10: *haec mutatio dexterae Excelsi.*

[120] This is Pressburg, on the boundary separating Hungary and the empire; cf. *Two Cities* VII.xiii.

self with a great throng of Hungarians followed them and hastened to the rescue of the castle. The counts who had preceded him made careful inquiry of the townsmen why they had inflicted so grave an injury on the king. They replied that they had done this neither for the prince of the Romans nor for their duke, but for their lord, Boris. Now Boris was the son of Koloman, formerly king of Hungary. As has been told in the former chronicle,[121] he was seeking to regain the aforesaid kingdom of Hungary by hereditary right. In order to accomplish this, he frequently importuned both emperors (I mean of the Romans and of the Greeks) for aid, and by paying money he induced many of our knights to support him. So the king of Hungary came up, pitched camp, and besieged the town, making use of various kinds of engines of destruction and surrounding the town with archers. Since the Germans had no consoling prospect of liberation from siege, because the duke was tarrying in the upper parts of Bavaria and because the sovereign remained in remote places of his realm, they began to treat with the Hungarians for terms of peace. And so, not to delay you with many words, after conferring together they received from the king under oath the promise of three thousand pounds in weight [of gold], restored the castle to him, and themselves returned to their own homes. But the king of the Hungarians, annoyed at the loss inflicted upon him by the Germans and having his suspicions of the Bavarian duke, denounced him as his enemy and collected a very large army throughout the entire extent of his realm.

However, before we speak of this expedition, it seems desirable to say certain things by way of preface concerning the geography of the land itself and the nature of the people.

xxxii (xxxi). Now this province, because it is shut in on all sides by forests and mountains and especially by the Apennines [Carpathians], was from ancient times called Pannonia.[122] In the interior there is a very broad plain seamed by rivers and streams. It has many forests filled with all sorts of wild animals and is known to be delightful because of the natural charm of the landscape and rich in its arable fields. It seems like the paradise of God, or the fair land of Egypt. For it has,

---

[121] *Ibid.* VII.xxi, xxiv.

[122] See the Introduction, p. 12, and below, II.xiii (cf. Isidore *Etym.* XIV.iv.16), where Otto's confusion between the Alps, Apennines, and Pyrenees is made clear. The reference here, however, seems clearly to be to the Carpathians.

as I have said, a most beautiful natural setting, but in consequence of the barbarous nature of its people it has only rarely the adornment of walls or houses; its bounds are set not so much by mountains and forests as by the course of its mighty rivers.

On the east, where that famous stream the Save empties into the Danube, it borders on Bulgaria. On the west lies Moravia and the East Mark of the Germans. On the south are Croatia, Dalmatia, Istria, and Carinthia. On the north are Bohemia, Poland, and Russia; to the southeast is Bosnia; [123] northeastward the open land of the Patzinaks and the *Falones*,[124] which comprises very fine hunting ground practically untouched by plow and hoe.

But as it has suffered frequent inroads of the barbarians, it is not surprising that the province remains crude and uncultured in customs and in speech. For first (as I have told at greater length elsewhere [125]) it was exposed to the depredations of the Huns, who, according to Jordanes,[126] had been the offspring of unclean spirits and harlots. Later it was subject to the devastation of the Avars, who eat raw and putrid meat. Finally, the land lay open to the inroads of the Hungarians from Scythia, who inhabit it to this day.

Now the aforesaid Hungarians are of disgusting aspect, with deep-set eyes and short stature. They are barbarous and ferocious in their habits and language. One seems justified in blaming fortune, or rather in marveling at divine patience, that has exposed so delightful a land to such—I will not say men, but caricatures of men. In one respect, however, they imitate the shrewdness of the Greeks, in that they undertake no important matter without frequent and prolonged deliberations. Finally, since in their villages and towns the houses are very wretched, made merely of reeds, rarely of wood, most rarely of stone, during the entire period of summer and autumn they live in tents. Thus they come together at the court of their king, each of the chieftains bringing his chair (*sella*) with him, and give due consideration and discussion to

---

[123] *Rama* or *Roma* in the text.

[124] Probably the Cumans; see *Two Cities* VI.x. Otto demonstrates a fair knowledge of the names of Hungary's neighbors, but his compass directions show an almost uniform error. Thus he places Bulgaria east instead of southeast, the Patzinaks northeast instead of east, Russia and Poland north instead of northeast, and so forth.

[125] *Two Cities* IV.xvi.

[126] *Getica* xxiv.122. For an English translation of this work, see Charles C. Mierow, *The Gothic History of Jordanes* (Princeton, 1915). Jordanes wrote in A.D. 551.

affairs of state. In the cold of winter they do the same thing in such abodes as they have.

They all render such obedience to their prince that every man regards it as wrong, I will not say to enrage him by open contradiction, but even to annoy him by secret whisperings. So it comes about that although the aforesaid realm is divided into seventy or more counties, from the proceeds of justice two thirds go to the royal treasury and only one third remains to the count; and in so vast an area no one but the king ventures to coin money or collect tolls. If anyone of the rank of count has even in a trivial matter offended against the king or, as sometimes happens, has been unjustly accused of this, an emissary from the court, though he be of very lowly station and unattended, seizes him in the midst of his retinue, puts him in chains, and drags him off to various forms of punishment (*tormentorum*). No formal sentence is asked of the prince through his peers, as is the custom among us, no opportunity of defending himself is granted the accused, but the will of the prince alone is held by all as sufficient.

If ever the king wishes to muster an army, all without protest are united as into one body. Every nine farmers who dwell in the villages furnish a tenth man (or even every seven furnish an eighth—or if need be a smaller number does the like) fully equipped for the campaign. All the rest are left at home to cultivate the soil. But those whose status is that of knight will venture to remain at home for none but the most urgent reasons.

In the king's own retinue there are great numbers of foreigners (*hospites*) who are called "princes" and are ever at the ruler's side for his defense. Almost all [the Hungarians] are hideous on the march, with rude weapons, save those already trained by, or even the sons of, the foreigners, whom we now call mercenaries (*solidarios*); they display a kind of valor not innate, but acquired, so to speak, by imitating princes and foreigners of our race in skill at arms and splendor of equipment.

But let this suffice for the customs of the aforesaid race.

xxxiii (xxxii). To resume, the king [Géza, in 1146] burst forth by the Moesian Gate with seventy thousand or more fighting men and pitched his camp in the plain between the aforesaid Gate and the river Leitha, called in the German tongue Virvelt: what we might term an open field. The duke also called his men together and with his retainers likewise marked out a camp not far from the other bank of the same stream, which is the boundary of the Roman empire and that kingdom [Hungary] on one side of the Danube, the river March being the boundary on the other side. He sent out scouts to learn by careful inquiry the disposition of the enemy's forces. The next day the king went to a certain wooden church in the plain I have mentioned and, having there received from the bishops the priestly blessing designed for this purpose, was girt with his arms; for up to that time, since he was still a youth, he had not yet been knighted.

After this the king drew up a line of battle and deployed his troops, placing at the head two detachments in which there were archers to repel from afar the enemy's assault, and directly behind them one great line commanded by his uncle, Duke Béla. It is said that he kept back more than twelve thousand cavalrymen in his own contingent.

Thereupon the king unexpectedly crossed the river Leitha by fording it (since the duke's scouts did not keep a good lookout, though sent for this purpose) and soon set fire to the region. The duke had likewise drawn up a battle line and was now taking counsel what he should do, waiting in vain for his scouts who (whether through treachery or indolence) were delaying. And while some advised him to fight, others to wait on the other side of the river Fischa—beyond which he was encamped only two German miles from the border—and investigate to better advantage the strength of the enemy, the sudden appearance of smoke gave certain evidence of fire and the presence of the enemy. Some of our men thought and declared that the enemy, being put to flight, had given over their own camp to the flames. Therefore the duke [of Bavaria]—for he is brave in action, keen of spirit, but impatient of delay—straightway took up arms and, contrary to military discipline and order, instead of advancing step by step rushed headlong upon the foe. His men advanced in groups and came up in confusion, disrupting the order of the legions. Finally, in consequence of the excessive speed of his charge, he anticipated the attack of the archers who had been stationed in two detachments in front and almost completely annihilated them, with the two counts who were in command. After this he rushed upon those two great battle lines of the king and of his uncle the duke; but in the king's contingent no man broke ranks, all remained as though rooted to the spot.

The Hungarians were now on the verge of flight and wanted to turn their backs. But lo! the Germans in the rear ranks of the duke's force began to flee. The duke was ignorant of this and could not see what was going on because of the clouds of dust, which in those regions is usually very great in a dry season.

Then for the first time the barbarians plucked up their courage and surrounded the duke—apparently deserted by his men. Only then was the duke obliged to turn his back to the foe. Thanks to his good right arm, as well as to the dust that darkened the air, he escaped from the perils of war and took refuge in the near-by town of Hyenis, which in Roman times was called *Favianis*.[127] The Hungarians pursued their foes only as far as the aforesaid river Fischa and thence returned to their homes.

In this battle a great many noble and illustrious men fell, and an innumerable multitude of the common people; still, it is reported that more of the Hungarians were slain. Vengeance for so disgraceful a deed as this has not yet been accomplished. It is expected hereafter, with the aid of God, by the victorious right arm of the present emperor.

xxxiv (xxxiii). At about the same time [1147] Roger of Sicily, having equipped in Apulia, Calabria, and Sicily triremes and biremes (which are now ordinarily called galleys or *sagitteae*) and other vessels carrying war equipment, dispatched the fleet against Greece. It was commanded by valiant leaders conversant with naval warfare. Now, after the ships had been prepared for action, they entered the bounds of Greece. After taking Methone without resistance or serious effort, they advanced as far as Corfu, a very strong fortress of Greece. Since they were unable to take it by assault, they had recourse to craft and trickery. Accordingly, having sent ahead (as the story goes) certain men to pretend that they were bringing a corpse for burial—for there is in the aforesaid stronghold a congregation of clerics or monks, as is customary among the Greeks—they burst into the town, seized the fortress, and, ejecting the Greeks, stationed their garrisons there. Next, advancing into the interior of Greece, they took by storm Corinth, Thebes, and Athens, renowned for their ancient glory. There they carried off a great amount of booty and, as an insult to the emperor and in compliment to their own prince, they led away captive even the workmen who are accustomed to weave silken goods. Establishing

---

[127] *Favianis* was on the Danube, between Tulln and Lorch, and was long erroneously identified with Vienna. Otto probably has Vienna in mind here.

them in Palermo, the metropolis of Sicily, Roger bade them teach his craftsmen the art of silk weaving. Thenceforth that art, previously practiced only by the Greeks among Christian nations, began to be accessible to the genius of Rome.[128]

But in order that my pen may return to that from which we have digressed a little, I must now speak briefly of the serenity of peace which suddenly shone forth again, contrary to the expectation of many, after this world conflict.

xxxv (xxxiv). While Eugenius was pope in Rome, Conrad reigning there and Louis in France, Manuel being emperor in the royal city, and Fulk ruling at Jerusalem,[129] Louis was impelled by a secret desire to go to Jerusalem because his brother Philip had bound himself by the same vow but had been prevented by death. He was unwilling further to postpone this resolve; he therefore summoned certain of his princes and revealed what he was turning over in his mind.

There was at that time in France a certain abbot of the monastery of Clairvaux named Bernard, venerable in life and character, conspicuous in his religious order, endowed with wisdom and a knowledge of letters, renowned for signs and wonders. The princes decided to have him summoned and to ask of him, as of a divine oracle, what ought to be done with reference to this matter. The aforesaid abbot was called and his advice requested regarding the wish of the prince I have mentioned. As he judged it unbecoming to give answer concerning so weighty a matter on the sole basis of his own opinion, he replied that it was best to refer the question to the hearing and the consideration of the Roman pontiff. Therefore an embassy was sent to Eugenius, and the whole matter was set before him. And he, pondering upon the example set by his predecessor—namely, the fact that Urban,[130] upon an occasion of this sort, had won back into the unity of peace the Church across the water and two patriarchal sees (of Antioch and Jerusalem) that had cut themselves off from obedience to the Roman see—gave his assent to the wishes of the aforesaid king for extending the observance

[128] See R. Lopez, "Silk Industry in the Byzantine Empire," *Speculum*, XX (1945), 2–3, 24.

[129] The rulers mentioned are Pope Eugenius III (1145–53), Conrad III (1138–52), Louis VII (1137–80), Manuel Comnenus (1143–80), and Fulk of Jerusalem. The last-named, however, had died in 1144 and had been succeeded by his son Baldwin II (1144–63). Otto commits this same error on Fulk in *Two Cities* VII.xxviii.

[130] Urban II (1088–99), who had proclaimed the First Crusade in 1095.

of the Christian faith. He granted to the abbot previously named, who was looked upon by all the peoples of France and Germany as a prophet and apostle, the authority to preach and to move the hearts of all thereto. Whence there is extant his letter directed to the king and his princes, as follows:

xxxvi (xxxv). "Bishop Eugenius, the servant of the servants of God, to his very dear son in Christ, Louis, the illustrious and glorious king of the Franks, and to his beloved sons, the princes, and to all God's faithful people that dwell throughout France, greeting and apostolic benediction.

"How greatly our predecessors, the Roman popes, have labored for the liberation of the Eastern Church we have learned from the recital of men of old and have found written in their histories. For our predecessor of blessed memory, Pope Urban, sent forth a voice like a heavenly trumpet and undertook to summon sons of the Holy Roman Church from the ends of the earth to deliberate about this. At his call those beyond the mountains, and in particular the most valiant and vigorous warriors of the kingdom of the Franks, and those also from Italy that were on fire with the flame of love, flocked together and—when a very great host had assembled—not without great shedding of their own blood, and accompanied by divine aid, freed from the defilement of the heathen that city in which our Savior willed to suffer for us and left behind for us as a memorial of his passion his glorious sepulcher—and how many other cities that, to avoid prolixity, we forbear to mention. These, by the grace of God and the zeal of your fathers, who in the intervening years have striven mightily to defend them and to spread abroad the name of Christ in those parts, have been held by the Christians down to our own times; and other cities of the infidels have been courageously stormed by them. But now, because of our own sins and those of the people, the city of Edessa—which we cannot mention without great grief and lamentation—the city of Edessa, called in our tongue *Rohais,* and which, it is said, alone served the Lord under the sway of the Christians when formerly all the land in the Orient was held by pagans, has been taken by the enemies of the cross of Christ, and many strongholds of the Christians have been seized by them. The archbishop of that city, with his clergy and many other Christians, has been slain there, and the relics of the saints have been given over to infidels to be trampled upon and scattered.

"How great a peril thereby threatens the Church of God and all Christendom we ourselves realize and, we believe, is not hid from Your Prudence. For it is evident that it will be the greatest proof of nobility and integrity if that which the might of the fathers won is mightily defended by you, their sons. But should it be otherwise—which God forbid—the valor of the fathers is shown to be diminished in their sons.

"Therefore we warn, we beseech, and we command every one of you and enjoin it for the forgiveness of your sins, that they that are God's, and in particular the more mighty and the noble, gird themselves manfully and strive thus to oppose the multitude of the infidels which is rejoicing at having secured a period of victory over us, and so to defend the Eastern Church, freed (as we have said) from their tyranny by the shedding of so much blood of your fathers, and to rescue out of their hands the many thousands of captives, our brothers, that the honor of the Christian name may be increased in your time and that your valor, which is praised throughout the entire world, may be kept whole and unimpaired.

"Let that good man Mattathias [131] serve as an example for you, who hesitated not at all to expose himself, with his sons and his parents, to death in order to preserve the laws of his fathers, and to relinquish all that he possessed in the world; and at last by the assistance of divine aid, though only after many labors, both he and his descendants triumphed manfully over their enemies.

"But we, making provision with a father's solicitude both for the peace of your people and the destitution of that Church, by the authority vouchsafed unto us by God grant and confirm, to those who in religious zeal have decided to undertake and to perform so holy and so very necessary a work and task, that forgiveness of sins which our aforesaid predecessor, Pope Urban, instituted. And we decree that their wives and their sons, their goods also and their possessions, shall remain under the protection of Holy Church, and under our own protection and that of the archbishops, bishops, and other prelates of the Church of God. Moreover we forbid, by apostolic authority, that any legal procedure be set in motion touching any property within their peaceful possession at the time when they accepted the cross, until there is sure knowledge concerning their return or their decease.

"Furthermore, since those who are soldiers of the Lord should by

---

[131] See I Maccabees 2.

no means give attention to costly clothing or personal adornment or dogs or falcons or other things which proclaim luxurious living, we admonish Your Prudence, in the Lord, that they who have reached a decision to undertake so holy a task give no heed to these things, but devote all their zeal and care, with all their might, to arms, horses, and other things whereby they may vanquish the infidels.

"Moreover, all they that are burdened by debt and have, with pure heart, undertaken so holy a journey need not pay the interest past due, and if they themselves or others for them have been bound by oath and pledge, by reason of such interest, by apostolic authority we absolve them.[132] It is to be permitted them also, in case their relatives or the lords to whom they are feudatory, upon being asked, are unwilling or unable to provide funds, to pledge their lands or other possessions to churches or ecclesiastical personages or others of the faithful freely and without any refusal.

"Forgiveness of sins and absolution we grant, in accordance with the precedent established by our aforesaid predecessor, by the authority of Almighty God and the blessed Peter, chief of the apostles, granted unto us by God; so that he who has devoutly undertaken so holy a journey and finished it or died there shall obtain absolution for all his sins of which he has made confession with broken and contrite heart [133] and shall obtain, from the Rewarder of all, the fruit of an eternal recompense.

"Given at Vetralla on the Kalends of December [1145]."

xxxvii (xxxvi). Accordingly, to return to the order of the narrative, the venerable abbot, Bernard, made no misuse of the authority of the apostolic see that had been granted him. He valiantly girded himself with the sword of the Word of God; and when he had aroused the hearts of many for the expedition overseas, finally [1146] a general assembly was summoned at Vézelay, a town of France, where the bones of the blessed Mary Magdalene are preserved. The great and illustrious of all the provinces of France were summoned to attend. There Louis, the king of the Franks, with great eagerness of spirit received the cross from the aforesaid abbot and volunteered for military service

---

[132] This is of significance as the first known papal action designed to protect debtors taking the cross. The absolution from oath to pay usury would prevent the creditor from suing in an ecclesiastical court on the basis of oath.

[133] Psalms 51:17.

across the seas, with counts Thierry of Flanders and Henry, the son of Thibaud of Blois, and other barons and noblemen of his kingdom.

xxxviii (xxxvii). Meanwhile the monk Ralph, a man who did indeed wear the habit of religion and shrewdly imitated the strictness of religion, but was only moderately imbued with a knowledge of letters, entered those parts of Gaul which touch the Rhine and inflamed many thousands of the inhabitants of Cologne, Mainz, Worms, Speyer, Strasburg, and other neighboring cities, towns, and villages to accept the cross. However, he heedlessly included in his preaching that the Jews whose homes were scattered throughout the cities and towns should be slain as foes of the Christian religion. The seed of this doctrine took such firm root and so grew in numerous cities of Gaul and Germany that a large number of Jews were killed in this stormy uprising, while many took refuge under the wings of the prince of the Romans. So it came about that not a few of them, fleeing from such cruelty, to save their lives betook themselves to a town of the prince which is called *Noricum* or Nuremberg and to others of his municipalities.

xxxix (xxxviii). But the aforesaid abbot of Clairvaux, giving instruction to beware of such teaching, dispatched messengers and letters [134] to the peoples of Gaul and Germany to point out clearly by the authority of the sacred page that the Jews were not to be killed for the enormity of their crimes, but were to be scattered. In this connection he called attention also to the testimony of the writer of Psalms who says in the fifty-seventh Psalm: "God shall let me see my desire upon mine enemies. Slay them not." And also, "Scatter them by thy power." [135]

xl (xxxix). Now, when countless throngs in western Gaul had been aroused for the expedition across the sea, Bernard decided to turn his attention to the eastern kingdom of the Franks, to stir it with the plowshare of preaching, both that he might by the word of sacred exhortation move the heart of the prince of the Romans to accept the cross, and that he might silence Ralph, who in connection with the Jews was moving the people in the cities to repeated outbreaks against their lords. Hearing of this, the prince called a general assembly to be held at the city of Speyer at the time of the Lord's Nativity [Christmas, 1146]. The aforesaid abbot, coming thither, persuaded the king with Fred-

[134] See below, I.xliii.   [135] Psalms 59:10–11.

erick, his brother's son, and other princes and illustrious men to accept the cross, performing many miracles both publicly and in private.

Coming to Mainz also,[136] he found Ralph living there in greatest favor with the people. He summoned him and warned him not to arrogate to himself on his own authority the word of preaching, roving about over the land in defiance of the rule of the monks. Finally he prevailed upon him to the point where he promised to obey and to return to his monastery. The people were very angry and even wanted to start an insurrection, but they were restrained by regard for Bernard's saintliness.

xli. Meanwhile, the most noble Duke Frederick, who had been detained in Gaul by a serious illness, cherished in his heart bitter anger against his lord and brother, King Conrad, because he had permitted his son Frederick—whom, as the first-born and only son of his most noble first wife, he had made the heir of his entire land and had committed to his charge his second wife with her little son—to accept the cross. The aforesaid abbot came to pay him a visit, blessed him, and prayed for him. But unable to endure the pain of his grief, he died not many days later. He was buried in the monastery which is called St. Walburg's, situated on the borders of Alsace.[137] His son, Frederick, succeeded him in his dukedom.

xlii (xl). After this the prince entered Bavaria and there held a general assembly in the month of February.[138] He took with him, in place of the abbot of Clairvaux, Adam, abbot of Ebrach, a devout and very learned man. He celebrated solemn Mass as was customary and then, having invoked the grace of the Holy Spirit, ascended the pulpit and after reading the letters of the apostolic see and of the abbot of Clairvaux, by a brief exhortation persuaded practically all who were present to undertake the aforesaid military service. For there was no need of persuasive words of human wisdom or the ingratiating use of artful circumlocution, in accordance with the precepts of the rhetoricians, since all who were present had been aroused by previous report and hurried forward of their own accord to receive the cross. In that same hour three bishops accepted the cross, namely, Henry of

[136] In November, 1146, prior to the court at Speyer just mentioned.
[137] Located at Walburg, just north of Hagenau.
[138] At Regensburg, February, 1147.

Regensburg, Otto of Freising, and Reginbert of Passau; also, the duke of the Bavarians, Henry, brother of the king,[139] and from the order of counts, nobles, and illustrious men, a throng without number. Moreover, so great a throng of highwaymen and robbers (strange to say) came hurrying forward that no man in his senses could fail to comprehend that this so sudden and so unusual a transformation came from the hand of the Most High, and comprehending did not marvel with amazement of heart. Welf,[140] also, the brother of Henry, the former duke, one of the noblest princes of the realm, had with many others vowed to undertake the same military service on the very eve of our Lord's Nativity, on his own estate at Peiting. Vladislav, duke of the Bohemians,[141] and Ottokar, margrave of Styria, and the illustrious Count Bernard of Carinthia, not long afterward also took the cross with a great following of their people. But the Saxons, refusing to set out for the Orient because they had as neighbors certain tribes that were given over to the filthiness of idolatry, in like manner took the cross in order to assail these races in war. Their crosses differed from ours in this respect, that they were not simply sewed to their clothing, but were brandished aloft, surmounting a wheel.

xliii (xli). The following is a copy of the letter which the abbot of Clairvaux sent to the eastern realm of the Franks [1146]:

"To the very dear lords and fathers, archbishops, bishops, and all the clergy and people of East Francia [?Franconia] and Bavaria, Bernard, called abbot of Clairvaux, an abundance of the spirit of valor.

"I speak to you of the things of Christ, namely, those wherein lies your salvation. This I say that the authority of the Lord may excuse the unworthiness of the person who speaks—as does also a consideration of the utility of the words uttered. I am indeed weak, but not weak is my desire for you in the love of Jesus Christ. That is now my reason for writing to you, that is the occasion for my venturing to confer with you

[139] It will be recalled that Conrad had deprived Henry the Proud of the duchy of Bavaria and had granted it to his half brother, Margrave Leopold of Austria, upon whose death in 1141 it had passed to Leopold's elder brother, Henry Jasomirgott.

[140] Welf VI, younger brother of Henry the Proud and claimant to the Welf lands in southern Germany after Henry's death in 1139. During the minority of Henry's son, Henry the Lion, Welf was the chief opponent of the Hohenstaufen. See below, I.xlv.

[141] Vladislav II, husband of Gertrude, a sister of Otto and half sister of Conrad III; he had been established as duke of Bohemia in 1142 with Conrad's backing. He is not to be confused with Vladislav II of Poland, who married Otto's sister Agnes.

all by letter. I would prefer to discuss this with you by word of mouth, if only as the will is not lacking so also were the opportunity afforded. 'Behold, brothers, now is the accepted time; behold, now is the day of salvation' in full measure.[142] 'For the earth shook and trembled' [143] because the God of Heaven begins to lose His land. His land in which He appeared and for more than thirty years went about as a man among men. His land, which He glorified by His miracles, which He consecrated by His own blood, in which the first flowers of the Resurrection appeared. And now, for our sins, the adversaries of the Cross have raised their accursed heads, ravaging with the edge of the sword that blessed land, the land of promise. The time is near, if none stay their hands, when they will burst into the city of the living God, to overthrow the very workshop where our redemption was wrought, to pollute the holy places with the crimson blood of the lamb without spot.[144]

"They pant—O the pity of it!—with sacrilegious jaws for the very shrine of the Christian religion and attempt to profane and to trample underfoot the very resting place wherein for us our Life slumbered in death. What do ye, valiant men? What do ye, servants of the Cross? Will ye thus give that which is holy to the dogs and your pearls to swine? [145] How many sinners there confessing their sins with tears have obtained pardon, since the filthiness of the heathen was eradicated by the swords of our fathers! The Evil One sees this and is envious and gnashes with his teeth and melts away.[146] He stirs the vessels of his iniquity [147] that he may leave no signs or traces of piety if ever—which God forbid—he has the strength to prevail. Truly this is for all ages to come an inconsolable anguish because the loss is irreparable, but to this wicked generation in particular it is an unending source of shame and an eternal reproach. Yet, what think we, brethren? Has the arm of the Lord been shortened or made powerless to save [148] because it summons us little worms to defend and to restore His own inheritance? Can He not send more than twelve legions of angels [149] or even speak the word only [150] and the land shall be freed? Surely the power is His whensoever He has the will.[151]

[142] II Corinthians 6:2.
[144] I Peter 1:19.
[146] Psalms 112:10.
[148] Cf. Isaiah 50:2, 59:1.
[150] Matthew 8:8.

[143] Psalms 18:7.
[145] Matthew 7:6.
[147] *Vasa iniquitatis;* cf. Genesis 49:5.
[149] Matthew 26:53.
[151] Wisdom of Solomon 12:18.

"But I say unto you, the Lord your God is making trial of you. He gazes forth over the children of men to see if perchance there is one who understands and makes inquiry and is sorry for Him.[152] For God has compassion on His people and provides for those that have fallen low the remedy of salvation. Consider how shrewd a device He employs to save you and marvel; contemplate the depths of His love and have faith, ye sinners! He desireth not your death, but that ye be converted and live, because He thus seeks an opportunity not against you, but for you . . ."

In these words and with reference to the same theme [the abbot of Clairvaux] busied himself in the manner and fashion of the orators. And that the Jews should not be killed he proved by reason and by authority. Whence we have the following passage: "Happy would I term that generation which obtains the opportunity of so rich indulgence: a generation which this acceptable year of the Lord,[153] and truly a year of jubilee, finds alive. For this benediction is poured out upon all the world, and all hasten toward this sign of life. Because, therefore, your land is known to be rich in brave men and filled with lusty youth, as your praise is in all the world and the fame of your valor has filled the earth, so gird yourselves also like men and take up your auspicious arms!"

And concerning the Jews he spoke thus: " 'God,' saith the Church, 'shall let me see my desire upon mine enemies, slay them not.' [154] For they are living tokens unto us, constantly recalling our Lord's passion"; and much else after this fashion.

xliv (xlii). And so, as countless peoples and nations, not only from the Roman empire, but also from the neighboring realms—that is, France, England, Pannonia—were moved to take the cross, suddenly almost the entire West became so still that not only the waging of war but even the carrying of arms in public was considered wrong.

xlv (xliii). Now Conrad, the king of the Romans, called together the princes at Frankfort (a town of East Francia [? Franconia]), which may be called in Latin *Vadum Francorum* because Charles, setting out to do battle with the Saxons, is said to have found there a ford of the river Main which empties into the Rhine at Mainz, for the holding of a general diet [March, 1147]. And there his son Henry, who was still a boy, was chosen king by vote of the princes. Conrad commanded that

---

[152] Cf. I Samuel 22:8.   [153] Isaiah 61:2.   [154] Psalms 59:10–11.

he should be anointed and crowned king in the palace at Aachen on Mid-Lent Sunday, and chose him as his associate in the kingdom.

To the aforesaid diet came Henry, the son of Henry, duke of the Bavarians, of whom mention has been made above.[155] He had now grown to man's estate and demanded by right of inheritance the duchy of Bavaria, which he claimed had been unjustly taken from his father by judicial decision. The prince, prevailing upon him by great prudence and skill, postponed a decision until his return and persuaded him to wait peacefully.

xlvi (xliv). And so, when the rigor of the winter cold had been dispelled, as flowers and plants came forth from the earth's bosom under the gracious showers of spring and green meadows smiled upon the world, making glad the face of the earth, King Conrad led forth his troops from Nuremberg, in battle array. At Regensburg he took ship to descend the Danube, and on Ascension Sunday he pitched camp in the East Mark near a town called Ardacker. There for two or three days he awaited his men who were already coming up. Proceeding thence almost to the limits of his realm, he halted not far from the river Fischa. After observing Whitsunday there, he crossed the Leitha with practically all his troops, some descending the Danube and others coming by land, and made camp in Pannonia. But he drew after him so great a throng that the rivers seemed scarcely to suffice for navigation, or the extent of the plains for marching. Louis, the king of the Franks, with his men followed not far behind him, bringing with him, of our people, the Lorrainers, whose princes or leaders were the bishops Stephen of Metz and Henry of Toul, and the counts Reinald of Mouzon and Hugh of Vaudemont; and from Italy Amadeus of Turin, his brother William, marchese of Montferrat, their uncles, and many others.

xlvii. But since the outcome of that expedition, because of our sins, is known to all, we, who have purposed this time to write not a tragedy but a joyous history, leave this to be related by others elsewhere. Moreover, how the Saxons attacked the neighboring tribes (as I have said) and then returned to their homes, because their leaders disagreed among themselves, has not yet faded from the memories of those who still survive. Nevertheless, lest we shroud in silence the good fortune of our present Emperor Frederick, which from his youth to this very day has never turned on him a completely clouded face, I wish to record

---

[155] Henry the Lion, now aged nineteen; see above, note 140.

one incident out of all, and to represent all, that happened to us on that march.

(xlv). When after Pannonia Bulgaria had been crossed, at the cost of much toil and difficulty of the way, and when upper Thrace was passed, after Mt. Hebrus had been surmounted, when now we had been marching for several days with much gladness of heart in the most fruitful regions of lower Thrace on our way to the royal city [Constantinople], on the seventh day before the Ides of September, that is, on the day [September 7] before the festival of the birth of the blessed Mary, we came to a certain valley near a town called Cherevach,[156] attractive because of its green fields and marked by the course of a little stream through the midst of it. Captivated by the charm of this spot, we all decided to pitch our tents there and to rest in that place that day, in order to celebrate with great jollity the glad birthday of the Mother of God, ever virgin. Only Duke Frederick with his retinue and his uncle Welf—for the troops of the Lorrainers had not yet united with us—marked out a camp near us on the side of a certain mountain opposite. Not far off was the Propontis, which is now called by the natives the Arm of St. George, and on its shores two small towns, Selymbria and Athyra, whence we expected opportunities for trade.

This sea was once called the Hellespont, from the well-known story of Phrixus and Helle,[157] or the Propontis (that is to say, the Fore-Pontus), because it is driven forth from the Pontus by the force of two mighty rivers, the Don and the Danube, like a gently flowing stream, so they say, and empties into the Adriatic or Tyrrhenian [158] Sea near ancient Troy.

I confess that during the entire time of our expedition we never had a pleasanter camp; never (so far as one may judge from sense impressions) had our encampment covered a wider circuit.

But look! about the time of the morning watch a certain little cloud appeared and sent down a gentle rain. Suddenly such a tempestuous storm of rain and wind ensued that it caused the tents to sway, tore them loose, and dashed them violently to the ground, arousing us from our beds, to which we had retired after matins. A tumult arose, filling all

---

[156] The present Catalca, just west of Constantinople.

[157] Isidore *Etym.* XIII.xvi.8. Phrixus and his sister Helle fled across the straits on a ram with a golden fleece, but Helle fell off and was drowned.

[158] A mistake. It empties into the Aegean.

the air round about. For the little stream—whether from the backwash of the neighboring sea or the downpour of rain or a cloudburst betokening the vengeance of the Majesty on high is uncertain—had swollen so greatly and in consequence of its swollen waters had so overflowed beyond its custom that it covered the entire cantonment. What were we to do? Considering this a divine punishment rather than a natural inundation, we were the more dismayed. Nevertheless, we hurried to our powerful steeds, each one seeking to cross the river as best he could. You might have seen some swimming, some clinging to horses, some ignominiously hauled along by ropes to escape the danger, some dashing in disorder into the river and sinking because they were heedlessly entangled with others. A great many, believing they could wade across, were swept away by the rush of the river, injured by the rocks, and, swallowed up by the force of the eddies, lost their lives in the river. Some, who had not learned how to swim, laid hold of those who were swimming and clung to them in order that they might escape and exhausted them, so hampered, until they ceased the motions of their arms and, flat on their backs, both alike were submerged and drowned.[159]

Now some of us betook ourselves to the tents of Duke Frederick, which alone remained entirely unharmed by this destructive flood. There, hearing the solemn service of the Mass, we sang "Let us rejoice," not with joy, but with much bitterness of heart, hearing the grief and the groans of our men. Finally, some managed to cross the torrent with great fear and effort; others, in their despair fastening together wagons and other equipment they could secure, placed this material as a bulwark against the onrushing water and awaited the cessation of the flood.

But how great a loss our army sustained there both in men and goods and in the utensils necessary for so long a journey I need not relate. On the following day, when the waters had subsided and the face of the land appeared, all of us being scattered here and there, you might have obtained as sad a picture of our encampment as on the preceding day you could have seen it glad. So that, not inappropriately, it appeared clearer than light how great is the power of the high Deity, and how human happiness is unstable and passes quickly. But enough of this.

[159] Much of this description is borrowed by Otto from Hegesippus *De bello Judaico* IV.xv. Cf. the account of this occurrence in Helmold *Chronicle of the Slavs* I.lx.

xlviii (xlvi). There was in those days in French Aquitania, in the city of Poitiers, a bishop named Gilbert.[160] He was born in the same city and from his youth to extreme old age pursued the study of philosophy in various places in France. Both in fact and in name he had performed the function of a teacher, and shortly before these days had been elevated to the dignity of bishop in the aforesaid city. He was accustomed by virtue of his exceedingly subtle intellect and acute powers of reason to say many things beyond the common custom of men.

While this man on a certain occasion was conducting a great gathering of the clergy of his diocese, he included in the address that he happened to be delivering for the purpose of exhortation certain remarks on faith in the Holy Trinity. Two of his archdeacons, namely, Arnold and Kalo, protested, summoning him to an examination before the supreme pontiff and the see of Rome as teaching a doctrine contrary to the accepted belief of the Catholic Church. So both archdeacons set out and met the Roman pope Eugenius (who was on his way from Rome to France) at Siena, a city of Tuscany. When the Roman pontiff had given them an audience and learned the reason for their journey, he replied briefly that he was on his way to France and desired there to learn more fully about this teaching, because he would there have a better opportunity of examining it on account of the great number of learned men dwelling in that region. The archdeacons returned to France and induced Bernard, the abbot previously mentioned, whom they consulted, to favor their cause against the bishop.

xlix (xlvii). Now the aforesaid abbot was both zealous in his devotion to the Christian religion and somewhat credulous in consequence of a habitual mildness, so that he had an abhorrence of teachers who put their trust in worldly wisdom and clung too much to human argument. If anything at variance with the Christian faith were told him concerning anybody, he would readily give ear. Thus it happened that not long before this silence had been imposed upon Peter Abelard,[161] first by the bishops of France, afterward by the Roman pontiff.

[160] Gilbert de la Porrée (*c.* 1070–1154), a teacher at the cathedral school of Chartres prior to his election as bishop of Poitiers in 1142; Otto's following account is one of the two extant sources for Gilbert's opinions and his trial, the second being John of Salisbury's *Historia pontificalis.*

[161] Abelard (1079–1142) was the most famous and most controversial figure in the intellectual life of the twelfth century.

This Peter was a native of that province of France which is now called by its inhabitants Brittany. This region is productive of clerics endowed with keen intellects, well adapted to the arts but almost witless for other matters, such as the two brothers Bernard and Thierry, very learned men.[162] This Peter, I say, had from an early age been devoted to literary studies and other trifles, but was so conceited and had such confidence in his own intellectual power that he would scarcely so demean himself as to descend from the heights of his own mind to listen to his teachers. However, he first had a teacher named Roscellinus [163] who was the first in our times to teach in logic the nominalistic doctrine. Afterward he betook himself to those very distinguished men, Anselm of Laon and William of Champeaux, bishop of Châlons-sur-Marne, but did not long endure the weight of their words, judging them to be devoid of cleverness and subtlety. Then he became a teacher and went to Paris, showing great capacity by his originality in discovering matters not only of importance for philosophy but also conducive to social amusements and pastimes. On a certain sufficiently well-known occasion he was very roughly dealt with, and became a monk in the monastery of St. Denis.[164] There devoting himself day and night to reading and meditation, from being a keen thinker he became keener, from being a learned man he became more learned, to such a degree that after some time he was released from obedience to his abbot, came forth in public, and again assumed the office of teacher. Accordingly, holding to the doctrine of nominalism in natural philosophy, he rashly carried it over into theology. Therefore, in teaching and in writing of the Holy Trinity he minimized too much the three persons which Holy Church has up to the present time piously believed and faithfully taught to be not merely empty names but distinct entities and differentiated by their properties. The analogies he used were not good, for he said among other things: "Just as the same utterance is the major premise, the minor premise, and the conclusion, so the same being is Father, Son, and Holy Spirit." On this account a provincial synod was assembled against him at Soissons in the presence of a legate of the Roman see

---

[162] Bernard and Thierry of Chartres, two well-known teachers at Chartres around the middle of the twelfth century and, like Abelard, Bretons.

[163] Roscellin of Compiègne, who was compelled in 1092 to retract his more extreme propositions, and who died as a canon at Tours *c.* 1121. His nominalistic teachings denied the reality of universals.

[164] The reference is to his mutilation by Canon Fulbert, the uncle of Heloïse, in 1119.

[1121]. He was adjudged a Sabellian heretic [165] by those excellent men and acknowledged masters, Alberic of Rheims and Letald of Novara, and was forced by the bishops to cast into the fire with his own hand the books that he had published. No opportunity of making a reply was granted him because his skill in disputation was mistrusted by all. These things were done under Louis the Elder, king of France.[166]

(xlviii). Then, after he had lectured again for a long time and had attracted a very great throng of pupils to him, while Innocent was pope at Rome, and in France Louis, the son of the former Louis, was king,[167] he was again summoned by the bishops and by Abbot Bernard to a hearing at Sens, in the presence of King Louis and Thibaud, the count palatine, and other nobles and countless numbers of the people [1140]. While his faith was being discussed there, fearing an uprising of the people, he asked that he might appear before the Roman see. But the bishops and the abbot sent a deputation to the Roman Church along with the articles because of which he was assailed and demanded a sentence of condemnation, in a letter of which this is a copy:

"To the most reverend lord and most beloved father, by the grace of God supreme pontiff, Innocent, S[amson], archbishop of Rheims, and Bishops Joscelin of Soissons, G[eoffrey] of Châlons-sur-Marne, A[lvise] of Arras send voluntary acknowledgment of due subjection.

"As your ears are busied with many matters, we make brief mention of a lengthy subject, all the more so that it is contained more fully and in greater detail in a letter of the lord [archbishop] of Sens.

"Peter Abelard strives to make vain the merit of the Christian faith, since he believes he can comprehend by human reason all that is God: he mounts up to the heaven, he goes down again to the depths; [168] there is nothing that is hid from him, whether in the depth of hell or in the height above.[169] The man is great in his own eyes, disputing concerning the faith against the faith, exercising himself in great matters and in things too high for him,[170] a searcher of his own glory,[171] a contriver of heresies. In the past he composed a book about the Holy Trinity,

---

[165] Sabellius was an African priest of the third century whose teachings were held to overemphasize the unity of the three persons of the Trinity.

[166] Louis VI (1108–37).

[167] Louis VII (1137–80) and Pope Innocent II (1130–43).

[168] Psalms 107:26. [169] Isaiah 7:11.

[170] Psalms 131:1. [171] Proverbs 25:27.

but by the authority of a legate of the Roman Church it was tried by fire because iniquity was found in it.[172]

"Cursed be he who rebuilds the ruins of Jericho.[173] That book of his has risen from the dead, and with it the heresies of many that were asleep have risen and have appeared to many.[174] Finally now she sends out her boughs unto the sea and her shoots unto Rome.[175] This is the man's boast, that his book hath where to lay its head [176] in the Roman court; by this is his error strengthened and confirmed. Hence he preaches with confidence everywhere the word of iniquity.

"Therefore, when the abbot of Clairvaux, armed with zeal for justice and for the faith, accused him of these matters in the presence of the bishops, he neither confessed nor made denial,[177] but that he might prolong his iniquity,[178] he appealed, without suffering any hurt or oppression, from the time, the place, and the judge that he had himself selected for himself, to the apostolic see.

"The bishops who had assembled for this sole purpose, deferring to Your Reverence, have taken no action against his person, but merely —through the necessity for remedial measures, lest the disease spread —have passed judgment upon the articles once condemned by the holy fathers. Accordingly, because that man draws the multitude after him and has a people that believes in him, it is necessary that you treat this disease with a swift-acting remedy:

'For too late is medicine active,
When from long delay sickness has gathered strength.' [179]

"We have gone as far as we dared in this matter. It is your care, Most Blessed Father, to provide for the rest, that the beauty of the Church be not marred by any spot of heretical depravity. To thee has been entrusted the Bride of Christ, O friend of the Bridegroom. Thine is the task of presenting her to one husband, 'a chaste virgin to Christ.' [180]

Innocent's reply was as follows:

---

[172] Cf. I Corinthians 3:13 and Ezekiel 28:15.

[173] Joshua 6:26. [174] Matthew 27:52-53.

[175] Cf. Psalms 80:11. [176] Matthew 8:20.

[177] Cf. John 1:20.

[178] Psalms 129:3; "they made long their furrows," in the King James version; Vulgate: *prolongaverunt iniquitatem suam.*

[179] Ovid *Remedia amoris* 91. [180] II Corinthians 11:2.

"Bishop Innocent, the servant of the servants of God, to the venerable brethren, the archbishops Henry of Sens and S[amson] of Rheims and their suffragans and to his very dear son in Christ, B[ernard], abbot of Clairvaux, greeting and apostolic benediction.

"From the testimony of the apostle we learn that as there is one Lord, so there is one faith,[181] on which as upon an immovable foundation, other than which no man can lay,[182] the stability of the Catholic Church rests unshaken. Hence it is that the blessed Peter, the prince of the apostles, for his notable confession of this faith was privileged to hear: 'Thou art Peter, I say, and upon this rock will I build my church,'[183] by rock quite evidently being meant the firmness of the faith and the solidity of Catholic unity. For this is our Savior's coat without seam for which the soldiers cast lots but could not rend it.[184] Against it in the beginning 'the heathen raged and the people imagined vain things. The kings of the earth set themselves and the rulers took counsel together.'[185] But the apostles, the leaders of the Lord's flock, and their successors, the apostolic men, aflame with the fire of love and zeal for righteousness, have not hesitated to defend the faith and to plant it in the hearts of the peoples by the shedding of their own blood. When at last the fury of the persecutors ceased, the Lord commanded the winds and there was a great calm[186] in the Church. But because the adversary of the human race ever walketh about, seeking whom he may devour,[187] he stealthily brought in the deceitful error of the heretics to combat the purity of the faith. Against these the true leaders of the churches manfully rose up and condemned their wicked teachings together with the authors of the same. For in the great Nicene synod the heretic Arius was condemned. The synod of Constantinople condemned the heretic Manichaeus with due sentence. In the synod of Ephesus, Nestorius received the condemnation befitting his error. The synod of Chalcedon also, by a most just sentence, confuted the Nestorian heresy and that of Eutyches with Dioscurus and his accomplices.

"And besides, Marcian, who though a laic was nevertheless a most Christian emperor, inflamed with love for the Catholic faith, writing to our predecessor the most holy Pope John against those who strove to profane the sacred mysteries, speaks as follows, saying (among other

---

[181] Ephesians 4:5.   [182] I Corinthians 3:11.   [183] Matthew 16:18.
[184] Cf. John 19:23–24.   [185] Acts 4:25–26; Psalms 2:1–2.
[186] Matthew 8:26.   [187] I Peter 5:8.

things) : 'Let no cleric or soldier or man of any other condition attempt hereafter to discuss the Christian faith in public. For one does an injustice to the judgment of the very reverend synod, if one seeks to agitate anew and argue again about matters once decided and properly settled. And those who transgress this law shall be punished as though they had committed sacrilege. Therefore, if there shall be any cleric who dares to discuss religion in public, he shall be removed from the company of the clergy.' [188]

"Moreover, we grieve that (as we learn from an inspection of your letters and the heretical articles sent to us by you, my brothers) in the last days when perilous times impend,[189] because of the pernicious doctrine of Master P. Abelard, the heresies of those whom we have mentioned and other perverse dogmas have begun to spring up in opposition to the Catholic faith. But in this we find particular consolation and for it we give thanks to Omnipotent God, that in your country He has raised up such sons to succeed such fathers, and that in the time of our apostolate in His Church He has willed that there should be such illustrious shepherds who are zealous to oppose the falsehoods of a new heretic, and to present to Christ a bride without spot, a chaste virgin, to one husband.[190] We, therefore, who are seen to sit, although unworthy, on the chair of St. Peter, to whom it was said by the Lord: 'and, when thou art converted, strengthen thy brethren,' [191] we, having conferred with the council of our brethren the cardinal bishops, have condemned the articles sent us by Your Discretion and all the perverse teachings of Peter himself, by the authority of the holy canons, together with their author, and we have imposed perpetual silence upon him as a heretic. We decree also that all followers and defenders of this error be sequestrated from the company of the faithful and restrained by the bond of excommunication.

"Given at the Lateran on the twelfth day before the Kalends of August [1141]."

li (xlix). When Peter learned that the condemnation of his teaching had been confirmed by the Roman church, he betook himself to the monastery of Cluny and wrote an apologetic denying the words of the aforesaid articles in part and the interpretation entirely. It begins thus:

---

[188] These words are contained in an edict of Valentinian III and Marcian issued in 452, and not addressed to Pope John (the pope in 452 was Leo I).

[189] II Timothy 3:1.　　　[190] II Corinthians 11:2.　　　[191] Luke 22:32.

"Not to waste time (as Boethius says) [192] in prefaces which contribute nothing, I must come to the point, that the truth itself rather than prolixity of words may testify to my innocence."

Now it may suffice to cite these few articles out of many adduced against him: That the Father has full power, the Son some power, the Holy Spirit no power; that the Holy Spirit is not of the substance of the Father; that the Holy Spirit is the world soul; that Christ did not become flesh to save us from the yoke of the devil; that they did not sin who crucified Christ in ignorance.

But he himself ended his days in that same monastery not long afterward, humbly setting forth his faith before his brethren.[193]

lii (1). Now, that my account may return to the point from which it has digressed, the aforesaid archdeacons, having associated with them the Abbot Bernard, a man of so great authority and held in high esteem, were attempting to condemn Bishop Gilbert in the same way as the aforesaid Peter. But there was neither the same reason nor like material. For Gilbert from his youth subjected himself to the instruction of great men and put more confidence in the weight of their authority than in his own intellect: such men as, first, Hilary of Poitiers; next, Bernard of Chartres; finally, the brothers Anselm and Ralph of Laon. From them he had secured not a superficial, but a solid education, not snatching his hand quickly from under the ferule.[194] His moral sense and the seriousness of his living were not at variance with his intellectual attainments; he had applied his mind not to jesting and jokes but to serious matters.

Hence it was that he was dignified in bearing and in utterance; as he showed himself to be serious in behavior so was his speech difficult, and what he meant was never clear to childlike minds, scarcely even to men of education and learning. He was called first to Auxerre, later to Paris. Among other teachings for which he was criticized were four articles concerning the divine majesty, to wit: that he asserted that the divine essence is not God; that the properties of persons are not the persons themselves; that persons (in the theological sense) are not predicated in any proposition; that the divine nature did not become flesh.

And beside these, there were others of less importance, namely: that

---

[192] *De syll. categ.* I.

[193] Abelard died April 21, 1142, not at Cluny, but at the priory of St. Marcel, outside Chalon-sur-Saône.   [194] Juvenal 1.15.

(belittling human merit) he said that no one save Christ possesses merit; that (making vain the sacraments of the Church) he said that no one is baptized unless he is destined to be saved. And others of this sort.

liii (li). And so when the supreme pontiff Eugenius sat with the cardinals, the bishops, and other venerable and learned men in the above-mentioned city of Paris, the aforesaid Bishop Gilbert was presented before the consistory to defend these articles. There were introduced as witnesses against him two teachers, Adam of Petit-Pont, a subtle man who had recently been made canon of the church of Paris, and Hugh of Champfleury, the chancellor of the king. They asserted and, as though under oath, declared that they had heard some of these statements from his own lips. Many of those who were present were surprised that such great men, skilled in the practice of debate, should offer an oath instead of an argument!

liv (lii). While many accusations were there being brought against Gilbert, from this side and from that, and he was being compelled by the insistence of many persons to reply concerning so ineffable a theme, he is said to have remarked, among other matters: "I confidently confess that the Father is in one aspect Father and in another is God, yet is He not this and this." Master Joscelin, bishop of Soissons, took such violent exception to the obscurity of this saying, as being a profanely novel expression, that in the words of the proverb, avoiding the middle, he ran into the bank. For he had not yet read that authoritative work of Augustine, or perhaps had read but not understood it, in which being eager to speak circumspectly of the same very high theme he says among other things: "Thus it is one thing for God to be, another thing to exist, even as it is one thing for God to be, another thing to be father or lord. For that He *is*, is said with reference to Him; but He is father with reference to a son, and lord with reference to a serving creation." [195] And so that aforesaid bishop says: "What is the meaning of your statement that for God to be is nothing?" Because there was in logic a tenet of certain philosophers that when one says that Socrates *is* he says nothing. The aforesaid bishop, following these philosophers, had inadvertently applied their statement to theology. By this remark he drew the fire of practically all his hearers from Gilbert to himself. Afterward, when the tumult quieted down, Bishop Gilbert was asked

[195] *De trinitate* VII.iv (ix).

by those in attendance if he would explain why he made so great a distinction of persons in theology. He replied briefly: "Because every person is a thing in itself." And so that day's meeting was adjourned, not without great amazement on the part of many who were present.

As he was again brought to trial the next day and was assailed for the novelty of his words because in his essay on the Holy Trinity he had called the three Persons three separate beings, N.,[196] archbishop of Rouen, aggravated the situation by saying that God ought rather to be called one separate being than three separate beings, not, however, without offense to many, since Hilary says in his book on the synods: "Just as it is unholy to speak of two Gods, so it is sacrilegious to speak of a separate and sole God"; and likewise in that same work: "Let us bring forth no single thing from the holy sacraments to arouse suspicion in our hearers and to give occasion for blasphemy." [197]

(liii). But the bishop of Poitiers testified that in his aforesaid writings he had had a simple meaning, affirming that by the word "single" he meant to convey the fact of their exalted uniqueness, just as by antonomasia we are accustomed to call St. Paul *the* apostle, the unique, the par excellence apostle, and we call the glorious Mother of God the unique virgin for the reason that there never was nor will there ever be a virgin like her who was at once a virgin and a mother. It was by analogy with these examples, he asserted, that when he spoke of three "singulars" he had in mind the uniqueness—the excellence—of the three Persons, since there is not, was not, nor shall there be such a Father who forsooth is Father and God, and after the same fashion such a Son, such a Holy Spirit.

But because we have said that the aforesaid man interpreted a person in theology as something unitary in itself, let us enter a little into his meaning, that a judgment concerning this same expression may be clearer to posterity. For an understanding of this it seems best to insert the following chapter by way of preface.

lv. In natural objects one property of a substance is universal, another is singular—whether individual or particular. Of the individual, one property is personal, another is not. I use the term "person" as though it were obtained by derivation from personality, not as the Greeks, from the mask placed before an actor's face, call it *prosopon*,

---

[196] Hugh of Amiens, archbishop of Rouen, 1130–64.
[197] The first quotation has not been found; the second is from *Liber de synodis* lxx.

or the Latins *persona* from the fact of speaking through it. But I use it in the same sense as Boethius, in his book on person and nature where he argues against Eutyches and Nestorius and (after the fashion of the Greeks) calls "person" that which the Greeks call "hypostasis," following not the etymology of the word but the meaning of the thing, and defines it as follows: "A person is the individual substance of a rational being." [198]

Now I call a thing universal not because one exists in many, which is impossible, but because by uniting many in similarity it may be called, from the union of assimilation, universal as though "turning into one." For example, from the likeness of many the greater is termed corporeity; the lesser, animal nature; the least or the last, humanity. Whence Boethius says: "The species is the form of individuals and the ultimate likeness." For after this occurs not likeness but unlikeness.[199] From this the other term is clearly revealed, namely, why I called a singular property individual or particular, that is, a property which does not render its subject like others—as humanity does—but divides, distinguishes, separates from others, like the quality which we are accustomed to call by the coined name of "Platonism." This is called "individual" from dividing, "particular" from separating, "singular" from distinguishing. Nor should one object that from dividing it should rather be called "dividual" than individual; for, since it does not merely separate its subject and differentiate it from others, but it also gives it permanent abidance in its own individuality and dissimilarity which are so great that there is not, was not, and shall not be another subject which can be assimilated to it, in so far as this property [viz., Platonism] is concerned. It is better called "indivisible" (*individuum*) from "separation" (*privando*) than "divisible" (*dividuum*) from "positing" (*ponendo*). As to its opposite, because it communicates more by dividing itself and divides by communicating, it ought more properly to be called "divisible" (*dividuum*).

But it must be observed that "individual" and "singular" are not convertible terms; for everything individual is singular, but not everything singular is individual. For this whiteness is singular, but is not individual. Finally, in the sphere of nature no simple thing can be indi-

---

[198] *Contra Eutychen* iii. Otto borrows the preceding account of the Greek and Latin words for "person" from this same source.

[199] *In Porphyrium comment.* iii (PL, LXIV, col. 104).

vidual. Likewise, not every individual thing is personal, but every personal thing is individual according to the preceding subdivision, wherein it was stated that one individual is personal, another not, which will very easily be apparent from the aforesaid definition of "person." For, since every being results from form, every subsistent thing owes both its reality and its name to its form. Likewise, although every definition belongs to one thing and fits another, yet it is not permissible without rational justification to use one for the other. "Person" therefore derives its name from its own being, which may be called by an invented name "personality"; but by definition mere individual substance is not called a person unless we add "endowed with a rational nature." On this account it is to be observed that among the Greeks, who are not without resource in language, one thing is called *ousia*; another, *ousiosis*; another, *ypostasis*.[200] But we may translate *ousia* as "essence"; *ousiosis* as "subsistence"; *ypostasis*, because of the poverty of the Latin speech, we cannot express by a single word. For, whereas among us as among them, substance or *ypostasis* gets its name from "staying under" (*a substando*), there is a difference in this, that our word "substance" (*substantia*) is so general as to include all things that subsist, but their word *ypostasis* is to be applied only to such things as subsist in rational nature. Therefore, the Latin translator, since he could not faithfully render the original, word for word, was satisfied with rendering the sense and preferred to use the word "person" rather than the word "substance." Whence the aforesaid definition of "person": "A person is the indivisible substance of a rational being."

It is clear, therefore, that not every indivisible thing is a person, because not every indivisible substance is a rational nature; just as the being of this crystal is singular, or to emphasize the association with reason, the crystal itself is an individual or an individual substance, nevertheless it is not a rational nature. Although, even if it were of rational nature, yet a crystal could not fully be termed an individual substance. For we are not accustomed to describe as individual substance a single thing which has the capability of uniting with another thing, likewise single, to form a certain whole, but does not in itself possess unity. For that exists as one in itself which, neither by act nor by nature, is able, has been able, or shall be able to unite with another

---

[200] This, and the remainder of this paragraph, is drawn from Boethius *Contra Eutychen* iii.

to form some whole. From this it comes about that a given soul, which is a substance of rational nature, yet because in this regard it is not of itself one and indivisible—since it unites with a given body to constitute a given man, cannot be said to be a person since, as we have known, the definition: "a person is the indivisible substance of a rational being" has been removed from it. And [if the definition has been removed] then the thing defined is also removed in accordance with the logical principle that "from whatsoever you remove the definition, from it you also remove the thing defined." This lion here, although it is in itself a thing, one and indivisible, yet because it is not a rational nature cannot be called "person" if we adhere to the precise meaning of the word. We conclude that a given angel and a given man alone among natural beings can with full right be called "person."

Accordingly, the aforesaid bishop set up two rules for natural beings, namely, "the subsistences of different subsistent things are different" and "the personal properties of different persons are different." One he excluded from theology, the other he admitted. For he entirely repudiated the first rule which states that there are as many subsistences as there are subsistent things [as he naturally would], since the orthodox view which falls between one extreme (that of Arius) and the other extreme (that of Sabellius) believes that there are three persons and one essence. The other statement he admits to theology, since in the Holy Trinity there is no personal property of the Father which is peculiar to the Son, and conversely.

Consequently, he declared that the term "person" was transferred to theology not from that which is called *prosopon,* but from the aforesaid use in the sphere of natural beings, frequently quoting Hilary's familiar saying: "Let not the same one, because of fictitious resemblance (as that of a mask), pretend to be now the Father and now the Son." Hence he also declares that these persons possess genuine unity. But as regards his saying that although He is in one respect Father and in another is God, nevertheless He is not the sum of two aspects (*hoc et hoc*),[201] what he means is: if we apply the predicament [the category] of substance He is God; but if we apply the category *ad aliquid* [i.e., relativity] then He is Father. That these diverse categories exist also

---

[201] *Hoc et hoc;* we may say "man is body" and "man is soul," soul and body being different, but in the case of God we may not say "God is power" and "God is wisdom" as though His wisdom were different from His power.

in theology is shown by the book of Boethius which he wrote concerning the Holy Trinity. And yet one may not on this account properly conclude that if He is in one respect Father and in another God, He is therefore this and that (*hoc et hoc*). This conclusion is not properly reached unless it be first conceded that both are substantial predicates of God,[202] as when we say: God is good, wise, omnipotent. These predicates are substantial; undoubtedly, if they were different God would be this and that (*hoc et hoc*). But since it is the same thing to declare "God is wise" as to say "God is good," so that (contrary to our practice with natural beings) one may well say: "He is good in wisdom, wise in goodness"—as though I were to proceed thus in the case of natural objects: "This pearl is shining in its whiteness, white in its sheen"— He is not this and that, but is this.

I have set down what he believed. Let others judge what should be believed. But enough of this. Now let us return to the order of the history.

lvi (liv). When the bishop, already so frequently mentioned, had for several days been questioned concerning his faith in the presence of the supreme pontiff in the city of Paris, the pope, being a cautious and pious man and realizing the difficulty of the case, decided that the matter should be postponed until the universal council. For a general council had been summoned to meet at Rheims, the chief city of that part of France, for the next Mid-Lent Sunday, both because the aforesaid pope was delaying in France [203] to avoid persecution from his own people and also because a certain would-be clergyman, affecting the honor of being a heretic "with the calves of the people," [204] was being held in chains and reserved for examination by the Church. This fellow had arrogated to himself the language of Scripture in the remote districts of France, that is, around Brittany and Gascony, because among populations remote from the heart of France simplicity, or rather folly (if I may be so frank), is rife and error can ordinarily find easy entrance. Calling himself "Him" (*Eum*),[205] as though he were

---

[202] Which they are not, since one of them was shown to be an accidental predicate.
[203] See above, i.xxviii.   [204] Psalms 68:30.
[205] Eon de l'Etoile, a Breton hermit and heretic who, as Otto notes in the next sentence, identified himself with the *Eum* of the phrase *Eum qui venturus est judicare vivos et mortuos* ("Him who will come to judge the quick and the dead"). See H. C. Lea, *History of the Inquisition of the Middle Ages* (3 vols., New York, 1888), I, 66; Jean Guiraud, *Histoire de l'inquisition au moyen âge* (2 vols., Paris, 1935, 1938), I, 14–16.

the Son of God, he drew after him a great multitude of the uneducated people, declaring that he himself was the one by whom every prayer concludes when we say: "By Him" (*Per eum*).

lvii (lv). And so in the course of time, when Mid-Lent [1148] arrived and while we,[206] dispersed by the Turks on our way to Jerusalem, were sailing on the high seas, the council met at Rheims in the basilica of the blessed Mother of God ever virgin, the supreme pontiff Eugenius presiding. There (to visualize the scene) the aforesaid "Him" was brought forth with his little writings, a man rustic and illiterate and undeserving of the name of heretic, and in punishment for his stubborn folly or his foolish stubbornness was committed to Suger, the abbot of St. Denis, who because of the absence of the king was administering the affairs of the kingdom of France,[207] in accordance with a prerogative of that monastery. Being held by him in strict custody, he soon ended his days.

There came to the aforesaid council with a golden bull the messengers of the younger king of the Romans, Henry, both to announce to the Roman pope his elevation to supreme authority [208] and to complain about the three brothers in Poland who, driving out the fourth, their senior, had divided the duchy among them, and about the bishops of that province who had in that matter sworn an oath to the father of these brothers.[209]

Mischievous rumor, also, swifter than all other moving things, according to the well-known line,

"Rumor, an evil than which no other is quicker in movement" [210]

by the speed of its nature flitting across the great expanse of water, was busied there in the ears or on the lips of all as it brought sure indications of the outcome of our expedition.

lviii (lvi). And so, when the synod was ended and wholesome articles had been issued for changes or confirmation of the ancient decrees there announced, the more prudent and those who lived not far

---

[206] That is, the crusaders, including Otto himself.

[207] Suger was regent during Louis VII's absence on crusade. He received custody of Éon, presumably not as regent, but in his ecclesiastical capacity as abbot of St. Denis.

[208] Henry is, of course, notifying the pope of his *election;* he had not been crowned emperor by the pontiff. It is, however, interesting to note Otto's phrase: *de sublimatione sua ad imperium.*

[209] See above, I.xxx and note 117.   [210] Vergil *Aeneid* IV.174.

away were detained to bring the case of Bishop Gilbert to a conclusion. When the week of Mid-Lent had passed, and the holy time of the Lord's passion was beginning, the bishop of Poitiers was again brought to judgment, the supreme pontiff still remaining at Rheims. He was summoned to the chamber in which the bishop of the City sat with the elders, and was subtly questioned by him as to his views concerning faith in the Holy Trinity. Gilbert caused to be read the authoritative passages in the orthodox fathers, which he had brought with him, not on bits of parchment in abbreviated form, but entire in the corpus of the books; he declared that he held the same faith as they. And as the day was being consumed by speech of this sort and by the long continuance of the reading, the Roman bishop, as though affected by weariness, said: "Brother, you say much, you have caused to be read much—and things which perhaps we do not understand. But I should like to learn from you in simple language whether you believe that the highest essence, wherein you declare the three persons are one God, is God." And he, tired by the long discussion and without taking thought, answered, "No." The secretary seized upon the word almost before it had escaped his lips, writing it down in this fashion: "The bishop of Poitiers has written and declared that the divine essence is not God." For his commentary on Boethius, *Concerning the Trinity*, where the author [i.e., Boethius], setting apart theological from natural categories, wrote among other matters "the substance *whereby* (*qua*) God is"; he [Gilbert] amplified the statement by adding "not ['the substance] which *is* God' (*quae Deus est*), that is, it is to be related not to the subsistent thing but to subsistence." [211]

And so the meeting on that day adjourned on these words. The bishop spent all the remainder of that day and the following night with those of the cardinals who were his friends—and there were many such.

On the next day, when the bishop was again placed on trial in the presence of the supreme pontiff, the written record was read. He was called on to justify his statement. He declared that he had not made so explicit an admission. For he stated that the name "God" is applied sometimes as a designation for the divine essence (*naturae*, i.e., *divinitas*), sometimes as a designation of a person and also of the person as *one*. As a designation for the divine essence, as when one says: "Thy God is one"; of a person, as when one says: "The Father is God, the

[211] Gilbert's commentary on the *De trinitate* of Boethius (PL, LIV, col. 1290).

Son is God"; of a person and of only one of the three, as in "God is gone up with a shout," [212] which (as no one can doubt) is said of the person of the Son. Now [he concluded, the statement he stood by and the one] he recognized as his own was [the following:] that the divinity is God only when God is taken in the first sense, when the name God is given to the essence (*natura*). But that he did not dare accept it without distinction (*absolute*). For obviously if he admitted without distinction that divinity is God, that is, any one of the persons, he would be obliged to grant anything without distinction concerning any one of the persons and concerning the essence, and so would fall into the absurdity [of admitting] that, just as had the person of the Son, so had divine essence without distinction become flesh and suffered. From this absurdity might easily emerge the heretical opinion of Sabellius, that the same thing is said to beget and to be begotten and to have begotten itself. But that reason distinguished between nature and person not by abstract mathematics but in some wise by theological considerations, he strove to prove both by logical arguments and by authority. By logical arguments, lest the religious tenets of the Christian faith should with Arius admit a plurality of essences as well as of persons, or with Sabellius restrict the plurality of the persons to the singleness of the essence, using as his authority the following quotation of Theodoret against Sabellius: "Now a man who desires spiritual riches and wishes to profess the teachings of Christianity ought not to be ignorant of the property of things, lest perchance he should sin against the teachings by interpreting one thing as something else. For he who understands nature and person as one and the same falls either into the Arian sunderance or into Sabellian fusion." [213] And that statement of Hilary: "Distinguish, therefore, O heretic, the spirit of Christ from the spirit of God, and the spirit of Christ raised from the dead from the spirit of God raising Christ from the dead. And I ask now whether you think in the phrase 'the spirit of God' a nature or a thing of nature is indicated. For 'nature' and 'thing of nature' are not the same thing; even as 'man' and 'what is of man' are not the same, nor is 'fire' and 'what is of fire' the same. And accordingly 'God' and 'what is of God' are not the same." [214]

---

[212] Psalms 47:5.
[213] Theodoret *De trinitate* (PG, LXXXIII, col. 1170).
[214] *De trinitate* VIII.xxi–xxii.

Likewise he pointed out on the authority of the council of Toledo [215] that we must believe it was not the nature but the person of the Son that became flesh: "Only the Word was made flesh and dwelt among us.[216] And although the Trinity as a whole formed the Man that was assumed, because the works of the Trinity as a whole are inseparable, yet [the Son] alone took upon Himself man in the singleness of His person, not in the unity of the divine nature. That is: the property of the Son, not what is common to the Trinity." And when Gilbert wanted to clarify this authority the abbot of Clairvaux injected certain words which displeased the cardinals. And the bishop of Poitiers said: "Let this also be written down." To which Bernard made answer: "Let it be written with a pen of iron, with the point of a diamond." [217]

And presently going out to the people [in the council] Bernard called together all whom he could. There, with the archbishops, the bishops, and the religious and learned men in opposition to the four aforesaid articles which were charged against the bishop of Poitiers, he set forth (he with them and the others with him) their faith after this fashion:

lix. "We firmly believe that the nature of divinity is God, and that it cannot in any catholic sense be denied that divinity is God and God is divinity. For if it is said that by wisdom He is wise, by greatness He is great, by eternity eternal, by unity one, by divinity God, and the like, let us then believe that He is wise only by the wisdom which is God Himself, great only by the greatness which is God Himself, eternal only by the eternity which is God Himself, one only by the unity which is God Himself, and is God only by the divinity which He Himself is: that is, that in Himself He is wise, great, eternal, one, God. When we speak of the three persons, Father, Son, Holy Spirit, we affirm that they are one God, one divine substance. And conversely, when we speak of one God, one divine substance, we affirm that the one God Himself, the one divine substance, is three persons. We believe that only God the Father, and the Son, and the Holy Spirit is eternal, and that there are no other things at all, whether they be called relations or properties or singlenesses or unities or other terms of this sort which attach to God, that are from eternity and are not God. We believe that divinity itself, whether one calls it divine essence or divine nature, was incarnate, but in the Son."

---

[215] In 638; see Mansi, X, col. 662.   [216] John 1:14.   [217] Jeremiah, 17:1.

lx (lvii). The holy senate of cardinals took so ill this conduct on the part of the Gallic church that they entered the papal court with great indignation of heart and, as though made one body, all said to their pope with one voice: "You must realize that, being raised to the supreme power over the Church by us cardinals, around whom as around its cardinal points [218] the axis of the Church universal moves, being made by us from a private person into the father of the entire Church, you cannot henceforth belong to yourself, but rather to us; you cannot any longer place private and recent friendships before those which are common and of long standing; you must, because of the obligations of your past, consider the advantage of all, and cherish and keep watchful eye upon the exaltation of the Roman curia. But what has your abbot done—and the Gallic church with him? With what effrontery, with what audacity has he raised his head against the primacy and the supremacy of the Roman see? For it is this see alone which shuts and no man openeth, openeth and no man shuts.[219] It alone has the right to conduct investigations of the Catholic faith and even though absent it can permit no one to infringe upon this unique privilege. But see! these Gauls, despising us even in our very presence, have without consulting us presumed to set down their profession of faith relative to the articles which have been discussed during these days in conference with us, as though they were adding the final touch to a definitive decree. Surely, if a matter of this kind were being dealt with in the East, at Alexandria or Antioch, in the presence of all the patriarchs, nothing would be held valid and established without our authorization. Nay, further, according to the decrees and precedents of the ancient fathers, it would have to be reserved for definite action by Rome. How then do these men dare in our very presence to usurp a prerogative which in our absence is not permitted to farther removed and more distinguished men. We desire, therefore, that you quickly assail so rash an innovation as this and defer not to punish their insolence."

The Roman pontiff, calming them by flattering speech, summoned the abbot into his presence and adroitly questioned him about this incident and the nature of it. The abbot replied in humility and reverence that neither he nor the lord bishops had made an authoritative statement about the aforesaid articles, but because he had heard from the

[218] A play on words in the Latin: *cardines* (hinges).
[219] Revelation 3:7.

bishop of Poitiers that an expression of his faith was to be given in writing, and being unwilling to do this by himself, he had, with their concurrence and cognizance, set forth in simple language what he believed. By this reply of his, so lowly and modest, the anger of the cardinals was allayed, yet on condition that the aforesaid document, as issued without the advice of the curia and lacking in weight of authority, should not be counted in the Church as a creed such as is customarily drawn up in councils convened against heresies.

Blessed in all things be God, who thus watched over His Church, His bride, and saw to it that neither the principal members should separate from their Head, nor so great a number of pious and discerning persons in the Gallic church be the occasion for a disastrous schism because they felt oppressed by some weighty judgment pronounced by the Roman see!

lxi. Let it suffice to have related these few out of the many proceedings of that council, with this additional statement, however, that because of the confusion previously mentioned, no definite conclusion could be reached about the first three articles. And no wonder. For in the fourth article Bishop Gilbert did not differ much from the others, since they acknowledged that the nature became flesh, but in the Son, whereas he said that the person of the Son became flesh, but not without its nature. What definition could they reach concerning the predication of the persons, when they did not consider his usage—what he termed "using the word, of course, in its proper sense"—at variance with other teachers, even in natural matters? Concerning properties, whether they are part of the person, both for the aforesaid cause and for theological theories which are held here and there, a decision was withheld. Only concerning the first point did the Roman pontiff determine that in theology no interpretation should make a distinction between nature and person, and that God should be referred to as divine essence not only in the relationship expressed by the ablative case but also in that of the nominative.[220] Whence up to the present time the more reliable disciples of that bishop maintain that reason may there make not a logical distinction but only a verbal one.

But the bishop, accepting with due reverence the aforesaid utterance of the supreme pontiff, having become reconciled with his archdeacons,

---

[220] That is, both are true; God is *by* divine essence, and God *is* divine essence.

returned to his own diocese with his episcopal status unimpaired and in the fullness of honor.

Whether the aforesaid abbot of Clairvaux in consequence of the frailty of human weakness, being a mere man, was deceived in this matter, or the bishop, being a very learned gentleman, escaped the condemnation of the Church by shrewdly concealing his view, it is not our task to discuss or to decide. For that holy and wise men, hampered by corruptible flesh, are frequently deceived in such matters is proved by both modern and ancient examples. For, not to mention the instance (which the blessed Gregory cites [221]) of holy David, on whom the Spirit of the Lord is said to have come [222]—as he was returning to his native land, from which he had been expelled by his son, he was taken unawares by the servant of Mephibosheth, who came to meet him with gifts [223]—in Christian times the blessed Epiphanius, bishop of Salamis in Cyprus, a man of such notable sanctity that he even restored a dead person to life, could yet be so violently incited by his foes against John Chrysostom, whose memory flourishes in the Church today, that beyond avoiding him in his own city and being unwilling to communicate with him, he even aroused against him, to the best of his ability, the very people who had been entrusted to him. This incident, taken from the *Tripartite History,* has been more fully related in our earlier account.[224] So much for that.

lxii (lviii). While these matters and others of this sort were taking place in France, our army, as has been said above, dotted the sea, being dispersed by the very effort of navigating the ships and each attempting in various places to reach land, as and when he could. For Louis, the king of the Franks, put in about Mid-Lent in a place called the Port of St. Simeon,[225] near Antioch, in the land of a prince who was his wife's uncle; [226] others of our forces at Ptolemaïs, which is also called Acre; others at Tyre; others, between Tyre and Sidon in Sarepta,[227] a town of the Sidonians, not without fear of shipwreck, reached

---

[221] *Dialogues* I.iv.   [222] I Samuel 16:13.

[223] II Samuel 9; 16:1–4; 19:24–30.

[224] *Two Cities* IV.xix; *Hist. Trip.* x (PL, LXIX, col. 1172).

[225] At the mouth of the Orontes.

[226] Raymond of Poitiers, prince of Antioch and younger son of William IX, duke of Aquitaine; Louis' wife at this time was Eleanor, daughter of William X of Aquitaine, and thus Raymond's niece.   [227] The Biblical Zarepath and modern Sarfend.

the desired haven. Some actually did suffer shipwreck; certain of them were swallowed up by the waters, the rest escaped half naked.

Now those that had reached shore so early entered the Holy City about Palm Sunday and celebrated our Lord's Passion and holy Resurrection with much devotion of heart, going about to the various places where those events occurred, and beholding them, as men say, eye to eye.

But Conrad, the prince of the Romans, still having in his company the princes Ortlieb, bishop of Basel; Arnold, his chancellor; [228] Frederick, duke of the Swabians; Henry, duke of the Bavarians; Duke Welf; and other counts and illustrious men and nobles, landed at Ptolemaïs in the very week of Easter. After a few days he came to Jerusalem, amid great jubilation on the part of clergy and people, and was received with much honor. At that time there died of the king's following Frederick,[229] that very famous advocate of the church of Regensburg; his body was borne to the Holy City and was buried in the cemetery of the Knights of the Temple, not far from the ancient temple of the Lord.

The king remained there for a few days in the palace of the Templars, where once the royal house, which is also the Temple of Solomon, was built, and after visiting the holy places everywhere returned to Ptolemaïs through Samaria and Galilee. As the knights arrived, he induced all that he could by gifts of money to remain. For he had agreed with the king [230] of that land and the patriarch [231] and the Knights of the Temple to lead an army into Syria about the following July to take Damascus. Wherefore he then assembled what troops he could by a lavish expenditure of money.

lxiii. King Louis of France also, pursuing the same course to the best of his ability, upon his return from Antioch remained at Tyre. Accordingly, the two met in the month of June around the nativity of St. John the Baptist [June 24 in 1148] at a place called Palma (taking its name from the tree) between Tyre and Ptolemaïs, to make plans concerning the time and place: where and when the army should be

[228] Arnold of Wied, Conrad's chancellor, who, as archbishop of Cologne, crowned Frederick in 1152; see below, II.iii.

[229] Frederick of Bogen, for many years a leading supporter of the Hohenstaufens against the Welfs in Bavaria.

[230] Baldwin III (1144–63).

[231] Fulcher, Latin patriarch of Jerusalem (1146–57).

mustered. Not yet, however, even after so many great tribulations, had royal pride in their case been consumed and laid to rest. Hence what issue and event this expedition to Damascus also experienced must be related elsewhere, and possibly by others.[232]

lxiv (lix). But upon the completion of this expedition the princes made their plans to return home, the Roman king through Greece, but the other by way of Calabria and Apulia. Accordingly, Conrad, the prince of the Romans, embarked at Ptolemaïs and sailing across the sea met his brother and friend Manuel, the prince of the royal city, in the territory of Achaea or Thessaly. He went to see him and, wearied by the long journey and weakened by its fatigues and suffering from no little exhaustion, he rested with him for some time.[233] There making arrangements for the return, he sent Duke Frederick, his brother's son, ahead to inquire into, or rather to strengthen, the condition of the empire. Making his way through Bulgaria and Pannonia, Frederick reached home in the month of April and, exercising the function of a good judge, in the interests of peace there executed by hanging certain of his own ministers. Thereupon his uncle, the king, after the lapse of a number of days during which he had rested in Greece, arrived within the confines of his own realm at Pola, a city of Istria, after sailing across the Illyrian and Dalmatian sea. He brought with him the aforesaid bishop of Basel and Chancellor Arnold and his brother Henry, duke of the Bavarians; for Duke Welf had returned by way of Calabria and Apulia. At Pola, Conrad mounted a charger and, traveling through Aquileia, he celebrated Whitsunday in *Iuvavia*, which is now called Salzburg and is known as the metropolitan see of Bavaria. Two years had elapsed since he had observed the same festival in the territory of Pannonia. After that he held a diet at Regensburg, attended by a great throng of princes.

lxv (lx). Now because some of the little brethren of the Church being offended marvel, and marveling are offended [234] at the effort of

---

[232] The siege of Damascus in July, 1148, was a complete failure. See the account in William of Tyre, *A History of Deeds Done beyond the Sea*, translated by Emily Atwater Babcock and A. C. Krey, "Records of Civilization," No. 35 (New York, 1943), II, 186–95.

[233] Conrad accompanied Manuel to Constantinople, where he remained until the spring of 1149. During this time an alliance was concluded by the two monarchs against Roger of Sicily (see above, i.xxxiv and note 115).

[234] Cf. Matthew 18:6; Luke 17:2; Mark 9:42.

our aforesaid expedition, inasmuch as starting out from so lofty and good a beginning it came to so pitiful a conclusion—not a good one—it seems that they must be answered as follows. Nothing can truly be called good save only that One who has what He is, not from some other source, but from Himself, and is said most truly to be and most truly to be good, according to the saying: "None is good, save one, that is, God." [235] All things else are called by him "good" not because they participate in His essence but because they proceed from His goodness. Now whatever among natural objects is called "good," that is so made either absolutely (*simpliciter*) or relatively (*secundum quid*). But if it is produced absolutely, then it is termed an endowment of nature, just as what is bestowed is called a gift of grace, according to the statement: "Every good gift and every perfect gift is from above." [236] The natural endowment which we called absolutely "good" may be considered as the most universal in earthly things.[237] And when we subdivide it by applying to it as an "informing" differentia [238] the gift of grace we obtain a species of virtue of whose existence we call things [no longer unrestrictedly good but] just and temperate. Therefore, when created things are spoken of as "good" in the absolute sense, doubtlessly we mean the "good" of nature. It is in the sense that "good" is used in the Biblical phrase: "God saw everything that he had made, and it was very good." [239] It is in this sense that we speak of stone or wood as being "good." If we narrow down the universality of the genus and restrict it so as to form rational nature by applying to the genus the differentia which we call the "gift of grace," then of this rational nature and only of this we can predicate "just" and "temperate." For though we call a stone "good" we can never call it "just" or "temperate." I conclude then with the words of Boethius who in his "Book of Rules" [240] says that "good" is the term of the genus and "just" of the species and adds: "Neither does the species descend to all things," meaning thereby [that the species cannot be predicated of] everything that is derived from the genus. Which is the same thing as

---

[235] Luke 18:19.   [236] James 1:17.

[237] Otto is here thinking of the *genus generalissimum*.

[238] See above, note 36.   [239] Genesis 1:31.

[240] *In libro regularum;* this is Boethius' treatise *Quomodo substantiae*, cited before by Otto as *Libri ebdomade* (see above, I.v and note 54). Otto's present title derives from the nine rules (*regulae*) with which Boethius opens. The quotation that follows occurs at the very end of the treatise.

saying *ex opposito* that the genus is predicable only of those derived things which have not been narrowed down into predicates of the species. So in accordance with the usage of logicians a valid statement is obtained by denying the genus and affirming the species.[241] And so then when I say that something is absolutely (unrestrictedly) "good," I mean that it is an endowment of nature (what nature gives) and [as unrestricted] it is univocally predicable of all the subordinate species. But when I say that something is relatively (restrictedly) "good," then I consider not the fact that it is given by bountiful nature but I look rather at the usefulness that it has [under any given circumstances]. [And understanding "good"] as "useful" [this useful good] becomes an equivocal [predicate and can be expanded] indefinitely. So that we call a horse "good" from its utility for riding, a garment "good" from the utility of wearing it, food "good" from the utility derived from nutrition. Likewise, for the same reason, what is called "good" for one species is called "bad" for another. For example, henbane nourishes a sparrow but kills a man. One and the same thing also, according as it changes from one aspect to another, will be good and will not be good for individuals comprised within the same species, or even for the same single individual. Whence we are accustomed to say: It is good for one who feels the heat of fever to drink water; it is good, according to the apostle, for another to use a little wine because of the weakness of the stomach. Nor does it follow from this that if a thing is good in a relative sense, for this man or for that, it is good absolutely; just as it does not follow if the Ethiopian is white of tooth, therefore he is white, or conversely, he is not black of tooth, therefore he is not black. This is evident also from the use we make of Holy Scripture, when we say it was not good for the Jews or for Judas to betray Christ or to crucify Him, although for us it was good. But as in our human philosophy having a white tooth does not take blackness from the Ethiopian, thus in Holy Scripture the badness of the Jews does not invalidate the fact that for all humanity Christ's Passion was good.

From this it follows by analogy for the same reason, with reference to our aforesaid expedition, that although it was not good for the en-

---

[241] Thus, to take the statement "if he is a man he is an animal": if we affirm the species and say "Plato is a man, therefore he is an animal" we have a valid statement. Likewise, if we deny the genus and say "Plato is not an animal, therefore he is not a man" the statement is valid. But we cannot correctly say "Plato is not a man, therefore he is not an animal," or "Plato is an animal, therefore he is a man."

largement of boundaries or for the advantage of bodies, yet it was good for the salvation of many souls, on condition however, that you interpret the word "good" not as an endowment of nature but always in the sense of "useful." And on condition that this usefulness emerge as a subdivision in virtue of which (as we have said above) "good" is sometimes used absolutely, sometimes relatively; and when it is used relatively equivocation appears because of the diversities of the useful. So the good [we are now concerned with] as identical with "useful" is considered sometimes absolutely, sometimes relatively. And yet, if we should say that the holy abbot [242] was inspired by the spirit of God to arouse us, but that we, by reason of our pride and arrogance not observing the salutary commandments, have deservedly suffered loss of property and persons, it would not be at variance with logical processes or with ancient examples; although it is also true that the spirit of the prophets does not always accompany the prophets.

But how the aforesaid good man, in writing on this subject, inserted in his book to Pope Eugenius *On Consideration* [243] an apologetic to defend himself, the curious investigator of events may discover.

(lxi). But how Pope Eugenius received the prince of the Romans with fatherly words of comfort, as he returned from so dire tribulation, is indicated below:

lxvi. "Bishop Eugenius, the servant of the servants of God, to his very dear son in Christ, Conrad, by the grace of God illustrious king of the Romans, greeting and apostolic benediction.

"Since the law of change impairs everything in this world, even as we should not be puffed up by prosperity, so too we ought not be broken by adversity, putting our faith in divine mercy, because the Mediator between God and men by an admirable dispensation is accustomed to scourge with adversities every son whom He receiveth,[244] that while He calls him to eternal rewards through love, the present world may repel his mind from itself by the tumults which it brings on, and that he may the more readily withdraw from the love of this world as he is the more under compulsion while being called. This is shown in the case of the people of Israel (when Moses called them) and Pharaoh. For Moses was then sent to call them when Pharaoh

[242] Bernard of Clairvaux.
[243] Bernard *De consideratione* II.1 (PL, CLXXXII, col. 741–45).
[244] Hebrews 12:6.

was oppressing them with hard tasks, that the one might draw them by his call, the other impel them by his frenzy, so that the people disgracefully held in slavery might be aroused either when enticed by the benefits or when moved by the hardships. Actuated, therefore, by this reasonable argument, we admonish and exhort Your Discretion in the Lord to endure with patience the tribulations which Omnipotent God has inflicted upon you and your army, and to set your hope on Him who permits whom He will to be afflicted and is accustomed mercifully to liberate them that put their trust in Him. For if you perfectly hold fast your patience and humility in adversity, you shall be led undismayed through the wilderness of this life under the protection of the pillar of cloud and fire, that is, the solace of patience and the flame of love.[245]

"Because, therefore, we cherish your person with true love and have firm confidence in you, it would have been particularly pleasing to us if, after your return, we could without delay have discussed with you in joint converse the matters which are known to tend toward the honor of Holy Church and of the empire. But because the circumstances of the time denied us this, and because we are concerned for your safety, we have felt that we should send certain of our brethren to Your Serenity, after we learned that by God's help you had come in safety to the region of Lombardy, as we have indicated to you through our venerable brothers Hartwig, archbishop of Bremen, and Anselm, bishop of Havelberg, to set forth to you the affection and good will which we feel toward you, and that we may know from their lips what we desire to hear about you. We have given them instructions to set forth to you, as our very dear son and Catholic prince and particular defender of the Holy Roman Church, the status of the Church itself and our own situation.

"Now these men, after proceeding as far as Tuscany, from which region they learned you had crossed over into German territories, fearing the length of the trip and the difficulty of the journey on account of the heat of summer, have returned to our presence. But, because we desire to know your situation and that of our beloved son Henry, the younger king, whom since your departure we have loved with fatherly affection and whose actions we earnestly desire in the Lord may prosper hereafter, and as our brothers could not endure the exertion of so

[245] Exodus 13:21.

long a journey on account of the summer's heat, we visit Your Excellency through our faithful Franco, the bearer of the present letter, and through apostolic letters. We admonish and exhort Your Nobility in the Lord that you hasten to inform us, through this same Franco, about the course of events with reference to you and him, and the state of the realm, and that you display at this time the devotion which you cherish toward your mother, the Holy Roman Church, that you may be seen to respond harmoniously to our affection, and that you may duly merit greater grace from our Creator, through the intercessions of blessed Peter, the chief of the apostles, to whom you should offer yourself wholly.

"Given at Tusculum on the eighth day before the Kalends of July [June 24, 1149]."

lxvii (lxii). At about the same time Henry, the king's son, whom he himself (as has been said above) had raised to the kingship, by election of the princes, died [1150]. There still remained another little brother, named Frederick. At that time also at Utrecht, a city of Frisia, upon the death of Hartbert,[246] the bishop of that church, a serious schism arose. Some chose Frederick, the son of Count Adolph,[247] others Herman, the provost of the church of St. Gereon situated in a suburb of Cologne, as bishop. But those who had elected Herman, anticipating the others, approached the prince at Nuremberg and received from him investiture with the regalia. The other party, following him as far as Speyer, a city of Gaul, obtained from him a postponement until the next Rogation days, at the palace in Nijmegen. Meanwhile Arnold, also, the archbishop of Cologne, departed this life; a man of no use for any ecclesiastical or secular affairs.

lxviii. Accordingly, King Conrad journeyed to the country of the Lower Rhine, both in connection with the succession at Cologne and to conduct an investigation for the settlement of that controversy that was raging in the church at Utrecht. He had with him the bishops Otto of Freising, from Bavaria, and Albert of Meissen, from Saxony. And when he had reached Boppard, a royal estate situated on the Rhine in the territory of the Treveri, he encountered ambassadors announcing that his chancellor, Arnold, had been elected to the aforesaid church of

---

[246] *Hardelibo;* Hartbert of Beron (1138–50).

[247] Adolph, count of Altena; Frederick was at this time provost of St. George of Cologne, and later became archbishop of Cologne (see below, II.liii, lvi).

Cologne, but had deferred until the king's arrival his assent to this action. The king received these tidings with gladness. Thereupon, digressing a little from his way, he captured two very strong fortifications. One of them, situated on the Moselle, was called Cochem; the other, on the bank of the Rhine, Rheineck. In Cochem he placed a garrison; the other he gave to the flames. There he received the aforesaid archbishop-elect of Cologne and, descending with him toward the lowlands, he had consecrated by the aforesaid bishops whom he had brought with him an elaborate chapel which Arnold had built on his own property not far from Cologne.

Then, taking ship and sailing down the Rhine, he came to Cologne, and was there received with the greatest rejoicing on the part of the clergy and the people. Thereupon, in accordance with custom, when the solemn procession was at an end, the king, sitting in the principal church of St. Peter, invested Arnold (who vigorously objected and protested) with the regalia of both the archbishopric and the duchy. And so he came to the palace at Nijmegen, to judge the case of the people of Utrecht.

The people of Utrecht proudly held Frederick in their city, having ejected Herman. Therefore, first seeking safe conduct for themselves, they came with a great number of ships from the Rhine through the river Waal, which—branching off from it—is known to be an arm of the Rhine. The king, calling them to account, desired to restore them to peace with their adversaries without a legal conflict; when unable to proceed in this fashion he finally offered them a judicial decision. They demanded provisions for their return, declaring that inasmuch as the case itself, being ecclesiastical, had been transferred to an ecclesiastical judge, that is, to the ears of the supreme pontiff, they could not appear before a belted judge.[248] The king complained bitterly against them, since he was unable to punish them immediately as guilty of treason in opposing the Roman emperor, because of the safe conduct granted them, and would soon have proceeded to their city to exact due vengeance for this presumption had he not by reason of the insolence of certain Bavarian counts been recalled into that country.

lxix (lxiii). Therefore, after observing with crown on head [249] the

[248] That is, a secular official.

[249] *Sub corona incedendo celebrans;* Otto employs this or a similar phrase on a number of occasions in the sense of "making a state appearance," in connection with the holding of a diet or other solemn or impressive gathering. See Introduction, p. 13.

next Whitsunday at Coblenz (where he also dismissed the messengers of the king of the Spaniards, who had tarried long with him), Conrad entered Bavaria. Holding a diet at Regensburg, he received into his presence two cardinals, legates of the Roman see, namely, Jordan and Octavian. Thereafter, he outlawed Count Palatine Otto because of excesses committed by his sons; he besieged a castle of his not far distant, called Kelheim, a place shut in by a sharp bend of the Danube; and he forced him to give one of his sons as a hostage.[250]

Returning thence into Gaul, he brought the affair of the people of Utrecht to a conclusion, to the honor of the empire, by summoning all to return to their obedience to Herman. And that no least doubt might in the future be entertained concerning this action, he secured from the Roman see its ratification.

lxx. Not long after, when everything had been set in good order in Gaul and Germany, and when he was also soon to receive the crown of empire by virtue of the expedition he had sworn to lead, Conrad was taken ill.[251] In this some suspicion fell upon certain physicians whom he had with him from Italy, that they had been instigated by Roger of Sicily because of his fear of the king. And thus he came, nevertheless, to Bamberg to hold court, unbroken by the great pain of his illness. There, reft of life amid the lamentations of many and retaining in his last trial the courage of his former endurance, he brought

[250] The Count Palatine Otto of Wittelsbach, whose family held the advocacy of Otto's church of Freising, a position that brought the Wittelsbachs into bitter conflict with the bishop. Our historian thought but poorly of the entire clan; see *Two Cities* VI.xx.

[251] Conrad had plans for an expedition to Italy against Roger of Sicily, in the course of which he would have been crowned emperor by the pope. He was the first German ruler in two centuries who had not been so crowned.

Otto's statement that all was in good order in the German realm at this time (*omnibus bene in Gallia et Germania compositis*) is too strikingly at variance with the truth to pass over unnoted. The young Duke Henry the Lion of Saxony, head of the Welf family, was in full revolt, and Conrad had just waged a disastrously unsuccessful campaign against him in Saxony. Otto gives us no hint of this situation. Nor does he mention the abortive rising of Henry's uncle, Duke Welf, in 1150. Welf had acted in at least tacit understanding with Roger of Sicily, a fact perhaps hinted at by Otto in noting that Welf had returned from the East not with Conrad, but through Calabria and Apulia, domains of Roger (see above, I.lxiv). These striking omissions in Otto's history seem to form a pattern; he was anxious to minimize the struggles between his Welf and Hohenstaufen relatives (see note 89 above). For a convenient summary of the state of Germany at the death of Conrad III, see *Cambridge Medieval History*, V, 357–58.

his life to a close on the Friday following Ash Wednesday, that is, on the fifteenth day before the Kalends of March [February 15, 1152], entrusting the insignia to Duke Frederick and his only son, likewise called Frederick. For, being a wise man, he cherished little hope that his son, who was still a small child, would be raised to the rank of king. Therefore he judged it more advantageous both for his family and for the state if his successor were rather to be his brother's son, by reason of the many famous proofs of his virtues. But when his followers, acting, as they claimed, in accordance with his wish, desired to take his body to the monastery of Lorch and to inter it there in his own plot next to his father, the church of Bamberg decided that this would be in derogation of its dignity and refused to permit it. Nay further, judging it most suitable and honorable both for that church and for the empire, they buried him in royal state next to the tomb of the Emperor Henry, the founder of that place, who was recently raised by the authority of the Roman Church into the holy places and is in the number of the saints.[252]

These and other matters, most invincible of the Augusti, are written to Your Excellency, some to you as for you, others to you but not as for you, which the sharp eye of your clerks should know how to differentiate. But since, in accordance with my plan, I have outlined in summary form the deeds of your grandfather, your father, and your uncle—not without some mention of you—and have now come to your exploits in particular, may I set an end to this first book for the sake of a little rest, in order that my spirit may proceed with greater power to the things that are to be said concerning Your Magnificence.

HERE ENDS THE FIRST BOOK

[252] Henry II had been canonized in 1146.

THE SECOND BOOK

HERE BEGIN THE CHAPTERS OF THE SECOND
BOOK

HERE END THE CHAPTERS

HERE BEGINS THE PROLOGUE OF THE BOOK THAT FOLLOWS

I am not unaware, O paragon of emperors and kings, that while I am attempting to portray the magnificence of your exploits, my pen will prove unequal to the material, as your victories increase. Yet of the two evils, so to speak, I have thought it better that my work should be surpassed by the subject (through my deficiency in expression) than that your glorious deeds should be veiled in silence and perish, were I to say nothing of them.

But because I brought my previous little book to an end with the beginning of your rule as king and emperor, at the death of your most glorious uncle, King Conrad, may this second book, that is to vie with the glory of your principate, now, with God's favor, take its beginning.

HERE ENDS THE PROLOGUE

HERE BEGINS THE SECOND BOOK

i. In the year 1800 since the founding of the City,[1] but 1154 [1152] from the incarnation of the Lord, the most pious King Conrad departed this life in the springtime, on the fifteenth day before the Kalends of March—that is, on the Friday following Ash Wednesday —in the city of Bamberg, as has been said. Wonderful to relate, it was possible to bring together the entire company of the princes, as into a single body, in the town of Frankfort, from the immense extent of the transalpine kingdom (as well as certain barons from Italy), by the third [fourth] day before the Nones of March [March 4]—that is, on Tuesday after *Oculi mei semper*. When the chief men took counsel together there concerning the choice of a prince—for this is the very apex of the law of the Roman empire, namely, that kings are chosen not by lineal descent but through election by the princes (this right it claims for itself as though by unique prerogative)—finally Frederick, duke of the Swabians, the son of Duke Frederick, was sought by all. By the favor of all he was raised to the rank of king.

---

[1] Otto dated the birth of Christ in the year 752 from the founding of the City (*Two Cities* III.vi), or 2 B.C., so that this date should read 1904 rather than 1800.

ii. The explanation of this support, the reason for so unanimous an agreement upon that person, was, as I recall, as follows. There have been hitherto in the Roman world, within the borders of Gaul and Germany, two renowned families: one that of the Henrys of Waiblingen,[2] the other that of the Welfs [3] of Altdorf. The one was wont to produce emperors, the other great dukes. These families, eager for glory as is usually the case with great men, were frequently envious of each other and often disturbed the peace of the state. But by the will of God (as men believe), providing for the peace of his people in time to come, it came about that Duke Frederick, the father of this Frederick, who was a descendant of one of the two families (that is, of the family of the kings), took to wife a member of the other, namely, the daughter of Henry, duke of the Bavarians, and by her became the father of the Frederick who rules at the present time.

The princes, therefore, considering not merely the achievements and the valor of the youth already so frequently mentioned, but also this fact, that being a member of both families, he might—like a cornerstone—link these two separate walls, decided to select him as head of the realm. They foresaw that it would greatly benefit the state if so grave and so long-continued a rivalry between the greatest men of the empire for their own private advantage might by this opportunity and with God's help be finally lulled to rest. So it was not because of dislike for King Conrad, but (as has been said) in the interest of a universal advantage that they preferred to place this Frederick ahead of Conrad's son (likewise named Frederick), who was still a little child. By reason of such considerations and in this way the election of Frederick was celebrated.

iii. When, therefore, all the princes who had thronged to that place had been bound by oath of fealty and homage, the king with a few men whom he considered suitable for the purpose, having dismissed the rest in peace, took ship, amid great rejoicing, on the fifth day of the week. He sailed by the Main and the Rhine, and disembarked at the royal seat at Sinzig. There taking horse, he came the next Saturday to Aachen. On the following day, that is, on that Sunday on which *Laetare Ierusalem* is sung, he was escorted by the bishops from the

---

[2] That is, the Hohenstaufen, so-called from the village of Waiblingen in Swabia; the Italians turned Waiblingen into "Ghibelline."

[3] The ducal family of Bavaria, Italianized as "Guelf"; see above I.xx.

palace to the church of the blessed Mary ever virgin. With the greatest applause of all who were present, he was crowned by Arnold, archbishop of Cologne, the others assisting, and was seated on the throne of the realm of the Franks that was placed in that same church by Charles the Great. Not a few marveled that in so short a space of time not only had so great a throng of princes and of nobles of the kingdom flocked together, but that some also had arrived from western Gaul, whither the report of this event was supposed not yet to have arrived.

I think I ought not to omit the fact that while the diadem was being placed on Frederick's head, after the completion of the sacramental anointing, one of his retainers, from whom for certain grave offenses he had withdrawn his favor before he was king, cast himself at his feet in the center of the church, hoping to turn the latter's spirit from the rigor of justice on so happy an occasion. But Frederick maintained his previous severity and remained unmoved and thus gave to all of us no small proof of his firmness, declaring that it was not from hatred but out of regard for justice that this man had been excluded from his patronage. Nor did this fail to win the admiration of many, that pride could not dissuade the young man (already, as it were, in possession of an old man's judgment) from virtuous firmness to the fault of laxity. What more need be said? Neither the intercession of the princes, nor the favor of smiling fortune, nor the present joy of so great a festival could help that poor wretch. He departed from the inexorable prince unheard.

But this, too, should not be veiled in silence, that on the same day and in the same church the bishop-elect of Münster (also named Frederick) was consecrated by those same bishops who consecrated the king. So it was believed that the Highest King and Priest was actually participating in the present rejoicing: and this was the sign, that in one church one day beheld the anointing of the two persons who alone are sacramentally anointed according to the ordinance of the New and of the Old Testament, and are rightly called the anointed of Christ the Lord.

iv. When all that pertains to the dignity of the crown had been duly performed, the prince retired to the private apartments of the palace and summoned the more prudent and powerful of the assembled nobles. After consulting them concerning the condition of the state, he arranged to have ambassadors sent to the Roman pontiff, Eugenius, to the City, and to all Italy, to carry the tidings of his elevation to the rank of king. Therefore Hillin, archbishop-elect of Trier, and Eberhard, bishop of Bamberg, prudent and learned men, were sent. Then the prince advanced upon the lower regions of the Rhine, to punish the people of Utrecht for the arrogance which, as has previously been related,[4] they had shown toward his uncle Conrad. After he had punished them by the imposition of a fine and confirmed Herman as bishop, moving back up the Rhine he celebrated holy Easter at Cologne. Thence he passed through Westphalia and entered Saxony.

v. In the kingdom of the Danes there arose at that time a serious controversy concerning the rule, between the two kinsmen Peter (who is also called Svein) and Knut. The king summoned them before him and held a great assembly in *Martinopolis*, a city of Saxony which is also called Merseburg, with a large number of princes. The aforesaid young men came there and humbly yielded themselves to his command. Their case is said finally to have been settled by the judgment or advice of the chief men as follows: that Knut (to whom certain provinces were left) should abdicate the royal title by surrendering his sword—for it is the custom of the court that kingdoms are bestowed by the prince or taken back again by the sword, provinces by the military standard—but that Peter, receiving the royal power at the sovereign's hand, should be bound to him by fealty and homage. So the crown of the realm was placed on his head by the hand of the prince, on Whitsunday, and he himself, wearing the crown, bore the sword of the king who marched in state wearing his crown.[5] Waldemar also, who was a member of the same family, received a certain duchy of Denmark.[6]

vi. At about the same time the church of Magdeburg (which is known to be the metropolis of Saxony), being bereft of its shepherd, determined to hold an election. And since some were for choosing Gerhard, the provost of that church, and others the dean, individuals

---

[4] See above, i.lxvii–lxix.

[5] . . . *ipse coronatus gladium regis sub corona incedentis portavit.*

[6] The emperors enjoyed a rather shadowy control over the states to the north and east: Denmark, Poland, Bohemia, Hungary. Though Otto's account leaves the impression that this settlement of the Danish throne was definitive, its actual effect seems to have been negligible. The struggle between Svein and Knut continued, and the former (Frederick's candidate) was driven into exile within two years. Svein had Knut killed in 1157, but the result was to put on the throne his counsin Waldemar, whom Otto has just mentioned.

being divided on this side and on that, they decided to approach the king, who was still tarrying in Saxony. The prince endeavored in many ways to lead them back to unity and the bond of peace. As he could not accomplish this, he persuaded one party—that is, the dean and his followers—to choose Wichmann, the bishop of Zeitz, a man still young but of noble blood, and having summoned him, invested him with the regalia of that church. For the court holds and declares that when the controversy between the empire and the papacy concerning the investiture of bishops was settled, under Henry V,[7] it was granted by the Church that when bishops died, if there happened to be a division in the choice of a successor, it should be the prerogative of the prince to appoint as bishop whomsoever he might please, with the advice of his chief men; and that no bishop-elect should receive consecration before having obtained the regalia from the prince's hand through the scepter.

The king, having brought all matters in Saxony into good order and inclined to his own will all the princes of that province, entered Bavaria and wore his crown in Regensburg, the metropolis of that duchy, at the festival of the apostles,[8] in the monastery of St. Emmeram; for the cathedral had burned down, together with certain quarters of the city. The ambassadors sent to the City, to Pope Eugenius, and to the other cities of Italy returned to that same diet with glad tidings. There indeed did the prince, having displayed a strong will in arranging all to his satisfaction within the confines of his empire, think to display abroad a stout arm. He wished to declare war on the Hungarians and to bring them under the might of the monarchy. But being for certain obscure reasons unable to secure the assent of the princes in this matter, and thus being powerless to put his plans into effect, he postponed them until a more opportune time.

vii. However, though all was prospering in his kingdom, the most serene prince was indeed very anxious to end without bloodshed that dispute over the duchy of Bavaria between his own relatives, that is, Duke Henry, his paternal uncle, and Duke Henry, his maternal uncle's son.[9] (For the latter was the son of the former Duke Henry of Bavaria,

---

[7] The Concordat of Worms, 1122.   [8] The apostles Peter and Paul, June 29.

[9] Henry Jasomirgott, brother of Bishop Otto, half brother of Conrad III, and paternal uncle of Frederick, who had received the duchy of Bavaria from Conrad, and Henry the Lion, son of Henry the Proud (Frederick's mother, Judith, was the latter's sister).

whom King Conrad had compelled to remain in Saxony after he had been outlawed, as has been told elsewhere.[10] His duchy he had bestowed first upon Leopold, the son of Margrave Leopold, and then upon this Henry, the younger Leopold's brother.) The king, therefore, to decide the aforesaid strife by judicial decree or by his counsel, appointed for them a diet at the city of Würzburg in autumn, during the month of October. Inasmuch as the one (that is, the son of Duke Henry) appeared there and the other absented himself, the latter was summoned again and again.

At that same diet exiles from Apulia, whom Roger had driven out from their native land, made tearful lament and cast themselves pitifully at the feet of the prince. Both because of the affliction of these people and that he might receive the crown of empire, it was solemnly agreed that an expedition into Italy should be undertaken within a little less than two years.

viii. Next, the provost Gerhard hastened to Rome and applied to Pope Eugenius. Setting forth the case of the church of Magdeburg, he charged Wichmann (who, as has been narrated above, had been installed in office by the prince after his election by the second party) with usurpation, on many counts. How greatly disturbed the Roman pontiff was by this matter we have learned both from the letter he sent (in reply to certain bishops who had written to the Roman Church on his [Wichmann's] behalf, out of love for the king) and by word of mouth from the cardinals who were afterward sent across the Alps. Now the content of the letter was as follows:

"Bishop Eugenius, the servant of the servants of God, to his venerable brothers, the archbishops Eberhard of Salzburg, Hartwig of Bremen, and Hillin of Trier, and the bishops Eberhard of Bamberg, Herman of Constance, Henry of Regensburg, Otto of Freising, Conrad of Passau, Daniel of Prague, Anselm of Havelberg, and Burchard of Eichstädt, greeting and apostolic benediction.

"The letter which Your Prudence dispatched on behalf of the church of Magdeburg we received in all due kindness. But in reading it and learning its contents we were filled with great surprise and amazement, because we perceived them to be far other than beseems you, in consideration of your office of bishop. For though you have by Divine

---

[10] *Two Cities* VII.xxiii.

Providence been set at the head of the Church, to remove from its midst such things as are harmful and to preserve with zealous care the things that are useful, in the present case (as has become known to us from the contents of your letter) you have heeded not what is expedient for the Church of God, what is in accord with the sanction of the sacred canons, what accordingly would be approved by the will of heaven, but rather that which is pleasing to earthly princes. And you, who ought to turn aside their hearts from their unrighteous intent and show where the way of the Lord is, have not advised them what is right, nor stood as a wall before the house of Israel. Nay even, as the prophet says,[11] when men were building a wall you 'daubed it with untempered mortar'; a thing that we can scarcely say without great bitterness of spirit. Not so did the prince of the apostles judge, who in consequence of the confession of his faith obtained the promise that he should be the foundation of the whole Church; but when the sons of this world menaced the apostles and threatened destruction and death if they preached in the name of Jesus, he made answer: 'We ought to obey God rather than men.'[12]

"But you, lest you should appear to disagree with earthly princes, bestow your favor upon that cause to which both the authority of ecclesiastical enactment and the test of the will of heaven is surely believed to be opposed. For whereas the expression of divine law does not permit the transferring of bishops without a proof of evident advantage and necessity, and whereas also a far greater harmony of clergy and people should precede [in such a transfer] than in other elections, in the transfer of our venerable brother Wichmann, bishop of Zeitz, we find none of these circumstances, but only the anticipated favor of the prince. Without investigating the needs of the Church, or considering the usefulness of the person, the clergy unwilling—nay more, with the majority of them, it is said, protesting it—you declare that he must be moved to the church of Magdeburg.

"We marvel the more at this, as we know from past experience how much weight and wisdom that person [Frederick] has, and likewise are not entirely ignorant of how useful he is to that church. Now whoever else may be moved by the breezes of temporal favor, we who are founded upon the stability of that rock which was worthy to be estab-

[11] Ezekiel 13:10.   [12] Acts 5:29.

lished as the foundation of the Church, both should not and desire not to be tossed about by 'every wind of doctrine,' [13] or to wander because of some impulse from the right way of the sacred canons. We charge you, therefore, by this present writing that you no longer lend your favor to that cause, and that you endeavor by your exhortations so to influence our very dear son Frederick (whom God has exalted at this time to the eminence of royal authority to preserve the liberty of the Church) that he himself desist from his purpose in this matter, and no longer bestow his favor upon that same cause in opposition to God, in opposition to the sacred canons, in opposition to demands of his royal dignity; but that he relinquish to the church of Magdeburg—as also to the other churches of the realm entrusted to him by God—the free privilege of choosing whomsoever it wishes, in accordance with God's will, and sustain that same election thereafter by his favor, as is seemly for royal majesty. For if we could see that what he is endeavoring to do concerning our aforesaid brother is supported by reason, we would not think that either his will or your request should at all be opposed. But there is no petition whatever to which we can grant our consent in opposition to God and the sanctions of the sacred canons.

"Given at Segni, on the sixteenth day before the Kalends of September [August 17, 1152]."

ix. Now the king, when he wore the crown in Bamberg the following Easter, had with him two cardinals, namely, the priest Bernard and the deacon Gregory, sent by the apostolic see for the deposing of certain bishops. So, while celebrating the next Whitsunday at Worms, he deposed through the instrumentality of the same cardinals Henry, archbishop of the see of Mainz (a man often reproved for weakening his Church, but never improved) [14] and replaced him by his chancellor, Arnold,[15] through election by certain of the clergy and people who had come thither. To the aforesaid court came the dukes previously mentioned, the two Henrys, contending for the duchy of Bavaria, as has been said. But as the one alleged that he had not been summoned in proper form, the matter could not there reach a due conclusion. More-

---

[13] Ephesians 4:14.

[14] Archbishop Henry seems to have raised the only dissenting voice at Frederick's election as king, and this is probably the reason for his removal.

[15] Arnold of Selenhofen, later murdered in a communal uprising at Mainz in 1160, and afterward canonized.

over, the same cardinals with the permission of the prince likewise removed Burchard of Eichstädt, a man weighed down by years, giving as their reason his inefficiency. And when, after this, they were thinking of passing sentence upon the archbishop of Magdeburg and certain others, they were prevented by the prince and bidden to return home (*ad propria redire*).

x. At that time Pope Eugenius, a just man and notable for his piety, departed this life [July 8, 1153] and left the see to Anastasius, who was of advanced age and experienced in the customs of the court.[16] When a certain cardinal, Gerard by name, had been sent by him to end the case of the archbishop-elect of Magdeburg, he had approached the prince in that same city while he was celebrating the Lord's Birthday.[17] As he tried to do certain things there against the will of the prince, he incurred the latter's anger and was compelled by stern command to return ingloriously, leaving unfinished the business for which he had come; indeed, he died on the road. But the prince sent messengers to Anastasius, together with Wichmann, and secured not only the ratification of his action but also the pallium for Wichmann, not without offending certain persons who had heard (from their own lips) that the Romans were immovably determined that this should never happen. Since that time the authority of the prince has very greatly increased in the administration not only of secular but also of ecclesiastical affairs.

xi. At about the same time, in the month of September [1153], the princes and the leading men of Bavaria were called together by the king at Regensburg. But nothing could be settled there with reference to the blessing of peace in that province, on account of the strife between the two dukes. Now the king, because he had been separated from his wife [18] by legates of the apostolic see not long before, on the ground of consanguinity, was negotiating for another marriage. Both on this account and for the overthrow of William of Sicily, who had recently succeeded his deceased father, Roger, the enemy of both empires, he arranged to send ambassadors to Manuel, emperor of the

[16] Anastasius IV, elected in July, 1153, and died December 3, 1154.

[17] Frederick celebrated Christmas of 1153 at Speyer; the meeting with the cardinal seems to have occurred at Magdeburg on the following Easter (April 4, 1154); see Simonsfeld, *Jahrbücher des deutschen Reiches unter Friedrich I*, I, 215.

[18] Adelaide, daughter of Dietpold, margrave of Vohburg and Cham.

Greeks.[19] And so, by the advice of his chief men, that mission was undertaken by Anselm, bishop of Havelberg, and Alexander, once count
of Apulia, but expelled by Roger with other nobles of that same province under suspicion of seeking the throne.

Then, in the following month of December [1153], both the dukes
(Henry and the other Henry) attended the prince's judgment seat in
the city of Speyer. But the case was postponed, because the one for the
second time claimed he had not been summoned in due legal form.
Frederick had now striven for almost two years to terminate the strife
between the two princes so close to him, as has been said, by blood relationship. Therefore, being at length moved by the insistence of the
one who desired to return to the land he had inherited from his father,
from which he had long been debarred, Frederick was compelled to
make an end of the matter because of the imminent task of the expedition in which he needed that same youth as a knight and companion of
his journey. Accordingly, holding court at Goslar, a town of Saxony,
he summoned both dukes by issuing edicts. Since the one came and the
other absented himself, the duchy of Bavaria was there by decision of
the princes, adjudged to the former, that is, to Duke Henry of Saxony.
After this the prince, betaking himself from Saxony into Bavaria and
thence proceeding through Swabia, in the third year of his reign assembled a military force on the plains of the river Lech, the boundary
of Bavaria, opposite the city of Augsburg, in order to enter Italy.
This was at about the beginning of the month of October, almost
two years having elapsed since the expedition had first been vowed.
Nor, by the judgment recently proclaimed against so great a prince of
the empire and the no little murmuring of other princes arising there-
from, was it possible to distract the illustrious spirit from so great a
deed, but disregarding all those things that were behind, and entrusting himself to God, he pressed on to the things that were before.
Therefore after crossing the passes of the Alps and passing through
Brixen and the valley of the Trent, he encamped on the plains of
Verona, near Lake Garda. When he was there taking counsel with his
princes concerning their further advance, he determined he must first
of all win the favor of the Prince of Heaven. In short, the army, being
unable on its passage through the mountain barriers to find things
necessary for the support of life, on account of the barrenness of the

[19] Roger died on February 26, 1154; he was succeeded by William I (1154–66).

country, while suffering great want (a thing that is always very grievous for troops) had violated certain holy places. To atone for this—
although they seemed to have the aforesaid excuse of necessity—the
king ordered a collection to be taken from the entire army. He decided
that the not inconsiderable sum of money thus amassed should be
taken back by certain holy men to the two bishops (of Trent, that is,
and of Brixen) and divided among the various places of the saints
which had suffered loss. Thus he provided nobly for the common
good, fulfilling nobly a leader's task. For being about to enter upon
very great undertakings, he decided that before all else he must placate
the Ruler and Creator of all, without Whom nothing is well begun,
nothing successfully completed, and that His wrath must be averted
from his people.

xii. Then, breaking camp, Frederick halted in the month of November on the plain of Roncaglia, on the Po, not far from Piacenza.
Now it is the custom of the kings of the Franks (who are also called
kings of the Germans), that as often as they have assembled a military
force to cross the Alps in order to assume the crown of the Roman
empire, they make a halt on the aforesaid plain. There a shield is sus-
pended on a wooden beam that is raised aloft, and all the knights that
are his vassals are summoned by the herald of the court to stand watch
over their prince the ensuing night. Accordingly the princes who are
in his company each likewise calls out his own feudatories, by heralds.
The next day anyone discovered to have absented himself from
the night watch is again summoned into the presence of the king and
the other princes and illustrious men. Thus all the vassals, both of the
sovereign and of the princes, who have remained at home without the
full consent of their lords are punished [by confiscation of] their fiefs.
The prince followed this custom, and not only the fiefs of some laymen
but also the regalia of certain bishops (namely, Hartwig of Bremen
and Ulrich of Halberstadt) were taken away from them: only from
these individuals, however, because they were bestowed in perpetuity
by the princes upon the churches but not upon individuals.

Now since mention has been made of this country, I shall say a few
words concerning its location and customs, and by whom it was previously inhabited, by what name it was called, by whom it was afterward possessed, by what appellation it was distinguished.

xiii. This land, shut in on this side and on that by the Pyrenees [20]

[20] See above, I, note 16.

and the Apennines, very high and rugged mountains that extend for a long distance, like the navel of these mountains—or rather of this range of mountains—extends as a very garden of delights from the Tyrrhenian Sea to the shore of the Adriatic Sea. It has to the north the Pyrenees mountains (as has been said); on the south the Apennines which presently, changing their name, are commonly called the Mount of Bardo; on the west the Tyrrhenian; on the east the Adriatic Sea. It is watered by the course of the Po, or *Eridanus* River, which topographers rate as on of the three most famous rivers of Europe,[21] and of other streams, and by reason of the pleasantness of the soil and the moderate climate it is productive of wine and oil, to such a degree, indeed, that it brings forth fruit-bearing trees, especially chestnuts, figs, and olives, like forest groves.

The colony of the Romans, once called Farther Italy, was separated into three provinces: Venetia, Aemilia, and Liguria. Aquileia was the metropolis of the first, Ravenna of the second, and Milan of the third. The district in the Apennines themselves—where the city of Rome also is known to be situated—which is now called Tuscany, was quite properly termed Inner Italy because, being surrounded by the Apennines, it holds in its lap the City itself as well. But that plain which succeeds when the mountains run out, and is for this reason still customarily called Campania, was once termed Hither Italy or Greater Greece; now it is named Apulia and Calabria. It extends to Faro di Messina, an arm of the sea unfavorable for ships on account of the sandbanks; for Sicily, the boundary of Europe, is counted with Sardinia and the other islands of Italy. But some, who count this and mid-Italy as one, have preferred to call Hither Italy and Greater Greece "Italy," enumerating not three (as aforesaid) but only two Italies: Farther and Hither.[22]

Some, indeed, hold that the aforesaid mountains, the Apennines and the Pyrenees, are one mountain range. For approximately where the city of Genoa (well versed in naval warfare) is situated, on the Tyrrhenian Sea, they enclose the aforesaid province by drawing close together. As a proof of their statement they declare that, according to

[21] The others being the Danube and the Rhone; see below II.xliii, xlvi.

[22] Otto himself does so; see below, II.xxvii and *Two Cities* VII.xiv.

Isidore,[23] Pannonia received its name from being enclosed by the Apennines; however, not the Apennines (now called the Mount of Bardo) but the Pyrenees [Alps] Mountains touch it. It is evident, I think, why I have previously called this land the navel of two ranges or of the one range.

But as it began to be subject to the invasions and the domination of the barbarians who, coming from the island of Scandza [Scandinavia] with their leader Alboin, first inhabited the Pannonias, from them it began to be called Lombardy. For to increase their army [by the drafting of women] they twisted the women's hair about the chin in such a way as to imitate a manly and bearded face, and for that reason they were called Lombards (*Longobardi*), from their long beards. Hence it came to pass that as the ancient inhabitants of that province were crowded together around the exarchate of Ravenna, that part of Italy (which was formerly called Aemilia) is commonly called even today *Romaniola*, which is known to be a diminutive, derived from "Rome."

But [the Lombards] having put aside crude, barbarous ferocity, perhaps from the fact that when united in marriage with the natives they begat sons who inherited something of the Roman gentleness and keenness from their mothers' blood, and from the very quality of the country and climate, retain the refinement of the Latin speech and their elegance of manners. In the governing of their cities, also, and in the conduct of public affairs, they still imitate the wisdom of the ancient Romans. Finally, they are so desirous of liberty that, avoiding the insolence of power, they are governed by the will of consuls rather than rulers. There are known to be three orders among them: captains, vavasors, and commoners.[24] And in order to suppress arrogance, the aforesaid consuls are chosen not from one but from each of the classes. And lest they should exceed bounds by lust for power, they are changed almost every year. The consequence is that, as practically that entire land is divided among the cities, each of them requires its bishops to live in the cities, and scarcely any noble or great man can be found in all the surrounding territory who does not acknowledge the authority of his city. And from this power to force all elements to-

[23] Etymologies XIV.iv.16.

[24] This is a sketchy attempt by Otto to indicate the class structure of the northern Italian towns. The captains are the great nobles.

gether they are wont to call the several lands of each [noble, or magnate] their contado (*comitatus*).[25] Also, that they may not lack the means of subduing their neighbors, they do not disdain to give the girdle of knighthood or the grades of distinction to young men of inferior station and even some workers of the vile mechanical arts, whom other peoples bar like the pest from the more respected and honorable pursuits. From this it has resulted that they far surpass all other states of the world in riches and in power. They are aided in this not only, as has been said, by their characteristic industry, but also by the absence of their princes,[26] who are accustomed to remain on the far side of the Alps. In this, however, forgetful of their ancient nobility, they retain traces of their barbaric imperfection, because while boasting that they live in accordance with law, they are not obedient to the laws. For they scarcely if ever respect the prince to whom they should display the voluntary deference of obedience or willingly perform that which they have sworn by the integrity of their laws, unless they sense his authority in the power of his great army. Therefore it often happens that although a citizen must be humbled by the laws and an adversary subdued by arms in accordance with the laws, yet they very frequently receive in hostile fashion him whom they ought to accept as their own gentle prince, when he demands what is rightfully his own. From this arises a twofold loss to the common weal: the prince is obliged to assemble an army for the subjugation of his people, and the people (not without great loss of their own possessions) are forced to obey their prince. Accordingly, by the same process of reasoning whereby impetuosity accuses the people for this situation, so should necessity excuse the prince in the sight of God and men.

xiv. Among all the cities of this people Milan now holds chief place. It is situated between the Po and the Pyrenees, and between the Ticino and the Adda, which take their source from the same Pyrenees and drain into the Po, thereby creating a certain very fertile valley, like an island. Located midway, it is rightly called *Mediolanum*, although some think it was named *Mediolanum* by its founders from a certain portentous sow that had bristles on one side and wool on the

[25] Otto is here trying to describe the north Italian city state, with its extensive control over the surrounding territories. See *Cambridge Economic History*, I, 323–43, and Plesner, *L'Émigration de la campagne à la ville libre de Florence au XIIIe siècle*.

[26] That is, the emperors.

other.[27] Now this city is considered (as has been said) more famous than others not only because of its size and its abundance of brave men, but also from the fact that it has extended its authority over two neighboring cities situated within the same valley, Como and Lodi. Furthermore—as usually happens in our transitory lot when favoring fortune smiles—Milan, elated by prosperity, became puffed up to such audacious exaltation that not only did it not shrink from molesting its neighbors, but recently even dared incur the anger of the prince, standing in no awe of his majesty. From what causes this situation arose I shall afterward briefly set forth.

xv. Meanwhile, it seems necessary to say a few words concerning the jurisdiction over the realm. For it is an old custom, maintained from the time that the Roman empire passed over to the Franks even down to our own day, that as often as the kings have decided to enter Italy they send ahead certain qualified men of their retinue to go about among the individual cities and towns to demand what pertains to the royal treasury and is called by the natives *fodrum*. Hence it comes about that, on the prince's arrival, most of the cities, towns, and strongholds that attempt to oppose this right by absolute refusal or by not making full payment are razed to the ground to give evidence of their impudence to posterity. Likewise, another right is said to have found its source in ancient custom. When the prince enters Italy all dignities and magistracies must be vacated and everything administered by his nod, in accordance with legal decrees and the judgment of those versed in the law. The judges are said also to accord him so great authority over the land that they think it just to supply for the use of the king as much as he needs from all that the land customarily produces that is essential for his use and may be of advantage to the army, only excepting the cattle and the seed devoted to the cultivation of the soil.

xvi. Now the king abode, it is said, for five days [November 30–December 6, 1154] at Roncaglia and held a diet, with the princes, consuls, and elders of almost all the cities assembled there, and diverse things became known from the complaints of this party or of that. Among them were William, marchese of Montferrat, a noble and great man, and practically the only one of the barons of Italy who could escape from the authority of the cities, and also the bishop of

[27] Isidore *Etymologies* xv.i.57. The derivation would be *medietas* ("half") and *lana* ("wool").

Asti. They made serious charges: one, concerning the insolence of the people of Asti; the other (that is, the marchese), concerning that of the inhabitants of Chieri.

(But we do not think that, in comparison with his other valiant exploits, it contributes much to the prince's claim to glory if, while hastening on to more important things, we speak of the fortified places, rocky strongholds, towns, and great estates destroyed since his coming, not only by those of knightly order but even by the assault of the unbridled sergeants.)[28]

There were present also the consuls of Como and of Lodi, making mournful lament over the arrogance of the people of Milan. They bewailed their long-continued misery of mistreatment in the presence of two consuls of that very city, Oberto de Orto and Gerardo Negri. Therefore, as the prince was about to visit the upper regions of Italy and wished to pass through the Milanese territory he kept the aforesaid consuls with him to guide his way and to make arrangements for suitable places for encampments.

There came also to the same court ambassadors of the people of Genoa, who not long before this time had captured Almeria and Lisbon,[29] renowned cities in Spain, very famous for their workmanship of silk cloths, and returned laden with spoils of the Saracens. They presented the prince with lions, ostriches, parrots, and other valuable gifts.

xvii (xiii b). Frederick, therefore, being (as has been said) about to set out for the upper regions of Farther Italy, led his forces from Roncaglia and pitched camp in the territory of the Milanese. And as he was conducted by the aforesaid consuls through wastelands where provisions (*stipendia*) could neither be found nor secured by purchase, he was moved to anger and turned his arms against the people of Milan, having first ordered the consuls to return home. Another circumstance aggravated his wrath. The whole army is said to have been so exasperated by a heavy downpour of rain that in consequence of this double annoyance—hunger and the inclement weather—all aroused

---

[28] This paragraph, seemingly out of place here, may be a later addition to the text.

[29] A Genoese fleet had operated in Spanish waters in 1147–48, and had assisted in the capture of Almeria and Tortosa. Lisbon also fell to the Christians in 1147, but the Genoese played no part in that enterprise. For the capture of Lisbon, see C. W. David, *De expugnatione Lyxbonensi: The Conquest of Lisbon* "Records of Civilization," No. 34 (New York, 1926).

the prince against the consuls as much as they could. There was likewise
another by no means trivial cause for this high feeling. The prince had
already perceived their swollen insolence in the fact that they were not
only unwilling to rebuild the cities which they had destroyed, but were
even trying to bribe and to corrupt his noble and hitherto untarnished
spirit to acquiesce in their iniquity. The king, moving his camp from
the barren region, betook himself to fertile places of this land, not far
from the city, and refreshed his weary soldiers.

xviii (xiv). There was in the vicinity a certain fairly well-populated
town, Rosate,[30] where the people of Milan had stationed a garrison of
about five hundred armed knights. These knights were then ordered
to return to the city, and all that was useful having been taken as
plunder, the town itself was given up to the flames. Thereupon certain
of the knights of the prince, advancing to the gates of the Milanese,
wounded some and took others captive. The people of Milan, not only
aghast at their present loss but also in fear for the future, in order to
assuage the anger of the prince destroyed the house of the consul,
Gerardo, as the author of this calamity. But the prince, taking no
thought of this incident, proceeded to the Ticino River to bring greater
disasters upon them. This river, rising (as has been shown above) from
the Pyrenees and emptying into the Po, or *Eridanus*, near Pavia (which
for this reason is called *Ticinus*), encompasses the island of the Milanese on the western side. There he seized two wooden bridges, which
they had built for an attack on the people of Pavia and of Novara, and
had fortified with bulwarks to check their assault. After sending his
army over them, he gave them up to the flames.

Then he captured and burned three of the fortified and excellent
strongholds, namely, Momo, Galliate, and Trecate,[31] which they had
established in the territory of the people of Novara for their subjugation. Now Novara is not a large city, but since its reconstruction (after
it was in times past destroyed by Emperor Henry [32]) it has been fortified with a new wall and a good-sized rampart. It has within its diocese Count Guido of Biandrate, who contrary to Italian custom rules
all the territory of this city, scarcely excepting the city itself, by authority of the people of Milan—these as yet insatiable Milanese, who had

[30] Ten miles southwest of Milan.
[31] Momo is to the north, Galliate and Trecate to the east, of Novara.
[32] By Henry V, in 1110.

heretofore desired to absorb both this city and Pavia, as they had the cities before mentioned. This victory was won in the month of December, and the Lord's birthday was celebrated by the prince with great rejoicing over the destruction of the aforesaid strongholds.

xix (xv). After this [1155] the prince, proceeding through Vercelli and Turin, crossed the Po there and directed his march to the lowlands, toward Pavia. But the townsmen of Chieri as well as the citizens of Asti, because they had not obeyed the command of the prince that they do justice to William, marchese of Montferrat, were proscribed as enemies convicted of rebellion. When the king led his army to punish their disobedience, they forsook their fortifications as though distrusting their strength, and fled to the neighboring mountains. The king, coming first to Chieri and finding sufficient supplies, remained there for several days. He destroyed the towers that were there—not a few —and burned the town. Then proceeding to Asti and finding it empty, not of resources but of inhabitants, he stayed there for several days and gave it up to fire and pillage. But before he moved his camp from there, the king took counsel with men of prudence and decided to enact some regulations advantageous to the soldiers in the future, on account of the frequent dissensions that had broken out in the army. He issued an order, not merely by public announcement but also through the administering of an oath to everyone of high and low degree, that none should venture to carry a sword within the confines of the camp to the possible hurt of a fellow soldier. He added as a penalty that whosoever wounded any of his fellows in violation of this peace regulation (*treugam*) should lose a hand or even have his head cut off. After this order—as wise as it was necessary—had been laid down, the thoughtless violence of youthful spirits was calmed.

xx (xvi). Not far from that place there was a city named Tortona, fortified by nature and art, friendly to the people of Milan and allied by treaty with them against the people of Pavia. Accordingly, as the people of Pavia complained that they were troubled more by Tortona than by Milan (for although the city of Pavia is, indeed, situated in the valley of the people of Milan, the chief extent of its territory is on the other side of the Ticino River, exposed to Tortona with no intervening mountain or stream [33]), Tortona was ordered by the prince to

[33] The Po also flows between Pavia and Tortona; what Otto means here is that much Pavian territory lay south of the Po, exposed to Tortonese attack.

withdraw from its alliance with Milan and to associate with Pavia.
When it refused to do this, it too was proscribed as guilty of treason and
numbered among the enemies of the empire, because it had chosen to
cling rather to a seditious and hostile city than to one that was peaceful
and loyal to the kings. The prince, in order to punish the insolence of
the people of Tortona in like fashion to that of the inhabitants of Asti,
moved his camp from Asti and pitched his tents at a certain town which
is called Bosco. After delaying there for several days, he decided to
send ahead certain of the knights in company with his brother Conrad,[34]
Berthold, duke of the Burgundians,[35] and his standard-bearer Otto,
the count palatine of Bavaria,[36] to investigate the situation of the city.
They crossed the river [Scrivia], hastened down to the city itself, and
after inspecting everything pitched camp not far from it on the aforesaid stream. On the third day after this, the king followed his men and
fixed his tents on the opposite bank of the stream, being unable to join
his companions because of the flooding of the aforesaid river, which had
increased to more than its usual size from a sudden downpour of rain.
Nevertheless, not long afterward, when the little stream had somewhat
subsided, he joined his men by managing to wade across, and hastened
to the city. At the first assault he stormed and took the suburbs, defended by a wall and towers. The citizens scarcely had an opportunity
to retreat to the citadel under cover of the night which was now coming on and a storm that was rising. Now Tortona is almost at the foot
of the Apennine mountains, being located at the point where the
Apennines and the Pyrenees are united, as has been said before, and
looks out upon the plain of Pavia and Milan as from a watchtower.
Placed on a smooth mountain whose rocky face projects over its precipitous sides, it glories in its towers. One in particular, of brick, was
built long ago by Tarquin the Proud [37] and is now called *Rubea*.
Tortona is notable for a suburb on the steep mountainside and gains
distinction from the circuit of its walls and the number of its lofty
towers and of its people, and for a certain little rivulet [Ossona] that
flows through its midst.

[34] Half brother of Frederick, who had made him count palatine of the Rhine.

[35] Berthold IV of Burgundy and Zähringen.

[36] Otto VI of Wittelsbach; see above, I.xlix.

[37] The seventh and last of the traditional kings of Rome. His reign would be placed
in the late sixth century B.C.

The prince having taken the suburb (as has been said) laid siege to the citadel, or the city itself. But this citadel had been garrisoned for defense not only by its own troops, but also by the forces of the Milanese [38] and of the neighboring barons (one of whom was the marchese Obizzo, surnamed Malaspina). Made confident by so much support, Tortona dared to prepare to ward off the anger of the prince. This famous siege of Tortona was begun early in the month of February [1155], in the first week of Lent, after Ash Wednesday.

xxi. Now when the people of Tortona had retreated to their narrow citadel, and so great a multitude was shut up, as it were, in one prison, the mountain itself was completely surrounded with siegeworks, that no way of escape might be open to the wretched inhabitants. The prince himself encamped on the west side, Henry, duke of Saxony, in the suburb (which faces south, toward the Apennines), the Pavians in the plain which extends to the east and north, toward Pavia and Milan. Without delay, machines and engines of various kinds were built; archers, balistarii,[39] and slingers watched the beleaguered citadel. The valiant prince tried everything, and where he saw weaker spots in the citadel, there he pushed forward with stronger hand. But the people of Tortona, shut up within the most confining barriers, having no place of escape, took courage from desperation. "For nothing makes a soldier bolder in war," as that renowned historian says,[40] "than the necessity of fighting under desperate conditions." They were assailed by lances, they were assailed by *balistae*. And, worse yet, they were tormented by their own consciences; for, as rebels against their own prince, they might expect, if captured, execution on the gallows which they could see already set up. For just as the consolation of a good conscience is a great reason for hope when wretched people are exposed to the enormities of a tyrant, so on the contrary, in default of a good conscience the fear of a just sentence heaps misery on misery for those at-

---

[38] About a hundred knights and two hundred archers had been sent by Milan into Tortona, according to the Milanese author of the *Gesta Federici I imperatoris in Lombardia*, p. 17.

[39] *Balista* seems to have been used rather loosely by medieval writers to refer to any mechanism for the propulsion of missiles. Otto employs it or its derivative *balistarius* three times in the present chapter. On this and the second occasion he probably has only crossbows in mind; on the third he is referring explicitly to a mangonel.

[40] Hegesippus *De bello Judaico* III.ix. In his account of the siege of Tortona, Otto borrowed heavily from this description of Titus' siege of Jerusalem (III.ix–xiii).

tempting to struggle against a prince who may be called not only a
righteous judge but also a pious ruler. Nevertheless, as though they
were burdened by no perilous fears, they made frequent sorties against
the encamped army. Youthful spirits, eager (as they ever are) for
praise, kept making trial of their strength on both sides, the one party
striving for survival, the other for glory. Nor was this without loss to
both parties. For of our men two young nobles, *Kadolus* of Bavaria
and John of Saxony, were slain, and many were wounded. And of the
besieged, besides those whom they concealed in the city when killed or
wounded, some were taken alive and paid a well-merited penalty by
being hanged in the sight of all. They say that on a certain day a stone
propelled by mechanical force (*vi tormenti*) from the balista, which is
now commonly called a mangonel (*manga*), fell on the upper part of
the fortifications. Being broken into three pieces by hitting the walls,
it struck and killed instantly three armed knights as they stood near
the cathedral amid the chief men of the city, conferring on the condition of their city.

But because the camp of the Pavians was being subjected to greater
attack than the rest, William, marchese of Montferrat, and certain other
of the Italian barons joined them by command of the prince. For on
that side there was a well or spring—the only one that the townsmen
could use. And since the Pavians prevented its use, the Tortonese, in
that most dire need of which the characteristic is indifference to the
hazard of peril, fought boldly, and a major combat ensued, indeed
almost daily. For the little river which, as has been shown above,
flowed through the midst of the suburb had been diverted from its
proper channel by the debris from the towers and other fortifications,
and was being sharply watched by the duke of Saxony and his men
lest, filthy though it was, it might minister to their need.

The prince, seeing that the siege was being prolonged beyond his
desire—for he longed to receive the crown of sole rule over the world
and the City—gave orders that not only should the towers be shattered
by his engines but even (employing a quite unusual device) that tunnels should be bored in the direction of the tower of Tarquin, which
was called *Rubea*, so that, by thus proceeding through these same sub-
terranean passages to the tower itself, by weakening the foundation
they might cause it to fall. For since the aforesaid city is not like other
cities fortified by a wall and a ditch, but is almost isolated by precipitous

cliffs on all sides—a natural defense—it is only in that quarter which is a little more accessible and without the protection of bristling crags that the skillfully devised protection of the aforesaid tower and the strength of the great moat serve as supports to its weakness. The townsmen (not without suspicion of treachery on the part of some of our men) learned in advance what was afoot and, employing guile, they also made tunnels near the foundation of the tower. Thus, after certain attackers who were advancing to overthrow the tower had been suffocated, the rest desisted from the attempt.

After this the king, desiring to vanquish nature by nature's aid, that is, to constrain by lack of drinking water those who were hedged in by nature's defenses, proceeded to make the aforesaid spring useless for human needs. There were thrown into it the rotting and putrid corpses of men and beasts. But not even thus could the pitiful thirst of the townsmen be restrained. Another device was found. Burning torches, with flames of sulphur and pitch, were cast into the aforesaid spring, and thus the waters themselves were made bitter and useless for human needs.

xxii (xvii). There was in the vicinity a certain stronghold of the people of Milan called N.,[41] fortified by nature and art. Ladders and other instruments useful for scaling walls were manufactured in the camp within sight of the people of Tortona, who supposed that these were being made to their own hurt. Certain shrewd and courageous men were selected from the order of knights, and two were set over them as leaders—Duke Berthold and the Count Palatine Otto—and they were dispatched to the aforesaid stronghold at a time when the undertaking could be concealed under cover of night. Putting their ladders to the wall without delay, they pushed on to the steep ascent of the upper citadel; they entered the stronghold. And undoubtedly, since almost all were sunk in sleep, they would have had what they desired if the inhabitants had not been aroused by a prematurely uttered shout. They prepared for flight, but barely took heart at last and rushed to their arms.

xxiii (xviii). Nor must we fail to mention the valor, the downright

----

[41] Apparently Otto did not know, or could not recall, the name of this stronghold. The *Gesta Federici . . . in Lombardia* (p. 17) mentions Milanese garrisons at several points in the territory of Tortona. Otto Morena (p. 24) speaks of such a garrison at Sarezanno, just southeast of Tortona.

audacity, of a certain sergeant (*strator*). Wearied by the long siege, he
wished to set the others an example by scaling the citadel! Using only
his sword and shield and a little axe, such as is carried after the fashion
of that class of men, fastened to the saddle, he approached the wall
which lies in front of the tower *Rubea*, and cutting with the axe a trail
on which to set his feet, he ascended the height. Neither the frequent
blows of stones, propelled from the prince's siege engines against the
tower by the force of the machines, nor the incessant thud of spears and
rocks that showered down from the citadel, could deter him. He
reached the tower, now half in ruins, and there, fighting manfully,
even brought down to earth by his blows a fully armed soldier, and
amid the hazards of so many perils was able to return to camp unhurt.
The king called the sergeant into his presence and decreed that for so
notable a deed he should be honored by the belt of knighthood. But
as he declared that he was a man of lowly station and wished to continue therein, his condition being satisfactory to him, the king permitted him to return to his own quarters, richly rewarded.

xxiv. But let us return to the point from which we digressed. The
townsmen, by reason of the poisoning of the springs, were suffering
from an intolerable lack of water, the grievous torment of thirst. The
Easter festival was approaching, and the prince, out of respect for religion, decided that he should cease from his assault on the citadel for
four days, that is, from the Thursday of the Lord's Supper to the
Monday following, in Easter week [March 24–28]. And so on the
next day (that is, Good Friday, the day on which the Lord's Passion
is observed by all Christians), the clergy and the monks who were shut
up with the townpeople, clad in their religious vestments, with crosses,
censers, and all the other paraphernalia of the Christian faith, opened
the gates, came forth, and desired to come to the prince's tent. The
king, catching sight of them from afar, sent bishops and men of letters
to meet them, and asked why and for what they came.

xxv. And they made answer:

Churchmen to fled.

"We, an unhappy part of Tortona, desired to come to the feet of
His Royal Excellency to bewail our calamities, which we endure
through no fault of ours, but by reason of our contact with a lost city
and its doubly lost citizens. But now, since we are not admitted to the
presence of the prince, may it be granted us meanwhile to grovel at the
feet of Your Benignity, importunately beseeching that in the name of

humanity you regard us as human beings and recognize in us the state of human misery as though it were your own. For we bring no pleas for the city or for its citizens, found guilty of treason. Would that our eyes had never beheld them, that chance had never united us with them, whose lot was destined to be so baneful to us. Must the guiltless with the guilty, the harmless with the harmful, the innocent with the condemned, be afflicted by a like penalty by a righteous judge? We are walled in by a siege of long duration; we are shaken by remorseless batterings; we are compelled by the parching pangs of thirst to drink pitchy and sulphurous waters unfit for human use. And there is one thing still more to be grieved over: it is not our pleasure to serve God at this very holy season of the Lord's Passion, because it is not possible. For as we stand at the sacred altars we are terrified by the arrow points, we are daunted by the crash of the stones, and so always frightened— even at every natural sound—we are distracted from peace of mind like men out of their wits. We are not free from care in our beds; we are not without fear in the place of prayer; we cannot muster in peace a spirit distracted by the immediacy of these dangers, so as to offer to God the sacrifice of peace. What have we done? For what are we making atonement? Have we ever, in association with Milan, borne arms against Pavia? Have we incurred the wrath of the prince by alliance with a seditious city? Nay we, as yet unacquainted with weapons, are allied with no rebels, indeed to no mortals; we are accustomed to fight for God alone, equipped not with carnal but with spiritual weapons. Without our counsel the soldier is armed; we are not consulted, nay we are ignorant, when battle is joined; that is the arrangement of the consuls and elders of the city: by their nod these things come to pass. 'All these things result from the decisions of the leaders,' [42] as the saying goes. Nothing is our concern save care for the watch kept in the churches and daily supplication to God, the King of kings, for the peace of kings and all others set in high places. But it will be said: 'From association with the enemy you too are adjudged an enemy. You should be his companion in punishment whose friend you were in wrongdoing. For "he that toucheth pitch is defiled." [43] He that abides with the froward becomes froward. For the Psalmist also says: "With the pure thou wilt shew thyself pure; and with the froward thou wilt shew thyself froward." ' [44] Is it then more by our own will than by Divine

[42] Lucan *Pharsalia* v.342.   [43] Ecclesiasticus 13:1.   [44] Psalms 18:26.

Providence that we are associated with these citizens—through the necessity of staying, not through acquiescence in their wrong doing? Cannot we, who are not Babylonians, be in one enclosure with the Babylonians, who are to be avoided as regards affection, not location? [45] One may be with an evildoer and yet may not justly be called the ally or friend of the evildoer. One may be so joined with a person by the law of necessity as not to be joined with him in his crime. One can by the law of nature in man so love a man's nature as to have an abhorrence for that nature's fall. For one who seeks proof from the testimony of the wise man and the Psalmist that was cited—namely, that a man becomes good by association with the good, bad by association with the bad—will not thus interpret the passage: as though it were *not* to be accepted of one so and of another not so, but individually and invariably so. But although one accept it as true of one and not of another, yet not true of each or always, he may yet think of it as spoken to cover the majority of cases. The art of physicists, not that of mathematicians, follows this practice in the study of nature. Nor can touching pitch properly be referred to on the basis of contact, but on that of consent. Although what precedes and what follows give to the passage of the aforesaid prophet a different meaning: that these words are applied not to us, but to the Creator, who, indeed, as He appears holy to the holy, justifying him by His mercy, thus by the perverse He is accounted perverse, though justly punishing him, in accordance with that manner of speech or method of relationship whereby a straight line when applied to a curved wall by the unreasonable verdict of sense perception does not seem straight. Whence the same prophet says elsewhere: 'Truly God is good to Israel, even to such as are of a clean heart.' [46] And he adds immediately: 'For thou wilt save the afflicted people; but wilt bring down high looks.' [47] Let the prince of the earth imitate the Prince of Heaven, and if in the same city the humble be found with the proud, yet let not the humble be punished with the proud. Therefore have pity on our lot, lords and fathers. Behold upon us the marks of Christ, which we bear, and may at least the sign of the Lord move those to pity whom the bitterness of our calamity has not moved. But alas for the lot of mortals! It is for the lies of Pavia you suffer the penalty, Tortona, not for your own transgressions. O Pavia, you accuse Tortona of evil deeds, whereas you—if the dissimilarity of

[45] Cf. *Two Cities* I.vii. [46] Psalms 73:1. [47] Psalms 18:27.

qualities admits a comparison—have done worse. But it will be said: 'You must in justice endure the punishment from a righteous prince for being united by treaty with a wicked city and one that oppresses all its neighbors in its stubborn pride.' Granted Tortona is allied with Milan. Why? Not as a favor to her, but out of fear of you. Not to rule by her might, but to be rescued from your violence by her strength. 'I perceived,' says Tortona, 'that my own safety was at stake when the nearest defense—I mean Lomello [48]—was on fire; I took refuge under the wings of Milan.' You condemn Milan because it destroyed Como for due cause. You take no heed to yourself, who felt no compunctions about leveling to the ground without excuse Lomello, an imperial town, garrisoned with a great and strong company of knights, famed as the dwelling place of your count palatine, after craftily summoning the townsmen themselves to a conference about peace and treacherously making them your prisoners. He who should have been lord, the most renowned among the nobles of Italy, has become your tenant. He now pays tribute to you, this man to whom you were accustomed to pay tribute when he represented the prince. Let the prince see and take note with what credit to himself and honor to the empire your tributary sits at his side to dispense justice to the Italians. Let him consider with what appropriateness the executioner's axe, whereby the guilty must in accordance with law be punished in Italy, is carried before him who now wars beneath your banners. Therefore by a just judge of the matter Pavia should first be weighed in the even scales of justice, and in accordance with this example the excesses of all the other cities of Italy should be corrected. But how do such matters concern us?

" 'None but the carpenters handle carpenters' tools.' [49] We, a wretched folk, we who are dedicated solely to the service of God, should contemplate our own lot. The lords of the earth are none of our concern. And O that an earlier age, all too happy,[50] and the golden centuries of Saturn, might return; [51] that the husbandman might battle with hoe and mattock and rake against the soil and not with man, nature's brother; and that thus the order which is consecrated to God might be free to devote itself to prayers and petitions! May he perish,

---

[48] About fifteen miles north of Tortona, and the same distance west-southwest of Pavia.

[49] Horace *Epistles* II.i.116.   [50] Boethius *De consolatione* II, meter 5.

[51] Cf. *Two Cities* I.xxv (end).

who brought forth arms to stain with blood the race of men, who with the ferocity of the beasts, not recognizing himself as a man, first shed human blood! [52]

"To return to ourselves. We have done nothing; we are punished for the sins of others. May the piety of the prince spare us, we entreat, and if he is unwilling to pardon the wretched city, let him at least permit us, unarmed, sick already from the foulness of pestilence and nigh unto death, to go our way, restored to freedom from so grievous a prison."

These were their words, and raising their hands to heaven, their cheeks wet with the starting tears, they cast themselves with loud wailings at the feet of those who had been sent to meet them.

xxvi (xix). When the prince was informed of this, he perceived that his heart was inclined toward mercy, but to avoid all suspicion of weakness he maintained the outward demeanor of perseverance in his previous severity, ordering the priests to return to the citadel. For he felt compassion for the pitiful lot of the clergy, but had only mockery for the fate of the insolent people whom he understood from this indication to be practically in despair and on the verge of destruction. But the townsmen, feigning that they were not yet vanquished by so many disasters, during the four days in which we have said the prince gave his foes peace for the observance of the Christian religion, craftily devised a machine for hurling missiles, without the knowledge of the prince, who supposed that they were duly observing the truce that had been granted. When the four-day period had elapsed (as has been said), the townsmen were again fired upon by engines of war. They withstood the force of the bombardment with the weapon that they had made, even striking and damaging one siege gun by which they were particularly harassed. It was repaired without delay, and they were assailed more sharply than before. Broken by fatigue from so many attacks and especially from thirst, and plunged into utter despair, the people of Tortona at last bargained for the surrender of their stronghold, making submission their means of defense.

(xx). Therefore in the third week after the Easter festival, in the month of April [April 10–16], their lives alone being restored to safety and freedom by the mildness and mercy of the prince, the city was first subjected to looting and then given over to destruction and

[52] Ninus; see *Two Cities* I.vi.

flames. There one of the nobles of the Greeks was rescued from the grievous captivity in which he was held: a man whom Obizzo, surnamed Malaspina, had basely seized in order to extort money from him, and was holding captive, immured in the citadel itself, in harsh confinement. You might have seen the wretched townsmen as they now came forth, with assurance of safety, from the pitiful prison house of the fortress to the freedom of the mild spring air, by their deathly pallor resembling corpses coming from their tombs, demonstrating in their persons the saying that to be besieged is the most pitiful fate of all! [53]

xxvii. After the victory was won, the king was invited by the people of Pavia to their city, that they might give him a triumph. And there, on the Sunday on which the *Iubilate* is sung [April 17], in the church of St. Michael, on the site of the ancient palace of the Lombard kings, he was crowned with much rejoicing on the part of the citizens.[54] Three days were spent there with great joy and large outlay on the part of the city. Then passing by Piacenza [55] he celebrated Whitsunday [May 15] near Bologna, and crossing the Apennines there traveled through Hither Italy, which is now usually called Tuscany. There he encountered the Pisans, men that are mighty in the islands and the lands across the sea, and gave them instructions to fit out ships against William of Sicily. At about the same time Anselm, bishop of Havelberg, returning from Greece, received from the prince, upon election by clergy and people, the archbishopric of Ravenna as well as the exarchate of the same province—a magnificent reward for his labor.

xxviii. Now on his way to the City the king encamped near Viterbo. Thither came the Roman pope, Hadrian,[56] with his cardinals, and was received with the honor due to his office. He was given a deferential

[53] Though Otto does his best to make Frederick's campaign seem successful, it is clear that essentially the attempt to reduce Lombardy had utterly failed. The very choice of Tortona rather than Milan as an example to the Lombard towns was a confession of imperial weakness. The reduction of Tortona enabled Frederick to turn southward without complete loss of face, but he left in his rear a Milan untouched, powerful, and in full opposition. Nor could he well afford the two months lost at Tortona; time will not now permit him to settle accounts with the Normans on this expedition. Perhaps only William of Sicily gained by this siege.

[54] See above, Frederick's letter; in Pavia he assumed the Lombard crown.

[55] According to the *Gesta Federici . . . in Lombardia* (p. 18), Frederick had hoped to capture Piacenza, but was foiled by the arrival of Milanese troops.

[56] Hadrian IV, the Englishman Nicholas Breakspear (1154–59). Frederick met the pope at Sutri, just southwest of Viterbo, June 8, 1155.

hearing as he uttered bitter complaints against his people. For the aforesaid people, since their endeavor to reinstate the order of senators, in their rash daring did not shrink from inflicting many outrages on their popes. There was this additional aggravation of their seditious conduct, that a certain Arnold of Brescia, of whom mention has been made above,[57] under guise of religion and—to use the words of the Gospel [58]—acting as a wolf in sheep's clothing, entered the City, inflamed to violence the minds of the simple people by his exceedingly seductive doctrines, and induced—nay, rather, seduced [59]—a countless throng to espouse that cause.

That Arnold, a native of Italy from the city of Brescia, a cleric ordained only as a lector of the church there, had once had Peter Abelard as his teacher. He was a man not indeed dull of intellect, yet abounding rather in profusion of words than in the weight of his ideas; a lover of originality and eager for novelty. The minds of such men are inclined to devise heresies and the tumult of schisms. Returning from his studies in France to Italy, he assumed the religious habit that he might deceive the more, assailing all things, carping at everything, sparing no one—a disparager of the clergy and of bishops, a persecutor of monks, a flatterer only of the laity. For he used to say that neither clerics that owned property, nor bishops that had regalia, nor monks with possessions could in any wise be saved. All these things belong to the prince, and should be bestowed of his beneficence for the use of the laity only. Besides this, he is said to have held unreasonable views with regard to the sacrament of the altar and infant baptism. While he was keeping the church of Brescia in uproar in these and other ways, which it would take too long to enumerate, and was maliciously defaming ecclesiastical personalities to the laity of that land, who have itching ears as regards the clergy, he was accused by the bishop and pious men of that city at the great council held at Rome under Innocent.[60] Therefore the Roman pontiff decided that silence should be imposed upon the man, that his pernicious teaching might not spread to more people. And thus it was done.

So that man, fleeing from Italy, betook himself to the lands beyond the Alps, and there assuming the role of teacher in Zurich, a town of

---

[57] I.xxviii.   [58] Cf. Matthew 7:15.

[59] *Post se duxit, immo seduxit.*

[60] The Lateran Council of 1139, held under Innocent II (1130–43).

Swabia, he sowed his pernicious doctrine for some time. But when he learned of the death of Innocent he entered the City, near the beginning of the pontificate of Eugenius.[61] As he found it aroused to rebellion against its pope, he incited it all the more to revolt, not following the counsel of the wise man who says of a situation of this kind: "Heap not wood upon his fire." [62] He set forth the examples of the ancient Romans, who by virtue of the ripened judgment of the senate and the disciplined integrity of the valiant spirit of youth made the whole world their own. Wherefore he advocated that the Capitol should be rebuilt, the senatorial dignity restored, and the equestrian order reinstituted. Nothing in the administration of the City was the concern of the Roman pontiff; the ecclesiastical courts should be enough for him. Moreover, the menace of this baneful doctrine began to grow so strong that not only were the houses and splendid palaces of Roman nobles and cardinals being destroyed, but even the reverend persons of some of the cardinals were shamefully treated by the infuriated populace, and several were wounded. Although he incessantly and irreverently perpetrated these things and others like them for many days (that is, from the death of Celestine [63] until this time) and despised the judgment of the pastors, justly and canonically pronounced against him, as though in his opinion they were void of all authority, at last he fell into the hands of certain men and was taken captive within the limits of Tuscany. He was held for trial by the prince and finally was brought to the pyre by the prefect of the City. After his corpse had been reduced to ashes in the fire, it was scattered on the Tiber, lest his body be held in veneration by the mad populace.

But that my pen may come back to the topic whence it has digressed, after the supreme rulers of the world had been united amid their retinue, they advanced together for several days, and pleasant converse was exchanged as between a spiritual father and his son. Both ecclesiastical and secular matters were discussed, as though a single state had been created from two princely courts.

xxix (xxi). But the citizens of Rome, learning of the prince's arrival, decided to sound out his inclinations in advance by an embassy. Therefore they appointed scholarly and learned men as their representatives to meet him between Sutri and Rome, having first received

---

[61] Eugenius III (1145–53).   [62] Ecclesiasticus 8:3.
[63] Celestine II (1143–44).

a safe conduct for their protection. And thus being presented before the consistory of His Royal Excellency, the men began to speak as follows:

"We the ambassadors of the City—no insignificant part of the City—O Excellent King, have been sent to Your Excellency by the senate and people of Rome. Hear with calm mind and gracious ears what is brought to your attention by the City that is the kindly mistress of the world—the City of which, by God's aid, you shall soon be prince, emperor, and lord. If you have come—nay, because, as I [the People] believe, you have come—in peace, I rejoice. You seek authority over the world; I arise willingly to give you the crown. I meet you with rejoicing. For why should not a prince come peacefully to visit his people? Why should he not treat with notable munificence the people who have awaited his coming with great and protracted expectation, in order to shake off the unseemly yoke of the clergy? I pray for the return of the former times. I ask for the return of the privileges of the renowned City. May the City under this prince take the helm of the world once more. May the insolence of the world be checked under this emperor and be subjected to the sole rule of the City! May such a ruler be adorned with the fame as well as with the name of Augustus!

"Now you know that the city of Rome, by the wisdom of the senatorial dignity and the valor of the equestrian order, sending out her boughs from sea to sea, has not only extended her empire to the ends of the earth [64] but has even added to her world the islands that lie beyond the world,[65] and planted there the shoots of her dominion. The boisterous waves of the seas could not protect those, nor could the rugged and inaccessible crags of the Alps defend these: indomitable Roman valor has subdued all. But, for our sins, since our princes dwelt at a great distance from us, that noble token of our antiquity—I refer to the senate—was given over to neglect by the slothful carelessness of certain men. As wisdom slumbered, strength too was of necessity diminished. I have arisen to reinstate the holy senate of the holy City and the equestrian order, to enhance your glory and that of the divine republic, that by the decree of the one and the arms of the other its

[64] Cf. Psalms 80:11 and 72:8.

[65] This would seem to be a reference to the conquest by Rome of England, which lay outside the seven climes into which ancient and medieval geography divided the habitable world.

ancient splendor may return to the Roman empire and to your person. Should this not please Your Nobility? Will not so notable a deed and one so in keeping with your authority be judged even worthy of reward? Hear then, O Prince, with patience and with clemency a few matters that have to do with your justice and with mine! About yours, however, before I speak of mine. For 'the beginning is from Jove.' [66] You were a stranger. I made you a citizen. You were a newcomer from the regions beyond the Alps. I have established you as prince. What was rightfully mine I gave to you. You ought therefore first afford security for the maintenance of my good customs and ancient laws, strengthened for me by the emperors your predecessors, that they may not be violated by the fury of barbarians. To my officials, who must acclaim you on the Capitol, you should give as much as five thousand pounds as expense money. You should avert harm from the republic even to the extent of the shedding of your blood, and safeguard all this by privileges, and establish it by the interposition of an oath with your own hand."

xxx. Hereupon the king, inflamed with righteous anger by the tenor of a speech as insolent as it was unusual, interrupted the flow of words of those ambassadors concerning the jurisdiction of their republic and of the empire, as they were about to spin out their oration in the Italian fashion by lengthy and circuitous periods. Preserving his royal dignity with modest bearing and charm of expression he replied without preparation but not unprepared.[67]

"We have heard much heretofore concerning the wisdom and the valor of the Romans, yet more concerning their wisdom. Wherefore we cannot wonder enough at finding your words insipid with swollen pride rather than seasoned with the salt of wisdom. You set forth the ancient renown of your city. You extol to the very stars the ancient status of your sacred republic. Granted, granted! To use the words of your own writer,[68] 'There was, *there was* once virtue in this republic.' 'Once,' I say. And O that we might truthfully and freely say 'now'! Your Rome—nay, ours also—has experienced the vicissitudes of time. She could not be the only one to escape a fate ordained by the Author of all things for all that dwell beneath the orb of the moon. What shall I say? It is clear how first the strength of your nobility was transferred

[66] Vergil *Ecologues* III.60 and *Aeneid* VII.219.
[67] *Ex improviso non inprovise.* [68] Cicero *In Catilinam* I.i.3.

from this city of ours to the royal city of the East, and how for the
course of many years the thirsty Greekling sucked the breasts of your
delight. Then came the Frank, truly noble, in deed as in name, and
forcibly possessed himself of whatever freedom was still left to you.
Do you wish to know the ancient glory of your Rome? The worth of
the sensatorial dignity? The impregnable disposition of the camp? [69]
The virtue and the discipline of the equestrian order, its unmarred
and unconquerable boldness when advancing to a conflict? Behold our
state. All these things are to be found with us. All these have descended to us, together with the empire. Not in utter nakedness did
the empire come to us. It came clad in its virtue. It brought its adornments with it. With us are your consuls. With us is your senate. With
us is your soldiery. These very leaders of the Franks must rule you by
their counsel, these very knights of the Franks must avert harm from
you with the sword. You boastfully declare that by you I have been
summoned, that by you I have been made first a citizen and then the
prince, that from you I have received what was yours. How lacking in
reason, how void of truth this novel utterance is, may be left to your
own judgment and to the decision of men of wisdom! Let us ponder
over the exploits of modern emperors, to see whether it was not our
divine princes Charles and Otto who, by their valor and not by anyone's bounty, wrested the City along with Italy from the Greeks and
the Lombards and added it to the realms of the Franks. Desiderius
and Berengar teach you this, your tyrants, of whom you boasted, on
whom you relied as your princes. We have learned from reliable accounts that they were not only subjugated and taken captive by our
Franks, but grew old and ended their lives in their servitude. Their
ashes, buried among us, constitute the clearest evidence of this fact.
But, you say: 'You came on my invitation,' I admit it; I was invited.
Give me the reason why I was invited! You were being assailed by
enemies and could not be freed by your own hand or by the effeminate
Greeks. The power of the Franks was invoked by invitation. I would
call it entreaty rather than invitation. In your misery you besought the
happy, in your frailty the valiant, in your weakness the strong, in
your anxiety the carefree. Invited after that fashion—if it may be
called an invitation—I have come. I have made your prince my vassal

[69] Frederick (or Otto?) is here presumably comparing the camp of the Roman
legion with that of the imperial army; cf. below IV.ii.

and from that time until the present have transferred you to my jurisdiction. I am the lawful possessor. Let him who can, snatch the club
from the hand of Hercules.[70] Will the Sicilian, in whom you trust,
perhaps do this? Let him take note of previous cases. Not yet has the
hand of the Franks or the Germans been made weak. By God's help,
if I live, that man will be able someday to test his own boldness. You
demand the justice that I owe you. I say nothing of the fact that the
prince should prescribe laws for the people, not the people for the
prince. I pass over the fact that any possessor who is about to enter
upon his possession should submit to no prejudicial conditions. Let us
argue reasonably. You propose, as I understand it, to exact three
oaths. I will discuss each separately. You say I must swear to observe
the laws of my predecessors, the emperors, that are guaranteed you
by their privileges, and likewise your good customs. You even add
that I am to swear to defend the fatherland at the very risk of my life.
To these two I make a single response. The things you demand are
either just or unjust. If they are unjust, it will not be yours to demand nor mine to concede them. If they are just, I acknowledge that
I am willing because of the obligation and that I am under obligation
because of my willingness. Wherefore it will be unnecessary to affix an
oath to an obligation to which I assent and an assent which is an obligation. For how could I infringe upon your just claims, since I desire
to preserve for even the lowliest that which is theirs? How could I fail
to defend the fatherland and especially the seat of my empire, even at
the risk of my life, when I have been giving thought to the restoration
of its frontiers so far as it is within my power, not without consideration
of that same danger? Denmark, recently subjugated and restored to
the Roman world, has learned this, and perhaps more provinces and
more kingdoms would have perceived it if the present undertaking had
not intervened.

"I come to the third provision. You declare that I should personally
swear to pay you a certain sum of money. How disgraceful! You,
Rome, demand from your prince what some sutler should rather seek
from a peddler. With us, these demands are made of captives. Am I,
then, held in captivity? Am I weighed down by the enemies' bonds?
Do I not sit on my throne, renowned and attended by a great force of
valiant soldiers? Shall a Roman emperor be forced against his will to

[70] Cf. Macrobius v.iii.16.

be anyone's purveyor and not his benefactor? Hitherto I have been accustomed to bestow my favors royally and munificently upon whom I pleased, and as much as was seemly, and particularly to those who have deserved well of me. For as due respect is properly demanded from inferiors, so a fitting service is justly repaid by superiors. This practice, received from my sainted parents, I have elsewhere observed. Why should I deny it to my own citizens? Why should I not make the City happy upon my entrance? All is justly denied to him who demands unjustly."

With these words, and not without a justifiable indignation of spirit, he brought his speech to an end and was silent.

xxxi. And when certain of the bystanders inquired of the ambassadors whether they wished to say anything more, after deliberating a little they deceitfully replied that they wished first to report to their fellow citizens the things which they had heard, and return to the prince only after taking counsel.

Thus dismissed, the ambassadors departed from court and returned in haste to the City. The king, anticipating treachery, decided that he should consult his father, the Roman pontiff, about this matter. The latter said to him: "My son, you will learn more about the guile of the Roman rabble as time goes on. For you will discover that in treachery they came and in treachery have departed. But aided by the clemency of God, Who says 'I shall take the wise in their own craftiness,' [71] we shall be able to circumvent their shrewd schemes. Accordingly, let brave and knowing young men of the army be quickly sent ahead to take possession of the church of the blessed Peter and the Leonine stronghold. Our knights are there within the fortifications; upon learning our wishes they will straightway admit them. Besides, we shall add to their number the Cardinal Priest Octavian, whose lineage is of the noblest blood of the Romans, a man most faithful to you." [72]

And so it was done. The next night almost a thousand armed knights were chosen, the very pick of the young men; and entering the Leonine city at the break of day they succeeded in occupying the church of the blessed Peter, its entrance and steps. Messengers returned to camp reporting these glad tidings.

[71] I Corinthians 3:19.

[72] Cardinal priest of St. Cecilia, and later the antipope Victor IV (1159–64); Octavian was the leader of the imperial party of the college of cardinals.

xxxii (xxii). After the sun had risen, and at the end of the first hour, Pope Hadrian led the way with the cardinals and the clergy and awaited the prince's arrival on the steps; the latter broke camp and fully armed descended the slope of Monte Mario [73] with his men and entered the Leonine city, in which the church of the blessed Peter is known to be situated, by the gate which they call Golden.

You might have seen the soldiery, gleaming so brightly in the splendor of their armor, marching so regularly in unbroken order that it might properly be said of them: "Terrible as an army with banners," [74] and that verse of Maccabees, "The sun shone upon the shields of gold, and the mountains shone therewith." [75]

Presently the prince, coming to the steps of the church of the blessed Peter, was received with all honor by the supreme pontiff and led to the tomb (*ad confessionem*) of the blessed Peter. Then after the solemnities of the Mass had been celebrated by the pope himself, the king, attended by his knights under arms, received the crown of the empire, with the appropriate blessing. This was in the fourth year of his reign, in the month of June, on the fourteenth day before the Kalends of July [June 18, 1155]. All who were present acclaimed him with great joy, and glorified God for so glorious a deed.

Meanwhile, the bridge near the castle of Crescentius, [76] which leads from the Leonine city to the entrance of the City itself, was being guarded by his men, that the rejoicing over this celebration might not be interrupted by the frenzied populace.

When all was finished the emperor, wearing the crown and mounted upon a caparisoned steed, rode alone, all the rest going on

[73] *Per declivum montis Gaudii;* Monte Mario, about five hundred feet in height, is situated on the Tiber, two miles north of Rome.

[74] Song of Solomon 6:4.   [75] I Maccabees 6:39.

[76] The reference is probably to Hadrian's Tomb, or the Castle of St. Angelo, which was held for a time by the patrician Crescenti family. The whole account of this uprising and its suppression is not clear. In his account Otto Morena (ed. Güterbok, pp. 29–31) appears to refer to the fight as having taken place at a point lower down the Tiber where the *Isola Tiberina* was connected with the mainland, on the left bank by the *pons Fabricius* and on the right bank by the *pons Cestius*. This was close to the *casa Crescentii* (also known as the *casa Rienzi*). Acceptance of this account would help to clear up some of the obscurities in the text of Otto of Freising, but it would give rise to others equally difficult to resolve. Simonsfeld, after consideration of the sources which mention the incident, rejects it. Simonsfeld, I, 689–98.

foot. By the same gate by which he had entered he returned to the camp, which adjoined the very walls. The Roman pontiff remained within the palace which he had near the church.

xxxiii. While this was going on, the Roman people with their senators had assembled on the Capitol. But upon hearing that the emperor had received the imperial crown without their assent, they became infuriated and crossed the Tiber in great force. Advancing to the church of the blessed Peter, they did not hesitate to kill within that sacred edifice certain of the sergeants (*stratores*) who had stayed behind. An outcry was raised. Upon hearing this, the emperor ordered the soldiers (who, parched by the great heat and exhausted by their thirst and labors, were eager to refresh themselves) to put on their armor. He made the more haste because he feared that the enraged populace had attacked the Roman pontiff and the cardinals. They joined battle: on one side, near the castle of Crescentius, with the Romans; on the other side, near the *Piscina*, with those from across the Tiber. You might have seen now the Romans driving our men toward the camp, now the latter pushing the Romans back to the bridge. It was to the advantage of our men that they could not be reached by the rocks and javelins hurled from the castle of Crescentius; even the women, who were watching, urged on their men (it is said), lest by reason of the boldness of the base commoners so respectable a company of disciplined knights might be smitten in the aforesaid ways by those who were in the fortification. And so, though the struggle was continued for a long time by both sides with varying fortune, the Romans were finally compelled to retreat, unable to bear the ferocious attack of our men. You might have seen our men ruthlessly and ferociously killing and wounding, wounding and killing, and seeming to say: "Take now, O Rome, Teutonic iron instead of Arabian gold. This is the price which your prince offers you for your crown. Thus do the Franks purchase empire. These are the gifts given you by your prince, these the oaths sworn to you."

This battle lasted from about the tenth hour of the day until nightfall. There were slain there or drowned in the Tiber almost a thousand, about six hundred were taken captive, the wounded were innumerable, all the remainder were put to flight. Of our men, strange to say, only one was killed, one taken captive. For the unhealthful climate and the very extreme heat at that season, especially in the neighborhood of the City, had more power to harm our men than the weapons of the enemy.

xxxiv (xxiii). After the conclusion of so magnificent a triumph, the emperor returned to camp, and there he and his men threw their weary limbs upon their beds. That night he rested. The next day, since he could secure no supplies from the embittered citizens, he led his army, who were suffering from lack of food, to higher ground, and proceeding a short distance to a level plain, pitched his tents. Then fording the Tiber near Mount Soracte (on which it is said the blessed Silvester once lay in hiding while fleeing persecution), he permitted his soldiers, exhausted by so frequent exertions, to rest for a little while in a certain valley not far from the city of Tivoli, made pleasant by the greenness of the fields and marked by the course of a certain river [the Aniene].

The festival of the apostles Peter and Paul [June 29], revered by the entire Church and especially by the pope and the emperor of the Roman city, now drew near. Accordingly, on that day the emperor wore his crown while Pope Hadrian celebrated Mass. It is said that there, during the solemnity of the ceremony, the pope of the Romans absolved all who had chanced to shed blood in the conflict fought with the Romans on the ground that a soldier fighting for his own prince and bound to obey him (warring against enemies not only of the empire but also of the Church), though he sheds blood may be declared, by divine as well as secular law, to be not a murderer but an avenger.

Moving his camp from that place, the emperor halted between the City and Tusculum.[77] Now the time was at hand [July 24] when the Dog Star must rise gleaming with morbid ray at the foot of Orion. All the air round about became heavy with the mists that rose from the swamps near by and from the caverns and ruined places about the City: an atmosphere deadly and noxious for mortals to breathe. The native of the City, accustomed at this season to fly to the mountains, and the soldier in camp, unused to such an unwholesome atmosphere, were alike burdened by this visitation. There is no doubt that the citizenry would have become obedient to the pope, submissive to their prince, if the army outside had been able to endure so great an inconvenience. But as countless numbers were stricken by most serious maladies in consequence of this corruption of the air, the prince, though

[77] Near Frascati, in the Alban hills, southeast of Rome.

distressed and unwilling, was obliged to move the encampment to the neighboring mountains merely to accommodate his men. Therefore, after separating from the Roman pontiff near Tivoli and turning over the prisoners to him, he ascended the near-by Apennines and pitched his tents above the river Nera, of which Lucan writes: [78]

"White Nar's sulphurous waters."

There he remained for several days and, taking the advice of prudent men, granted the army as much rest as possible, that they might counteract by medicines the corrupt air they had been breathing.

xxxv. While the prince was spending several days there, the people of Spoleto incurred his wrath when the *fodrum* [79] was demanded from the neighboring cities and strongholds and towns. Their offense was twofold. Being held responsible for the sum of eight hundred pounds, they defrauded him of part and in part gave bad money. He was the more angered by the fact that they had dared to seize and hold captive Count Guido, surnamed Guerra, one of the wealthiest of all the nobles of Tuscany, while he was lodging in Spoleto on his return to the emperor from a mission in Apulia. What was the worse for them, they ignored a command of the prince that Guido be released. Therefore the emperor, moved more by the captivity of his distinguished follower than by the deceit in the money matter, turned his arms against the people of Spoleto. The latter were not content [to remain] within their encircling walls and their many high defending towers, but issued forth from the walls with slingers and archers, thinking to attack the prince. Whom they could they slew, and whom they could they transfixed. Upon seeing this, the prince said: "This seems like a game of boys, not a conflict of men." He spoke, and ordered his men to rush bravely upon their adversaries. This was done without delay, and by reason of their courageous enthusiasm the obstructing walls were surmounted like level ground. The men of Spoleto were cut to pieces and, though they resisted manfully for some time, were forced to give way. As they sought to retreat to the protection of the city, the soldiers who pressed hard upon them from the rear gained admittance at the same time, fortune aiding the brave. The city was given over to plunder, and before anything that would be of use to the men could be carried off,

[78] Not Lucan, but Vergil *Aeneid* VII.517.

[79] See above, II.xv, and below, III.xlvii and note 135 where the term is explained.

was set on fire by someone and burned. The citizens who could escape
sword and flame made off, half-naked, to the neighboring mountains,
saving only their lives.

This battle lasted from the third to the ninth hour [July 27]. In
that conflict none fought more energetically than the prince, no one,
not even a common knight, was quicker to take up arms, no professional
soldier was more ready than he to undergo dangers. Finally, from the
side where the city seemed particularly impregnable because of the
slope of the mountain—just opposite the principal church, the bishop's
seat—he not only urged his men to the attack by encouragement, and
compelled them by threats, but even afforded a personal example to
others. Not without the greatest danger, he ascended the mountain
himself and broke into the city.

xxxvi. The downfall of the Spoletans having been thus accomplished, the victorious prince remained there that night. On the next
day, because the entire atmosphere in the vicinity, corrupted by the
burning of corpses, was producing an intolerable smell, he moved his
army a short distance away. There he stayed for two days, until the
spoils saved from the fire might be available for the needs of the army
—not for the wretched citizens of Spoleto.

After this the army moved on to the coast of the Adriatic Sea. There
the emperor pitched camp on the borders of Ancona and met Palaeologus—whose name means what we may call "an old story"!—the
noblest of the Greeks and a prince of the royal blood, and Maroducas,
a distinguished man.[80] They came as representatives of their prince of
Constantinople, bearing no small gifts. Having given them an audience
and learned the purpose of their journey, he kept them with him for
several days. Then taking the advice of the princes who were with
him, he dispatched to Greece Wibald, royal abbot both of Corvey and
of Stablo, a man of prudence and eminent at court, to undertake an
embassy to the prince of the royal city.

xxxvii (xxiv). Meanwhile, the prince [Robert] of Capua, Andrew,
count of Apulia, and the other exiles from that province, entering
Campania and Apulia with the emperor's embassy, received back without opposition the cities, castles, and other possessions which they once

---

[80] Michael Palaeologus and John Ducas, sent by the Emperor Manuel Comnenus to
treat with Frederick for joint action against the Normans of southern Italy, as Frederick
has told us in his letter prefixed to this history.

had, the inhabitants supposing that the emperor would follow them. Now the prince, in long consultations with the leaders and more distinguished persons of the army, strove earnestly to prevail upon their hearts to descend into Apulia. But as the Dog Star's fury [81] blazed forth the more upon the army, and there were scarcely any left who did not feel the debilitating effects of the burning heat and the unwholesome air, and as many also had been wounded and several killed in the taking of the cities, strongholds, and towns, he was obliged—not without bitterness of heart—to return to the lands across the Alps.

xxxviii. Therefore the signal was given, and all were granted permission to go back to their native land. Some took ship, to return home by way of the Adriatic Sea and the island which is now called Venice. Among those the most distinguished were Pilgrim, patriarch of Aquileia; Eberhard, bishop of Bamberg; Count Berthold; Henry, duke of Carinthia; and Ottokar, margrave of Styria. Others made their way to the western parts of Lombardy, some to cross by the Great St. Bernard, some through the valley of Maurienne. Many still remained with the emperor.

xxxix. Frederick, therefore, victorious, renowned, and triumphant,[82] moving his camp from the territory of the people of Ancona, passed through Sinigaglia (where the Romans say the Senonian Gauls once abode), Fano and Imola, crossed the Apennines, and halted in the plain of Farther Italy, on the Reno near Bologna. Thence he traversed the Italian plain, crossing the Po in boats near the monastery of St. Benedict,[83] and reached the fields around Verona near the beginning of the month of September [1155].

(xxv). Now there is an old custom of the people of Verona, granted

[81] *Canis rabie;* cf. Horace *Epistles* I.x.16.

[82] Despite Otto's eulogy, it is clear that Frederick had accomplished little in Italy. The one exploit upon which Otto chose to dwell in great detail, the siege and capture of Tortona, was quickly neutralized by the reconstruction of that town with Milanese aid. Frederick had not come to grips with William of Sicily, who in 1156 suppressed the uprising in Apulia, hinted at by Otto above, and dealt effectively with the Byzantine intervention (see below, II.xlix). Hadrian IV, abandoned by Frederick with Rome still in revolt, collaborated briefly with Byzantium against William, but was soon forced to terms; his treaty with William in 1156, a direct result of Frederick's failure in Italy, marks the beginning of the emperor's contest with the papacy as well as the triumph of the anti-imperial party in the papal councils. On the credit side, it can only be said that Frederick had been regularly crowned emperor, and had learned much of Italy that would be useful in his later expeditions.

[83] San Benedetto, southeast of Mantua.

by the emperors, of which they avail themselves as a sort of privilege of long standing. The princes of the Romans, whether in coming to the City from the transalpine regions or returning thence, cross the Adige a little above the city on a bridge of boats made by the citizens, that they may not be subjected to looting because of the emperor's coming through their city. The people of Verona, craftily observing this custom, had indeed built a bridge of boats, but one so insecure as regards the connecting links that one might rather have termed it a mousetrap than a bridge. They had also employed another pernicious device. On the upper reaches of the stream they had gathered great heaps of logs into several piles, that they might thereby deceive an army unaware of this scheme: namely that, after one detachment had crossed, the second, held back after the destruction of the bridge by this diabolical plot, would be attacked alone. The wicked fell, as the Scripture says,[84] into the pit which they had made. For, by the will of God, providing for the safety of the emperor and his army, it came to pass that the soldiers made the crossing—perilously indeed yet without a casualty— and the aforesaid heaps of logs, coming down the stream, destroyed the bridge and cut off certain of the enemy who had followed the army, thinking to return by the same way they had come. All these were soon slain as traitors. That night the soldiers, tired from their exertions, camped in the neighborhood.

xl. There was a narrow mountain pass near by and a tremendous boulder, almost inaccessible on the sloping wall of rock, overlooking the road. It was necessary for the army to pass beneath this. For the nature of this place is as follows: on one side flows the Adige, an unfordable stream; on the other, precipitous cliffs of the mountain narrow the way and leave scarcely a bare trail. On this height, at the instigation of a certain Alberic, a noble knight of Verona, a band of brigands had flocked together for the purpose of securing plunder. Now as the army approached, certain of the troops who desired to pass on the same day on which the Adige was crossed were permitted by the brigands to go through the narrows unmolested—a sly trick. As others came by on the following day, the robbers dashed up to the massive rock and prevented their passing. This could not escape the attention of the prince. There were still in his company two illustrious knights—Garzabanus and Isaac—citizens of Verona, who had ac-

84 Psalms 7:15.

companied him to the City and had followed him thence as far as this place. The prince thought that by sending them to the aforesaid robbers, the latter might, at the advice of their fellow citizens, be more readily persuaded to desist from such evil. The robbers would not listen to them, but drove them off with blows. The emperor sending others to the robbers again ordered them to abandon their undertaking. But they persisted in their obstinate determination, and began as before to throw stones, saying that the emperor should never pass there unless they got from every knight his armor and his horse, and no small sum of money from the prince besides. When he heard this, the emperor said: "This is a hard condition. It is hard for a prince to pay tribute to a robber." What was he to do? Whither could he turn? Was he to ford the river? But nature had rendered it unsuitable for fording. Was he to cross by other means? The bridge had been destroyed. Should he descend toward the city? But there too the mountain, coming close to the river, had created an obstruction which Veronese troops were guarding. He recalled the familiar examples of his valor in times past. For he must scale the aforesaid height by some means or other. He ordered the baggage to be set down, as though tents were to be put up and camp was to be pitched there that night.

"Here," he said, "where the very gates of our fatherland may be said to smile upon us in welcome, here, after having undergone so many dangers, we shall have the end of our labors." Thus he addressed his men, as though he were quoting that famous passage from Vergil: [85]

O my companions, no strangers are we heretofore to misfortune,
Ye who have suffered worse trials, to these too will God grant an ending.
—Sometime, perchance, even this may it give us joy to remember!

Then he ordered all to arm themselves. Next he summoned Garzabanus and Isaac and by shrewd questions sought information concerning the lay of the land and how the road might by some means be opened.

And they said: "Do you see that rock of awe-inspiring height that overhangs the pass, practically inaccessible because of the uneven ground and jagged rocks? If you are able to get possession of it first, while they are off their guard—unless perchance it is being watched by them—you will achieve your purpose." There was no delay. About

[85] *Aeneid* I.198–99, 203.

two hundred picked young men under arms were sent with his standard-bearer, Otto. They went by devious ways through the woods and the mountains, through the hollows and boulder fields of the Alps, and at last, by the expenditure of much sweat, arrived at the aforesaid crag. As this afforded a soldier no possibility of ascent, being severed as though by a sword, one man bent over so as to lift a comrade on his back, and another offered his shoulders to raise his fellow soldier. After this, making a ladder of spears—for with this natural ladder, so to speak, the fully armed knight was heavily burdened—all attained the summit of the crag. Otto raised the emperor's standard, which he had been carrying concealed. At this signal, which seemed to presage victory, shouts and songs were raised. The army that remained in the valley hastened to the attack. The brigands who had been careless about this—for they thought the aforesaid crag was inaccessible to mortals and could be attained only by the birds—seeing that they were assailed from below and from above, were seized with despair and thought of flight. But there was no room for flight. For any one of them who entrusted himself to the protection of the precipice was crushed and mangled by striking against the rocks in his fall, losing his life out in space, even before he struck the ground. So great was the height of the rock, so great the rough spite of the jagged cliff. Why say more? With only a single exception it is said, a man who lurked concealed in the caves, all were slain, twelve (including Alberic) being captured and held for punishment. Practically all who were caught and held in chains were of the order of knights.

Accordingly, when the aforesaid men were brought into the presence of the prince and condemned to the penalty of death on the gallows, one of them said: "Hear, most noble emperor, the lot of a most miserable man. I am by birth a Gaul, not a Lombard; although in station a poor knight, by condition a free man. By accident, not deliberately, I became associated with these robbers, for the purpose of repairing my lack of an estate. They promised that they would conduct me to such places where my need might be remedied. I, poor wretch, believed them and gullibly consented. I was led and misled by wicked men into this misfortune. For who would suspect in any human being the folly of so rash a spirit, who would suspect the recklessness of so unrestrained a temper? Who would believe that such guile was devised by his own subject against the prince, the lord of the City and of the

world? Pardon, O prince, pardon one so wretched, pardon one pitifully led astray!"

The glorious emperor decreed that of them all only this man should
be saved from the sentence of death, imposing upon him as penalty
merely this, that he should adjust the noose about the neck of each
man and inflict upon his comrades the punishment of the gallows. And
so it was done. The large sums of money that they promised for the
redemption of their lives were of no avail to those poor wretches.
They were hanged on the gallows by an unyielding judge. All the rest,
who lay strewn along the slopes of the mountains, were piled in heaps
on the very path to afford to all passers-by the warning example of their
fate. There were, it is said, about five hundred of them.

xli (xxvi). The prince, having passed this narrow defile, with all
perils now at an end, joyfully pitched his camp that night in the territory of Trent. Advancing thence through Trent and the valley of
the Trent, he came to Bolzano. This town, situated on the borderline
of Italy and Bavaria, sends to the Bavarians a sweet wine and one naturally suited for export to the foreign districts. Thence, while many
scattered to their own homes, he continued his march through Brixen
and returned to the Bavarian plain just about a year after his departure
from that place [September, 1155].

Let it suffice to have narrated these incidents of the progress and success of that expedition—a few out of many. For not all the brave deeds
there accomplished could be related by us with such orderly coherence
and charm of style as if we had seen them with our own eyes. For it is
said to have been a custom of the ancients that those who had perceived
with their senses the actual events as they took place should be the ones
to write about them. Whence also it is customarily called "history"
from *hysteron*, which in Greek signifies "to see." [86] For everyone will
be competent to speak more fully of the things which he has seen and
heard. Being in need of no man's favor, he is not carried hither and
thither in search of the truth, dubiously anxious and anxiously dubious.
Truly, it is hard for a writer's mind to depend on another's judgment,
as though incapable of making an investigation of its own.[87]

xlii (xxvii). Now, when the toilsome journey was successfully

[86] Cf. Isidore *Etymologies* I.xli.1.

[87] An interesting revelation of the writer's conception of the ideals and function of
the historian.

brought to a conclusion, the prince returned to his ancestral home. He held a conference with his uncle, Duke Henry [Jasomirgott], on the borders of Regensburg, to persuade him to reach an agreement with the other Henry [the Lion], who now (as has been said) had obtained possession of the duchy of Bavaria by the judgment of the princes. When Henry did not give him his assent at this time, another date was set to treat with him about the same matter through intermediaries—in Bavaria near the Bohemian frontier. The prince coming there met with Vladislav (*Labezlaus*), duke of Bohemia, Albert [the Bear], margrave of Saxony, Herman, count palatine of the Rhine, and other great men. For by reason of the splendor of his exploits so great a fear had come upon those who had stayed behind that all came voluntarily, and everyone endeavored by obedience to secure the favor of his friendship. Moreover, how much terror the memory of his deeds inspired in the Italians can be estimated from the ambassadors of the people of Verona. This, by God's grace, must be more fully related hereafter.[88] But although we who there played the part of mediators strove in many ways to effect a reconciliation, they [the two Henrys] separated from each other without a word at parting, leaving the matter still unsettled.

xliii (xxviii). After this, in the middle of October [1155], the emperor entered Regensburg, the metropolis of Bavaria, to hold a diet, having with him Henry [the Lion], the son of Duke Henry, that he might put him in possession of the duchy. This city is situated on the Danube (which is called by topographers one of the three most famous rivers in Europe), at the spot where two navigable rivers, the Regen and the Naab, flow into the aforesaid stream. It is called *Ratisbona* or *Ratispona*, either because it is favorable and good for ships, or from the mooring of ships there. It was once the seat of the Bavarian kings and is now that of their dukes.

To that diet came Arnold, archbishop of Mainz, and the aforesaid Herman, count palatine of the Rhine, each to make complaint of the other. In fact, during the time that the prince was in Italy, practically the entire transalpine realm felt the absence of its head, being torn by uprisings and thrown into confusion by fire and sword and open warfare. Notably these two princes, so much the more effective in committing injuries as they were the more powerful, had stained almost

---

[88] See below, II.xlv.

the whole Rhineland and especially the renowned territory of the city
of Mainz by pillage, bloodshed, and burning. At this public assembly
the oft-mentioned Duke Henry [the Lion] received from the emperor
his lands and the seat of his fathers. And the chief men of Bavaria
bound themselves to him through homage and oath, and the citizens
not only by an oath but also by giving surety, that they might have no
chance of wavering.

xliv. There charges were brought against Hartwig, who had recently received the bishopric of that same city [Regensburg] through
election by the clergy and people and consecration by his metropolitan.
For he had disposed of the regalia which, according to the regulations
of the court, it is not permitted to bestow upon any vassal of the bishops
before they are received from the hands of the prince. Hartwig, being
unaware of this rule, had inadvertently disposed of them while the
prince was still tarrying in Italy. Being brought to trial for this, he
incurred the penalty of a fine, since he could neither deny the fact nor
justify his conduct. All the others, also, who had received fiefs from
him, were condemned to undergo a like penalty, greater or less according to their condition and station. For this is a law of the court, that
whosoever of the rank of the princes incurs the anger of his sovereign
and is obliged to pay a fine is held responsible for a hundred pounds;
all other men of lesser rank, whether gentry, freemen, or servitors,[89]
ten pounds.

xlv. To that same diet came the bishop of Verona [Tibaldo], who
had been sent to the emperor by his people, having with him the two
aforesaid knights, Garzabanus and Isaac.[90] When he had been admitted to the presence of the prince he said:

"Most glorious prince, your most loyal subjects of Verona have sent
us to Your Magnificence. Nor was I, who have the title of bishop of
that city, though I am unworthy, willing to undertake this embassy
until all, assembled in the cathedral, as though making God their witness, unanimously declared that what they professed with their lips
they also cherished in their hearts. And indeed it is incredible that a
people distinguished for intellectual integrity, and in possession of an
abundance of wealth, should make the shepherd of their souls a lying

[89] *Ingenui sive liberi vel ministri;* the first two of these terms are often used interchangeably in the twelfth century, but Otto clearly has a distinction in mind.
[90] See above, II.xl.

messenger. They might have found some other more suitable as a minister of deceit. Besides, these persons are associated with me as colleagues, of whose good faith in matters of business and valor in battle you have had proof in your recent expedition. Believe therefore, my Lord, believe what we say. Your people of Verona are your own peculiar people,[91] most loyally devoted and most devotedly loyal to you as their lord and emperor. They have heard that while you were passing through their territory certain brigands had dared to seize the pass. They know that you punished them with a fitting penalty. Verona heard this and rejoiced. She does not count as her citizens those who waylaid Your Majesty. Heaven forbid that she should consider as citizens those who practice brigandage. She has heard, however, a thing that causes her no little grief: that you harbor this suspicion concerning your city. For this reason we have been sent. Whosoever has made this insinuation to Your Serenity was a slanderer, envious of the happiness of others. You may know him to be a spreader of falsehood, not a knower of truth. Is not Verona bound to you by a pledge of loyalty? Was she not still in your favor when you withdrew from her? Would Verona, under the cloak of good faith, treacherously harm her own prince, though not accustomed to harm her equals in this fashion? Do you wish more? But if it does not please you to believe the arguments we have set forth, Verona makes its apologies for this occurrence. She is prepared to clear her name, to prove her innocence by a judgment of the court in the presence of Your Majesty's Excellency. Therefore let the good prince accept the vindication of the innocence of his devoted people, and turn the keen edge of his wrath against the arrogance of the people of Milan and of Rome."

After receiving this embassy, the emperor took counsel with the princes. Thereafter, as we know, Verona was received back into favor. For she both contributed a large sum of money and promised under oath to lead against the people of Milan as many troops as she could raise.

xlvi. Thence proceeding to the Rhineland, the emperor celebrated the Lord's Nativity at Worms. For that region which the Rhine, that very noble stream, one of the three most renowned of Europe, intersects—for one bank marks the limits of France, the other of Germany —is rich in grain and wine and affords abundance of hunting and fish-

[91] Cf. Deuteronomy 14:2.

ing. For it has on the Gallic side the near-by Vosges and the Ardennes, and on the German side no small forests that still retain their barbaric names. It can maintain the sovereigns for a very long time when they remain in the transalpine regions.

To this court came Archbishop Arnold, of Mainz, and the count palatine, Herman. They were brought to trial because (as has been said above) in the absence of the emperor they had terrorized that land by pillaging and burning. Both were found guilty, together with their accomplices. The one was spared because of his advanced age and his dignity, and out of respect for his episcopal station. The other was subjected to the due penalty. Now an old custom has gained the status of a law among the Franks and the Swabians, that whenever a noble, a *ministerialis,* or a peasant (*colonus*) has been found guilty by his judge of such offenses, before he is punished by sentence of death the noble is obliged to carry a dog, the *ministerialis* a saddle, the peasant (*rusticus*) the wheel of a plow, from one county into the next in token of his shame. The emperor, observing this custom, compelled that count palatine, a great prince of the realm, together with ten counts, his accomplices, to carry dogs the distance of a German mile. When this stern judgment was promulgated throughout the breadth of the transalpine empire, so great terror came upon all that everyone desired rather to keep the peace than to promote the confusion of warfare. To augment so great a blessing there was added the fact that the prince energetically destroyed the camps, fortifications, and hiding places of several robbers in the neighborhood. Certain of those he caught he condemned to capital punishment, others to be broken on the rack.[92] Bavaria alone did not yet merit becoming a participant of his favor on account of the strife previously mentioned.

xlvii (xxix). In that same year [1156], between Easter and Whitsunday, Archbishop Arnold of Cologne, an honorable man and the restorer of his church, died. The emperor, returning to Bavaria, spent Whitsuntide in retirement at a stronghold of the Count Palatine Otto.[93] On the next Tuesday [June 5] he had a conference with his uncle, Duke Henry [Jasomirgott], not far from the city of Regensburg, and then finally induced him to come to terms with the other

[92] *Patibuli tormento torquendo.* The rendering is free, but obviously some form of physical punishment short of death is indicated.

[93] Otto of Wittelsbach, count palatine of Bavaria and the emperor's standard-bearer,

Henry [the Lion]. The prince prized this more highly than the successes of all his other undertakings: the fact that, without the shedding of blood, he was able to bring to friendly relations princes of the realm so mighty and so closely related to himself.

xlviii. Then in the following week, at Würzburg, a city of Franconia (*orientalis Franciae*), he celebrated in royal state, with many princes assisting, his marriage with Beatrice, the daughter of Count Rainald. This Rainald, who traced his lineage from the ancient and illustrious stock of the Burgundians, was called count of that former kingdom of Burgundy which had once been bequeathed by King Rudolph to Emperor Henry, Conrad's son.[94] It is this same province of which Duke Conrad [of Zähringen] and his son Berthold were customarily called dukes.[95]

Now I shall relate in a few words what was at issue here. In that country a custom has persisted which is observed in practically all the provinces of Gaul, that authority over a father's inheritance always passes to the elder brother and to his children, whether male or female, the rest looking upon him as their lord. In consequence of this practice it came about that William, who was termed "the Child" (Rainald's kinsman on his father's side but a son of Duke Conrad's sister), had the authority in that province as long as he lived. But when he was reft of his earthly existence by the craft of his kinsmen, the dominion fell by hereditary right to Count Rainald. This came to pass under Henry V or Lothar II [III].[96] But the aforesaid count, putting too much faith in the justice of his claim—for he was an easy-going man and in consequence of his excessive mildness rather negligent—failed to attend the diets of the emperor. From this it resulted that, being moved to anger, the emperor granted the aforesaid land to Duke Conrad,[97] and thus each of them laid claim to this neighboring country. And so the controversy was prolonged almost to the present in a long-drawn-out feud, to such an extent that they even fought openly on the battlefield; until recently, as we know, it was settled by the emperor in such wise

[94] Rudolph III of Burgundy (993–1032), after whose death Conrad II had his son, the later Henry III, crowned king of Burgundy.

[95] See above, I.ix.

[96] Under Lothar (1125–37), since Count William was murdered in 1127.

[97] By this act, Lothar had strengthened the Zähringen, chief rivals in Swabia of his Hohenstaufen enemies, and won them over to his support.

that Berthold, the son of the aforesaid Conrad, received in settlement of the affair three cities between the Jura and the Great St. Bernard (*montem Iovis*), Lausanne, Geneva, and N. [Sion]. All the rest were left to the empress. Now this province extends almost from Basel (that is to say, from a stronghold which is called Montbéliard) to the Isère River, of which Lucan writes:[98]

"They left the fords of the Isère."

Joined with its dominion is the land which is properly called Provence, extending from that river to those places where the Rhone enters the sea, and where the city of Arles is located. But that Rainald, taking in marriage the daughter of Duke Simon of Lorraine, had by her only this girl. When he died not long afterward [1148] he left her (in accordance with the aforesaid custom) as the heir of his entire land. The emperor, selecting her in marriage, as has been indicated, began in his wife's name to hold personally (as will be more fully related hereafter[99]) not only Burgundy but also Provence, long alienated from his empire.

xlix. To that court came Wibald, abbot of Corvey, returning from Greece.[100] For the ambassadors of the Greeks, who had been sent with him to the emperor, were left at Salzburg and not admitted to the presence of the prince. The reason for this was as follows: When they had departed from him near Ancona, they had surreptitiously secured certain letters sealed with his seal and when the prince returned to the transalpine country, the Greeks entered Campania and Apulia and, displaying the imperial letters, falsely declared that the regions along the seacoast had been granted them by the prince. And so they subjected the entire province to their overlordship, not merely by frightening some of the natives by the emperor's authority but also by bribing them with gold. Proceeding thence as far as Bari, they even captured the citadel where a garrison of William [of Sicily] was stationed. There Palaeologus died and was borne to his own land. They were aided not only by assistance from the exiles—namely, the prince of Capua, Count Andrew, and others who had recently recovered their lands[101]—but also by the help of a certain Count Robert of Bassavilla [*Cavillen-*

[98] *Pharsalia* I.399.   [99] See below, III.xii.   [100] See above, II.xxxvi.
[101] See above, II.xxxvii.

sis],[102] a great man of that land, whom they had won over by money. In addition, practically all the inhabitants of the cities and towns supported them, because they had for so long been oppressed by the tyranny of this William and his father, Roger, and longed to be freed from so heavy a yoke. Not only was it being noised abroad through the neighboring regions, but a rumor had even reached us that William had either died or lost his reason through illness, and that the Greeks now held possession of all those provinces. The emperor heard this, and being moved by indignation took the matter under advisement for a very long time: whether the aforesaid ambassadors, who had come on behalf of their emperor, Manuel, should be admitted to his presence, or punished as traitors, or being treated with contempt should receive permission to depart. Finally, he was influenced by the entreaties of certain persons and arranged to grant them an audience. For this a day was appointed for them in the month of July, in Nuremberg.

(xxx). Now, although he hated William, Frederick was nevertheless unwilling that the frontiers of his empire—seized by Roger's tyrannical frenzy—should be taken by foreigners, and he had an expedition against that land vowed under oath. Yet not long afterward, upon learning that William had put the Greeks to flight and had retaken Apulia and Calabria [May-June, 1156], he changed his plan and directed his wrath against the people of Milan, to quell their arrogance. Whence we find a letter of his directed to the princes, as follows:

1. "Frederick, by the grace of God emperor of the Romans and august forever, to his beloved uncle Otto, bishop of Freising, his favor and all things good.

"Since by the providence of divine clemency we hold the helm of the City and the world, we must provide for the holy empire and the divine commonwealth in accordance with the varying turn of events and the exigencies of the times. For inasmuch as measures that were taken under necessity ought to be abrogated if the necessity ceases to exist, we annul the expedition which we recently ordered at Würzburg to be vowed on account of the invasion of Apulia by the Greeks. We relieve you and the other princes of your oath since their flight, that we may

[102] Count of Conversano and Loritello, and cousin of William I of Sicily: see *Cambridge Medieval History*, V, 191–92, 194; Simonsfeld, I, 322, note 137, 323, note 139, 409, note 416; and William of Tyre *History* XVIII.ii.

find you the more ready for other tasks of the empire. But because the arrogance of the people of Milan has long since raised its head against the Roman empire and is now striving to overthrow all Italy by its might or subject it to its dominion, we intend to muster for their destruction all the strength of the empire, in order to meet future exigencies like men, lest so great presumption should prevail in our time, or an impious folk be able to usurp or to trample upon our glory. Therefore, in accordance with a decision of the princes, we call upon you for an expedition against Milan, which is vowed to take place within a year from next Whitsunday [May 19, 1157], asking and directing in all friendliness that you meet us without fail at Ulm a year from the eve of Whitsunday [June 7, 1158], to participate in it with us. However, be assured that we shall compel neither you nor any of our princes to cross the Apennine range.[103]

li. Now, when the prince returned to the transalpine regions, just as his presence restored peace to the Franks,[104] so his absence deprived the Italians of it. For not only did Apulia and Campania participate in this misfortune (as has been shown), but even Farther Italy, feeling the absence of its prince, could not be immune from this turmoil. For the people of Milan, soon rebuilding Tortona, renewed the war against the Pavians. Building two bridges over the Ticino, they entered Pavian territory, besieged a certain town called Vigevano [105] (where there were many Pavians, together with the Marchese William [of Montferrat]), and finally, having deceitfully induced them to surrender, compelled them to seek peace and give hostages. But when they had heard the excessively severe terms of peace, the Pavians attempted to renew the struggle. Therefore the people of Milan, crossing by means of the bridges which they had made, rebuilt Lomello [106] and cruelly ravaged almost the entire territory of the Pavians.

lii (xxxi). At that time, upon the death of Archbishop Arnold of Cologne (which has been mentioned), the clergy of that church, assembling to hold an election, were very seriously divided. The provosts and abbots selected Gerhard, the provost of Bonn, but the canons of the cathedral, who at that time were without a provost and a deacon, chose

---

[103] Otto acknowledges receipt of this command in his letter to the emperor prefixed to the revised version of the *Two Cities* in 1157.

[104] That is, the region of Burgundy and Provence; see above, II.xlviii(end).

[105] Twenty miles southwest of Milan and the same distance northwest of Pavia.

[106] See above, II.xxv.

Frederick, the son of Count Adolph.[107] Therefore, as the emperor was staying during the month of July [1156] in Nuremberg, where the Greeks were to be presented to His Majesty, each of these parties came to set forth its case to the prince.

liii. Not long before this time the emperor of the Greeks, sending troops with Boris [108] against the Hungarians, suffered a great loss to his army, so serious that Boris himself was struck and killed by an arrow [from the bow] of a certain Cuman (that is, a Scythian) who had come with him. Therefore, the aforesaid messengers had come to the emperor, not only to arrange for a marriage,[109] but also to seek vengeance by the authority of the prince for the injury they had suffered from the Hungarians. In both of these aims they failed. For the emperor had not only married another (as has been said before), but an expedition against the Hungarians could not be set in motion so quickly (for they demanded that it be undertaken the next September). Nevertheless, they were admitted to his presence, and their papers were received. The emperor sent back with them his chaplain, Stephen, that through him he might learn more fully the will of the Greek prince. But let what has been said concerning the Greeks suffice at this point.

liv. The disputants of Cologne put in an appearance and asked for advocates; both parties argued and wrangled for three days before the prince concerning their election. Finally the emperor, having heard the claims of both, on advice and judgment of the bishops and the other princes whom he had with him, decreed that the aforesaid case should be postponed to the diet at Regensburg, where his plan for terminating the conflict of the two dukes was to be made public.

(xxxii). Therefore, as it was already mid-September, the princes assembled at Regensburg and for several days awaited the arrival of the emperor.

lv. When the emperor met his uncle on the field where the latter was encamped under tents nearly two German miles from the town, with all the great and important men present, the plan which had for so long been kept secret was announced. Now this, as I recall it, was the essential part of the agreement. The elder Henry [Jasomirgott] resigned the duchy of Bavaria to the emperor by the surrender of seven banners. These were handed over to the younger [Henry the Lion]. The latter gave back, by two banners, the East Mark, with the

---

[107] See above, I.lxvii.   [108] See above, I.xxxi.   [109] See above, II.xi.

counties that pertained to it from of old. Thereupon, by the judgment of the princes the emperor made of that Mark, with the aforesaid counties (there are said to be three of them), a duchy, and handed it over not only to Jasomirgot but also to his wife, with two banners, and ordained that it might not be changed or infringed upon in the future by any of his successors.[110] This was done in the fifth year of his reign as king, the second of his rule as emperor [1156].

lvi. So having, as he had hoped, brought to an end without the shedding of blood the controversy between his paternal uncle and the son of his mother's brother, he returned to the city rejoicing. On the very next day, sitting in public assembly, he caused to be solemnly sworn a truce for a year from the next Whitsunday, that henceforth Bavaria might not be without a share in the peace of the entire realm. Thereafter, from that day to the present time, so great a felicity of peace smiled upon the entire transalpine empire that Frederick may rightfully be called not only Emperor and Augustus but also Father of his Country. For before this diet came to an end, both parties from the church at Cologne presented themselves before him again, and he confirmed as the more valid of the two elections that one which had been held by the canons of the cathedral. He invested with the regalia Frederick, the son of Count Adolph, and so sent him to the City to be consecrated by the Roman pontiff.

So great are the things that might be said of Your Majesty's valor, O best of the Augusti, that if they were to be ineptly poured forth all at once, without a break, they might stifle the writer's capacity for expression. Wherefore let an end be set to this second book, that a place may be reserved in the third for the things which remain to be said.

[HERE ENDS THE SECOND BOOK]

[110] This is, of course, the creation of the duchy of Austria, held by the Babenberg family to 1238, and by the Hapsburgs from 1276.

THE THIRD BOOK

HERE BEGINS THE PROLOGUE OF THE WORK THAT FOLLOWS [1]

To the very discreet men, experienced in peace and in war, the lords Ulrich and Henry, the one chancellor, the other notary of the sacred palace,[2] Rahewin, by profession a canon of the holy church of Freising, in rank a deacon, although unworthy, wishes plenitude of understanding and of the spirit of piety. Inquiring of the former age, and diligently searching the traditions of the fathers,[3] I find it established by many examples that there is nothing enduring in human events, nothing eternal,[4] but the days of man are swifter than a weaver's shuttle, and his life passes more swiftly than the shadow or the wind.[5] While this is clear from many notable instances, even the page of this present book affords us its proof. Begun by its author, of blessed memory, in charming style, now that he himself—O Sorrow!—has been cut off by an untimely death, it has been entrusted to so insignificant a person as myself, like a child born prematurely, and as though torn from the body of its parent,[6] by his own command and likewise at the behest of the most serene and divine Emperor Frederick, to be fostered and furthered.

Accordingly, I considered that I must obey preceptors so powerful,

[1] Namely, Rahewin's continuation of Bishop Otto's *Gesta Friderici I Imperatoris*. See Introduction, pp. 3–4, 7. Strictly speaking, this Prologue introduces the whole of Rahewin's work and might have been so indicated in the format. For purposes of convenience, however, it has been included with the third book.

[2] Ulrich was chancellor 1159–62; Henry was chief notary 1157–67.

[3] Job 8:8.

[4] Josephus *De bello Judaico* III.viii.8. This and subsequent references are to the Whiston translation, and the citation will be in English: *Wars*. It should be noted that Simson's text follows an edition of the Latin version of Josephus, ascribed to Rufinus, in which divisions into books, chapters, and sections differ from those employed in most editions and translations of the work. References here given do not, therefore, accord with those in the text by Simson. Both systems of numbering may be found in the edition of the text by Hudson (1720), Vol. II.

[5] Job 7:6–7.   [6] Ovid *Tristia* I.vii.38.

preferring rather to incur criticism for the formlessness of my rude style than to be branded for disloyal idleness or idle disloyalty, if I were to allow a work that had been begun on so noble a theme and a memorial of a man so renowned and my own most dear lord to pass with him to destruction and oblivion.

And, indeed, that task ought preferably to be entrusted to your wisdom, since in you there is to be found accurate and trustworthy knowledge of history. But since responsibility for various duties is a hindrance to you in this regard, there is not so much time to apply your distracted minds to writing as to accord to the writings of others criticism or due praise. For, as Josephus says,[7] some are accustomed to write not of what they have personal knowledge, but rather, in the manner of orators, taking uncertain and contradictory accounts from hearsay; others, eyewitnesses, produce a false account either to flatter the victorious prince, or from hatred of the vanquished.

From both of these faults I consider myself to be free, since in the things that I have heard I have not permitted myself to be deceived indiscriminately by the tales of any rumormonger, nor in the things that I know at first hand have I added anything untrue to please the prince or out of prejudice for my own people.[8]

But if anyone should compare the eloquence of the preceding work with the dull style characteristic of my ability, may he graciously make allowance. For I confess that my utterance is too slight to sound even a little flute, to say nothing of filling so tuneful a trumpet of writing and of speech as that of the previous writer, my venerable bishop. But when the burden of eloquence and style overcomes me, the understanding and full truth of the deeds recounted will by God's favor make atonement.[9]

Therefore in this task I choose you both as my instructors, witnesses, and critics, asking that you accept without reproach the work you exacted of me. And since you, familiar with, and participants in, privy matters, were present at the actual events, be not slow to emend in accordance with the rule of truth whatever needs correction, and to erase or add a sufficient amount where too much or too little has been

[7] *Wars*, Preface (from which the end of the preceding sentence is also drawn).

[8] Cf. Jordanes *Getica* lx.316.

[9] Most of the last two sentences of this paragraph is taken from the Prologue to the *Getica* of Jordanes, who had in turn borrowed it from Rufinus. See Mierow, *Gothic History of Jordanes*, p. 143.

said. For truly I would sink beneath this load if I did not rely on your help and interest. In vain would I attempt by myself to portray the exploits of so great an emperor. Were one to compare the greatness of his spirit and of his power with his years, one would deem them beyond his age. For so widely and so nobly has he waged war throughout the entire world, so great are his deeds in peace and in war, that he who reads his history will think them the achievements not of one king or emperor, but of many.[10]

HERE ENDS THE PROLOGUE

HERE BEGIN THE CHAPTERS OF THE THIRD BOOK

[10] In this sentence, Rahewin has borrowed and slightly adapted to his needs the eulogy of Rome with which Florus begins his *Epitome*.

HERE END THE CHAPTERS

HERE BEGINS THE THIRD BOOK

i. When the empire had been set in order with the utmost wisdom in the German lands,[11] all that region enjoyed an unwonted and long unknown peace. There was in Germany such tranquility that men seemed changed, the land different, the very sky milder and gentler.[12]

---

[11] *Alemanniae;* this term was normally used by Otto for "Swabia," but he noted (above, I.viii) that in his day some were using it in the sense of "Germany." Rahewin seems to employ it regularly in the latter sense (below, III.xvii, xx, etc.).

[12] Florus *Epitome* II.xxx.

However, the emperor did not misuse so great quiet for idleness, or for enticing pleasures. For he thought it an unworthy thing to permit his powers, practiced in warfare, to be relaxed in sloth without advantages to the empire.

Therefore in the year 1157 since our Lord's incarnation, in the month of August, he took the field against the Poles. Poland, which the Slavs now inhabit, according to geographers lies within the borders of Upper Germany, having on the west the river Oder, on the east the Vistula, on the north the Russians and the Scythian Sea,[13] on the south the forests of Bohemia. The land is particularly well fortified by natural defenses; the people—both because of their own ferocity and through contact with the neighboring tribes—are practically barbarous and very warlike. For they say that the inhabitants of the provinces by the sea which washes the shore of that land are such as devour one another in time of famine, and, as they suffer from the rigor of perpetual cold and therefore can carry on no agriculture in some regions, they are devoted to hunting and killing. Moreover, they all practice piracy, and trouble the islands of the ocean, Ireland and Britain, and Denmark as well, although they are found upon another shore.[14] Through their nearness to such peoples, the Poles, as usually happens, have acquired by intercourse no little ferocity—like the dust from rusty iron.[15] Hence they are not known to display fidelity to their princes or due affection to their neighbors.

ii. Now the reason for this expedition was as follows: Boleslav, Casimir, and a third [Vladislav] (who had married the emperor's niece Gertrude, a daughter of Margrave Leopold of Austria), should have held the whole land by the bond of inheritance, the elder (whom we have put in the last place) possessing the title and dignity of duke.[16] After the last named was forcibly expelled by his brothers, together with his wife of royal blood, had betaken himself to Conrad, then prince of the Roman empire, and had been graciously received, frequent embassies were sent to the aforesaid tyrants, asking that they

---

[13] The Baltic; see Helmold *Chronicle of the Slavs* I.i.

[14] This description seems to best fit the *Rani* or *Rugiani,* inhabitants of the island of Rügen, noted for their piratical activities until their conquest by the Danes in 1168.

[15] Cf. Seneca *Epistles* vii.7.

[16] See above, I.xxx, lvii, and note 117. Gertrude, however, was the wife of Vladislav II of Bohemia; it was her sister Agnes who married Vladislav II of Poland. She was a niece of Conrad III.

restore their brother to his former rank. But the king was treated with contempt, and the duke's exile continued until the death of the king. And when the divine Prince Frederick assumed control of the government, in like fashion they supposed they might with impunity ignore his behest. But this resulted differently for them than they had thought. For repeated insults did not permit this more high-spirited and valiant prince to overlook the offense any longer. Besides, there was the fact that they had now ceased to proffer the customary oath of fidelity and to bring to the public treasury the tribute of five hundred marks due each year. By such acts they were openly declaring that they had seceded from the empire and were planning not a secret but an open rebellion.

iii. The emperor accordingly invaded Poland in great force, although it is strongly fortified by nature and art, so that previous kings and emperors had with great difficulty barely reached the river Oder. Relying upon divine aid, which visibly preceded the army, he penetrated the barriers which they had erected in narrow places by cutting densely growing timber and cleverly heaping it in great piles as obstructions. On the eleventh day before the Kalends of September [August 22, 1157], contrary to the expectation of the inhabitants, he crossed with his entire army the aforesaid stream, which on that side encompasses all Poland like a wall and by the depth of its waters wards off all approach. For so great a desire to cross took possession of all, that some went over by swimming, others by using as a boat whatsoever contrivance chance afforded. Upon seeing this, the Poles, shaken by so unexpected a calamity and greatly frightened, since they now saw nothing ahead save their own doom and the destruction of their country (although by the aid of neighboring tribes—namely, the Russians, the *Parthi,*[17] the Prussians, and the Pomeranians—they had assembled a very great army), sought safety in flight. They were so smitten with despair that they laid waste their own soil, their own fatherland, setting fire to it with their own hands, and even destroyed strongholds and fortifications. Among others they burned the strongly fortified camps, Glogów and Bytom, which had not previously been taken by an enemy, lest garrisons should be placed there by our men. The emperor, following the fugitives and traversing the territory of a bishopric which is called Breslau (*Frodezlau*), came to the diocese of

[17] Possibly the Hungarians, but more likely one of the neighboring Slavic tribes.

Posen. All that land he also ravaged with fire and sword, thinking it incongruous to spare those who had been found such cruel foes to themselves.

iv. Duke Boleslav, seeing his plans in utter ruin, and his land and people in peril and near destruction, opened negotiations, both in person and through emissaries, with our barons and princes. With many prayers, tears, and promises he sought to merit return to the yoke of Roman dominion and to the favor of the prince, prudently abandoning his rebellion in the face of irreparable disaster. He might disdain lesser lords, but not him under whose sway lay the Roman empire.[18] The emperor, having long since learned that it is noble "to spare the prostrate and to overthrow the proud," [19] unwilling to soil with blood a victory that was quick, sudden, and vouchsafed by God, decided that the duke's surrender should be accepted.

v. And so in the aforesaid territory of the bishopric of Posen, near the limits of Krzyszkowo (*Crisgowe*), the aforesaid duke, casting himself at the emperor's feet, was at the intercession of the princes received back into favor on the following terms: First he swore, for himself and all the Poles, that his brother had not been driven out as an exile in derision of the Roman empire. Then he promised to give to the emperor two thousand, to the princes one thousand, to the empress twenty marks of gold, to the court two hundred marks of silver, for his failure to appear at the diet, and to give the oath of fidelity for his land, as was due. He swore also to participate in the Italian expedition. Then he swore that at the next celebration of the Nativity of the Lord he would be under obligation to come to the diet to be held at Magdeburg, to answer fully, in accordance with the judgment and sentence of the Poles and the Bohemians, the complaints of his exiled brother. And so, upon swearing fidelity to the prince, as is the custom, and when the latter had received hostages (namely, Casimir, the duke's brother, and other nobles) for the faithful fulfillment of all the above terms, the emperor, having won a glorious victory under God's guidance, made a triumphant return.[20] But the duke himself, full of wiles and cherishing in his heart a burning desire for dominion, even then was planning

[18] Cf. Josephus *Wars* v.ix.3.   [19] Vergil *Aeneid* vi.853.

[20] Up to this point, Rahewin's account in chapters iii–v has followed almost word for word Frederick's letter to Wibald, abbot of Stablo and Corvey (printed in Jaffé, *Bibliotheca rerum Germanicarum*, I, 601 ff.)

to be unfaithful to his promises, as afterward became evident.[21] For he did not come to the diet nor did he send representatives empowered to act for him. He was deceitful about the Italian expedition also, violating his oath.

vi. Not long afterward [September, 1157], at the city of Würzburg, legates of Alexius [Manuel], the emperor at Constantinople, set forth in the presence of the prince the purpose of their embassy, bringing gifts. But because their words in certain respects appeared to smack of royal pride and (in their overornate speech) of the arrogance of the Greeks, the emperor scorned them. Had they not thought better of it and safeguarded their own interests more (although the prince dissembled his personal feelings), they might well have received from some a humiliating and annoying reply, if this had been possible without violation of the rights of ambassadors.

Appeased by their many entreaties and tears, however, the emperor granted them his forgiveness for these offenses, having received their pledge that henceforth, abjuring bombast, they would bring him in their salutations only such reverence as befits a Roman prince and the ruler over the City and the world. After obtaining his indulgence and favor, they asked and were granted that Frederick, duke of Swabia, the son of King Conrad, who was still a youth, be girt with a sword and knighted in their presence. For his aunt, the empress of Constantinople,[22] had previously, as now, honored this boy by the bestowal of many magnificent gifts, and is said to have charged the legates never to return to Greece unless this matter had been accomplished. Her husband heartily supported her in this on account of the good will and friendship of long standing he had enjoyed with King Conrad, the boy's father.

vii. In that place there were then present also ambassadors of King Henry of England,[23] to bestow varied and precious gifts, enhanced by much graceful language. Among these gifts we beheld a tent, very large in extent and of the finest quality. If you ask its size, it could not be raised except by machinery and a special sort of instrument and props; if you ask its quality, I should imagine that neither in material nor in workmanship will it ever be surpassed by any equipment of this

---

[21] See below, III.xiii.

[22] Bertha, sister-in-law of Conrad III (see above, I.xxiv–xxv), who, after her marriage to Manuel, had changed her name to Irene.　　[23] Henry II (1154–89).

kind. He had also sent a letter full of honeyed speech, of which the following is a copy:

"To the friend dear to his heart, Frederick, by the grace of God the most invincible emperor of the Romans, Henry, king of England, duke of Normandy and Aquitaine and count of Anjou, greeting and the harmony of true peace and love.

"We express to Your Excellency the utmost thanks within our power, O best of rulers, because you have deigned to visit us through ambassadors, to greet us in letters, to anticipate us in bestowing gifts, and—a thing we cherish even more dearly than these—to enter into treaties of peace and love with us. We have exulted and have felt our spirit somehow grow within us and be carried to greater heights, since your promise, whereby you have given us hope in the matter of setting in order the affairs of our realm, has made us more alert and more ready. We have exulted, we say, and have with all our heart arisen before Your Magnificence, making you this answer with sincere and heartfelt affection, that we are prepared to bring to pass according to our ability whatever we know tends toward your glorification. We lay before you our kingdom and whatever is anywhere subject to our sway, and entrust it to your power, that all things may be administered in accordance with your nod, and that in all respects your imperial will may be done.

"Let there be, therefore, between us and our peoples an undivided unity of affection and peace, safe commercial intercourse, yet so that to you, who excel us in worth, may fall the right to command; while we shall not lack the will to obey.

"And as the generous bestowal of your gifts arouses in us the memory of Your Serenity, so do we also fondly desire that you may remember us, sending you the most beautiful things we could find, and what was most likely to please you.

"Consider therefore the affection of the giver, not the gifts, and receive them in the same spirit in which they are given.

"Regarding the hand of the blessed James,[24] concerning which you have written us, we have placed our reply on the lips of Master Herbert [25] and William, our clerk.

[24] That is, a relic of St. James.

[25] Herbert of Bosham, secretary and biographer of Thomas à Becket, and later archbishop of Benevento and cardinal.

"Given at Northampton, the Chancellor Thomas [26] serving as witness."

viii. There were present also various embassies of different nations: for instance, from Denmark, Pannonia, Italy, and Burgundy. Their representatives, beholding each other and vying in the bestowal of gifts and petitions, were the cause of mutual amazement and admiration.

In the middle of the month of October [1157] the emperor set out for Burgundy to hold a diet at Besançon. Now Besançon is the metropolis of one of the three parts into which the renowned Charles the Great divided his empire for distribution among his three sons, all enjoying the royal title.[27] It is situated on the river Doubs. In this city practically all the chief men of that land had assembled, and also many ambassadors from foreign lands, namely, Romans, Apulians, Tuscans, Venetians, Franks, English, and Spaniards, awaited the emperor's arrival. He was received with the most festive display and solemn acclaim. For the whole world recognized him as the most powerful and most merciful ruler, and undertook, with mingled love and fear, to honor him with new tokens of respect, to extol him with new praises.

But before our pen addresses itself to an account of the affairs of this province and its management, we must speak of the ambassadors of the Roman pontiff, Hadrian—why they came and how they departed—because the authority of this delegation was very great and their errand very serious. No one will complain at the prolixity of this account who considers carefully the importance of the matter and the length of time that this tempest has raged and still rages. The personnel of the embassy consisted of Roland, cardinal priest of the title of St. Mark and chancellor of the Holy Roman Church,[28] and Bernard, cardinal priest of the title of St. Clement, both distinguished for their wealth, their maturity of view, and their influence, and surpassing in prestige almost all others in the Roman Church.

Now the cause of their coming seemed to have an air of sincerity; but it was afterward clearly discerned that unrest and an occasion for mischief lay beneath the surface. One day, upon the prince's retiring

---

[26] Thomas à Becket, archbishop of Canterbury from 1162, murdered in 1170, and canonized in 1173.

[27] After the death of Charlemagne and his son Louis the Pious, the empire was divided among the latter's three sons. Besançon fell to the portion of Lothar.

[28] Roland Bandinelli, later Pope Alexander III (1159–81).

from the uproar and tumult of the people, the aforesaid messengers were conducted into his presence in the more secluded retreat of a certain oratory and—as was fitting—were received with honor and kindness, claiming (as they did) to be the bearers of good tidings.[29]

But the beginning of their speech appeared notable at the very outset. It is said to have been as follows: "Our most blessed father, Pope Hadrian, salutes you, and the College of Cardinals of the Holy Roman Church, he as father, they as brethren." After a brief interval they produced the letter that they bore. Copies of this and other letters which passed back and forth in this time of confusion, I have taken pains to insert in this work that any reader who may wish to judge, attracted and summoned not by my words or assertions but by the actual writings of the parties themselves, may choose freely the side to which he desires to lend his favor.[30] Now the content of the letter was as follows:

ix. "Bishop Hadrian, the servant of the servants of God, to his beloved son Frederick, the illustrious emperor of the Romans, greeting and apostolic benediction.

"We recollect having written, a few days since, to the Imperial Majesty, of that dreadful and accursed deed, an offense calling for atonement, committed in our time, and hitherto, we believe, never attempted in the German lands. In recalling it to Your Excellency, we cannot conceal our great amazement that even now you have permitted so pernicious a deed to go unpunished with the severity it deserves. For how our venerable brother E[skil], archbishop of Lund, while returning from the apostolic see, was taken captive in those parts by certain godless and infamous men—a thing we cannot mention without great and heartfelt sorrow—and is still held in confinement; how in taking him captive, as previously mentioned, those men of impiety, a seed of evildoers, children that are corrupters,[31] drew their swords and violently assaulted him and his companions, and how basely and shamefully they treated them, stripping them of all they had, Your Most Serene Highness knows, and the report of so great a crime has already spread abroad to the most distant and remote regions. To avenge this

---

[29] *Boni nuncii baiolos* (II Samuel 18:22).

[30] Note this interesting and diplomatic device on the part of the historian. His two books do contain much primary material in the form of letters. For similar opportunities afforded the reader to reach his own decisions, see below, iii.xvi, and iv.lix, lxxv.

[31] Isaiah 1:4.

deed of exceptional violence, you, as a man to whom we believe good deeds are pleasing but evil works displeasing, ought with great determination to arise and bring down heavily upon the necks of the wicked the sword which was entrusted by divine providence to you 'for the punishment of evildoers and for the praise of them that do well,' [32] and should most severely punish the presumptuous. But you are reported so to have ignored and indeed been indifferent to this deed, that there is no reason why those men should be repentant at having incurred guilt, because they have long since perceived that they have secured immunity for the sacrilege which they have committed.

"Of the reason for this indifference and negligence we are absolutely ignorant, because no scruple of conscience accuses our heart of having in aught offended the glory of Your Serenity. Rather have we always loved, with sincere affection, and treated with an attitude of due kindness, your person as that of our most dear and specially beloved son and most Christian prince, who, we doubt not, is by the grace of God grounded on the rock of the apostolic confession.

"For you should recall, O most glorious son, before the eyes of your mind, how willingly and how gladly your mother, the Holy Roman Church, received you in another year, with what affection of heart she treated you, what great dignity and honor she bestowed upon you, and with how much pleasure she conferred the emblem of the imperial crown, zealous to cherish in her most kindly bosom the height of Your Sublimity, and doing nothing at all that she knew was in the least at variance with the royal will.

"Nor do we regret that we fulfilled in all respects the ardent desires of your heart; but if Your Excellency had received still greater benefits [33] at our hand (had that been possible), in consideration of the great increase and advantage that might through you accrue to the Church of God and to us, we would have rejoiced, not without reason.

"But now, because you seem to ignore and hide so heinous a crime, which is indeed known to have been committed as an affront to the Church universal and to your empire, we both suspect and fear that perhaps your thoughts were directed toward this indifference and neglect on this account: that at the suggestion of an evil man, sowing

---

[32] I Peter 2:14.

[33] *Beneficia;* the emperor and his attendants took this in its feudal sense of "benefice," thus concluding that the pope claimed overlordship of the empire. For the pope's attempt to offer another interpretation, see below, III.xxiii.

tares,[34] you have conceived against your most gracious mother the Holy Roman Church and against ourselves—God forbid!—some displeasure or grievance.[35]

"On this account, therefore, and because of all the other matters of business which we know to impend, we have thought best to dispatch at this time from our side to Your Serenity two of the best and dearest of those whom we have about us, namely, our beloved sons, Bernard, cardinal priest of St. Clement's, and Roland, cardinal priest of St. Mark's and our chancellor, men very notable for piety and wisdom and honor. We very earnestly beseech Your Excellency that you receive them with as much respect as kindness, treat them with all honor, and that whatever they themselves set forth before Your Imperial Dignity on our behalf concerning this and concerning other matters to the honor of God and of the Holy Roman Church, and pertaining also to the glory and exaltation of the empire, you accept without any hesitation as though proceeding from our mouth. Give credence to their words, as if we were uttering them." [September 20, 1157.]

x. When this letter had been read and carefully set forth by Chancellor Rainald [36] in a faithful interpretation, the princes who were present were moved to great indignation, because the entire content of the letter appeared to have no little sharpness and to offer even at the very outset an occasion for future trouble. But what had particularly aroused them all was the fact that in the aforesaid letter it had been stated, among other things, that the fullness of dignity and honor had been bestowed upon the emperor by the Roman pontiff, that the emperor had received from his hand the imperial crown, and that he would not have regretted conferring even greater benefits (*beneficia*) upon him, in consideration of the great gain and advantage that might through him accrue to the Roman Church. And the hearers were led to accept the literal meaning of these words and to put credence in the aforesaid explanation because they knew that the assertion was rashly made by some Romans that hitherto our kings had possessed the imperial power over the City, and the kingdom of Italy, by gift of the popes, and that they made such representations and handed them down

---

[34] Matthew 13:25.

[35] Probably an allusion to the pope's agreement with William of Sicily in 1156 (see above, Bk. II, note 82).

[36] Rainald of Dassel, archbishop of Cologne and imperial chancellor.

to posterity not only orally but also in writing and in pictures. Hence
it is written concerning Emperor Lothar, over a picture of this sort in
the Lateran palace:

> Coming before our gates, the king vows to safeguard the City,
> Then, liegeman to the Pope, by him he is granted the crown.

Since such a picture and such an inscription, reported to him by those
faithful to the empire, had greatly displeased the prince when he had
been near the City in a previous year [1155], he is said to have received
from Pope Hadrian, after a friendly remonstrance, the assurance that
both the inscription and the picture would be removed, lest so trifling
a matter might afford the greatest men in the world an occasion for
dispute and discord.

When all these matters were fully considered, and a great tumult
and uproar arose from the princes of the realm at so insolent a message,
it is said that one of the ambassadors, as though adding sword to
flame,[37] inquired: "From whom then does he have the empire, if not
from our lord the pope?" Because of this remark, anger reached such
a pitch that one of them, namely, Otto, count palatine of Bavaria (it
was said), threatened the ambassador with his sword. But Frederick,
using his authority to quell the tumult, commanded that the ambassadors, being granted safe-conduct, be led to their quarters and that
early in the morning they should set forth on their way; he ordered
also that they were not to pause in the territories of the bishops and
abbots, but to return to the City by the direct road, turning neither to
the right nor to the left. And so they returned without having accomplished their purpose, and what had been done by the emperor was
published throughout the realm in the following letter [October,
1157]:

xi. "Whereas the Divine Sovereignty, from which is derived all
power in heaven and on earth, has entrusted unto us, His anointed, the
kingdom and the empire to rule over, and has ordained that the peace
of the churches is to be maintained by the imperial arms, not without
the greatest distress of heart are we compelled to complain to Your
Benevolence that from the head of the Holy Church, on which Christ
has set the imprint of his peace and love, there seem to be emanating
causes of dissensions and evils, like a poison, by which, unless God avert

---

[37] Cf. Horace *Satires* II.iii.276.

it, we fear the body of the Church will be stained, its unity shattered, and a schism created between the temporal and spiritual realms.

"For when we were recently at the diet in Besançon and were dealing with the honor of the empire and the security of the Church with all due solicitude, apostolic legates arrived asserting that they bore to Our Majesty such tidings that the honor of the empire should receive no small increase. After we had honorably received them on the first day of their arrival, and on the second, as is customary, had seated ourself with our princes to hear their tidings, they, as though inspired by the Mammon of unrighteousness,[38] by lofty pride, by arrogant disdain, by execrable haughtiness, presented a message in the form of a letter from the pope, the content of which was to the effect that we ought always to remember the fact that the lord pope had bestowed upon us the imperial crown and would not even regret it if Our Excellency had received greater benefits (*beneficia*) from him.

"This was the message of fatherly kindness, which was to foster the unity of Church and empire, which was to bind them together in the bonds of peace, which was to bring the hearts of its hearers to harmony with both and obedience to both! Certain it is that at that impious message, devoid of all truth, not only did Our Imperial Majesty conceive a righteous indignation, but all the princes who were present were filled with so great fury and wrath that they would undoubtedly have condemned those two wicked priests to death, had not our presence averted this.

"Moreover, because many copies of this letter were found in their possession, and blank parchments with seals affixed that were still to be written on at their discretion, whereby—as has been their practice hitherto—they were endeavoring to scatter the venom of their iniquity throughout the churches of the Teutonic realm, to denude the altars, to carry off the vessels of the house of God,[39] to strip crosses of their coverings, we obliged them to return to the City by the way they had come, lest an opportunity be afforded them of proceeding further.

"And since, through election by the princes, the kingdom and the empire are ours from God alone, Who at the time of the passion of His Son Christ subjected the world to dominion by the two swords,[40] and since the apostle Peter taught the world this doctrine: 'Fear God, honor the king,'[41] whosoever says that we received the imperial crown as a

[38] Luke 16:9.   [39] Daniel 1:2.   [40] Luke 22:38.   [41] I Peter 2:17.

benefice (*pro beneficio*) from the lord pope contradicts the divine ordinance and the doctrine of Peter and is guilty of a lie. But because we have hitherto striven to snatch from the hand of the Egyptians [42] the honor and freedom of the churches, so long oppressed by the yoke of undeserved slavery, and are intent on preserving to them all their rights and dignities, we ask Your University to grieve at so great an insult to us and to the empire, hoping that your unwavering loyalty will not permit the honor of the empire, which has stood, glorious and undiminished, from the founding of the City and the establishment of the Christian religion even down to your days, to be disparaged by so unheard-of a novelty, such presumptuous arrogance, knowing that— all ambiguity aside—we would prefer to encounter the risk of death rather than to endure in our time the reproach of so great a disorder."

xii (xi). Having dealt thus with this matter, Frederick turned his attention to ordering the affairs of the empire in the kingdom of Burgundy. And as Burgundy had formerly had its own valiant kings, by whom it had been used to being ruled, it had long since (in consequence of that thirst for freedom which, as is said,[43] is beyond price) become insolent and disobedient. But now that land, which—it had been supposed—could only be subdued with much toil and strife, became (by God's ordinance) so obedient that the emperor might have proceeded peacefully and almost without escort as far as Arles, its capital, had not other pressing matters called him elsewhere. Finally a thing happened which men now living cannot recall as having ever before occurred. Stephen, archbishop of Vienne and archchancellor of Burgundy, and Heraclius, archbishop and primate of Lyons, the bishops Odo of Valence and Geoffrey of Avignon, and Silvio, the great and powerful prince of Clérieux, coming at that time to the court, pledged their fidelity to Frederick and did him homage, and with all respect received their fiefs (*beneficia*) from his hand. Moreover, the archbishop of Arles and all the other archbishops, bishops, primates, and nobles would have come and done the same, had they not been hindered by the brevity of the emperor's visit. Nevertheless, in letters sent by very reliable and zealous messengers, they promised complete subjection and due fidelity to the Roman empire. Louis [VII] also, the king of France, had come as far as Dijon for a conference with the emperor, but as the latter turned his course toward Germany, the attempt came

[42] Exodus 18:9; I Samuel 10:18.   [43] *Digest* L.xvii.106.

to nothing. But each prince sent ambassadors (the emperor dispatching the afore-mentioned Chancellor Rainald and Count Ulrich of Lenzburg, and the king his own chancellor, Master Aldericus [44]) and greeted the other through them. But though the embassy was apparently designed for useful purposes, actually it seemed on both sides to be devoted rather to regal display. For as I have learned from a report of that venerable man Henry, bishop of Troyes, upon hearing how vigorously Frederick had conducted himself in those parts, Louis feared that he was coming not to confer (which he doubted) but to fight. He had quietly assembled no small forces, so that the aforesaid bishop related that one night nine bishops with their military following were lodged in Troyes. And since that entire land cowered in no small fear, that very trepidation was regarded as a victory for us.

xiii (xii). Having thus successfully established his authority over the lands of his empress (of whom we have spoken above [45]), the emperor on his return from Burgundy proceeded to Saxony, and observed the days of the Lord's Nativity in the city of Magdeburg. He now learned something of the Poles, who, as we have said previously,[46] should at this time have carried out their promises; but blinded by avarice and ambition, they set little value on their good faith and their oaths. Then, moving to Bavaria, he held a diet at Regensburg, with a great attendance of princes, on the octave of Epiphany [January 13, 1158]. Among the many present there were ambassadors of King N. of Hungary.[47] For his brother, N.[Stephen] by name, had by certain men been accused before the king of aspiring to royal power. In this he was thought to have been instigated by Duke Béla, an uncle of them both, a very shrewd and scheming man, who seemed to be feeding the pride of a young man already accustomed to too much honor. But the king, suspicious of the great attention paid to his brother, and fearing worse things from him than was needful, now openly accused not the man himself so much as his friends and those of his household, and turned all that they said or did against him. After many accusations had been aired and many persons induced to bear false witness, the king was said to be planning to have his brother killed. The latter, having learned that the Roman empire is an asylum for the whole

---

[44] Hugh of Champfleury, bishop of Soissons, was chancellor of France, 1150–72; Luchaire (*Études sur les actes de Louis VII* [Paris, 1885], p. 57) believes that Aldericus acted as chancellor for this trip of the king.

[45] See above, II.xlviii.　　[46] See above, III.v.　　[47] Géza II (1141–61).

world, escaped by fleeing to the emperor and tearfully bewailed his fate and his brother's bitter cruelty toward him. To counter the charges made against him, he branded them as false, declaring that the truth of his denial was apparent to all, and that slanderers would never be lacking so long as there existed a man open to persuasion. It was most unjust (he said) that his brother was not content with having driven him from their ancestral realm, but would also inflict capital punishment upon him and take an absolutely innocent life.

Frederick, moved by such entreaty, sent ambassadors into Hungary, and took thought for the young man's reinstatement, adding the weight of imperial authority to his requests. Therefore the king sent to the court to oppose his brother two of the nobles of his kingdom, Bishop Gervase of Eisenstadt [48] and Count Heidenrich, wealthy men and well trained to speak. Through them he endeavored to lull criticism and to turn the odium of the brother's exile upon the brother himself. He set forth the many injuries and wrongs he had suffered: his brother had participated with him in joint rule, and only in name had he been superior to him, as long as the brotherhood between them had remained inviolate. Then, in his youth, his brother had, under evil influences, given himself over to the worst pursuits. The result was precisely the same as in the body, where it always follows that when some part is inflamed and by its corruption weakens and infects the whole body, and a cure is despaired of, an amputation is necessary. He had made war without provocation, and when he was conquered he complained because he had been unable to inflict injury.[49] He pretended that he had had to flee, though he had been permitted to remain in his country [50] until he had so drawn upon himself the hatred and enmity of all that they believed he was plotting against the kingdom and should be expelled as a cruel foe before, by his misdeeds, the kingdom should be rent by bloody strife.

The emperor, having heard both sides, saw that matters had reached such a pass that the dispute must be terminated either by a division of the realm or by the condemnation of one or the other. But in consideration of other pressing matters he decided to defer to a more suitable time the settlement of this quarrel. Therefore, at the young man's

[48] *De Castro-ferreo.* Simonsfeld (p. 603, note 20) suggests that this was his surname; he was bishop of Raab.

[49] Sallust *Jugurtha* xv.1. Much of the preceding account is taken from Josephus *Wars* I.xxvi.1–3.   [50] Sallust *Jugurtha* xiv.20.

request, he sent him to Greece by way of Venice. He also permitted the ambassadors of the king to return to their prince with a message of peace. Having received from them gifts to the value of practically a thousand talents, he honored them likewise with his liberality.

xiv (xiii). At this same diet N., the duke of the Bohemians,[51] a man of great talents, distinguished for his physical strength [52] and courage, great in counsel and action, many instances of whose zeal and loyalty had previously been shown (his exceptional valor had been recently demonstrated in the Polish expedition), so that he was endeared to all by his merits, was made king instead of duke by the emperor and the princes of the empire, in the year 1158 since the incarnation of the Lord. Therefore, after being privileged to use a crown and other royal insignia, he returned rejoicing and accoutered himself for the Italian expedition, that as king he might set forth, together with the emperor, in regal splendor.

There also the emperor brought back into peaceful and brotherly accord his uncles, Bishop Otto of Freising and Duke Henry [Jasomirgott] of Austria, who were at variance because the aforesaid bishop had resisted the attempts of the duke, his brother, to seize unlawfully lands of the Church.

xv (xiv). After these things had been done in Bavaria, Frederick entered the territories of the Ripuarians [53] and, traveling through the country of the Lower Rhine, let no days pass in idleness, thinking those lost on which he had not made some enactment to the advantage of the empire, for the preservation of law and justice among all peoples. That was the reason why he had so consistently striven for so strong an empire on this side of the Alps, had calmed the spirits of such strong peoples by great discretion, without warfare, and—marvelous to relate —was now regarded not as the ruler of the realm, but as father and governor of one home, one state.

xva. After celebrating Easter at N. [Maastricht], Frederick retraced his way to the upper regions of the *Vangiones*,[54] and turning aside to the royal palace which he had built at Kaiserslautern, devoted several days to his home and to setting his family affairs in order.

Now the time was drawing near at which kings are accustomed to

---

[51] Vladislav II (1140–73).   [52] Sallust *Jugurtha* vi.1.
[53] The Ripuarian Franks; the territory meant is the Rhineland.
[54] The area of Worms.

go forth to battle,[55] and he himself was shortly to lead his army over the Alps. Fixing his trust in God,[56] he summoned religious and saintly men and consulted them as though they were divine oracles, and on their advice conferred many gifts upon the churches, with imperial prodigality. In these matters he had as his special adviser and faithful confidant for his soul's welfare Hartmann, bishop of Brixen [1140–64], a man then preeminent among the bishops of Germany for his sanctity and the austerity of his life. Calling this man to his presence, he reverently submitted his private affairs to the counsels of this pious prelate, thereby acting the part of a devout and most Christian prince, in order that, when about to go to war, he might fortify his soul with spiritual weapons before arming his body, preparing himself with heavenly instruction before himself giving military instruction to the soldiers setting forth to battle. Moreover, he set forth the reasons for the war, and as the aforesaid bishop as well as the rest of the priests acknowledged them as just, lest the imperial dignity be diminished by the unworthy, and thus the peace and tranquillity of the churches be disturbed, they aroused him to set forth against the rebels, forewarned and forearmed with their wholesome precepts.

xvi (xv). Meanwhile, the legates of the apostolic see, Roland and Bernard, had returned [to Rome] and set forth the great insults they had sustained, the great danger they had undergone, adding even more serious charges to what was serious enough, in order to provoke the bishop of the Roman city to seek vengeance for the things they said they had endured. In this matter the Roman clergy were divided among themselves, so that a number of them favored the party of the emperor and blamed the thoughtlessness or inexperience of those who had been sent; however, a certain group upheld the wishes of their pontiff. Now, being about to speak of this commotion, we desire (as we said above) that the reader shall not depend on our words, but that, as we place on record the letters sent back and forth, he may decide from them what side he should favor or to whom he wishes to remain loyal. But we seek indulgence for ourself, who venerate with due respect both persons, namely, the priestly and the royal, too much to venture to make a rash judgment concerning one of them. And so the following is a copy of a letter sent by the supreme pontiff to the archbishops and bishops concerning these matters:

---

[55] II Samuel 11:1.   [56] Psalms 78:23.

"As often as any attempt is made in the Church directed against the honor of God and the welfare of the faithful, the solicitude of our brothers and fellow bishops, and of those in particular who are led by the spirit of God, must be aroused, that matters which have been wrongly done may receive the correction that is pleasing to God.

"Now at this time, a matter of which we cannot speak without the deepest sorrow, our very dear son Frederick, emperor of the Romans, has done such a thing as we do not know to have been done in the times of our predecessors. For when we had sent to his presence two of our very good brothers, Bernard, of the title of St. Clement, and Roland, our chancellor, of the title of St. Mark, cardinal priests, he seems to have received them gladly when first they came into his presence. But on the following day, when they returned to him and our letter was read in his hearing, taking umbrage at a certain expression therein employed, namely, 'we have bestowed upon you the benefice (*beneficium*) of the imperial crown,' [57] he blazed forth with such great anger that it was disgraceful to hear and would be painful to repeat the insults that he is said to have hurled at us and our legates, and to recall in how humiliating a fashion he obliged them to retire from his presence and with all speed from his land. And as they departed from his presence, he issued an edict that no one from your realm should approach the apostolic see, and is said to have set guards throughout all the bounds of that same realm who should forcibly detain those who desired to come to the apostolic see.

"Although we are somewhat disturbed by this act, yet at heart we draw very great consolation from the fact that he did not do this on your advice and that of the princes. Hence we are confident that by your counsel and persuasion his wrath may easily be calmed.

"Wherefore, brethren, inasmuch as your own interests, and those of all the churches—not our interest only—are clearly at stake in this matter, we admonish and exhort Your Love in the Lord to interpose yourselves as a wall before the house of the Lord,[58] and strive to lead back our aforesaid son to the right way as soon as possible. See especially that he cause his chancellor Rainald and the count palatine, who had the presumption to spew forth great blasphemies against our aforesaid legates and your very holy mother, the Roman Church, to offer

---

[57] The text here is *beneficium coronae*, whereas in Chapter ix we read *imperialis insigne coronae.*   [58] Cf. Ezekiel 13:5.

such apology and to do it so openly that, as the bitterness of their speech has offended the ears of many, so also their apology may tend to recall many to the right way.

"Let not our same son give heed to the counsels of the ungodly, let him consider what is behind and before,[59] and walk in that way in which Justinian and other Catholic emperors are known to have walked. For by imitating the example of those men he will be able to lay up for himself both honor on earth and blessedness in heaven.

"You also, if you lead him back to the right way, will both serve the blessed Peter, prince of apostles, and will preserve your own liberty and that of your churches. Otherwise may our aforesaid son learn from your admonition, may he learn from the truth of the Gospel promise, that the Holy Roman Church founded by God on an immovable rock [60] will be steadfast forever, under the Lord's protection, by whatsoever tempests it may be shaken.

"Moreover, as you know, it was not seemly for him to have attempted so steep a path without your counsel; hence we believe that upon hearing your admonitions he can the more easily be brought back —like a man of discretion and a Catholic emperor—to a more reasonable frame of mind."

xvii (xvi). Upon the receipt of this letter and an embassy to the same purport, the bishops of Germany took counsel and replied to the apostolic see in the following words:

"Although we know and are sure that neither wind nor storm can overthrow the Church of God, founded upon a firm rock, yet we, being weak and faint-hearted, are shaken and tremble whenever blows of this kind befall. Hence we are, of course, gravely disturbed and alarmed at these developments which seem likely to prove—unless God avert it —the source of great evil between Your Holiness and your most devoted son, our lord, the emperor. Indeed, in consequence of those words which were contained in your letter, which you sent by your messengers, those most prudent and honorable men, the Lord Bernard and the Lord Roland, the chancellor, venerable cardinal priests, our whole empire has been thrown into confusion. Neither the ears of the emperor nor those of the princes could endure to hear them. All have so stopped their ears [61] that—saving Your Holiness' grace—we dare not and cannot uphold or approve in any way those words, by reason

[59] Psalms 139:5.   [60] Cf. Matthew 16:18.   [61] Acts 7:57.

of their unfortunate ambiguity of meaning, because they were hitherto unknown and unheard of. We received and welcomed, however, with due reverence your letter, and have advised your son, our lord the emperor, as you ordered, and—thanks be to God!—have received from him the following reply, worthy of a Catholic prince, namely:

" 'There are two things by which our realm should be governed, the sacred laws of the emperors, and the good customs of our predecessors and our fathers. The limits set by them on the Church we do not wish to overstep, nor can we; whatever is not in accord with them, we reject. We gladly accord to our father the reverence that is his due. The free crown of empire we ascribe solely to the divine beneficence (*beneficium*). We recognize first in the election the vote of the archbishop of Mainz, then those of the other princes, according to their rank; the anointing as king we recognize as the prerogative of the archbishop of Cologne; the final anointing, as emperor, indeed pertains to the supreme pontiff. "Whatsoever is more than these cometh of evil." [62]

" 'It is not to show disrespect for our most beloved and reverend father and consecrator that we obliged the cardinals to depart from our land. But we did not wish to permit them to proceed further, to the disgrace and shame of our empire, with their letters, written or blank.[63] We have not closed the way in and out of Italy by edict, nor do we wish in any way to close it to those going to the Roman see as pilgrims or on their own necessary business, in reasonable fashion, with testimonials from their bishops and prelates. But we intend to resist those abuses by which all the churches of our realm have been burdened and weakened, and almost all the discipline of the cloisters killed and buried. In the chief city of the world God has, through the power of the empire, exalted the Church; in the chief city of the world the Church, not through the power of God, we believe, is now destroying the empire. It began with a picture, the picture became an inscription, the inscription seeks to become an authoritative utterance.[64] We shall not endure it, we shall not submit to it; we shall lay down the crown before we consent to have the imperial crown and ourself thus degraded. Let the pictures be destroyed, let the inscriptions be withdrawn, that they may not remain as eternal memorials of enmity between the empire and the papacy.'

"These and other matters—for instance, concerning the agreement

---

[62] Matthew 5:37.   [63] See above, III.xi.   [64] See above, III.ix, x.

between the Ro[mans] and W[illiam] of Sicily, and other pacts made in Italy—which we do not venture to recount in detail, we heard from the lips of our lord the emperor. In the absence of the count palatine, who has already been sent ahead to make preparations for the expedition into Italy, we have heard nothing from the chancellor, who is still present here, save that he was of meek and peaceful bearing, except when he defended the ambassadors with all his might when their lives were threatened by those present, as everyone there could attest.

"As for the rest, we humbly ask and beseech Your Sanctity to pardon our weakness and, like a good shepherd, calm the high spirits of your son with a letter more conciliatory than that former one, that the Church of God may rejoice in tranquil devotion and that the empire may glory in its sublimity, with the mediation and aid of the 'Mediator between God and man, the man Christ Jesus.' " [65]

xviii (xvii). The emperor began his expedition propitiously, and pitching camp at Augsburg, a city of Rhaetia, on the river Lech, he awaited for seven days the soldiery who poured in from various directions [June, 1158].

Meanwhile the Roman bishop, being informed of the coming of the prince—for his legates, the above-mentioned Chancellor Rainald and Count Palatine Otto, had entered Italy long before—now changed his attitude for the better and sent ambassadors to calm Frederick's spirit, namely, Henry, cardinal priest of the title of Saints Nereus and Achilles, and Hyacinth, cardinal deacon of St. Mary-in-the-Greek-School,[66] men of prudence in secular matters, and much better qualified for dealing with affairs of state than those previously sent.

xix (xviii). But before we give our attention to their journey and their mission, it is not out of place to give by way of foretaste a few items of many concerning the characters and deeds of the aforesaid royal ambassadors. In particular, these illustrious men possessed a pleasant and imposing presence, nobility of family, an intellect strong in wisdom,[67] unperturbed spirits; in fact, they were men to whom no task was too unfamiliar, no post too dangerous, no armed foe too terrible.[68] They permitted themselves no misdeeds, no passions; [69] they were eager for praise, generous with money; they wished for great

---

[65] I Timothy 2:5.
[66] Later Pope Celestine III (1191–98).
[67] Sallust *Catiline* vi.6.　[68] *Ibid.*, vii.5.　[69] Cf. *ibid.*, lii.8.

glory and honorable wealth.[70] They were youthful and remarkably eloquent; similar in manner, save that one was marked by the gentleness and pity consonant with his clerical status and rank, whereas the sternness of the sword that he bore not in vain [71] had added dignity to the other. The one offered a refuge to the wretched, the other doom to evildoers.[72]

With such characters and such pursuits they had won for themselves praise, for the empire glory and no small advantage at home and abroad, so that at that time almost nothing great—no especially courageous achievement—was accomplished on that expedition, wherein I have failed to discover these men to have been either foremost or among the foremost.

xx (xix). And so, on their first entrance into Italy, the ambassadors accepted the capitulation of a stronghold which is called Rivoli, situated above the pass of Verona,[73] impregnable because of its natural setting; for they thought that through the possession of it our men would find the passage easier, both coming and returning, in so narrow a defile. Received by great throngs and with marked respect on the part of the bishop and citizens of Verona, both there and in other cities (namely, Mantua, Cremona, Pavia) they exacted an oath of fidelity to the emperor and a promise of assistance in the expedition sworn on the Holy Gospels. Preparing the way for the emperor, they proved themselves trustworthy and valuable precursors of his arrival. Now this is the formula of the oath to which all swore:

"I swear that from this time forth I shall be faithful to my lord Frederick, the emperor of the Romans, against all men, as is my lawful duty to my lord and emperor, and I shall aid him to retain the crown of empire and all its prerogatives in Italy, namely and specifically the city of N. and whatever jurisdiction he is entitled to have in it, or in his power over the county or bishopric of N. I shall not deprive him of his

---

[70] *Ibid.*, vii.6.   [71] Romans 13:4.

[72] For the preceding two sentences, cf. Sallust *Catiline* liv.1–3. Rahewin's fulsome praise of the count palatine, Otto of Wittelsbach, contrasts rather sharply with Otto of Freising's adverse judgment; see *Two Cities* vi.xx.

[73] *Super clausuram Veronensium:* the modern *Chiusa di Verona*, the pass on the Adige, ten miles northwest of Verona, where Frederick had had difficulties on his earlier expedition (see above, ii.xl). Rivoli is located at the northern end of this narrow and rocky defile.

royal rights here or elsewhere, and if they should be taken from him I shall in good faith aid him to recover and retain them. I shall be party to no plot or deed to cause him the loss of life or limb or honor or to be held in dire captivity. Every command of his, given me personally, or in writing, or through his representative rendering justice, I shall faithfully observe, and I shall by no evil means evade hearing or receiving or complying with it. All these things I shall observe in good faith without deceit. So help me God and these four Holy Gospels."

(xx). From Verona the ambassadors passed through Mantua, and coming to Cremona held a well-attended conference or, if you will, diet. There came to meet them at this city the archbishops of Ravenna and Milan and fifteen of their suffragan bishops, and also counts, margraves, consuls, and the leaders of all the surrounding cities. And this I can truthfully say: many kings have been denied the splendor and honor shown these upright envoys.

Thence making their way through Romagna and Emilia, the ambassadors visited the exarchate of Ravenna, everywhere actively and industriously advancing the interests of the prince and the realm. Thence they turned toward Ancona, through Rimini. For they had learned that the logothete or Palaeologus,[74] with other envoys of the emperor of Constantinople, was staying there, ostensibly to recruit, by largess of money, troops known as mercenaries (*solidarii*) to serve against William of Sicily, but actually (as rumor had it at the time) to bring the coast cities by force or by guile beneath the sway of the Greeks—a thing which we know has often been attempted before. And when they departed from Ravenna, they met, not far from the city, a number of the leading men of the region, who had gone to the aforesaid ambassadors of the Greeks and had conferred privately with them. Disturbed and angered by this—for they seemed to have disdained the emperor and (in their hope of profit) to have preferred the Greeks—the Count Palatine Otto, disregarding their large numbers and his own smaller force, drew his sword, and laying hands upon the best and noblest of all the men of Ravenna, William, surnamed Maltraversar,[75] threatened to lead him away captive, all the rest being silent for fear and terror, and offering no objection. How great and amazing was the spirit

---

[74] Actually the Protostrator Alexius, whom Rahewin here confuses with Michael Palaeologus; see Simonsfeld, pp. 718–19.

[75] William *Traversarius*, podesta of Ravenna.

of the aforesaid count, who was intimidated neither by the numerous following of the noble in question, nor by the proximity of his city! He made use indeed of the imperial authority, as legate of the empire, when the occasion demanded. But being finally appeased and placated by gentler words and much entreaty, he resumed his journey.

Against the Greeks, who (as we have said) were then tarrying at Ancona, the envoys assembled no small military force and pitched camp near that city. Summoning the Greeks before them, they sternly and vehemently demanded by what audacity they had presumed to commit such acts without the prince's knowledge. They were not unaware, they said, of the Danaans' wiles [76] and of Greek cunning. Feigning friendship, the Greeks had intended evil; with the most subtle trickery they had contrived against friends devices better directed against foes. And since by manifest proofs they were exposed as enemies of the Roman empire, nothing was left save to inflict upon them the full punishment for treason. The Greeks were thrown into terror and consternation by such invectives as these. With great humility they babbled excuses, defending themselves as best they could. They were, they said, by no means ignorant of the Julian law of treason,[77] aimed at those conspiring against the emperor or the state; but of this, their consciences declared them free. Fiction should not be accepted as fact; rather, credence should be put in the kindness and honor so frequently demonstrated by the Greeks toward our people. All Germany is witness of this; witness of this is the emperor himself, now prince of the world, who once saw and experienced it himself.[78] Fairness to the living, compassion for the dead, honor to the prince, liberality toward the great—these are most certain evidences of their affection for our people, more reliable than false accusations.

By these and similar protestations, and with great contrition of heart, the Greeks defended themselves against the charges. Since no proof of deceit could be found, after receiving from them munificent gifts, they were permitted to return to Greece in peace. The imperial envoys then returned to Modena.

xxi. Meanwhile, Henry and Hyacinth, the aforesaid legates of Pope Hadrian, had come to Ferrara, and hearing that the envoys of

[76] Vergil *Aeneid* II.65.

[77] The *lex Iulia maiestatis;* see *Institutes* IV.xviii.3, and below, IV.xliii.

[78] Apparently a reference to the hospitality Frederick had received on the Second Crusade.

the emperor had returned to Modena, they made show of humility (hitherto rare) and came there—having no hope of being themselves visited. After setting forth the reason for their embassy, namely, the cause of peace and the honor of the empire, they were dismissed. But by this time throughout all those regions where they had to cross the mountain passes, rumor had reported their coming, and the cupidity of many had been aroused by the fact (of which scarcely a man was unaware) that the imperial majesty was hostile to the Romans. And according as each was inflamed by the vice of greed, he audaciously threatened them as though in compliance with the wishes of the king, hoping that in this case brigandage might be extenuated under a more honorable name. And so they proceeded from Ferrara to Verona, from Verona through the valley of the Trent, having with them, for greater security, Albert, the venerable bishop of Trent. But "the accursed lust for gold" [79] prevailed; once it has possessed a man, it never permits him to contemplate or to seek anything honorable or reasonable. For Counts Frederick and Henry,[80] whose deeds of violence in those parts were not a few, taking captive both the cardinals and the bishop, robbed them and kept them in chains until a noble man, N., the brother of Hyacinth, giving himself as a hostage, freed the Romans; but it was evidently divine power that freed the bishop. This outrage, however, was properly avenged not long afterward, by the most noble duke of Bavaria and Saxony,[81] out of love for the Holy Roman Church and to the honor of the empire. For he both freed their hostage and forced the counts to surrender and make restitution, after inflicting much evil upon them.

xxii. Accordingly, when Frederick had pitched his camp in the plains of Augsburg (as has already been said), he admitted to his presence those same legates and, receiving them graciously, asked the cause of their coming. With due reverence and downcast eyes [82] they began their mission in these words: "The bishop of the Holy Roman Church, Your Excellency's most devoted father in Christ, salutes you as the very dear and spiritual son of St. Peter. Salutations also from our venerable brothers, your clergy, all the cardinals, to you as lord and em-

---

[79] Vergil *Aeneid* III.57.   [80] Of Eppan, in the Tyrol.

[81] Henry the Lion.

[82] Cf. the phraseology of Sallust *Catiline* xxxi.7. It is interesting to note Rahewin's borrowing from Sallust to describe these events, at which he was himself apparently present.

peror of the City and of the world. With what great love the Holy Roman Church esteems the dignity and honor of your empire, how she has—though unwillingly enough—endured your anger without consciousness of guilt, both this present writing and the words placed upon our lips shall declare."

They then produced a letter which was given to the venerable Bishop Otto of Freising to read and to interpret—a man who felt a peculiar grief at the controversy between the state and the Church. This is a copy of the letter:

xxiii. "Since we assumed the care of the Church Universal by God's will and pleasure, we have been careful to do honor to Your Magnificence in all matters, that your love of us and veneration for the apostolic see might daily increase. When we heard that your feelings had been roused against us by certain people, we sent to you, to ascertain your will, two of our best and most distinguished brothers, the Cardinal Priest R[oland], the chancellor, of the title of St. Mark, and B[ernard], of the title of St. Clement, who had always been solicitous in the Roman Church for the honor of Your Majesty. Hence we learned with great astonishment that they were treated otherwise than behooved the imperial dignity. For your heart was stirred to anger, it is said, by the use of a certain word, namely *beneficium*. Yet this should not have vexed the heart of even one in lowly station, to say nothing of so great a man. For although this word *beneficium* is by some interpreted in a different significance than it has by derivation, it should nevertheless have been understood in the meaning which we ourselves put upon it, and which it is known to have possessed from the beginning. For this word is formed of *bonus* (good) and *factum* (deed), and among us *beneficium* means not a fief but a good deed. In this sense it is found in the entire body of Holy Scripture, wherein we are said to be ruled and supported *ex beneficio Dei*, not as by a fief (*feudum*) but as by His benediction and His 'good deed' (*bono facto*). And indeed Your Highness clearly recognizes that we placed the emblem of imperial dignity upon your head in so good and honorable a fashion that it merits recognition by all as a good deed. Hence when certain people have tried to twist that word and the following formula, namely, 'we have conferred upon you the imperial crown,' from its own proper meaning to another, they have done this not on the merits of the case, but of their own desire and at the instigation of those who by no means love the concord of Church and state. For by 'we have conferred' (*contulimus*) we meant nothing else than when we said before 'we have placed' (*imposuimus*). As for the report that you afterward ordered the turning back of ecclesiastical persons on due visitation to the sacrosanct Roman Church, if it be so, we believe that Your Discretion, O very dear son in Christ, must realize how unseemly an act that was. For if you harbored any bitterness toward us, it should have been intimated to us by your envoys and letters, and we would have taken care to safeguard your honor, as that of our very dear son. Now therefore, as we have, at the advice of our beloved son H[enry], duke of Bavaria and Saxony, sent into your presence two of our brothers, Henry, cardinal priest of the title of Saints Nereus and Achilles, and Hyacinth, cardinal deacon of St. Mary in Cosmedin, truly wise and estimable men, we urge and exhort Your Highness in the Lord that you receive them with honor and kindness. Know also that what is imparted to Your Magnificence by them on our behalf has proceeded from the sincerity of our heart. And therefore may Your Highness so strive to reach an agreement with these our sons, through the mediation of our aforesaid son, the duke, that there may remain no seed of discord between you and your mother, the Holy Roman Church."

xxiv (xxiii). When the letter had been read and set forth with favorable interpretation, the emperor was mollified, and becoming more gracious he indicated to the legates certain specific matters to be considered later [83] which might lead to dispute unless properly corrected. When to this they made answer agreeable to the prince and in all respects satisfactory, and promised that the bishop of Rome would do nothing derogatory to the royal dignity, but would always preserve inviolate the honor and the just claims of empire, he guaranteed peace and friendship both to the supreme pontiff and to all the Roman clergy, and certified it for the absent by giving them also, through those who were present, a kiss in token of peace. So the ambassadors were gladdened and enriched with royal gifts, and set forth for the City.

xxv (xxiv). At the same time, ambassadors of N.[Waldemar], the recently elected king of Denmark, came to the prince, requesting that he deign to send to the king the investiture of his realm and to ratify the choice that had fallen upon him. The emperor gave them an au-

---

[83] See below, IV.xxxiv–xxxvi.

dience, and accepted their sworn assurance that within forty days after his return from Italy the king would come to court and receive at the prince's hand authority to administer his realm, after swearing the oath of due allegiance.

xxvi (xxv). Meanwhile, as a numerous army poured in to him from all sides, envoys of the various princes filled the court and inquired of the emperor at which points each detachment was to cross over the mountain passes. Indeed, the many roads could scarcely accommodate the great multitude of troops, namely, of Franconians, Saxons, Rhinelanders, Burgundians, Swabians, Bavarians, Lorrainers, Bohemians, Hungarians, and Carinthians, and with these some other Celtic or Germanic peoples, valiant men, warriors in untold numbers, with varied equipment of arms, young men strong and unafraid of war. Frederick, after taking counsel and employing great foresight, determined that the roads and passes of the Alps should be assigned to them as follows: Duke Henry of Austria and Duke Henry of Carinthia, together with the Hungarian force (about six hundred picked archers), and the counts and barons of those lands, were to go by way of the valley of Canale, Friuli, and the march of Verona; Duke Berthold of Zähringen (or rather of Burgundy) with the Lorrainers by the route of Julius Caesar, now called *mons Iovis* [Great St. Bernard]; a large part of the Franconians, Rhinelanders, and Swabians by Chiavenna and the lake of Como. The emperor himself, having in his following the king of Bohemia; the duke of Swabia (Frederick, the son of King Conrad); his brother Conrad, count palatine of the Rhine; the archbishops Frederick of Cologne, Arnold of Mainz, and Hillin of Trier; the bishops Conrad of Eichstädt, Daniel of Prague, Herman of Verden, Gebhard of Würzburg; the abbots of the royal monasteries (namely, Fulda and Reichenau)—I say nothing of the margraves, the famous and very powerful counts (to mention only their names might weary the fastidious or unwilling reader)—attended by all these forces, nay more, by divine protection, divine Augustus entered the Alpine passes, ready for battle.

xxvii. The army issued rejoicing from the passes of the mountains, and camp was pitched in the plains of Italy. Brescia was the first that rashly ventured to oppose their onward thrust, confident in its fortifications and the valor of its soldiers; but it was quickly broken and subdued. Weakened by the king of the Bohemians, upon the arrival of the emperor it was granted terms of surrender, giving up sixty hostages and no small sum of money.

xxviii (xxvi). The emperor now rested, awaiting the troops that were coming from various cities of Italy, wisely and prudently occupying himself with the affairs of peace before turning to war. Summoning the princes, he ordained the following regulations for maintaining order in the army:

"[1]. We have decreed and desire to have it strictly observed that no knight or sergeant shall presume to provoke strife. But if one man quarrel with another, neither shall utter the rallying cry of the camp, lest his people be incited thereby to battle. But if strife shall have started, no one shall run up with weapons (sword, spear, or arrows); but, clad in breastplate, shield, and helmet, let him bring to the fight nothing but a staff with which to separate the combatants. No one shall shout out the rallying cry of the camp save when seeking his quarters. But if a soldier (*miles*) shall have caused strife by shouting out the rallying cry, all his accouterment shall be taken from him, and he shall be expelled from the army. If a varlet (*servus*) shall have done so, he shall be shorn, flogged, and branded on the cheek, or his lord shall buy him off with all his accouterment.

"[2]. Whosoever shall have wounded anyone and deny it shall then have his hand cut off if the wounded man can convict him by two truthful witnesses, not related to him. But if witnesses are lacking and he wishes to clear himself by an oath, the accuser may, if he please, refuse to accept the oath and challenge him to a duel.

"[3]. Whosoever shall have killed anyone, and shall have been convicted by two truthful witnesses not related to the slain man, shall suffer death. But if witnesses are lacking, and he wishes to purge himself by an oath, a close friend of the slain man may challenge him to a duel.

"[4]. If a strange knight shall come peacefully to the camp, riding a palfrey, without shield and weapons, if anyone injure him, he shall be judged a violator of the peace. But if he come to camp riding a charger, with a shield slung from his neck and a lance in his hand, if anyone injure him he has not broken the peace.

"[5]. A soldier who has despoiled a merchant shall make twofold restitution for what has been taken, and swear that he did not know he was a merchant. If he be a varlet, he shall be shorn and branded on the cheek, or his lord shall restore the plunder on his behalf.

"[6]. Whosoever sees anyone robbing a church or a market ought to prevent him, yet without strife; if he cannot prevent him, he should bring accusation against the guilty man in court.

"[7]. No one is to have a woman in his quarters; but he who dares to do so shall be deprived of all his accouterment and be considered excommunicated, and the woman's nose shall be cut off.

"[8]. No one shall attack a stronghold that has a garrison from the court.

"[9]. If a varlet commit a theft and is detected, if he was not previously a thief he shall not be hanged for it, but shall be shorn, flogged, and branded on the cheek, and expelled from the army, unless his lord buy him off with his entire accouterment. If he was previously a thief, he shall be hanged.

"[10]. If any varlet be accused, but not caught in the act, of theft, on the following day he shall purge himself by the ordeal of red-hot iron, or his lord shall swear on his behalf; but the accuser shall swear that he cited him for theft for no other reason than because he thought him guilty.

"[11]. If anyone find another's horse, he shall not shear it or disguise it, but shall tell the marshal, and shall not secretly keep it and place his pack upon it. But if he who has lost the horse come upon it on the road carrying a burden, he shall not pull off its pack but follow it to camp and recover his horse.

"[12]. If anyone set fire to a village or a house, he shall be shorn and branded on the cheeks and flogged.

"[13]. A smith shall not burn charcoal in a village but shall carry the wood to his quarters and burn it there; but if he does it in a village, he shall be shorn, flogged, and branded on the cheeks.

"[14]. If anyone injure another, charging that he has not sworn to keep the peace, he shall not be guilty of breaking the peace unless the other can prove by two satisfactory witnesses that he did swear to keep the peace.

"[15]. No one shall receive in his quarters a varlet who is without a master. If he does so, he shall return twofold whatever the varlet has carried off.

"[16]. Whosoever finds a buried treasure (*foveam*) may enjoy it freely. But if it is taken away from him, he shall not render evil for evil,[84] shall not exact vengeance for the wrong done him, but shall lodge a complaint with the marshal in order to secure justice.

"[17]. If a German merchant enter a city and buy goods and convey them to the army and sell them at a higher price in the army, the chamberlain shall take away from him his entire stock and shall flog him and shear him and brand him on the cheek.

"[18]. No German is to have an Italian as a comrade unless he understands German; but if he does have [such a comrade], all that he has shall be taken from him.

"[19]. If a knight utter insults to a knight, he may deny it upon oath; if he does not deny it, he is to pay him a fine of ten pounds in that money current in camp at the time.

"[20]. If anyone find vessels full of wine, let him drain off the wine so carefully that he will not break the vessels, or cut the bindings (*ligamina*) of the vessels, lest all the wine be drained off, to the loss of the army.

"[21]. If any fortress be taken, let the goods that are therein be carried off, but let it not be set on fire, unless perchance the marshal should do this.

"[22]. If anyone hunt with hunting dogs, he shall have the wild animal he has found and run down with the dogs, without opposition on the part of any.

"[23]. If anyone start a wild animal with greyhounds, it shall not of necessity be his, but shall belong to the one who seizes it.

"[24]. If anyone kill a wild animal with a spear or a sword, and before he lift it in his hand another seize it, it shall not belong to the latter, but the one who killed it shall have it without dispute.

"[25]. If anyone while hunting kill a wild animal with bow or crossbow, it shall be his."

This peace ordinance the archbishops, bishops, and abbots ratified, offering their right hands in token, and promised that violators of the peace would be chastised by the severity of the priestly office.

xxix (xxvii). The entire army had now assembled from both sides of the Alps, and a throng of men of keen intelligence and most learned in the law had gathered, and all were eager to learn where or against

---

[84] I Peter 3:9.

whom the prince would first direct their efforts. Then the emperor, combining with youthful vivacity the gravity of a king, that he might deserve to be both feared and loved, is said to have taken his stand where he could be clearly heard [85] and to have spoken as follows before the assemblage:

"We acknowledge that we owe great, inexpressibly great, thanks to the King of Kings, by Whose will we govern the kingdom as His servant and yours. He has bestowed upon us such great confidence in your probity and your prudence, which has been so often demonstrated, that, with your support and counsel, we can confidently face whatever may happen, anything that may threaten the security of the Roman empire. The Roman empire, we say, whose servant we recognize ourself to be, and whose authority lies with you who are the princes of the realm. Let no one suppose we wage wars at our whim; wars whose outcome is doubtful [86] and whose consequences—famine, thirst, loss of sleep, and at last death in many a form—we know to be terrible and fearful. It is not a lust for domination that drives us to battle but a fierce rebellion. It is Milan that has called you forth from your ancestral homes, that has snatched you from the dear embraces of your children and your wives, that has brought all these hardships down upon your heads by her impiety and defiance. It has given us just cause for war, since it stands revealed as rebellious against lawful authority. You will thus engage in warfare, not from greed or cruelty, but eager for peace, that the insolence of the wicked may be restrained, and that the good may be fittingly rewarded. [87]

"But if through sloth or cowardice we did not reply with avenging sword to the insult inflicted upon us by Milan, we would now undoubtedly be bearing it in vain, [88] and our patience in the matter would not so much be deserving of praise as our negligence worthy of execration. It is therefore in the service of justice that we justly claim your support, that the defiance of our adversaries may fail of effect and that the repute of the empire that has endured to our own times may be maintained under our rule. We are not inflicting injury, but are re-

---

[85] Josephus *Wars* III.x.2 and VI.ii.1.   [86] Vergil *Aeneid* X.160.

[87] In this statement the emperor seems to have in mind Gratian's *Decretum* C. XXIII. qu.i c.6. Material in the following paragraph also suggests familiarity with the *Decretum*, C. XXIII. qu.iii. c.1, 7 and qu.ii. c.1. The emperor's appeal to canon law in support of his advocacy of a "just war" is of some interest.

[88] That is, the sword; Romans 13:4.

moving it. And since the war is just, and waged at the command of a higher power, let all act now to secure the highest praise of knighthood, and the reward of your merits and efforts; be obedient to the needs of the state and perform with all your might whatever is commanded you to her advantage. With God's gracious aid the hostile city will not find us slow or weak in preserving what was added to the empire by our predecessors Charles and Otto—the first emperors beyond the mountains (the former of the West, the latter of the East Franks) to extend the bounds of the empire."

He spoke thus, and his words were applauded by the entire army. A kind of divine enthusiasm inspired the soldiers,[89] and they offered prayers to the Giver of salvation and encouragement to the Emperor Frederick, each in his native tongue. But the learned men and the jurists advised that the people of Milan, though wicked and infamous, should nevertheless be cited to judgment by lawful procedure, lest it should appear that violence had been practiced against them or sentence pronounced unlawfully in their absence. Now by lawful procedure they meant a judge's summons, followed by a second and a third, or a single summons in place of all three, which is termed a "peremptory" summons. Thus it was done.

xxx (xxviii). When the people of Milan saw the full force of war directed against them, they sent as envoys to the court men of learning, very skilled in speech. These, seeing that they were faced with prosecution and the punishments of a rigid law, and that the emperor could not be appeased by a large sum of money, and after seeking in vain the support of the princes, returned to their people with their mission unaccomplished.

The emperor, with the approval of the judges and the most eminent men of Italy, pronounced sentence of condemnation against the Milanese, declared them enemies, and made ready, with every device, to besiege the city. When this became known in Milan, the city was thrown into confusion and the very appearance of the town was changed. After the pleasures and delights produced by a long peace, all were suddenly filled with dismay. Restless and alarmed, each appraised the peril in his own fashion and according to his fear. The women, too, with a terror of war unusual in their powerful city, were greatly troubled, raised suppliant hands to heaven, bewailed the fate of their little

---

[89] Josephus *Wars* III.x.3.

children, and trembled at everything.[90] Yet there were many who with obstinate hearts set out to destroy themselves and the city. For in cities, those who have no property and cannot pay their debts invariably covet the goods and the tranquillity of others. They are eager for change; out of hatred for their own lot they seek to upset everything. In times of sedition they do not suffer, since, as it is said, "poverty is easy to bear; it has nothing to lose." Moreover, the young men who lived miserably by manual labor in the fields were tempted by the public doles, and preferred an idle life in the city to such unpleasant work. And thus this rabble, in control by virtue of its great numbers, as little solicitous of the city as of themselves, awaited with joyous spirits the outcome of the war, the nobler and better citizens acquiescing in silence through fear of such fellows. This was the state of affairs in the city.

xxxi (xxix). But Frederick, with royal clemency, delayed for several days, waiting to see whether perchance a saving penitence might recall the Milanese from their seditious attempt; whether perchance the fear of destruction and disaster might induce them to alter their plans. For the tranquil spirit of the emperor was prepared rather to grant gracious pardon to the repentant than to triumph over a ruined people after the devastation of the province. As they persisted in their previous stubbornness, however, he zealously set forth to undertake a siege, accompanied by all his forces. Moving his camp, he advanced as far as the river Adda. This stream, whose mid-channel separates the territories of Cremona and Milan, has very often checked their violent assaults upon one another. And, indeed, at that time it had become greatly swollen because of the melting snow in the Alps. Its bridges had been swept away, and it seemed impossible for the army to cross it. Besides, about a thousand armed horsemen, the most warlike of the troops of Milan, were marshaled on the farther bank of the river. They supposed that by the aid and assistance of the raging torrent they could easily defend its fords and bridges. But

"Meeting courageous hearts, courage no longer is safe." [91]

---

[90] This description of Milan as the emperor approached would be somewhat more impressive were it not borrowed almost word for word from Sallust's picture (*Catiline* xxxi.1–3) of Rome at the time of Catiline's conspiracy. The remainder of the paragraph is drawn almost entirely from *ibid.*, xxxvi.4 and xxxvii.3–8.

[91] Ovid *Met.* X.544.

For they were foiled when the king of Bohemia and Duke Conrad of Dalmatia,[92] with their men, suddenly dashed into the water, despising the danger. Although with great difficulty, and not without the loss of some of their men, they forded the bed of the raging stream undaunted, or rather swam across. The number of those whom the violence of the waters overwhelmed and drowned was estimated at about sixty.[93] The Milanese, after they learned that the king had effected a crossing, contrary to their hope and expectation, scattered in flight without fighting and returned to the city. Their baggage was left behind, and all this booty was plundered by our men.

From this first inauspicious endeavor, some prophesied disaster for the people of Milan, judging the outcome of the conflict from its beginning. The remainder of the army followed the Bohemians—a part by repairing the bridges, a part by braving the mad torrent—and set both themselves and their packs on the other side [July 24, 1158].[94]

xxxii (xxx). There was not far from this spot a certain stronghold of the Milanese called Trezzo, situated on a slight eminence rising above the level plain. The aforesaid stream, the Adda, washed it on one side; the other was fortified by a very strong encircling wall and a strong tower. A solid bridge, suited for the passage of a large military force, united it with its suburbs. The emperor, considering that its capture would ensure control of the passage [over the river], invested it, attacked it, and in a short time took it by storm. For the defenders of the castle, though utterly terrified by the discipline and skill of the soldiers, did indeed sustain the first attacks for a little while. Then, as they could hope for no opportunity for flight and no help from the city, knowing too that their very lives were at stake, they asked for peace, received it, and surrendered the fortress, counting it a great thing that in such evil case they had saved themselves. Frederick, placing a garrison there, made ready for the siege of the city.

xxxiii (xxxi). As he advanced into hostile territory, certain in the army, anxious for praise and distinction, rivaled one another in search

[92] Count Conrad of Dachau, titular duke of Dalmatia; see above, I.xxvi, and below, IV.xvii.

[93] One manuscript reads "two hundred" rather than "sixty."

[94] Otto Morena (pp. 48–50) gives a somewhat different version of this action, saying that the Milanese barred the passage over the bridge of Cassano until threatened from the rear by the Bohemians, when they fled. The bridge was passable, but gave way under the weight of the crossing troops.

of means to display their valor.[95] Among them were Count Ekkebert
of Pütten, a man distinguished for nobility, wealth, and strength of
mind and body, and certain other nobles and knights of the royal
household. They all combined, about a thousand mounted men, in the
hope of accomplishing some memorable deed, and rode almost to the
gates of the city. Their valor should have met with better reward; although they failed, yet one must give heed not to the outcome, but to
what was intended.[96] For they encountered a strong detachment of the
enemy. They first contended with spears, then fought with drawn
swords. And in the conflict one could scarcely distinguish on which
side each was fighting, since the men were in disorder and confusion
because of the narrow space. The dust that was stirred up blinded their
vision like the night. Moreover, the confusion rendered unintelligible
a word of command. There was no room for flight or for pursuit, but
those who had taken their stand in the front rank were under the necessity of killing or being killed; it was not in their power to retreat, for
those in the rear of each party were crowding their companions ahead,
and had left no empty space between the combatants. But when the
numbers of the enemy overcame the courage and skill of our men, and
the entire company was being driven back, the aforesaid Count Ekkebert, seeking to bear aid to one of his followers who had been thrown,
leaped from his horse, freed the knight, and practically alone routed
the victorious foe and pursued them as far as the city wall. For they all
fled, unable to withstand the man's might and daring. But doubtless
the fates—which a man cannot escape—dogged the hero. For being
surrounded on all sides by a throng of adversaries, he was brought to
the ground by a lance and, after his helmet and breastplate had been
pulled off, was decapitated. No one came to his rescue because the narrow place prevented anyone from bearing aid. And so this most noble
count and man of royal blood was grievously slain, greatly lamented
not only by his own people, but also by strangers. But I remember that
it was said by some that he had been taken alive and cruelly beheaded
inside the city. Certain other nobles were slain there, and the royal

[95] Cf. Sallust *Catiline* vii.6 and ix.2.

[96] Josephus *Wars* VI.I.8. Rahewin's account of this engagement (to the end of the
present chapter) is in all essentials borrowed from the same place. To make the
passages apply, Rahewin places the battle at the very walls of Milan; both Otto Morena
(p. 53) and the Milanese *Gesta Federici in Lombardia* (pp. 29–30) put it at some
distance from the city.

vassals N. and N. Some were taken captive. The rest returned to camp.

xxxiv. But the reproaches of the princes and an angry emperor assailed the returning soldiers. He spoke after this fashion: "The people of Milan do everything deliberately and prudently, devising stratagems and pitfalls, and fortune favors their wiles. But our people, usually served by fortune because of their discipline and their habit of obeying their leaders, now err by the opposite conduct. Not undeservedly, therefore, they are defeated and beaten back, for the worst fault of all is to fight without a leader in the emperor's presence, for even to be victorious without the leader's command is reprehensible." [97]

He announced that he would punish to the full extent of the law all who in future should act presumptuously or make even the least move contrary to orders. But the troops that surrounded him made entreaty for their fellow soldiers and besought him to condone the rashness of a few in view of the obedience of all; they would atone for their present guilt by compensatory good conduct in the future. The emperor was placated by their entreaties, and besides thought that he ought to pardon the deed in the interests of the army as a whole; he earnestly admonished them to act more prudently hereafter. But since he had been provoked, he now gave more earnest thought to the means whereby he might take vengeance upon his adversaries.

xxxv (xxxii). Therefore on the following day, the dawning of the eighth before the Kalends of August,[98] Frederick led his army to the siege of the city, dividing his troops into seven divisions. He put in charge of each, from his princes, divisional leaders, whom the ancients used to call centurions or hekatonarchs or chiliarchs, together with standard-bearers and other custodians of discipline and order. Moreover, soldiers were sent ahead to accompany the road workers (*stratoribus viarum*), to make the roads level and remove obstacles, lest the army be exhausted by a difficult march. Grouped about the eagle and the other standards were the trumpeters and hornblowers. The servants of the several companies, bringing along on mules and other beasts

[97] This address was made not by Frederick Barbarossa at Milan, but by Titus at Jerusalem; all the present chapter (save for necessary minor alterations) is taken from Josephus *Wars* v.iii.4.

[98] It would seem that the engagement just narrated took place on August 5, and the following day would thus be the eighth day before the Ides rather than the eighth day before the Kalends (July 25). Much of the account following in this chapter is taken from Josephus *Wars* iii.v.5 and vi.2.

of burden the baggage of the soldiers, proceeded with the infantry. Following these came the men who conveyed machines and other devices for the capture of cities. Last of all the companies was the throng of mercenaries. When the order of march had been thus set, and the troops warned that no one should leave his place, filled with martial spirit they loudly invoked divine aid. Then they advanced quietly and with all decorum, each man keeping to his own place, as if in battle. Had an open-minded spectator happened to witness the maneuver, I think he might have understood more clearly the saying: "Fair as the moon, clear as the sun, and terrible as an army with banners." [99]

xxxvi. At the end of the march,[100] Frederick with his entire army of about a hundred thousand or more armed men reached Milan. There he pitched camp, although keeping the soldiers ready for battle, lest any attack be made on that day. But those who had come forth from the city stood, fully armed, on top of the wall, making no outcry whatever. It is uncertain whether the appearance of the emperor inspired awe and silence, or struck all with terror. Stationing the troops around the city, facing each gate, he made ready for the siege.

xxxvii (xxxiii). Although in a previous book [101] mention has been made of the situation and characteristics of this city, it seems necessary to add that it stands out from all sides because of the level plain, and is very large by the nature of the ground.[102] Its circumference comprises over a hundred stadia.[103] It is surrounded by a wall, around which, in place of a river, there is a very broad and water-filled moat,[104] which their consul had prudently constructed only the year before, in fear of the coming war, though many opposed it and were indignant. They do not set as much store as other cities on the height of their towers. For, placing their confidence in the numbers and valor of themselves and their allies, they thought it impossible that their city could be invested with siege by any king or emperor. Whence this city

---

[99] Song of Solomon 6:10.

[100] Much of this chapter is borrowed from Josephus *Wars* III.vi.3.

[101] See above, II.xiv.

[102] Orosius II.vi, viii–x, also quoted in *Two Cities* II.xi.

[103] A stadium was about six hundred feet, so that this would be a circumference of some twelve miles, which would be a very considerable exaggeration.

[104] The moat thus formed is the present *Naviglio Grande.* Rahewin's phraseology here is drawn from Orosius, *loc. cit.*

is said to have been hostile to the kings from ancient times, practicing such insolence as constantly to plot rebellion against its princes and take delight in the division of the realm. It preferred two lords rather than one justly reigning over it; and, being a fickle city, it mocked at the fortune of both and was loyal neither to the one nor to the other. If anyone seek proof of this, let him turn to Liutprand, who wrote of the exploits of the Lombards.[105]

xxxviii (xxxiv). After the various gates of the city had been assigned to the princes of the army (as has been said), all vied in speedily securing the camp by means of a wall, stakes, palisades, and other defenses against surprise assaults of the enemy. For they supposed that so great a city could not be attacked by mantlets, towers, rams, and other such machines,[106] but rather it would be forced to surrender when exhausted by a long siege, or might be overcome in battle if they sallied forth through confidence in their numbers.

The townsmen no less actively attended to their interests,[107] deranging the fortifications of the camps and making frequent sallies, while their archers and slingers wounded many. Stationed at the extreme wing of the army were Conrad, count palatine of the Rhine, brother of the emperor, and Duke Frederick of Swabia, with the Swabians and other troops, carrying on the siege around the gate assigned them. Hoping that they would win an easy victory or, after performing some deed of valor, might purchase fame at the cost of their lives, the Milanese thought it opportune to attack them either because they were fewer in number than the other detachments and their leaders younger, or because, being separated from the chief strength of the army, they could not obtain aid. Therefore, after sunset, when all the soldiers (excepting only the sentinels) hoped by quiet sleep to refresh their bodies exhausted by toil, the Milanese opened the gates and sent forth their most warlike men, who scattered the pickets and advanced to the camp of the aforesaid leaders,[108] attacking and inflicting wounds. When the Germans became aware of the arrival of the enemy, they were at first thrown into confusion by the sudden and unexpected event, producing on all sides fear and commotion.[109] Then they called to one

---

[105] Liutprand of Cremona *Antapodosis* I.xxxvii.

[106] Cf. Sallust *Jugurtha* xxi.3.   [107] Cf. *ibid.*, liv.6 and lxxv.10.

[108] Josephus *Wars* III.vii.17.

[109] Sallust *Jugurtha* liii.7. In the following ten sentences, Rahewin has borrowed extensively from this same work, liii.8, lx.2, lvii.4, lii.6, l.6, li.4.

another, shouted encouragement, took up arms, and met and drove
back their assailants. Outcry was mingled with exhortation, the din of
arms rose to the heavens, missiles flew in all directions. Each fought
as he best knew how, some at close quarters with swords, some with
stones or other objects. Not far from here the king of Bohemia was
encamped. As soon as he heard the uproar, he decided that he ought
to go to the assistance of his struggling comrades. Therefore he ordered his men to take up arms and to mount with what speed they
could. He himself, with picked knights and trumpeters and drummers,
led the way. The mounds and dirt walls of the vineyards did not delay
them, the unevenness and strangeness of the ground did not check
their advance. Indeed, the horses of the Slavs, accustomed to such obstacles, easily avoided them. When our men learned, from the sound
of the trumpets and drums, of the approach of their friend the king,
they stood their ground more boldly and hopefully, exhorting one another not to yield or to suffer the enemy to prevail when now on the
very verge of flight. The Bohemians came up. Then at length the
fighting was marked by the utmost exertion. Uttering violent cries
they dashed together with opposing standards. The king himself
pushed boldly forward to fight at close quarters, aided the hard-
pressed, struck down the foe, playing the part of a valiant soldier as
well as that of a good king. When the townsmen saw that, contrary to
their plans, they had plunged into the very midst of the enemy [110] and
that they could not withstand the king's attack, they turned their backs.
Our men kept at their heels as they fled and pursued them to the very
passageways of the gates. Thus they secured for themselves immunity
from future attacks. Some of the enemy were killed, many taken captive, a large proportion wounded.[111]

xxxix (xxxv). But because our age cannot recall having seen so famous a siege of so haughty a city [112] (for not only the fighting forces of
the German but also those of the Italian realm were there united), all
the most famous and those eager for praise strove to gain renown by
outdoing one another in some outstanding deed. And so Otto, count
palatine of Bavaria, of whom mention has often been made, with his
two brothers, Frederick and Otto the Younger, and other knights associated with them, observed with close attention the activities of the

[110] Sallust *Catiline* ix.2–5, with Catiline played by the king of Bohemia.
[111] Sallust *Jugurtha* lx.2.   [112] Cf. Josephus *Wars* Prologue.

enemy in the vicinity of a gate which they themselves had barricaded. Now on a certain day, when they had noticed that the defenders were loitering about and that there were but few guards at the gate, it seemed the proper time to try their fortune. So, as evening came on, they secretly ordered the knights to arm themselves, and the varlets to have ready fire with a bundle of dry kindling, that when the signal was given they might suddenly dash forth and burn both the bridge and, if possible, the gate itself. They obeyed the word of command and, at the nod of their officers, rushed quickly forward and reached the defenses of the bridge on a small rise, and (as instructed) were not slow to hurl the fire. The people of the city, roused by the sudden tumult, were thrown into a panic and in their terror were uncertain what could best be done.[113] When they saw the defenses and the ramparts ablaze with leaping flames, they feared lest the fire, finding dry fuel, might in its swift course destroy not only the bridges and the gate but the city itself. Shouting and confusion filled the city, and men ran about wildly, armed and unarmed, to check the fire. The two forces clashed and strove with all their might; the conflagration and torches and brands illumined the dark night. The crash of blows, the groans of the smitten, the cries of encouragement resounded. Our men strove mightily for the success of their attempt, the enemy to extinguish the blaze and dislodge our men from the gate. The counts, leaders of the fighting in this combat as in many others, exposed themselves to all dangers. Like outstanding warriors they made their strength of body and greatness of spirit so clear in the sight of all that even the enemy testified to their valor, and every spectator bore witness to it. Now, after great effort had been expended and the strife had continued into the night, the soldiers returned to camp. Many on both sides were wounded; but the protection of darkness lessened the extent of the losses.

xl (xxxvi). The Milanese, deeming it shameful to be slack in attacking us, sought to display their great temerity and daring at the proper time and place. They roused our soldiers against them, wounding them whether alert or off their guard, not by a numerous band, but by a few—archers, slingers, or even swordsmen. And, indeed, those who had participated in previous conflicts acted with greater caution; but others, as though less experienced, were ready to fight at any time.

---

[113] Sallust *Jugurtha* lxvii.1.

And so, as they frequently carried on this harmful practice at the gate which Duke Henry [Jasomirgott] of Austria was guarding (a man renowned for the nobility of his family and of his spirit, and the emperor's uncle), not thinking it seemly to let this conduct pass unpunished he made ready to amend and chastise it when the opportunity presented itself. Therefore, calling his own men to arms, and adding to them the Hungarian auxiliaries (very good archers) and the other forces associated with him, he prepared to storm the gate with all his might. This could not be concealed from the people of Milan, and as they perceived the preparations of our men, they judged it disgraceful if, though equal—nay, superior—in numbers, they should be inferior in courage when they met. Marching forth accordingly in their companies and cohorts, they joined battle; and with the utmost violence the combatants slew, wounded, captured, and pursued one another. Then ensued a horrible spectacle of pursuit, flight, slaughter, and capture.[114] Men and horses were struck down and many who had been wounded were unable to flee or to lie still, now striving to rise only to fall straightway. Finally, the whole ground was strewn with missiles, weapons, and corpses, and was drenched with blood. Again the fighting on the part of the townsmen was inferior, and the duke himself, whose prowess was there amazingly displayed, was undoubtedly victorious.[115] He drove them within their fortifications and thereafter had a respite from their customary sallies. Among others of the people of Milan who fell in that battle, there was slain one of their noblest, whom, as rumor then had it, they had thought to choose as their ruler.[116] Upon hearing of his death, the whole city went into mourning. They ransomed the dead man's body with the living prisoners they had taken and much money besides, and buried him, paying him the honor of a royal funeral.

xli (xxxvii). It is perhaps not inappropriate to mention [117] that a certain townsman, a man well pleased with himself, came toward the emperor's camp and made many boastful remarks. Taunting our men

---

[114] This and the two following sentences are taken from Sallust *Jugurtha* ci.11.

[115] *Ibid.*, cii.1.

[116] One manuscript names him as *Stasius*, who is probably the Milanese captain Tazo de Mandello, whose death in a sally against the Bohemians is recorded by Otto Morena (p. 55).

[117] The following chapter is largely taken from Josephus *Wars* vi.ii.10 and Liutprand *Antapodosis* i.xxi.

with lack of skill in riding, he challenged all the bravest and those most experienced in horsemanship to single combat. And he began now to give his responsive steed its head, in furious gallop, now with tight rein to guide it in circles, as is customary in this type of horsemanship, and presently to ride about in various involved figures. Many of those who stood near showed their scorn, but there were among them (as usually happens) some who were afraid. Some, indeed, were struck by the not unreasonable thought that one ought not to fight with a man desirous of death; and to come to blows with those whom it would not be a great thing to conquer, and by whom one might even be shamefully defeated, seemed a proof not of valor but of folly. But as no one made a move for a long time, and he indulged in much mockery of the cowardice of our men, the noble Count Albert of Tyrol, ready for any display of his courage, sitting a palfrey and unarmed save for his shield and spear, came to meet the aforesaid Ligurian and unhorsed the empty boaster. He disdained to kill him where he lay, content with the praise of having shown that he could. So Count Albert, having vindicated our men, returned without boasting to his own people. He was a man of little ostentation, who always wished to be found more ready of hand than of tongue. So from day to day various contests for the display of courage and for fame were waged among our princes against the Ligurians.

xlii (xxxviii). Meanwhile, the emperor himself strove unceasingly for the destruction and overthrow of the city. He went around the walls now with only a few, now with many picked knights, seeking its weakest points,[118] and tried in every way to provoke the besieged to an encounter and to battle. By these circuits he so subdued and held in check the opposite side of the city (which had not yet been so straitened and subjugated by the siege as to prevent the citizens pasturing their cattle outside and to deny them opportunity for ingress and egress) that at length the citizens bowed their necks and learned by experience what it meant to be besieged. When the emperor went his rounds, tumult arose in the city in expectation of an assault. There was great trepidation; signals sounded, trumpets blew, the strong took up arms, women and feeble old men took to lamentation. But no one dared come forth; it was only for the defense of the city that the armed and undaunted youths took their stand in a circle about it.

[118] Josephus *Wars* v.vi.2.

They made no sallies at the gate where the prince's own soldiery carried on the siege. It is uncertain whether they were restrained by fear or through respect for the emperor.

xliii. There was, not far from the wall—that is, about a bowshot off—a certain very strong tower built of squared stones solidly constructed. But it was the size of the stones that was remarkable. For the tower did not consist of ordinary small stones, or such as it was credible that men could carry. But it was so fashioned by the hands of the builders, that being supported by four columns, like Roman workmanship, nowhere—or scarcely anywhere—could a joint between stones be discovered.[119] Hence also it was called the "Roman arch," whether erected by some ancient emperor of the Romans for ornamentation and commemoration as a triumphal arch or, as we find recorded in the Exploits of the Lombards,[120] devised by one of our kings for the capture and destruction of the city. There were in it living quarters for men and sleeping chambers large enough for forty or more beds.[121] There had been collected there supplies both of arms and of food such as a consideration of their need rendered desirable for the time of the siege. There the Ligurians had placed their reserves with a double purpose: both to keep the tower from being of use to the enemy (for from it whatever went on in the city might be seen as though from a watchtower) and also that they might learn whatever was taking place in our camp and whatever our army was devising.

Frederick, for opposite considerations, decided to storm this tower. But since it seemed that because of its strength it could not be shattered by siege engines or machines or any sort of artillery, he encircled it with a triple line of slingers and archers, and so great was their number and their skill in shooting that anyone who put in an appearance on the battlements would be seeking certain death. Accordingly, forced by dire necessity, they sought terms of surrender and asked that their lives be spared. Upon receiving safe conduct, they surrendered the fortification and withdrew. Thenceforth that citadel was of use to our men.

xliv (xxxix). No one displayed greater zeal and courage in this siege than the forces of Cremona and Pavia, and to none of the besiegers did the besieged show more hostility and bitterness. For in the course

---

[119] The description of this tower is mostly taken from Josephus *Wars* v.iv.4. It was situated just southeast of the city.   [120] Liutprand *Antapodosis* III.xiv.
[121] From Josephus *Wars* v.iv.4, with the figure of "one hundred" reduced to "forty."

of the long enmity and strife between Milan and these cities, many thousands of men had been killed or subjected to dire captivity by both sides, lands had been laid waste by pillage and fire. And since they had been unable to even accounts with Milan, which was superior in its own strength and in its allies, seizing this timely opportunity those cities determined to avenge their wrongs. Therefore, these kinsmen raged against each other not as a related people, not as in civil war, but as if against enemies from without, against foreigners, with such cruelty as would be unseemly even against barbarians. The vineyards, fig plantations, and olive groves of the Milanese were torn up by the roots, cut down, stripped of their bark, and used as fuel. When they battled at close quarters and some luckless wretch was captured on either side, if by the besiegers, they would plunge a dagger into his throat or transfix him with a spear in sight of the enemy,[122] and if by the besieged, not to be outdone in cruelty, they would dismember a captive and cast him forth as a pitiful spectacle to his people. And such was the intercourse of the Italians (*conlatinorum*) with one another.

xlv (xl). And now the people of Milan were afflicted by many misfortunes. Moreover, despair grew with hunger in the city, and from day to day both evils increased.[123] For there was a countless throng, assembled from the entire region, and the food supply varied, since the stronger had more, while the weaker complained of a lack. Indeed, famine is considered the supreme disaster, for in time of famine men neglect what deserves reverence.[124] To this was added the punishment of divine vengeance, and disease and pestilence afflicted practically the entire city. Therefore, under compulsion of famine, sword, and pestilence alike,[125] the people were inclined to surrender, and already a great number of them were thinking of flight. But those of more valiant spirit were intent on sedition, saying that they were willing to barter their lives for their city's freedom and honor. As such disagreements arose, some of the more reasonable, preferring peace to war, determined to call the people together to consider the common advantage, and to dissuade them from rebellion at so great a peril.

The author of this scheme is said to have been Count Guido of Biandrate,[126] a prudent man, an accomplished speaker, and skilled in

---

[122] Sallust *Jugurtha* c.i.
[124] *Ibid.*, v.x.3.
[126] See above, ii.xviii.

[123] Josephus *Wars* v.x.2.
[125] Cf. Sallust *Jugurtha* xxiv.3.

persuasion. A native-born citizen of Milan, he had at this time conducted himself with such moderation and prudence that he was both beloved by the court and not an object of suspicion among the citizens —a very difficult thing to manage under such circumstances. Well suited, therefore, to be a trustworthy mediator, he is said to have spoken as follows before the assembly:

xlvi. "If I have hitherto kept faith with you, if I have wished that the position and the honor of Milan should continue unharmed and unshaken, I have done what I should. From my early youth so much kindness has been shown, so many benefits have been conferred upon me by you, that I know myself to be incompetent and unable to express my thanks, unless perchance a clear conscience and good will have won me some merit in your sight. Of these things, relying on your probity, I confidently make you my witness. Hence I do not fear being criticized by any good citizen in the present turn of circumstances, even though he hears from me something contrary to his liking and desires. For I deem myself free from those faults which ought to disqualify one for deliberation on critical matters. These are, as a certain writer says, 'hate, friendship, anger, and pity. Where these are present, the mind does not easily perceive the truth.' [127] Your dignity, fame, and fortune hitherto have not been in obscurity, but on the heights; all men know your deeds. But it was fitting that in the greatest good fortune there should be the least license.[128] We know what and how many kings Milan has set up; we know what and how many kings she has driven from power. But surely fortune rules everything; 'She exalts and diminishes all things by whim rather than by merit.' [129] This fortune has changed a little; for she is changeable, and she is consistently fickle and impermanent. Let us move with the wheel. Perhaps he who is now swept to the ground shall again be carried aloft to the stars. He was of my opinion who said: 'Change is the characteristic of all things. [130] I know there are those that say: 'Liberty is a priceless possession.' [131] It is a fine thing to fight for liberty. I admit it. Yet this should be done at the beginning; if one has been subdued and long obedient and then shakes off the yoke, he seems rather to yearn for an

---

[127] Sallust *Catiline* li.1–2.

[128] For this and the preceding sentence, see *ibid.*, li.11–12.

[129] *Ibid.*, viii.1.   [130] Terence *Eunuchus* ii.276.

[131] *Digest* L.xvii.106, quoted above, III.xii. The remainder of this speech is largely drawn from an address of Josephus to the besieged Jews in Jerusalem (*Wars.* v.ix.3–4).

evil death than for liberty. It is a very powerful law, binding upon wild beasts as well as upon men, to yield to the mightier. Victory is at the command of the powerful. He who resists power, resists also the ordinance of God.[132] Therefore, you have reason to fear that you are resisting not only the emperor, but even God. It is hard, I admit, after long peace, after a long habit of freedom, to bear the yoke and the bridle. But the greatness of the empire and the nobility of its ruler will solace the disgrace of subjection. Our fathers and our ancestors were superior to us in honesty, righteousness, and other good traits; they sought for glory, honor, and liberty as much as we, or more; nevertheless they were unable to withstand the empire across the Alps. Remember Charles the Great and Otto, the first German emperor. Therefore, having already experienced some of the varying hazards of war, it is best to change your minds before an utter disaster, and, while you may, act upon wise counsel. There is great hope for us in the mercy of an emperor who will not be angry with us to the end, unless we ourselves have defied him to the very end. Moreover, though our walls cannot be forced quickly, famine and pestilence will fight for them. I entreat each one of you to call up before his eyes the children, wives, and parents whom in a little while—unless you change your intention—war or famine will destroy. No one can suppose it is through cowardice that I give this advice, but upon consideration of the dangers. I myself am prepared to die for my people, for my city, and I shall gladly pay my blood as the price of your safety."

xlvii (xli). After Count Guido had ceased speaking, the Milanese showed their assent or disagreement, one by word, another by gesture.[133] But the advice of the more sensible prevailed over folly. Accordingly, becoming of one mind, they negotiated through their consuls and the leaders of the city, first with the king of Bohemia and the duke of Austria, then (with these as intermediaries) with the other princes, and finally sent them to the emperor to plead for peace. The prince, with royal clemency and his natural humanity, desiring to save the citizens for the city and the city for the citizens, rejoiced when he learned that the people were thinking of peace. He called a council and upon seeing that the hearts of all sought this with the greatest eagerness, he dealt with them concerning an agreement and terms of peace.

[132] Romans 13:2.　　　　[133] Sallust *Catiline* lii.1.

A document (of which this is a copy) was thereupon drawn up [September 1, 1158], which shows that the terms were as follows:

"In the name of our Lord Jesus Christ. This is the agreement, in accordance with which the people of Milan are to return to and remain in the favor of their lord the emperor:

"[1].[134] They will not prevent the rebuilding of the cities of Lodi and Como, and henceforth will not attack or destroy them. They will also exempt them, throughout their entire domain, from the *fodrum* [135] and subsidy (*viaticum*) and from every kind of exaction, and will interfere with them no more, that they may be free cities (even as the people of Milan are free from them) save in ecclesiastical affairs, wherein they have relationship with the archbishop and church of Milan.

"[2]. All the people of Milan, from the least of them even to the greatest, from the age of fourteen years to the age of seventy, shall swear fidelity to the lord emperor without evil intent, and shall keep it.

"[3]. They shall erect a royal palace in honor of the lord emperor under the direction of competent men, and shall keep it in good condition with due respect and in good faith.

"[4]. They shall pay to the lord emperor or the lady empress or to the court the money they have promised in reparation for damages, at fixed times: that is, a third within thirty days from the time at which this agreement is confirmed, another third within a week of the festival of the blessed Martin [November 11], and the third part remaining in the week of Epiphany [January 6]. And after these sums have thus been paid, they are to be bound by no private promises. This is the sum total of money promised: nine thousand marks of silver or of gold or in the coinage of the same value and worth.

"[5]. For the faithful performance and observance of these briefly outlined conditions, they shall give three hundred hostages, captains, vavasors, and common people, such as shall be approved by the lord archbishop of Milan and the count [Guido] of Biandrate and Marchese William of Montferrat and three consuls (if these arrangements are

---

[134] The numbering of the twelve articles that follow has been inserted by the translator.

[135] A tax, in kind or in money, for the support of an army; see above, II.xv, xxxv.

pleasing to the lord emperor), who have sworn to make this selection
faithfully. All the hostages are to be kept in the land of Italy except
fifty or less, who at the instance of Vladislav, king of the Bohemians,
and of the other princes, are to be transported beyond the mountains,
if it shall please the lord emperor. But those to whom hostages are
entrusted in Italy are to swear in the presence of citizens of Milan
appointed for this, that after a predetermined lapse of time, if the
aforesaid conditions have been observed, the hostages are to be freed
within a week after the Milanese have asked it. Furthermore, three
German princes shall guarantee that those hostages taken beyond the
mountains (if any are) shall on like terms be faithfully restored.

"[6]. The consuls who are now in office are to continue in office by
virtue of the authorization and permission of the lord emperor until the
next Kalends of February [February 1, 1159], and are to take oath
for their consulship to the lord emperor. But the succeeding consuls
are to be elected by the people, and the election is to be confirmed by
the emperor himself. Half of them are to come to him, so long as he is
in Lombardy. But when he is elsewhere, two of the consuls are to come
to him and after taking oath are to receive the office of their consulship
from the lord emperor, for themselves and for their associates, who
are to swear the same oath of allegiance to the lord emperor in the
presence of the people of their city. But if a legate has been sent into
Italy by the lord emperor, the same shall be done in his presence and
by him.

"[7]. Moreover, legates of the lord emperor who are sent into
Italy, if they enter the city, are to sit in the palace and decide for the
honor of the empire the cases brought to them.

"[8]. Before the besieging camp is removed, all captives are to be
placed in the power of the king of Bohemia, who shall give them security, both for himself and for the honorable princes, that he will turn
over those captives to the lord emperor, if the lord emperor makes
peace between them [the Milanese] and the people of Cremona, Pavia,
Novara, Como, Lodi, and Vercelli—and not only the Milanese, but
also their allies, the people of Tortona, Crema, and Isola— [136] saving
the honor of the lord emperor, and the friendships of the Milanese
continuing untarnished and unchanged. But if peace is not made by
them with the above-mentioned cities, these former captives are to be

---

[136] Isola Comacina, in Lake Como; see below, IV.xxx.

returned to them, nor shall they and their friends be deprived of the favor of the lord emperor on this account.[137]

"[9]. The imperial regalia, such as coinage, market tolls (*theloneum*), transit tolls (*pedaticum*), gate tolls (*portus*) [138] countships, and other similar matters if there be any, the commune of the people of Milan is to relinquish and not to administer hereafter. And if anyone shall resolve to keep these by reason of old custom,[139] and shall refuse to seek justice before the lord emperor or his representative, the people of Milan shall exact retribution, according to their ability, from his person and his possessions, and shall restore the royal prerogatives to the lord emperor without deceit or evil intent.

"[10]. By the terms of this agreement and ordinance, the lord emperor shall receive back into his favor the people of Milan and (with a penalty of one hundred and twenty marks) the people of Crema, and shall publicly absolve them and their allies from the ban, in full court, and shall restore to them all their captives, old and new, into the hand of the king of the Bohemians. Moreover, after the hostages and captives have been given, on the second or third day the army will raise the siege, and the lord emperor will deal graciously with the people of Milan and their allies.

"[11]. The commune of Milan shall fully observe the aforesaid conditions in good faith, without deceit or evil intent, save when it shall withhold compliance through lawful impediment or by agreement reached with Frederick, the Roman emperor, his representative, or his successor.

"[12]. The people of Milan may collect the aforesaid money from those with whom they were customarily allied, except the people of Como, Lodi, and the county of Seprio,[140] who recently swore allegiance to the lord emperor."

[137] This article would apply to the prisoners taken by the Milanese from Frederick's Italian allies, the cities of the first group. The emperor is bound to seek peace between them and Milan, but if he fails, the prisoners will be handed back to Milan. In the meantime, they will be held by the German princes.

[138] The English equivalents of these various terms are approximations. The *theloneum* may cover any tax on goods; the *pedaticum* was a toll collected from foot travelers, as distinct from *vectigalia* (mentioned IV.vii) which was employed in the sense of tolls on wagon transit; the *portus* might be, among other things, either a gate or a harbor toll.

[139] *Per usum;* but two manuscripts read *per divisum*, and a third, *per violentiam*.

[140] Twenty miles northwest of Milan.

xlviii (xlii). After these terms of peace had been accepted by both sides, upon receiving safe conduct the Milanese came to the court to be restored to favor, in the following order and array: at the head, all the clergy and their attendants, with the archbishop, crosses borne before them, their feet bare, and in lowly attire. Then came the consuls and elders of the city, likewise in disheveled garb, barefooted, bearing drawn swords upon their necks. It was a great sight; there was a very great crush of onlookers, and, on the part of many who were of a milder disposition, a feeling of compassion, when they beheld those, shortly before so arrogant and boastful of their deeds of wickedness, now so humble and trembling. So great change was pitiable, even in an enemy.[141] All the soldiery had taken early possession of such places as afforded so much as standing room, leaving the emperor and the princes barely sufficient room to look on, and allowing those who came up scarcely the necessary access.

Thereupon the divine emperor, looking upon them with gracious gaze, said[142] he was glad that God had led so renowned a city and so great a people to prefer peace to war, and that they had relieved him of the bitter necessity of punishing them. He preferred to rule over devoted and willing subjects, rather than men under compulsion. And if they had acquiesced in this from the beginning, they would have suffered no hurt but would have received many advantages. But since it had pleased Divine Providence that they should make trial both of the power and of the friendship of the empire, they must endeavor (the more easily to atone for their mistakes) to show repentance for what they had done. He could be won over more quickly by obedience than by war; anyone—even a coward—could start a fight, but the outcome rested with the victors.[143]

In reply they uttered a few words in defense of their conduct, with downcast eyes and suppliant voice.[144] They had not taken up arms with intent hostile to the empire, but had been unable to permit the lands of their fathers, by every legal right now their own, to be laid waste by their neighbors. As for the rest, if they were spared, they were

[141] This and the preceding sentence are drawn from Josephus *Wars* VI.viii.4. The following sentence comes from the same work, VII.v.3.

[142] The remarks here attributed to Frederick are essentially those ascribed to Sulla in Sallust *Jugurtha* cii.2–11, while the rejoinder of the Milanese which follows comes largely from the same work, cii.12–15, the reply of King Bocchus to Sulla.

[143] Cf. *ibid.*, lxxxiii.1.   [144] Sallust *Catiline* xxxi.7.

willing to exert themselves (being free from fear of evil) that the emperor's benevolence and favor toward them might the more readily be maintained.

xlix (xliii). Presently, the conditions of peace, which had been reduced to writing, were read, and when all who were there had indicated their favor and assent thereto, they obtained peace and friendship, and the imperial banner was flown over the city in token of the victory. There was great and prolonged rejoicing in the camp and in the city, and among the captives. When they came, in a great and long file to the emperor's feet, their friends and relatives received them with tears of joy. They commiserated their pale faces, their soiled clothing, their dreadful emaciation. Those whom they had known as beardless youths were now unrecognizable by reason of age, white hair, and prison squalor.[145] What happiness was there, and how much running to and fro, when a father found his long lost son, a brother his brother, a father-in-law his son-in-law, a relative his kinsman. Upon finding, they hailed the lost one with joyful greetings and embraced him, gladly calling one another by name, and speaking together in friendly conversation. Had there persisted in our mild and pious emperor any trace of the haughtiness of kings of olden time, he must have ordained that the gladness of this day should be forever celebrated by the Italians with the other festive occasions. This triumph was solemnized on the sixth day before the Ides of September [September 8, 1158].

l (xliv). The Roman prince, moving his camp from Milan, wore the crown at Monza, the seat of his Italian realm.[146] Its church, long ago subjugated by the people of Milan and almost destroyed, he restored to its former freedom and gave orders that the cathedral should be restored in magnificent style at his own expense. And since he hoped that, in consequence of the subjection of so great a city, the uprisings of the Italians would for the most part be checked, he permitted a large part of the army to return home with their leaders. Foremost among these was the king of Bohemia, also the duke of Austria with

---

[145] This colorful description may be regarded with some suspicion; the siege of Milan had lasted barely a month.

[146] Monza, eight miles north of Milan, was the capital of the Lombard kings. The *coronatur* refers to the ceremonial wearing of the crown rather than to the coronation with the Italian crown, which took place at Pavia three years previously. See above, II.xxvii; cf. also Simonsfeld, I, 305, note 83.

the Hungarians, Arnold, archbishop of Mainz, Duke Berthold of Burgundy, counts and margraves, and a great number of the nobles.

After dismissing them with the greatest cheerfulness, Frederick turned his attention to settling all the other affairs of Italy. But by this time so great terror and fear had taken hold of the entire land that no one, indeed, offered open rebellion, though secretly many had malice in their hearts.

li (xlv). For a citizen of Verona named *Turisindus* had, with his adherents, occupied the royal castle called Garda.[147] When certain of the Veronese were ordered to restore it to the emperor, they refused, and were declared enemies. They involved certain other citizens of Verona as associates and partners in their temerity. Therefore, the emperor moved in that direction, unexpectedly forded the river Adige below Verona, marched through their territory (which had long been inviolate and had feared no foe), and for a time permitted his soldiers to devastate the fields, to plunder and burn the castles. And rightly so, that he might inspire his enemies with a fear of rebellion, and provide for the safety of those people of the region who were loyal.[148] Returning again, he crossed the Adige by ford, as he had before, using no bridge or boat. For so great was the mildness of the weather, so great the fertility of the soil, so dry were the greatest streams and so diminished their currents, that the elements themselves were declared to be serving the fortune of the divine emperor and favoring his wishes.

lii. And thus when, during these days, hostages were taken from all the cities, and Otto, the count palatine of Bavaria, had been sent to Ferrara for this purpose, he crossed without boats the bed of the Po (where it divides, to the protection of the city), coming upon the city suddenly and unexpectedly, and having set everything in order as he desired, returned with forty hostages. This incident terrified most of the region. It seemed incredible, from the fact that Ferrara, trusting in its natural defenses (since the Po is stagnant there and creates impassible swamps), is fearless and proud, and mocks at and despises the entire vicinity.

Afterward, when the emperor crossed the Po River to administer

---

[147] On the eastern shore of the lake of Garda, northwest of Verona.

[148] All this, however, does not seem to have gained Frederick the castle of Garda, for *Turisindus* still held it five years later (Otto Morena, pp. 164, 171).

the royal estates of the house of Matilda,[149] he decided (following the example of the emperors of old) to expel and bar the throng of soldiers' servants, prostitutes, and camp followers who had attached themselves to the army in great numbers and might enervate the spirits of the soldiers.

liii (xlvi). Meanwhile, as all Italy was quiet and seemed to have exchanged the unrest of war for the tranquillity of peace, Frederick, thinking time lost in which he had not produced some memorial of his greatness, began to build a new city for the people of Lodi, where, if perchance the people of Milan should renew their former enmity and fall upon them, they might be safer from their attack. Therefore, with the greatest foresight, and amid the liveliest expressions of gratitude, he chose a place near the river Adda, defended on all sides by the circuit of the river, save only one inconsiderable point of approach to be enclosed by a wall and a breastwork. By expending a very large sum on the construction of this city, he afforded a remarkable proof of his generosity.

Next he proclaimed a general diet for all the Italian cities and nobles to be held at Roncaglia at the feast of the blessed Martin [November 11], where he would both proclaim the laws of peace and would discourse (with the very necessary collaboration of scholars) on the rights of the kingdom, which had now for a long time been veiled in obscurity among them and had fallen into neglect, and would elucidate what had long been ignored.

liv (xlvii). At about the same time, while Manuel, the emperor of Constantinople, was staying in the territory about Antioch with an army, opposing the Turks, one of the servants of the palace, namely, the *caniclinus,* whom we may call the chancellor, plotted treachery against his prince. For he had corrupted three young men of the most reckless daring by payment of an enormous sum of money and had induced them to kill the emperor. He himself, on the day appointed for the perpetration of this deed, was waiting, accompanied by great forces, to seize the imperial power in the city, together with the imperial palace. When this great danger to the king had been divulged

---

[149] Countess Matilda of Tuscany (1046–1115) had left her states to the Church, but they had been claimed by the emperors; see below, iv.xiii.

to the empress [150] by a secret informer, terrified by the enormity of the crime, she made the treachery known to her husband as quickly as possible. And so after the plot was discovered, the assassins were arrested, the author of the crime was forestalled and taken captive, and the punishment they deserved was inflicted upon them all. For the *caniclinus*, first having his eyes dug out and his tongue drawn through his pierced throat, died a pitiful death—but unpitied.

[150] See above, I.xxiv–xxv; III.vi.

HERE ENDS THE THIRD BOOK

THE FOURTH BOOK

HERE BEGIN THE CHAPTERS OF THE FOURTH BOOK

HERE END THE CHAPTERS

HERE BEGINS THE FOURTH BOOK

i. Now came the day [November 11, 1158] of the assembly, which brought the Roman emperor to the plains of Roncaglia, as had been announced. Arriving, therefore, with a large following, he pitched his tents on the shore of the Po. The people of Milan, those of Brescia, and many others pitched camp opposite him, on the other bank of the river. There came together from all parts of the realm in great numbers archbishops, bishops, and many other men of ecclesiastical status, dukes, margraves, counts, and notables, consuls and judges of the cities. What a diversity of languages and peoples there was among them the variety of tents made evident. Now as it was not chance but the order of reason and the reason of order that is accustomed to designate their arrangement at all times, I think I must not lightly pass over the subject at this point.

ii. For the army of the Roman empire still observes the ancient custom of the Roman soldiery, namely,[1] to give attention first to the fortification of a camp whenever they enter hostile territory. They neither set it up on uneven ground nor mark it off in irregular fashion, but place it in a level field. If the ground is uneven, it is leveled down as much as possible. Moreover, it most frequently takes the form of a circle or a square. For the throng of smiths and artisans and tradesmen, that follow an army in proportion to its needs, with their tents and workshops give the appearance of suburbs when the camp is square; or, if it is round, their shops built in a circle about it resemble a wall. Inside, they divide the camp into accurately measured quarters and mark out streets and gates, easy of access for the pack animals and sufficiently wide for themselves to run in if anyone beset them. So it is a sort of improvised city. In the center is the tent of the duke or prince, very much like a temple, and around it those of his commanders and chief men, according to the rank of each. The knights in armor live in tents in friendly companionship, decently and pleasantly. They are under military discipline in the leisure times of peace just as when ready for battle.

So after these arrangements had been made, a connecting bridge (completed within two days by order of the emperor) joined the camp of the Ligurians and of those Italians who had encamped on the other bank of the Po with the camp of our men.

iii. Now the princes and notables whom we saw [2] in attendance upon that diet were, as we recall, the following: from our side of the mountains, Frederick, archbishop of Cologne, and bishops Eberhard of Bamberg, Conrad of Eichstädt, Daniel of Prague, Gebhard of Würzburg, Herman of Verden, and Conrad of Augsburg. From the lands beyond the mountains, Guido of Crema, a cardinal deacon and legate of the apostolic see; [3] Pilgrim, patriarch of Aquileia; N[Ubertus], archbishop of Milan; and the bishops of Turin [Charles], Alba [Peter], Ivrea [Germanus], Asti [Anselm], Novara [William], Vercelli

---

[1] The rest of this paragraph is drawn from Josephus *Wars* III.v.1–3.

[2] The use of the first person would seem to imply that Rahewin had been present.

[3] Rather, cardinal priest of St. Calixtus, though until the previous April he had been cardinal deacon of St. Mary *in Porticu*. He was later the antipope Pascal III (1164–68).

[Uguccio], Tortona [Obertus], Pavia [Peter], Como [Henry], Lodi [Alberic], Cremona [Ubertus], Piacenza [Hugo]—a mortal illness kept the bishop of Parma [Lanfranc] at home—Reggio [Alberic], Modena [Henry], Bologna [Gerard], Mantua [Carsidonius(?)], Verona [Ognibene], Brescia [Raymond], Bergamo [Gerard], and Concordia [Gervicus]. The exarchate of Ravenna was without a metropolitan at that time.

As all these, with a throng of lay princes (namely, dukes, margraves, counts, and consuls and judges from all the cities in Italy), surrounded Frederick, he enjoined upon the bishops only—together with a very few princes who were secretly cognizant of his plan—that they deliberate with him in the fear of God for a sound administration of affairs in Italy, that they might rejoice at the peace and tranquillity of the Church of God, and that the royal power and glory of the empire might be advanced with due honor. This conference occupied three whole days. Finally, on the fourth day, the most serene emperor came into the assembly and, seated on a higher place, whence he might be seen and heard by all, with the venerable leaders whom we have named sitting in a circle around him, he spoke through an interpreter:

iv. "Inasmuch as it has pleased the divine ordinance, whence comes all power in heaven and upon earth,[4] that we should hold the helm of the Roman empire, we not unreasonably lay claim—in so far as we can of God's grace—to what is recognized as pertaining to the status of that office. And as we are not unaware that this is the duty of imperial majesty, that the wicked and disturbers of the peace be held in check by our zealous vigilance and the fear of punishment, the good raised up [5] and sustained in the tranquillity of peace, so we know what rights and what honors the sanction of divine as well as of human laws has assigned to the pinnacle of regal excellence. But we, though having the name of king, desire to hold our authority under the law and for the preservation of each man's liberty and right [6] rather than—in accordance with the saying, 'to do all things with impunity, this is to be a king' [7]—to become arrogant through freedom from responsibility and to transform the task of ruling into pride and domination.[8] By God's help, we shall not change our character with our fortune.[9] We

---

[4] Matthew 28:18.
[5] Gratian *Decretum* C. XXIII. qu.i. c.6.
[6] Cf. Sallust *Catiline* vi.6–7.
[7] Sallust *Jugurtha* xxxi.26.
[8] Sallust *Catiline* vi.7.
[9] *Ibid.*, ii.5.

shall take care to maintain our authority by the very qualities through which it was first obtained.[10] Nor shall we, by any negligence on our part, permit anyone to diminish the glory and the excellence of the empire. Since, therefore, one may become renowned either in war or in peace,[11] and it is an open question whether it is better to safeguard one's country with arms or to govern it with laws (since the one requires the aid of the other [12]), now that war's alarms have been allayed by a propitious Deity let us direct our efforts to the laws of peace. Now you know that the civil laws, brought to perfection by our benevolent interest, strengthened and confirmed by the customs of their users, have sufficient authority; but the laws of the states, wherein that which previously prevailed was afterward obscured through neglect, must needs be illumined by imperial action and your own wisdom.[13] Whether, therefore, our law or yours be reduced to writing, in establishing it we must take thought that it may be honorable, just, possible, necessary, useful, suited to the place and the time. And therefore both we and you, while we are forming the law, must very cautiously exercise foresight, because when the laws have been promulgated it will not be permissible to express a judgment about them, but it will be necessary to pass judgment in accordance with them."

v (iv). When Frederick had spoken, all were very favorably impressed. They marveled and were amazed that one who was not a scholar and who was as yet little more than a youth had displayed the gift of so great wisdom and eloquence in his speech. And arising one after another (as is the custom of that people [14]), to make known individually to their emperor their affection and a very willing devotion to him, or to acclaim his proficiency in speaking, in which they are accustomed to glory—first the bishops, then the secular princes, afterward the consuls and envoys of the several cities—they occupied that entire day with the most eloquent speeches, until nightfall. And this was the opinion of all, as expressed by the archbishop of Milan:

" 'This is the day which the Lord hath made; we will rejoice and be glad in it.' [15] Truly this day is a day of grace, a day of gladness, on which the renowned victor, the peaceful conqueror, not intent on threats of war, not thundering forth anything cruel or tyrannical, but

[10] *Ibid.*, ii.4.   [11] *Ibid.*, iii.1.   [12] Cf. *ibid.*, i.7.
[13] Cf. *Institutes, prooemium* 5.   [14] Cf. Sallust *Jugurtha* vi.1.
[15] Psalms 118:24.

planning the laws of peace, deigns to abide—a most indulgent ruler—
in the midst of his people. Finally, after many centuries, you are found
happy, O Italy, since you have now been privileged to obtain a prince
who looks upon us as men—nay, as kinsmen and brothers! Truly it is
you, O most illustrious prince and sole emperor of the world and the
City, who have realized again the long-lapsed freedom vouchsafed the
first man when it was truly said: 'Be fruitful and multiply, and have
dominion over the fish of the sea, and over the fowl of the air.' [16] For
our sins, man rules over man, but by divine ordinance man rules over
the fish of the sea and over the fowl of the air. O Italy, how many
kings—nay, tyrants—have you endured, who have taken this command
in an opposite sense. Turning it about, they rule over men, nay, they
oppress all the good and the wise who, as rational beings, desire to use
their reason. But the fish of the sea, that is to say, smooth rascals,
grasping and given over to filthy pleasures, and those who know only
the lofty void [17] they favor. And being unjust they favor the unjust
in their impious acts, contrary to law and equity.[18] We know what
unfair, arrogant, cruel government we have sometimes endured. We
know that under such inequitable sway the innocent, no less than the
guilty, have been ill-treated.[19] We recall proscriptions of the rich,
perpetrated without the justification of the commission of a crime;
magistrates and priests superseded by wicked and shameful agreement;
and many other acts, which the lust of the rulers decreed, impiously
performed before our very eyes.[20] Therefore, 'let us be glad and
rejoice and give honour' [21] to God, that after such troubles, a serene
peace has dawned upon us, since it is your pleasure, our most serene
lord, rather to preserve and protect your realm by righteousness than
to grow great through crime [22] and be stained with the blood of your
subjects. Thou shalt rule, O most august emperor, over the fish of the
sea and over the fowl of the air. For even the divine decree 'resisteth
the proud but giveth grace unto the humble.' [23]

"So far as we, your loyal subjects, your people, are concerned, Your
Wisdom is pleased to consult us about the laws and justice and the
honor of the empire. Know, therefore, that all authority in establishing laws for the people is vested in you. Your will is law, in accordance

---

[16] Genesis 1:28.

[17] That is, the "fowl of the air."

[18] Sallust *Catiline* xv.1.

[19] *Ibid.*, xvi.3.

[20] Most of this sentence is from *ibid.*, xxi.2.

[21] Revelation 19:7.

[22] Sallust *Jugurtha* xiv.7.

[23] James 4:6; I Peter 5:5.

with the statement: 'What pleases the prince has the force of law, as the people have yielded and granted to him all their authority and power. For whatever the emperor has established by letter, or taken cognizance of and decreed, or enjoined by an edict, that is accepted as the law.' [24] 'It is natural that the profits should accrue to him on whom the losses fall,' [25] so you who bear the burden of care for all of us ought to rule us all."

At the conclusion of the address, the diet (which on this day had been prolonged into the evening) was adjourned. There were there also some who publicly extolled the emperor's deeds in songs of praise.

vi (v). During the following days the emperor was occupied from morning until evening, in full and solemn court, dispensing judgments and justice. He listened attentively to complaints and appeals of rich and poor alike. He had four judges, namely, Bulgar, Martin, James, and Hugo, eloquent and pious men, most learned in the law, doctors of law in the city of Bologna and teachers of many students.[26] With these and other jurists present from various cities, he heard, deliberated, and decided matters. Remarking the great number of those who carried crosses—for this is the custom of the Italians, that those who have grievances carry a cross in their hands—he felt sorry for them and said that he marveled at the wisdom of the Latins, who gloried much in their knowledge of law, yet were so often found to be its transgressors. How niggardly they were of justice was clearly apparent from the number of those who were hungering and thirsting for righteousness.[27] Therefore, by divine inspiration, he appointed particular judges for each diocese, not, however, from its own city, but either from the court or from another city. He did so for this reason: he feared that if a citizen were appointed to judge his own fellow citizens, he might readily be diverted from the truth by favor or hatred. And so it came about that of this great number of plaintiffs, there was scarcely any who did not rejoice at having secured either a complete victory in his suit, or his rights, or a satisfactory agreement with his adversary.

[24] *Institutes* I.ii.6.   [25] *Digest* L.xvii.10.

[26] Bologna was already the great center of legal studies in the West, and these four doctors were its leading lights. For them, see Savigny, *Geschichte des römischen Rechts im Mittelalter*, IV, chap. xxviii *passim*. According to Otto Morena (p. 60), they were accompanied on this occasion by twenty-eight Bologna masters of law.

[27] Matthew 5:6.

vii. Then the emperor spoke earnestly about the justice of the realm and the regalia which, for a long time past, had been lost to the empire, either by reason of the impudence of usurpers or through royal neglect. As they could find no defense whereby to excuse themselves, both the bishops and the secular leaders and cities with one voice and one accord restored the regalia into the hand of the emperor. The people of Milan were the first of those who resigned them. Upon being asked what this right included, they assigned to him dukedoms, marches, counties, consulates, mints, market tolls (*thelonea*), forage tax (*fodrum*), wagon tolls (*vectigalia*), gate tolls (*portus*), transit tolls (*pedatica*), mills, fisheries, bridges, all the use accruing from running water, and the payment of an annual tax, not only on the land, but also on their own persons.[28]

viii. When all these had been assigned to the imperial treasury, the prince displayed such generosity toward the former holders that whoever had documentary proof that he possessed any of these things by royal grant, he should even now, by imperial grant and in the name of the empire, hold the same in perpetuity. However, from those who had appropriated regalia unjustifiably, by sheer presumption, there accrued to the public revenues annually thirty thousand talents, more or less.[29]

ix (vi). Furthermore, this also was adjudicated to him by all and recognized as his right: that he should himself select, with the consent of the people, the podestas, consuls, and all other magistrates, who (being both loyal and wise) would know how to maintain both the emperor's honor and due justice for the citizens and their native state.

Moreover, that all these agreements might be accepted and observed in good faith and without deceit, all the states bound themselves under

---

[28] Cf. above, iii.xlvii, par. [9] and note 138.

[29] Frederick's attempt to establish his power in northern Italy could be effective only if the cities, bishops, and nobles of the region were deprived of cherished and long-standing rights (hence his reliance upon Roman law and the jurists trained in it). The chief losers would be the cities, which had naturally gained their rights through gradual usurpation; the bishops and nobles would be better able to produce the documentary proofs demanded, and also to obtain from the emperor the preferential treatment accorded a few favored towns (the faithful Lodi, Cremona, and Pavia). Frederick had previously enjoyed the support of many Lombard cities against Milan; these cities gradually became increasingly aware of the dangers to themselves from the imperial power. The Lombard League of 1167 and the imperial disaster at Legnano in 1176 were the results of Frederick's program.

oath and furnished hostages at the emperor's pleasure. Next, a common peace was sworn, that city would not war on city, nor man on man, save at the emperor's command.

x (vii). Finally, with reference to feudal law, because it had not yet been satisfactorily expressed in writing among the Latins and almost all had converted the justice of the fiefs into injustice, he promulgated laws the provisions of which we have set down in the present chronicle:

"Frederick, by the grace of God emperor of the Romans and august forever.

"It is in keeping with imperial foresight so to exercise care for the state and so to scrutinize the welfare of our subjects that the advantage of the realm may continue to be unblemished, and the status of individuals be preserved constantly unharmed. Wherefore, since we have (in accordance with the custom of our predecessors) sat in judgment over the general diet at Roncaglia, we have received from the Italian princes —both the rulers of the churches and other faithful adherents of the realm—serious complaints because their vassals have mortgaged, and by some trickery of legal transaction have sold, without permission from their lords, the benefices and the fiefs which they held from them. Hence they were losing the services due them, and the honor of our empire and the results of our successful expedition were being diminished. Therefore, having taken counsel with the bishops, dukes, margraves, and counts, and also with the imperial judges and other leaders, by this edict and law, which by God's favor will prevail forever, we decree:

"[1]. That no one be permitted to sell a fief in whole or in part or to mortgage or in any wise to alienate it or to bestow [30] it for his soul's salvation, without the permission of his overlord, to whom the fief is known to pertain. Now Emperor Lothar promulgated such a law, merely taking precautions that this sort of thing should not happen in the future.[31] But we, making provision for the greater advantage of the realm, do not merely annul for the future but by this present decree render void and declare of no effect illicit alienations of this kind previously perpetrated. Despite any lapse of time, one who made the purchase in good faith is to have the right to bring suit for the pur-

[30] The word is *iudicare*, but *legare* seems to be what is meant.

[31] Lothar III, in 1136 (Doeberl, IV, 23–24; *Constitutiones*, I, 175 *seq.*).

chase price against him who sold. Furthermore, in order to thwart the shrewd machinations of certain men who, taking the purchase price, sell fiefs and transfer them to others under pretense of investiture, which they declare permissible, we absolutely forbid that such a fiction or any other be hereafter devised to evade this our enactment. By the full authority that is ours we decree that seller and buyer who shall be found to have made so unlawful an agreement shall lose the fief, and that it shall return freely to its lord. And the scribe who shall knowingly draw up the deed in such a case shall, after losing his office, lose his hand as a mark of infamy.

"[2]. Further, if a feudatory who is more than fourteen years of age shall, by his carelessness or his neglect, let a year and a day pass without seeking investiture of his fief from his overlord, after such time he shall lose the fief and it shall return to the lord.

"[3]. We also strictly ordain, in Italy as well as in Germany, that whosoever, upon public proclamation of a [military] expedition, is summoned by his lord to the same expedition and neglects to come within a reasonable time or to send another, acceptable to his lord, in his stead, or who fails to supply his lord with half of one year's income from his fief, he shall lose the fief that he holds from a bishop or other lord, and the lord of the fief shall have full authority to apply it to his own uses.[32]

"[4]. Further, a duchy, march, or county shall not be divided hereafter; but another fief, if the participants wish it, may be divided, provided that all who have part of the fief that is now divided or is to be divided take oath of fealty to the lord; yet in such wise that the vassal be not obliged to have more lords nor the lord permitted to transfer the fief to another without the consent of the vassals. And besides, if the son of a vassal injure the lord, his father (when required by the lord) shall bring his son to give the lord satisfaction or shall part from his son. Otherwise he shall be deprived of his fief. But if the father is willing to bring him to render satisfaction, but the son refuse, upon his father's death he shall not succeed to the fief unless he shall first have given his lord satisfaction. And a vassal shall act in like fashion for all members of his household.

"[5]. This also we enjoin, that if a vassal have another as vassal for a fief, and the vassal's vassal injure his lord's lord, unless he has done

---

[32] Up to this point, we have only a repetition of an imperial ordinance issued December 5, 1154 (Doeberl, IV, 85–86; *Constitutiones*, I, 207 *seq.*).

so in the service of his other lord whom he truly had previously, he shall be deprived of his fief and it shall revert to the underlord from whom he held it; unless upon summons he shall be ready to render satisfaction to the overlord, whom he has injured. Unless the underlord when required by the overlord has summoned the vassal to render satisfaction, he too shall lose the fief.

"[6]. Furthermore, if there be a dispute between two vassals over a fief, let the decision rest with the lord and the controversy be terminated by him. But if strife arise between a lord and a vassal, it shall be settled by the peers of his court who have been duly bound by the lord under oath of fealty.

"[7]. This also we decree, that in every oath of fealty the name of the emperor be specifically included."[33]

"I, Frederick, by the grace of God emperor of the Romans and ever august, command all subjects of our empire by this edict and law, to have effect forever:

"[1]. That all subjects of our empire shall observe a true and perpetual peace with each other, and that it shall be kept forever inviolate among all of them. Dukes, margraves, counts, captains, vavasors, and rulers of all places, with the great and small of all places, between the ages of eighteen and seventy, shall be bound, under oath, to keep the peace and to assist the rulers of the places in maintaining and preserving peace, and at the end of every five years the oaths of all to observe the aforesaid peace shall be renewed.

"[2]. If anyone believe that he have any claim against any person for any reason or any deed, let him have recourse to legal authority and seek through it his proper rights.

"[3]. But if any rashly presume to break the aforesaid peace, if it be a city, it shall be punished by a fine of one hundred pounds of gold to be paid into our treasury. A town shall be fined twenty pounds of gold. Dukes, margraves, and counts, however, shall pay fifty pounds. Captains and the greater vavasors shall be penalized twenty pounds of gold; but the lesser vavasors and all other violators of the aforesaid peace shall be obliged to bring in six pounds of gold and shall make restitution to the victim, in accordance with the laws.

"[4]. Violence and theft shall be punished by law. Homicide and

---

[33] That is, the vassal's oath of fealty to the emperor takes precedence over his oath to any other lord, and his liability for military service can never oblige him to serve against the emperor.

mutilation or any other offense shall be atoned for as the laws prescribe.

"[5]. Judges and the defenders of places, or whatever magistrates have been appointed or confirmed by the emperor or by virtue of his authority, if they neglect justice and fail to punish by law a violation of the peace, shall be obliged to make good all loss and damage to the injured parties and, in addition, if it be a higher magistrate, he shall pay a fine of ten pounds of gold into the sacred treasury, but a lesser official shall be assessed a fine of three pounds of gold. But he that is known to be too poor to pay the aforesaid fine shall suffer bodily chastisement with stripes and shall live for five years at a distance of fifty miles from the place of his home.

"[6]. We also absolutely forbid that there be associations and any sworn brotherhoods, in and outside the cities, even on the ground of blood relationship, whether between city and city, person and person, or a city and a person, and we abolish those formed in the past, individual members of the sworn brotherhoods to be assessed a fine of one pound of gold.

"[7]. It is our will also that the bishops of the several localities visit violators of this edict with ecclesiastical censure until they be brought to render satisfaction.

"[8]. Those also who harbor malefactors who have broken the aforesaid peace are to be subject to our wrath and to suffer the same penalty.

"[9]. Furthermore, the goods of that man shall be confiscated and his house shall be destroyed, whosoever shall be unwilling to swear and to keep the peace, and who does not observe the terms of the peace.

"[10]. Besides, we absolutely condemn and prohibit unlawful exactions in the cities and fortified towns, especially by the Church, an abuse which is now of long standing; and if such have been imposed, they shall be restored twofold.

"[11]. Likewise, the free oaths of wards concerning the validity of contracts involving their property shall be inviolably observed. But we decree that oaths extorted by violence or unlawful intimidation, even from those of full age, and especially such as stipulate that they shall make no complaint of the wrongs committed, shall have no binding force.

"[12]. And finally, whosoever shall sell his allod shall not presume to sell the emperor's rights and jurisdiction, and if he does so it shall not be valid."

xi (viii). Among all who brought suit against one another before the emperor, the inhabitants of Cremona and Piacenza were most bitterly disposed toward each other. There existed between these two cities, situated not far apart and separated only by the Po, grievances of long standing, because of their relations with the people of Milan. But now there was added the fact that as the people of Cremona were coming to the court with the emperor, the soldiery of Piacenza had sallied forth and challenged them to a contest which they now commonly call a tournament (*turnementum*). And there, some of either side were wounded, some taken prisoner, some killed. On this account they brought charges against one another. The people of Cremona declared that while they were in attendance upon the emperor and in his very retinue, they had been hostilely attacked. It was not so much they as the royal majesty that had been outraged, and thus the offense should be of concern to the illustrious princes. It was the responsibility of the empire that the men of Piacenza, as enemies of the state, should pay a heavy penalty for their impious conduct toward them, and for their treachery and temerity toward the emperor. However, the men of Piacenza maintained that they had set forth, not against the emperor, but against their most deadly foes, who (though they had committed many depredations in their territory by rapine and burning) now falsely alleged that they had suffered injury. Frederick gave both parties an opportunity to make their accusations and, after he had listened sufficiently to what each had to say, declared that the men of Piacenza had not satisfactorily cleared themselves of the charges, especially considering that their deceit and treachery toward the empire had been detected on many occasions in the past. And so the verdict of the judges went against them, and finally they were received back into his favor on these terms, that besides the contribution of no small sum of money they were to fill in the great trench around their city (which they were accused of having made recently in order to rebel against the emperor) and destroy all towers.[34] And so it was done, and this condign punishment inflicted upon the seditious city of Piacenza ac-

---

[34] Otto Morena (p. 63) notes the order to fill in the moat around the city and to destroy all towers more than twenty palms in height; he adds that the Piacenzans did not obey this command. See also below, IV.xxxi.

cording to the measure of their crime struck fear into the other cities. There, too, the august Frederick brought suit against the people of Milan over the possession of Monza where (as has been said) the seat of the Italian kingdom is known to be. By the decision of the chosen judges, justice triumphed gloriously in this suit.[35]

xii (ix). After all business had been duly transacted and the interests of the state wisely served at Roncaglia, Frederick adjourned the assembly and, having settled things near by, turned his royal attention toward the islands of the sea that were under the royal jurisdiction. Accordingly, he sent chosen ambassadors, namely, Bishop Conrad of Eichstädt and Count Emico,[36] to Sardinia and Corsica, commending them to the people of Pisa and of Genoa for escort, because these two cities appear to have the greatest power in the Tyrrhenian Sea. But why this embassy remained of no effect may be conjectured by those who know what profits Pisa and Genoa derive from the island of Sardinia. Hence it is not unreasonably supposed that the voyage of the envoys was hindered by their guile and deceitful machinations. For the emperor threatened to bring punishment on Genoa and, approaching its territories with marvelous speed and ease, he intimidated them and forced them to ask terms of peace. They were as follows: to pay a thousand marks of silver into the public treasury and to desist from building a wall which they had started. Now it is not illogical to believe that this terror and fear were divinely inspired in them lest by their audacity they should induce many to revolt. For the natural setting of their city was particularly calculated to afford the people of Genoa hope of safety and to cause its assailants to hesitate. Its site had so fortified the city on all sides that, because of the precipitous and trackless Alps on one side and the waves of the Tyrrhenian Sea which wash it on the other, it could not easily be approached. But the emperor was moved by none of these things and did not hesitate to contend even with nature, so that what she had made inaccessible he thought was to be overcome by his mighty spirit and his courage.

xiii (x). Hereupon Frederick decided to pass the winter in the rich regions of Italy that were as yet untouched by war, in order to refresh

---

[35] See above, III.1. Monza had been under Milanese control, and was claimed by Frederick as the traditional seat of the kings. We may perhaps question the impartiality of the judges in this case; it is an additional explanation of the early Milanese revolt.

[36] Count of Leiningen, in the Rhineland (see above, I.xiii).

his soldiers. Celebrating the Nativity of our Lord [1158] at the city of Alba,[37] he dispatched messengers throughout all Tuscany, the coastal region, and Campania, to collect the *fodrum*. He also sent the princes around to install consuls or podestas in the various cities. With them he associated scribes to report in full detail the exact sum of the regalia that had accrued to the treasury. He also recovered the imperial revenues of the house of Matilda, that had been dissipated and dispersed by Duke Welf and by others.[38] These he is known to have later generously restored to that same most noble prince, united and augmented. Those who have traveled along the banks of the Po are aware of the great extent of these estates and the abundant wealth of this land.

xiv (xi). Although the Roman emperor enjoyed good fortune in all else, yet he experienced the cruelty of fate in the death at this time of several princes. Their noble lineage, wisdom, and virtues both of mind and body forbid that there be no record of them among posterity.

In the number of these the foremost was Otto, venerable bishop of the church of Freising, the author of this book before you, who would have brought it to a happier conclusion had not (as certain writers complain) [39] the fates been envious of his virtues. And since my land was smitten by a twofold disaster in the death of so renowned a man as this and in the burning of the church of Freising, let no one criticize me if I give a rather detailed account both of the disaster to my native town and the lamentable death of my most gracious lord and benefactor,[40] but let him make allowance for my grief as I recall how my city attained such joy and happiness and now has been brought down to almost the last extremity.[41] But, as a certain writer says, "if anyone be too stern a critic of sympathy, let him attribute the facts to history, and the lamentations to the writer." [42]

Accordingly, in the year 1158 from our Lord's incarnation, in the seventh indiction, in the third year of the reign of our most serene Em-

---

[37] In Piedmont, midway between Genoa and Turin.

[38] Welf VI, son of Henry the Black and uncle of Henry the Lion, had inherited the Welf holdings in Italy (see above, iii.lii and below, iv.xlvi).

[39] Cf. Sallust *Catiline* lviii.21, and Josephus *Wars* vi.i.5. This lengthy chapter is our chief source of information for the life of Otto of Freising.

[40] Einhard *Vita Karoli magni*, Prologue.

[41] Rahewin here grieves for Freising in the words of Josephus grieving for Jerusalem (*Wars*, Prologue). [42] *Ibid.*

peror Frederick as emperor and the fifth of his rule as king,[43] the aforesaid bishop was called by God and departed this life.

When he first was sent, as if by God and from heaven, Otto found this church practically bereft of all goods, its resources dissipated, its buildings in ruins, its clergy in sad plight, with little or no remem- brance of its monastic tradition. When he was finally removed from this life he had, by divine aid, brought it back to such a condition that he had restored religion to the clergy, freedom to the community, abundance to the revenues, and beauty to the buildings. His care, his labor, his services to his see and his flock, were so great that he became not so much its restorer as its founder. His lineage, his integrity, and the esteem he inspired, contributed strength and assistance for this task. For he was the grandson of the Emperor Henry IV, brother-in- law of Henry V, half brother of King Conrad, and paternal uncle of this most august Emperor Frederick, now auspiciously reigning. His father was that most illustrious prince of the realm, the Margrave Leopold. His mother was Agnes, daughter of the Emperor Henry IV. They were also the parents of his brothers—Conrad, bishop of Passau; Leopold, duke of Bavaria; and Henry, duke of Austria—and of his sisters—Gertrude, duchess of Bohemia; Bertha, duchess of Poland; [44] and Ita [Judith], marchesa of Montferrat,[45] the mother of N., the empress of Spain.[46] From so great and so illustrious a family did he, its noblest scion, trace his descent. He had no common or ordinary education in the field of letters, being considered the first, or among the first, of the bishops of Germany. This was so far true that apart from his knowledge of Holy Writ, in whose cryptic and hidden meanings he was notably well versed, he was virtually the first to bring to our land the subtlety of the philosophers and the Aristotelian books of the *Topics, Analytics,* and *Elenchics.* Because of these and many other ac- complishments, and sure of his knowledge of secular affairs and of his most eloquent tongue, he frequently spoke with great assurance on ecclesiastical matters before kings and princes. His consequent fame

[43] Otto died September 22, 1158, which would be the sixth indiction, and Frederick's fourth year as emperor and seventh as king.

[44] Bertha married the burgrave Henry of Regensburg; another sister, Agnes, was duchess of Poland.

[45] The wife of Marchese William of Montferrat, often mentioned in this work.

[46] Richildis, or Rica, daughter of Agnes, duchess of Poland, married Alfonso VII of Castile in 1152. Alfonso had taken the title of emperor in 1135.

won him praise, and the praise—as is usually the case—aroused no little
envy; yet, unperturbed, he avoided the traps of his adversaries and
escaped their slanderous remarks unscathed, being a thoroughly good
man. He had, indeed, patterned his way of life upon that of the Cistercian Order, and at first was abbot of Morimund. He was found there
so good and excellent that it was deservedly said to him: "Friend, go
up higher." [47]

Upon being made bishop, with the ardor of youth past and the temptations of the dangerous age lulled to rest, he avoided the oil of the
wicked [48] and, counting it of little worth to do what was just in the
sight of men,[49] he endeavored rather to please God to whom our consciences and hearts are known, giving heed to the precept of the Gospel:
"Let not thy left hand know what thy right hand doeth." [50] Hence it
came to pass that he was now freed and cleansed of whatever little
earthy stain he might have contracted from his worldly associations,
through the instrumentality of the tongue of his detractors, which is
like a sharp sword.[51] When the aforesaid Emperor Frederick, his
nephew, was setting forth on his expedition into Italy, although Otto
should have gone, being very necessary and valuable in affairs of state,
it came to pass by the divine will that he absented himself from the
journey, so that as a pious man, breathing his last in the arms of his
brethren rather than amid the din of warriors, he was able to say: "O
Lord, take me, that I may be with my brethren, with whom," and so
forth. But being graciously excused by the emperor, with many sobs he
commended his church to the prince, and prophetically foreseeing his
own death, he besought Frederick not to oppress this church in any
wise after his decease, nor deprive it of the right of election, as was said
frequently to have been done in the case of other churches. After receiving assurances that his praiseworthy petition would be granted, he
returned to his home.

But when Otto learned from the reports and warnings of certain
clerics that his death had been revealed to them, in visions or in dreams,
he saluted his brethren with sincere brotherly love and bade them
farewell. Then he set forth to attend the Cistercian chapter general,[52]

---

[47] Luke 14:10.   [48] Cf. Psalms 141:5.   [49] Cf. Ecclesiasticus 1:29.
[50] Matthew 6:3.   [51] Psalms 57:4.
[52] *Cisterciense capitulum*—the annual chapter general of the Cistercian Order, held
each September at Cîteaux.

and being long since exhausted by his weakness and his bodily ailment, though as yet his friends who were with him had no anxiety about him, after a wearisome journey he arrived at the aforesaid monastery of Morimund.[53] There he lay in bed for several days, and having now no doubt that he was at the point of death, when he had been anointed with the consecrated oil, as is the custom, and had disposed of his estate in a proper will, he gave instructions, among other dispositions wherein he anxiously made provision for his soul's salvation, that this present book should be placed in his hands. He then entrusted it to learned and pious men, that if he seemed to have said anything in favor of the views of Master Gilbert (as expressed in the preceding books [54]) which might offend anyone, it might be corrected in accordance with their decision, and he declared himself to be an adherent of the Catholic faith in accordance with the rule of the Holy Roman—and truly the universal—Church. Then, after first acknowledging his sins with great contrition of heart and humble confession, he received the very holy sacrament and, in the midst of a great company of holy men, both bishops and abbots, he gave back his spirit to the Lord.

Happy indeed and justly rewarded, that by divine favor he was taken from life before seeing the church which he loved so much, to which he was joined by a spiritual and heartfelt love, turned to live coals and ashes, and utterly destroyed.

But though he had, while still alive, pointed out to the brethren with his finger a place for his tomb outside the church in a humble spot, where indeed he would have been trodden upon by all the brethren, it was thought best to ignore this last request of his, and he was interred with due honors inside the church near the high altar, and his tomb is held worthy of respect and veneration by all the brethren.[55]

And I, who took down the beginning of this book from his lips and, at the emperor's command, have undertaken to finish it, closed his

[53] In Champagne, just northeast of Langres; it was in this house that Otto had become a Cistercian monk.

[54] See above, I.xlviii–lxi. It would be interesting, but futile, to speculate on whether the "corrections" alluded to in this paragraph were actually made in the chapters of Book I.

[55] When the translator visited the church of Freising in 1934 he was shown the ancient crypt, and was assured that the remains of Bishop Otto are interred there, though the exact spot is not known.

eyes at the last with my own hand and composed this epitaph and had it inscribed on his tomb: [56]

"Phoebus entered the lists to encounter the scythe-bearer. Night prevailed over light, as daylight departed. Life was vanquished as death prevailed, when Otto—alas! how suddenly—was smitten and fell.

"This man, if you ask his status, was in rank a bishop. His appearance? Comely, proper; a young man in years. His lineage? Distinguished by the lofty majesty of kings. His character? Worthy of praise for its marvelous integrity.

"Religion? He was a monk. His viewpoint? He set forth ideas. May the Virgin, whose intercession he merited, commend him to Him whom she bore.

"Often philosophy occupied his leisure. His training in theology was even greater. He was closely tied to literature. Now may the supreme vision serve as his mirror!

"Let Germany lament him with general lamentation! But you more especially, Freising, bereft of such a man, you who were granted so much by him should mourn him with endless complaint.

"Through his zeal, study flourished within you; pleasant disputations stimulated many. There was no one who did not perceive the distinction between custom and reason.[57] Error and quibbling [58] were laid bare.

"This man exalted the holy service of the Church. He set the battle of wits in motion. All this is buried with his dust. No one can mourn sufficiently such a man.

"Who now will attribute such charm to forms? Who will recall tropes to importance? Or who will assign elegance to language? Alas! what opinions will the school now offer in vain,

[56] This epitaph is in the form of a poem of twelve stanzas, the first eleven of which are composed of four thirteen-syllable rhyming verses. The final stanza is a ten-verse poem in a different meter. Little can be said for the literary or intellectual merit of this labored and obscure venture into verse.

[57] *Quid mos aut quid ratio;* one manuscript offers this gloss: *id est moralia et logica predicamenta.* The number of glosses the manuscripts offer on this epitaph would seem to indicate that Rahewin's contemporaries had some difficulty in following him.

[58] *Cavillatio;* a gloss explains, *id est sophistica.*

"While it meticulously scrutinizes the constitution of things, while it considers what mathematical abstraction (*mathesis*) is? [59] While it is proved thereby that removal is nothing, we may learn from death what the activity of both is.

"His native city, rightly distressed by his death, grieving that the glorious structure is bereft of its director, seeing the man who has merited well of her is reduced to ashes, goes with him to destruction.

"At the funeral of one so illustrious a great throng of people shed pious tears, leading the sad chorus! In response to their endless prayers and lamentations, may He who makes happy the souls of the just now grant him salvation! Amen."

[In another meter:]

"Whatever it is that blesses upright and illustrious men on earth has amazingly lavished honors on Otto, the bishop. If honorable birth, religious office, and influence could remove from us the grievous pangs of death, he would never have died, so notably was he endowed with these blessings. Alas, that such a man must pass, with our common humanity, to ashes! How eloquent was his tongue, how sincere his love of wisdom, we may learn from his chronography, composed at the bidding of kings. His city mourns him in the midst of its own ruins. May God and the holy Virgin Mary be gracious unto him! [Amen.]"

xv (xii). Bishop Otto died on the tenth day before the Kalends of October [September 22, 1158], which is about the time of the winter solstice. A few months thereafter, on the Nones of April [April 5, 1159], which was then Palm Sunday and is near the spring solstice, during the hour of matins the city of Freising was entirely destroyed by fire. So complete was the destruction that, not to mention the greater churches [60] which perished with all their adornments, together with the bishop's seat and palace, not a single one of the smaller chapels and oratories was left. Even the houses and workshops of the canons and the houses of the knights—except a very few—were burned. This church was at that time in such prosperous circumstances

---

[59] A word used by medieval writers in the varying senses of learning in general, mathematics, and the occult arts.

[60] *Maioribus aecclesiis:* the term is usually in the singular and refers regularly to the cathedral. That the cathedral may here be meant is suggested by *haec aecclesia,* five lines below, which seems to refer to the *maioribus aecclesiis.*

that in property, buildings, and treasures it equaled or surpassed practically all the adjacent and neighboring bishoprics. It was so distinguished for the integrity of its clergy that in good character and discipline, in generosity and knowledge of letters, few in the Roman world were its equals and none were considered superior.

xvi (xiii). A number of omens and prodigies had preceded this manifold calamity of the city of Freising and the disaster of melancholy outcome. For on a certain occasion, on the day of our Lord's circumcision [January 1], as the priest was standing at the high altar for the solemn Mass, and had already brought to an end the silence observed at the close of the holy sacrament, the chalice with the blood was entirely overturned and poured out upon the altar in the sight of all, so that not a drop was left. But the most discreet bishop, feeling that such an omen presaged no good, urged that divine wrath be averted and placated by fasting and prayer. At the same time, also, certain four-footed monsters and other phantoms of the night were seen flying hither and thither—by trustworthy clergymen as well as by laymen. Wild beasts, such as foxes and hares, entering the shrines (*pastoforia*) of the church and the workshops of the canons as though tame, were captured without resistance. Boys and girls frequently marched in procession through the midst of the city and by their parodies of actual litanies foretold in jest the bitter truth. For in the following year the very place where the cathedral and the bishop's seat were to be erected was struck by lightning and consumed by fire from heaven. Screech owls, hoopoes, and horned owls uttered their mournful cries on the roofs all year long, and filled the ears of all with their lugubrious notes. The hairy creatures that they call satyrs were often heard in the houses.

From the ruin and desolation foretold by such omens, the aforesaid church of Freising by divine aid and under Otto's successor, the most pious pastor Albert, who governs and directs it at the present time, awaits restoration and hopes through his efforts to revive once more.

xvii (xiv). Moreover, in that same year the splendid church at Speyer, a magnificent building, was similarly destroyed by fire and, besides, when a retaining wall gave way, buried a great many people in its ruins.

During these days Frederick, archbishop of Cologne, of whom

mention was made in the previous book,[61] died [December 15, 1158] in the third year of his episcopate, to the sorrow of many. His flesh and organs were interred at Pavia, but his bones were brought to the city of Cologne. He was a noble and learned man, and one who by his gentleness and kindliness had won the affection of many, far and wide.

Also the bishop of Würzburg, N [Gebhard], overcome by a desire to see his native land again, was graciously dismissed by the emperor and upon the seventh day after his return to his city was taken ill and died. We learn by this example that neither a safer country nor a more comfortable manner of life enables one to escape the long arms of death.

At that time, also, Conrad, duke of Croatia and Dalmatia, a Bavarian by origin, from the town of Dachau, brought his life to a close at Bergamo. His body was transported to his own land and buried in the monastery of Scheiern. His generosity and his great spirit, tested by many perils, deserve to secure for him a long remembrance among posterity, though he has been removed from this life.

There were also many other nobles and very valiant soldiers, whose names do not occur to me as I write, who perished at that same troubled period, either through the varying fortunes of war, or through sickness.

xviii (xv). While Frederick was in winter quarters, Hadrian, the bishop of the city of Rome, prompted by certain people, began to stir up anew the hostilities between himself and the emperor that had been lulled to rest at Augsburg.[62] He complained of the insult to his envoys, of the insolence of those who had been sent to collect the *fodrum*, and of the injury done to his castellans. He had, he claimed, received evil for good, and the emperor was ungrateful for his acts of kindness. As he was seeking provocation, when he heard that the regalia had been sent to the emperor by bishops and abbots and by cities and notables, he sent a letter concerning the matter, quite mild at first sight, but (when carefully considered) full of sharp criticism. A certain unworthy messenger—a low fellow—presented it and disappeared before it was read.[63]

---

[61] See above, II.lvi.   [62] See above, III.xxii–xxiv.

[63] Judging from the letters printed below (IV.xxii, xxxiv), Rahewin is here confused between two distinct papal letters. The one he describes here was properly presented by two cardinals; another, dealing with a dispute between the cities of Brescia and Bergamo, was presented in the manner here depicted.

Aroused by this and moved by youthful ardor to retaliate, Frederick conceived the idea of replying to him through an honorable rather than through a lowly envoy. The bishop of Vercelli had been sent to the apostolic see even before this, bearing a friendly request that the pope would confirm and consecrate Guido, a noble youth, the son of Count Guido of Biandrate (of whom we have made mention above [64]), whom the emperor had had named in Anselm's place in the church at Ravenna.[65] For this young man was in sacred orders, and had already been made a clerk in the church at Rome and ordained (*consecratus*) as subdeacon by Pope Hadrian. It was thought that only by his permission and assent could he be transferred to another church. But when this request was refused by the Roman bishop, who wished to render void what had been done, Herman, bishop of Verden, was sent on the same mission, and his effort likewise failed of success. If anyone wishes fuller knowledge about it, let him study the letters sent by both parties. He will find the following to be copies: [66]

xix (xvi). "Frederick, by the grace of God emperor of the Romans and august forever, to Hadrian, the venerable pontiff of the Church of Rome.

"Since our beloved and faithful Anselm, of blessed memory, is dead, that our court might not for too long a time be without such a prince, we have taken pains that a person be chosen in his stead who seemed qualified, considering the circumstances, to make good the loss that that church has suffered and to render service to us. Above all else, however, we have kept before the eyes of our mind and have heard with an ear that is not deaf this: 'In honor preferring one another.' [67] So we have endeavored to raise to a loftier station, out of respect for you and for the Church of Rome, the son of the count of Biandrate, whom you, at our request, accepted as a clerk and a son of the church at Rome; to advance him in that particular church which, apart from the Holy Church of Rome, we regard as the greatest, or one of the greatest. And, as divine clemency favored our wish, the entire church of Ravenna, voluntarily and with one accord, agreed upon his election

[64] See above, II.xviii, III.xlv–xlvi.

[65] As archbishop of Ravenna; Anselm had died in August, 1158. It was noted above that the archbishopric was vacant in September (IV.iii).

[66] This letter and the pope's reply which follows it cannot be dated more exactly than early in 1159.   [67] Romans 12:10.

in the presence of those most honorable men, our legate, Bishop Herman of Verden, and yours, Cardinal Hyacinth. And while learning and character are united with noble lineage in the person of the aforesaid archbishop-elect, this choice was the more commendable and acceptable to us because you, father, have accorded him a testimonial that we greatly respect. We rejoice that he is so beloved and so honored by you, but hope it will be in the manner and fashion in which fathers are accustomed to love their sons. For in due time they give them their freedom and permit them to provide for a home of their own. And surely it is most fitting that the Holy Roman Church, as the mother of all churches, should gather her sons, who are the fruit of her womb,[68] and should scatter those thus assembled in other houses and families to the embellishment of the house of God. And our empire has both the obligation and the desire of bestowing appropriate honors upon them, as proceeding from the womb and the lap of our mother. Accordingly, may Your Wisdom, upon more mature consideration, decide what under the circumstances is appropriate to your majesty and honor as well as to our own."

xx (xvii). "Bishop Hadrian, servant of the servants of God, to his very dear son in Christ, Frederick, the illustrious emperor of the Romans, greeting and apostolic benediction.

"We recall how we previously received in friendship and companionship, out of regard for our heavenly Creator and upon the recommendation of Your Excellency and of our beloved son Guido, count of Biandrate, our beloved son Guido, our subdeacon, the son of that same count, and how in consideration of his integrity and for the honor and advantage of the Very Holy Church of Rome, as though he had already been ordained a deacon, we have expressly assigned a church to him, and we believe it has not escaped the memory of Your Serenity.

"But now, we have considered his honorable character, and his advancement in learning if he lives,[69] and what great advantage may yet accrue to the Very Holy Church of Rome through him and through his noble and powerful family, and what high office he himself may attain in that same Church of Rome, if his life accord with his lineage; he has been advanced by the apostolic see to the office of subdeacon, and (as has been said above) a church has been expressly assigned him by us, as though he were already a deacon. Therefore, having taken coun-

---

[68] Cf. Psalms 127:3.   [69] *Si vita comes fuerit* (II Kings 4:16).

sel with our brethren, we cannot comply with Your Excellency's petition and remove from our side so valuable a pledge. But we purpose, as opportunity affords and by God's grace, to ordain him in the Church of Rome to the honor of that same Church and of the empire, so that (as divine grace shall determine) he may either at the proper time attain to higher rank in it or, by the Lord's help, pass from it to the very pinnacle of ecclesiastical station elsewhere. For it is more suitable that he who is a son and clerk of the Church of Rome should not depart from her bosom, and that she herself should bestow upon him a worthy position near her, and afterward provide him with loftier status. For she gladly calls to herself men of character and learning, endowed with honor and distinguished by noble blood, and is more accustomed to seek them elsewhere than readily to give up such persons when she has them in her bosom.

"Therefore, because we consider this more seemly and more honorable, and are confident that it must also be pleasing, agreeable, and acceptable to the imperial majesty, we have felt that we should not accede to your demand, hoping and believing that from the moment you know our will in the matter, you will yourself commend our intention and decision."

xxi (xviii). The prince, thus provoked, relieved his anger by ordering his notary that in writing documents he should place his name before that of the bishop of Rome and address the latter in the singular. This custom of writing, though commonly used in antiquity, is supposed to have been changed by the moderns out of a certain reverence and respect for the persons addressed. For the emperor said that either the pope ought to observe the custom of his predecessors in writing to an imperial personage, or he himself should in his letters follow the style of the emperors of old. This struggle of words and letters gave rise to such enmity between them that certain letters sent by the apostolic see, urging the people of Milan and certain other cities to revolt again, are said to have been seized. The tenor of the letters which follow will reveal the truth of this matter. They were written by various persons.[70]

[70] Three letters follow. The first is from Cardinal Henry (see above, II.xviii, xxi, xxiii) to Bishop Eberhard of Bamberg; the second, from Eberhard to the cardinal; the third, from Eberhard to the pope. None is dated, but all seem to fall in the period February–April, 1159.

xxii (xix). "To the venerable father and brother, his dearest friend Eberhard, by the grace of God bishop of Bamberg, Henry, by that same grace cardinal priest of the title of Saints Nereus and Achilles in the Holy Roman Church, greeting in the Lord.

"Even as the emperor's character is shown by the conduct of those around him, so also those on whose counsel he depends ought to give heed to their own conscience and sense of honor. For their own honor clearly reflects credit upon their lords, just as their lord's adversity undoubtedly involves and overwhelms them.

"Therefore, beloved father, venerable brother, and very dear friend, we do not so much instruct as urge Your Prudence constantly to guide the imperial majesty—as much as you can—along a course of peace and honor. For in matters that pertain to God and the freedom of justice, your reason and good judgment have a more subtle and sincere intelligence and knowledge than other princes, however noble they may be, if they are ignorant of the sacred canons and those matters which were long ago settled and ordained by the fathers. You yourself were present as a most faithful mediator at the negotiations in Germany with the lord emperor concerning peace between the Church and himself, and at those which, on another occasion, we conducted most faithfully with him, and he most graciously with us, with reference to the same peace.

"But now because of the letter which it pleased his highness to send my lord after my return, a letter which certainly observed neither the style nor the ancient custom of imperial letters, we greatly fear that he has changed, and that now his countenance and his feelings have altered. This transformation has filled my heart with bitterness and covered my face with confusion.[71] Whatever honor and happiness and prestige I had brought back with me seem to have been lost and buried by that letter.

"Therefore, most beloved brother and dearest friend, may the office of bishop and the order of priesthood in which Divine Providence has placed you so move and instruct Your Discretion that you will fight for God's honor and your own, and for the liberty of the Church, that the Church may be preserved untouched within its ancient compass, lest in your time its hitherto untarnished honor be tarnished by new devices.

"What we were seeking to effect by your counsel has completely

[71] Cf. Ruth 1:20; Psalms 69:7.

failed and we assure you that so long as these matters are handled by men who are ignorant of things divine, the peace that has been inaugurated cannot stand firm. But if you and the lord provost of Magdeburg will undertake the task of making peace through God's love and the great knowledge of both of you, and your zeal and assiduity, a peaceful settlement, to the glory of God, the Church, and the emperor, can very easily be reached. Otherwise, if in the time of wrath no conciliator is found,[72] who by his words will smooth out the difficulties, this situation may perhaps call forth another, and the greater force of necessity may break what is still intact today." [73]

To the same Henry:

"Eberhard, by the same grace bishop of the church of Bamberg, however unworthy, manifold devotion in word and deed.

"Having read and reread your fatherly letter, I cannot marvel enough what that thing was, nay, what that woe was, concerning which you had written when as yet it was entirely hidden from me. But by seeking I have found that which I did not wish and whereof I have grieved deeply. As God is my witness, I have grieved deeply. I heard it, and was disturbed and saddened; all my bones shook,[74] my skin clave to my bones.[75] And indeed I knew and understood that amid the good seed—not mine, but your counsel of peace and concord—an enemy had sown tares.[76] All evil things spring from good beginnings.[77] As we read in Holy Writ, 'the Lord prepared instruments of death and burning arrows,' [78] so also in the emperor's deeds and words, as well as in his writings, are to be found many things that lead some astray and edify others. The records of another time are consulted, the imperial titles are read perhaps in the form which suited that age and the goodness as well as the simplicity of those times when men spoke right out, neither exchanging one number for another nor confusing person with person.

"But now all things are changed. Yet is not the gold become dim, nor is its color changed, nor are the stones of the sanctuary poured out

---

[72] Cf. Ecclesiasticus 44:17.

[73] These words seem deliberately obscure, and appear to carry a threat of some stronger action by the papacy.   [74] Jeremiah 23:9.

[75] Lamentations 4:8.   [76] Cf. Matthew 13:24–5.

[77] Cf. Sallust Catiline li.27.   [78] Psalms 7:13.

in the top of every street.[79] If any alteration has taken place in modern custom, it is by this example and from this occasion: because the flame that had died down was revived by the breath of the letter which the lord pope recently dispatched to the lord emperor concerning the dispute between Brescia and Bergamo over the possession of two fortresses.[80] This a certain beggarly fellow, a kind of enemy and spy, thrust scornfully upon the lord emperor, and was seen no more. The letter seemed rather harsh and apparently forbade in strong terms the lord emperor to exercise judgment in that case.

"But I am writing this to you, not to hide what must not be hidden, but that you and other prudent and God-fearing men may the more readily treat the malady, when you know its cause. On either side we say and write daily: 'Come, come,' and 'We are coming, we are coming.' We sit—with great respect for Your Holiness be it said—we sit and yawn. We sit, I say (to quote from a certain writer of the Roman republic), waiting by night [81] for the day and by day for the night, and, despite our prudence and learning, we are well on the road to ruin.[82] As regards myself, I say to you, speaking in confidence: I will not be the bearer of bad tidings,[83] nor will I come to hear or to report bitter tales. Words clash with words like threatening weapons.[84] Where is wisdom, where is prudence, in the empire and in the papacy? May God keep us from the number of those of whom it is said: 'They are at their wits' end.' [85] Say no more to us, 'Come,' but rather do you who have the keys of knowledge [86] anticipate us. Come without invitation and teach your sons, not in bitterness of spirit but in gentleness and in great mildness. God forgive them who add, as it were, oil to the flames,[87] and who sow discord between father and son, between empire and papacy. 'I am become a fool; ye have compelled me.' [88] In God's name, let good envoys come bringing peace, as wise men teaching us to 'be instant in season, out of season.' [89] With the Lord's aid, let letters be written in the customary manner.

---

[79] Lamentations 4:1.

[80] This letter is not extant. For the dispute between Bergamo and Brescia, see Giesebrecht, V, 218–19.   [81] Conificius *Rhet. ad Herennium* iv.48.

[82] Cf. Terence *Eunuchus* i.72–73.

[83] *Mali nuncii esse baiolus* (cf. II Samuel 18:22).

[84] Lucan *Pharsalia* I.7.   [85] Psalms 107:27.

[86] Luke 11:52.   [87] Horace *Satires* II.iii.321.

[88] II Corinthians 12:11.   [89] II Timothy 4:2.

'Better is ever the end that follows a mournful beginning.' [90]

and 'your sorrow shall be turned into joy.' [91]

"The lord emperor, when your envoy arrived, suddenly left the camp on some private business. Therefore I could not by my representations elicit a definite reply from him, nor could you have a letter from him immediately. You know the kind of man he is. He loves them that love him,[92] and is estranged from others, because he has not yet completely learned to love even his enemies." [93]

(xx). A letter of the same man [Eberhard] to the pope:

"As there is both 'a time to keep silence and a time to speak,' [94] when a common danger threatens, it is the part of despair rather than of piety to keep still. It is the duty of all to cry out, to assemble, and to bear aid. But when a hostile attack or a fire threatens a city, it is particularly the concern of the city's watchmen to arouse those that are in the citadel, and the father of the household as well, for help in the time of need. In consideration of this duty of mine and of the many ties by which I am bound to the Holy Roman Church, I, though the least of the bishops, not worthy even to be called a bishop, cry out to you just as impudently as imprudently, most reverend father and lord, at this time at which it appears to us weaker brethren that a danger threatens which we greatly fear. And indeed from that pot which the prophet once saw seething toward the north [95] a certain fire has begun to burst forth from hidden sparks, but as yet it is veiled in smoke, and, thank God! has not yet burst into flame. Between you, Lord, and your son, our lord emperor, there is some disagreement as yet confined to words. It is greatly to be feared and dreaded that words clashing with words may finally by their friction strike forth a flame which will spread far and wide in the Church and the empire. God forbid! This your son, as you know, is our lord; but you, like Christ, are our master and lord. No one of us dares to say why you act or speak thus. We only wish and ask for the things that pertain to peace. Even if it were permissible—with all due respect for Your Reverence—to weigh each word and to seek each meaning (I speak foolishly [96]), it would not, I think, be expedient; it would be better to put out the fire at once than

---

[90] Ovid *Met.* VII.518, cited above by Otto (I.xxii).

[91] John 16:20. [92] Proverbs 8:17.

[93] Cf. Luke 6:27; Matthew 5:44. [94] Ecclesiastes 3:7.

[95] Jeremiah 1:13. [96] II Corinthians 11:21.

to investigate its source. I know that I am speaking of matters that are beyond me, but in the simplicity of my heart and in the presence of Him who is above all and is aware of all secrets I say these things and, now that I have once begun, shall continue to speak to you, as to my father and lord.

"Putting aside such matters as may be interpreted in different ways by different persons, may you, as a father, deign to write again, gently and kindly, to your son, our lord emperor, and with paternal affection recall him to himself, for he is ready to show you all reverence. Let Samuel embrace his David and let him not be separated from him, that there be no rift in the mantle, that God may be honored, and that the Catholic Church may rejoice in tranquil devotion."

xxiii (xxi). Meanwhile, two or more nobles had been sent by the emperor from his court to each city to install the podestas and consuls. It happened that Chancellor Rainald and Otto, count palatine of Bavaria, frequently mentioned already, and Count Gozwin [97] came to Milan, being ordered to this task in that and in other cities. Thereupon the people rose against them, rushed upon the houses in which the ambassadors were believed to be, and with threats and insults hurled stones and other missiles. Nor could either the count of Biandrate, who was there himself, or the rest of the nobles deter them. For in that city, and in most other towns of Italy, all these disturbances come not from the nobility but from the people.[98] They are of a restless temperament, seditious and lovers of discord, eager for a change, opposed to peace and quiet. Many nobles, too, were inclined to find pleasure in sheer disorder and rebellion.[99] The ambassadors, some of whom were within the walls of the city, distraught by the unexpected danger, and not knowing what was best to do, were terrified, since they could not resist armed men in great numbers (being themselves but few and unarmed) nor could they escape, since the gates of the city had been closed.[100] But the counts, toward whom the crowd was especially hostile, were less alarmed, being lodged outside. Upon hearing the uproar, without delay they withdrew unhurt and untouched. On the fol-

[97] Gozwin of Heinsberg, installed as count of Seprio and Martesana after the expulsion of the Milanese from those places; see below, IV.lviii.
[98] Cf. Lucan *Pharsalia* V.342 and above, II.xxv.
[99] This and the preceding sentence are taken bodily from Sallust *Jugurtha* lxvi.2, 4.
[100] Much of this sentence is from *ibid.*, lxvii.1.

lowing day both the bishop and the chancellor followed them, with their mission unaccomplished.[101]

So the people of Milan, having broken the peace, violated their oaths, and transgressed an immunity which the *ius gentium* has established for ambassadors even among barbarians, revealed by this reckless act the poison of another revolt, which they harbored in their hearts and plotted secretly.

xxiv (xxii). At that same time, or rather during these days, ambassadors from the emperor of Constantinople, who were come to court, asked for safe conduct. For they feared they might be mistrusted on account of the death of Wibald, abbot of Stablo, who had been sent to Greece and had died there. Legates also from Louis, king of France, and from Henry, king of England, having arrived in close succession, vied with each other in striving by many flattering words and with gifts to induce Frederick to favor and support their respective princes. For between these kings incessant enmities and dissensions had been rife since the time of the divorce between Louis and the companion of his bed and her proud marriage to the aforesaid ruler of the English [102] —whether on account of the delimitation of their respective territories or because of some other less evident cause. Each thought that he would secure a powerful ally if he could win the favor of the Roman emperor. The king of Hungary also, upon learning by rumor only of the audacity of the people of Milan, dispatched two honorable and learned ambassadors, Master Matheus and Master Primogenitus, to the court, voluntarily promising anew to his prince auxiliary forces, in greater numbers than before. All these the emperor dismissed after cheering them with prudent words and royal gifts, and permitted them to return to their princes.

xxv (xxiii). As Frederick was celebrating Candlemas [February 2, 1159] in a town called Occimiano,[103] and many of the nobles of Hesperia [Italy] had flocked to him, he made open mention of the treachery and insolent pride of the people of Milan, so well known to all,

---

[101] It is clear from Rahewin's account that this embassy included other dignitaries than the chancellor and the two counts, but the identity of the bishop mentioned in the text is not known. This affair occurred in late January, 1159.

[102] Henry II of England had married Eleanor of Aquitaine in 1152, after her divorce from Louis VII of France.

[103] About ten miles northwest of Alessandria.

wearing an expression of countenance that indicated at once his just resentment and his royal indignation, and saying:

"We find ourselves obliged to execrate in your hearing, O princes, the crime of treachery (*lesae maiestatis*), of which that impious city, that worthless and accursed people—the Milanese—have been found guilty not once but repeatedly. I would recount to you their still recent act, if not only your ears but the ears of all in the Roman world were not tingling with the tale. The insult that the pride and presumption of those most iniquitous men have evilly inflicted upon us—nay, upon you and upon the empire—seems, by God's inscrutable decree, to have this purpose: that those who commit acts of madness to their own and others' destruction be properly repressed by the condemnation of others, by imperial authority, and by the full rigor of the laws. Where, I ask, is that fidelity which the Milanese boasted they possessed still inviolate and (as contrasted with the other cities) of virginal purity? Where is the justice on which they vaunted themselves hitherto, especially as regards the observance of law? It is not we who will summon them to justice, but their breach of good faith. They will find arrayed against them their worthless oaths, the broken treaty, and the laws protecting ambassadors that must be observed with integrity and the most holy respect not only by us and by you, but even by barbarians. Wherefore, if the praises I hear of your good faith, your justice, and your valor, be true, behold in the midst of your land the abomination of desolation,[104] that used to fill you with terror, and arise with your united strength to destroy our common foe—not so much our enemy as yours. Support the Roman empire of which—though we are the head—you are the members. Use us in this undertaking as you please, whether as soldier or commander.[105] By God's grace repeated punishment will follow hard upon repeated offense. What they have done to injure us—nay, you—and the glory of the Roman empire will be visited with such penalties that no hope may spring up among the base and seditious, and the offense of those who have not kept their promise to you or their reverence and good faith toward us may not remain unpunished. These men have abused our clemency and our patience, and have not been ashamed to adopt persistence for penitence and duplicity for simplicity."

xxvi. As he uttered these words, all showed their approval and, as

---

[104] Matthew 24:15; Mark 13:14.　　[105] Sallust *Catiline* xx.16.

though moved by some divine impulse, were eager to anticipate one
another in making a reply, each thinking it best not to be the last.[106]
There were there, besides lay princes, the bishops Eberhard of Bamberg, Albert of Freising, Conrad of Eichstädt, Herman of Verden,
Daniel of Prague, and, from beyond the mountains, the bishops of
Pavia, Vercelli, Asti, Tortona, Piacenza, Cremona, and Novara.[107]
Though each of them in speaking individually displayed his zeal in his
own way to gain favor, yet they offered the following single expression
of opinion in an eloquent speech by the bishop of Piacenza:

(xxiv). "Your Excellency, O prince dearest to us after God, we
condole with you with all-becoming seriousness and with indignation
in our hearts at the injury done by the people of Milan. But as we
know that your sincerity and your spirit have been preserved free from
blame in this matter, we express our thanks to Almighty God, who will
be able to accomplish much to your glory in consequence of the offenses
of the people of Milan, and will bring it to pass that—by contrast with
their proud cruelty and their cruel pride—your mildness and your most
praiseworthy humility may be the more conspicuous.

"O shameless pride, O luckless arrogance, that cast an angel from
heaven and man from paradise! I fear that this bane must be preparing
a deadly doom for the people of Milan. Too little on his guard against
this vice of pride was he of whom it was said: 'Thou sealest up the sum,
full of wisdom and perfect in beauty. Thou hast been in Eden the garden of God.' [108] Too little also was he [on his guard], to whom it was
granted to eat from every tree of paradise.[109] You, Milan, have been
no more careful than he, and to you these and many other sayings can
be applied because of a certain measure of similarity. He was first
among the angels and was called Lucifer. You are the first among the
cities of Italy, one of the first among the cities of the world. He amid
the delights of paradise, you amid the delights of this world, wanted
for nothing. He was full of wisdom and perfect in beauty, whereas
you have many wise men and philosophers. I fear that it may appropriately be said of you: 'They are at their wits' end.' [110] We know that
very great and ancient cities—Babylon and Nineveh—have been conquered in war and have become at last haunts of dragons, the habita-

---

[106] This sentence is taken from Josephus *Wars* VII.ix.1.

[107] Respectively, Peter, Uguccio, Anselm, Obertus, Hugo, Ubertus, and William.

[108] Ezekiel 28:12–13.   [109] Genesis 2:16, referring to Adam.

[110] Psalms 107:27, cited above, IV.xxii in the second letter.

tion of owls.[111] Upon you surely will the same fate descend tomorrow, so that unless you repent, in your halls shall the horned owls reply to one another with mournful voice, and satyrs shall dance.[112] Yet may it not be so! May God avert it from you! Indeed, in this matter I would rather utter a lie than to be found a true prophet.

"To you, our most serene lord, we believe we must in all loyalty suggest that in requital for the injuries done you by the people of Milan, you, as an upright judge, strive to perform the duty of punishment with a good heart.[113] For not in vain were the king's power, the soldier's arms, and the executioner's rack devised for the discipline of a ruler and the severity of a good father.[114] As a certain writer says: 'All these things have their means, their causes, their reasons, their uses. When these are dreaded, the wicked are held in restraint and the good live peacefully amid the wicked.' [115] The Milanese are mistaken if they suppose that in your case alone the saying does not apply:

'Do you not know that kings have long arms?' [116]

You came and you conquered. Nor will it be less easy for you to conquer the conquered than to have vanquished them without difficulty when they rebelled for the first time. You have the same empire, the same vigor of body and mind, the same valiant army, the same devoted soldiers. It merely remains for you to decide by what punishment, by what penalty, they who are so often disobedient to the laws and the lawfully constituted empire are to be chastised.

"But although they should justly be visited with an extraordinary penalty, yet imperial clemency will becomingly exercise such moderation that you will exact a penalty for the wrong not as they deserve but as is fitting for you. The guilt of the Milanese should not have more weight with you than your own dignity, lest you appear to have been swayed more by your wrath than by your self-respect or by justice. If a punishment commensurate with the enormity of their deeds be sought, we should in truth require new penalties far beyond our power of invention. Therefore I advise employing against them only what the laws prescribe.[117] You will be revealed as a good emperor and a just

---

[111] Cf. Isaiah 13:21–2; *Two Cities* VIII.xx.   [112] Cf. Isaiah 13:21.

[113] Cf. Gratian *Decretum* C.XXIII.qu.v.c.16.   [114] *Ibid.*, C.XXIII.qu.v.c.18.

[115] *Ibid.* (quoting from St. Augustine).   [116] Ovid *Heroides* xvii.166.

[117] These last three sentences are largely taken from Sallust *Catiline* li.7–8.

judge if you deal with your foes in accordance with the laws before you make war upon them."

Thus he spoke, and the emperor himself and all the nobles approved his sentiments.

xxvii (xxv). Therefore edicts were issued, and again the people of Milan were summoned to court in due legal form. On the appointed day, while Frederick was at a royal estate called Marengo,[118] the Milanese envoys presented themselves—their archbishop and certain other men of much eloquence but little wisdom. But the archbishop, whether because of an actual or a pretended illness, withdrew from their company. Now when the others were being closely questioned concerning the oaths that had been sworn, the rest of the treaty of peace and its violation, since they could make no other excuse, they said: "We did, indeed, swear but we did not promise to keep our oath"! An appropriate answer, a speech consistent with their character! Those accustomed to live and to act basely and treacherously could not have spoken otherwise than treacherously and basely; their disreputable speech was in keeping with their dishonorable life. And when they had given vent to these and many other shameless words,[119] they departed, leaving the negotiations unfinished, and another day was appointed for them.

xxviii (xxvi). Meanwhile, seeing that the insolence of the people of Milan could be held in check only by a strong and heavy hand, and since (as we have recorded above) [120] he had dismissed the army and remained with only a small force, the emperor decided that aid against the iniquitous city must be summoned from beyond the mountains.

Accordingly, he summoned by messengers the empress, Duke Henry of Bavaria, and others, both bishops and nobles of the realm, reminding them of their allegiance lest they have the temerity to think they could forsake their duty with impunity. He sought to learn whether they had a loyal desire to sustain the empire and to resist the attacks of its foes. Upon receiving the commission they prepared themselves with alacrity for a new expedition in the following spring.

xxix (xxvii). In the meantime, Frederick permitted himself no rest

---

[118] Some five miles southeast of Alessandria; Frederick was at Marengo February 7-22, 1159.

[119] Most of this and the two preceding sentences is copied from the *Invective against Sallust* (attributed to Cicero) 1.l.   [120] III.50.

and gave the enemy no security. Untiringly and wisely he devoted himself alike to his own and the enemy's affairs, and investigated what of good or ill there was on each side. Therefore (since the army had been dismissed) he made a circuit of the lands in company with a few of his men, and reviewed his new troops and auxiliaries. As a threat to the enemy and a base for his own men, he shrewdly established strongholds and fortifications, such as Verruca, Serralonga,[121] and others, which in that country appeared to be practically impregnable and not easily to be taken by storm. New Lodi he fortified with the greatest ardor all during Lent [February 25–April 11, 1159]. He made there an enormous moat and located gates and outworks, thinking it expedient for the conduct of the impending war if he were able at short notice to station and have ready a large number of soldiers in a city so near at hand (New Lodi being only twenty miles from Milan). Then advancing as far as Como where he was received with the utmost respect, he asked and received alliance and aid.

xxx (xxviii). There is in Lake Como an island,[122] abounding in wealth and thronged with warlike men. It was thought that it would be difficult for anyone to take it except by a very bloody victory. It was, moreover, friendly toward Milan and long allied with it. The emperor thought it best for the coming and going of his troops to detach this ally from the mutinous city. Filled with hope and confidence, he gave warning that he would enter the island as an enemy or, if the people chose, as a kindly emperor coming to his allies and friends. Without delay, embarking in boats with the few whom he had with him, he began the passage across. When the islanders perceived the emperors' spirit and audacity, smitten with foreboding they came to meet his vessel, sought peace, and upon his arrival received him with joy and just acclaim, swearing fealty and honoring him with gifts. For the future those people were found to be quite faithful to us. It was the intent of the emperor that those fierce islanders, much given to piracy,

---

[121] The site of these places is not certain; Giesebrecht (VI, 374) would place them near Lodi.

[122] Isola Comacina; see above, III.xlvii. Several passes over the Swiss Alps converged on Lake Como, to take advantage of its long water passage through difficult terrain; it had, thus, considerable strategic importance, and Frederick had in mind rendering this route to Germany secure for his troops. Below in this chapter Rahewin tells us that the Isolans practiced piracy; this doubtless explains their enmity with Como, whose prosperity depended upon this trade route, and their consequent alliance with Milan. In 1169 Isola was captured and utterly destroyed by Como.

might be won over to the advantage and benefit of our men in the narrow mountain passes.

What is the more to be marveled at in this victory? The emperor's courage in attempting so difficult a feat or his good fortune in bringing so perilous an undertaking to a victorious conclusion? But both are marvelous: that he dared make the attack, and that he so successfully won a glorious victory.

xxxi. Similar action was taken at Piacenza. This city too, an ally of Milan, had shown various signs of hostility, and its defection had long been suspected. Hence (as we have recorded above [123]), the citizens had been ordered, on the basis of the emperor's right of possession, to fill up their moat and level their towers, that the turbulent faction in the city might be held in check by fear rather than by punishment. But at that same time robbers had issued from Piacenza, and had ambushed imperial agents and seized the promised money from Genoa [124]—about five hundred talents—which they were carrying. Because of this and other evidences of guilt, the emperor suspected Piacenza of being surely inclined to revolt, yet he fearlessly entered the city with but few men. He observed Palm Sunday [April 5] with due solemnity, suitably performed whatever else needed to be done there, and at the entreaties of the citizens took back the stolen money.

xxxii (xxix). In the year 1159 since our Lord's incarnation, Frederick celebrated Easter at Modena [April 12]. When the festival was over he journeyed into the territory of Bologna, where his army was then encamped, and gladdened all by his coming. For since the day [125] when it is customary to strew ashes upon the heads of the faithful until then he had come but once to his army, being so occupied with the aforesaid undertakings. But he had put the venerable man Eberhard, bishop of Bamberg, in his stead to hear those who came and had business to transact, and to decide their cases after careful investigation. For that same bishop was distinguished for his piety, learning, and purity of life. And since he was known to be above all zealous for the honor and the good name of the empire, his name was widely known in many lands. He was so completely absorbed in the interpretation of Scripture and theological questions that in the midst of battles he would meditate earnestly on various problems of that nature. And

---

[123] See above, IV.xi.   [124] See above, IV.xii.
[125] Ash Wednesday, February 25, 1159.

while the emperor loved all bishops and men of any ecclesiastical rank, and considered them worthy of very great honor, yet he depended particularly upon the counsel of the aforesaid man as the wisest of them all, and deemed him worthy of being entrusted with his problems for opinion and judgment, sharing with him both the burden and the honor.

xxxiii (xxx). Now the day was at hand that had been appointed for the Milanese—the third or fourth time set. The emperor, calling together the judges and jurists (who were numerous in that city [Bologna]), ordered the people of Milan summoned to the bar of judgment. But when no one put in an appearance, to give a satisfactory excuse for their absence, they were severely sentenced as contumacious rebels and traitors to the empire. They were declared enemies, their goods subject to pillage and their persons to servitude. And on this occasion the question was fully discussed in the emperor's hearing and a clear decision reached as to the punishment that should be meted out to those found guilty of rebellion or high treason.

xxxiv. Besides other princes, nobles, and scholars there were present at this deliberation legates of the apostolic see sent by Pope Hadrian, namely, the cardinal priests Octavian, of the title of St. Cecilia, and Henry, of the title of Saints Nereus and Achilles, and the cardinal deacons William (previously archdeacon of Pavia [126]) and Guido of Crema.[127] The reasons for their coming, and also for the coming of legates from the senate and Roman people, are contained in the subjoined copy of a letter of that venerable man Eberhard, bishop of Bamberg, reading as follows:

"To the most reverend father and lord, Eberhard, archbishop of the church of Salzburg, Eberhard, by the grace of God bishop of Bamberg, however unworthy, sends assurance of most loyal devotion, with every prayer.

"I know, most holy father, that in your love of holy piety you sympathize with me in my labors and wish me salvation for my soul and peace for my body. But that you may know to what extent you should sympathize with me, I tell you that my soul is now weary of life.[128]

---

[126] Rather, cardinal priest of St. Peter in Chains.

[127] Rather, cardinal priest of St. Calixtus; see above, IV.iii.

[128] Job 10:1.

I carry in my heart two very heavy burdens, because I am girt and led whither I would not,[129] and I know not how long it must still endure. I desire to be aided by your prayers and those of others of the faithful, that I may be separated from those to whom the Lord hath sworn in his wrath: 'They shall not enter into my rest.' [130]

"Besides, perilous times seem to be coming,[131] and the breaking out of a conflict between the empire and the papacy is near. And, indeed, when cardinals were sent by the lord pope to the lord emperor, namely, Lord Octavian and Lord William, formerly archdeacon of Pavia, after a mild beginning and an apparently peaceful introduction, the most severe demands were made. For example: Envoys must not be sent by the emperor to the City without the pope's knowledge, as all the magistrates there with all the regalia are under the jurisdiction of blessed Peter. *Fodrum* is not to be collected from the pope's demesne, except at the time of the coronation. The bishops of Italy may render the lord emperor an oath of fealty only, without doing homage, nor are the emperor's envoys to be received in bishops' palaces. Possessions to be restored to the Church of Rome include Tivoli, Ferrara, Massa, Ficarolo,[132] all the land of Countess Matilda, all the land which extends from Acquapendente to Rome, the duchy of Spoleto, the islands of Sardinia and Corsica.

"The lord emperor steadfastly offered to submit these issues to trial and judgment, if they would do the same. But they desired only to receive and not to give concessions, on this ground, that they were not empowered to subject the lord pope to judgment. On the other hand, the lord emperor uttered many reproaches concerning the breach of the agreement, which had been entered into in good faith, to make peace with the Greeks, the Sicilian, and the Romans only by common consent. He spoke further of the cardinals who, without imperial permission, traveled about freely through the realm and entered the regalian palaces of the bishops and burdened the churches of

---

[129] Cf. John 21:18.   [130] Psalms 95:11.   [131] II Timothy 3:1.

[132] *Massae, Ficorolii.* There is some doubt as to these places. Most authorities seem to agree that Ficarolo, northwest of Ferrara, is intended, and that the *Massa* referred to may be near it, or may, as Doeberl (IV, 132, note *a*) suggests, be Massafiscaglia, an ancient papal property twenty miles due east of Ferrara. It is also possible that these two names should be joined and rendered as "Massafiscaglia."

God; concerning unjust appeals,[133] also, and many other matters that cannot be briefly set forth.

"When the aforesaid cardinals, with the approval of the emperor, sent both an envoy and letters to the pope, urging him to send additional cardinals to smooth out these matters with his legates and the princes of the court already present, he refused. So for our sins, the long-desired word of unity and concord remained unuttered.

"And while these things were going on, envoys of the Romans arrived and, desiring conditions of peace,[134] were well received and sent home again. Nevertheless, at the request of the cardinals the lord emperor is about to send ambassadors to the lord pope and to the City, that peace may first be ratified with the pope, if he wishes it; but if not, with the senate and the Roman people. The lord emperor is in great glory. He awaits her ladyship, the empress, and the duke of Bavaria and Saxony, with the other princes and troops expected,[135] and is keeping in chains some of the leading citizens of Milan and Brescia. Farewell."

xxxv. The emperor made the following reply to these words of the cardinals:

"Since I am well aware that I ought to reply to such important matters, not in accordance with my personal feelings but upon the advice of my princes, I give this answer without prejudice to them, not having consulted them.

"I am not eager for the homage of the bishops of Italy—if, that is, they do not care to hold any of our regalia. If they take pleasure in hearing the bishop of Rome say: 'What have you to do with the king?' let them consequently not grieve to hear from the emperor: 'What have you to do with worldly goods?' [136]

"He [the pope] declares that our envoys are not to be received in bishops' palaces. I agree—if perchance any bishop has a palace that

---

[133] That is, the pope is charged with improperly entertaining appeals from lower courts not falling within the jurisdiction of the papal curia.

[134] Luke 14:32.

[135] The empress and the duke joined Frederick late in July, which would indicate that this letter was written early in that month. Rahewin inserts it here, out of place chronologically, apparently to show the results of the papal legation treated in the preceding and following chapters.

[136] Gratian *Decretum* C.1.Dist.VIII (quoting from St. Augustine); cf. *Two Cities* IV, Prologue.

stands on his own land, and not on ours. But if the bishops' palaces are on our land and alod, then, since certainly everything that is built upon it goes with the land,[137] the palaces are ours. Therefore, it would be an injustice to debar our envoys from royal palaces.

"He states that ambassadors are not to be sent by the emperor to the City, since all the magistrates there, together with all their regalia, are under the jurisdiction of the blessed Peter. This is, I admit, a great and serious matter, which requires more serious and more mature consideration. For since, by divine ordinance, I am emperor of Rome and am so styled, I have merely the appearance of ruling and bear an utterly empty name, lacking in meaning, if authority over the city of Rome should be torn from my grasp."

xxxvi (xxxi). When the emperor had made this and other subtle replies to the aforesaid articles, it was determined that six cardinals should be chosen for the pope, and for the emperor, six bishops—pious, wise, and God-fearing—to obtain from all possible sources full information about matters of such importance, and to find for so great a dispute a satisfactory solution. But, as has been set forth above, this plan, too, is said to have been rendered vain by the Romans. On this point hear the letter of the emperor addressed to Eberhard, archbishop of Salzburg, as follows:

"As we have often had proof of the constant fidelity you have always displayed toward the empire, we make known to Your Discretion the state of our affairs and ask the advice of Your Prudence.

"Well then, there have come to us two cardinals, sent by the pope for the purpose of creating harmony between us and him. They said the pope desired that peace and harmony which had been made and written between Pope Eugenius and ourself.[138] We replied that we had in fact kept that peace inviolate until now. As for the future, however, we desired neither to keep it nor to be bound by it, because he himself had been the first to violate it in respect to the Sicilian, with whom he should not have been reconciled without our agreement. But, we added that we were ready to render or to receive justice whether in accordance with human or divine law. And if judicial procedure appeared to him too stern, we would gladly submit to the judgment of the princes and men of religion, out of love for God and the Church.

[137] *Digest* XLI.i.7.10.

[138] The Treaty of Constance, made in 1153 between Frederick and Eugenius III.

Our words pleased the cardinals, but they said they could not and dared not take any action in the matter without first knowing the pope's will. The pope learned of our proposal through messengers and declared, as before, that he desired no other harmony than that which had existed between Pope Eugenius and us. We refused this, in the aforesaid fashion, and, in the presence of all the German and Lombard bishops and lay princes and barons and vavasors, bearing witness thereto, we offered to submit these issues to trial or judgment, that we might be assured of justice. There were present on that occasion the envoys of the citizens of Rome, who were amazed and indignant at what they heard. For the pope made new and serious and hitherto unheard-of demands, which cannot be discussed without your counsel and that of others loyal to the empire. These we have communicated to Your Discretion, so that you may know the facts—which may be of value in case reports of these matters should reach you. We ask also that, if it should be necessary, and if we summon you on so grave a matter, you will come to us without delay."

xxxvii (xxxii). The Milanese now brought their revolt into the open. While the Easter festival was not yet at an end, they set out with all their forces and hastily attacked the town of Trezzo, where, as we have said,[139] Frederick had stationed troops during his previous expedition. For to besiege it while the emperor was in the province seemed to them hazardous. In their desire to obtain possession of this stronghold, they had prepared beforehand inside their city the machines and other things needed for the attempt,[140] and thus their intentions and their guilt were the more concealed.[141] After preparing the equipment to their satisfaction, suddenly they surrounded the town in great numbers.[142] Some sought to undermine the wall, some to scale it with ladders; others fought at long range with slings, stones, or javelins.[143] The Roman soldiers were alarmed by the uproar; some took up arms, some reassured the frightened, some rolled down rocks on the nearest assailants and threw back the missiles fired at them from a distance. So few shooting at so many could hardly have missed their mark had

---

[139] See above, III.xxxii. Trezzo, about fifteen miles northeast of Milan, was of value to the emperor for the passage it commanded over the Adda.

[140] Cf. Sallust *Jugurtha* xxxvii.4.

[141] *Ibid.*, xxxviii.2.   [142] *Ibid.*, xxxviii.4.   [143] *Ibid.*, lvii.4.

the Ligurians come nearer.[144] The ferocity of both sides made the action appallingly violent. Each was in peril,[145] and the victory at first uncertain.[146] Indeed, the fighting continued for three whole days. But at length the defenders, exhausted by the day-and-night activity, by fasting and exertion,[147] could no longer withstand the assault of the enemy; whereas the latter fought in relays and were able to aid one another when hard pressed, not one of the former could leave the spot which he had been assigned to defend.[148] When they all had become wearied, exhausted, and weak, the enemy was able to effect an entrance; all the Ligurians burst in, and all the defenders [149] were either killed or captured. The victors treated their own countrymen there with more violence than they showed our men. No mercy was granted their fellow Latins. But, whether out of respect for the prince or through fear, about eighty of the emperor's knights were reserved for captivity. Even for the triumphant foe the victory was by no means a joyous one, as many of them were killed or mortally wounded. So Trezzo, previously a town of the Milanese, was captured, burned, and utterly destroyed by them.[150]

xxxviii (xxxiii). Upon hearing of this Frederick, though saddened for a time,[151] concealed his anger and held in check the ardor of his knights. He held the previously announced diet at Roncaglia with great display, and there assembled a numerous host of warriors. Only then did he zealously turn his attention to exacting vengeance for that affront.[152] He invaded Liguria with his entire army, burned and laid

[144] These last two sentences Rahewin has pieced together from *ibid.*, xxxviii.5, lvii.5, and lviii.3; hence the "Roman soldiers"—but Sallust's Numidians become Ligurians. The borrowing from the accounts of two separate engagements explains the inconsistencies, such as having the Ligurians both scaling the walls and not coming close enough to be much bothered by fire from within the town.

[145] *Ibid.*, xxxviii.5. [146] Cf. *ibid.*, li.2.

[147] Sallust *Catiline* xxvii.2.

[148] Sallust *Jugurtha* xxxviii.6, from which most of the following sentence is also copied.

[149] *Oppidani*, but "defenders" seems to be meant.

[150] Trezzo fell April 13, 1159. Otto Morena gives us a more valuable, if less poetic, account of this action (pp. 65–66). He notes that the Milanese captured there a large store of Frederick's money, and that the emperor, hearing of the attack, hastened northward from Bologna to relieve the fortress. Learning at Lodi of its fall, he turned back.

[151] Sallust *Jugurtha* lxviii.1. [152] *Ibid.*

waste the fields, destroyed vineyards, uprooted fig trees, ordered that all fruit-bearing trees be cut down or stripped of their bark, and ravaged the entire region. He decided not to besiege the city until the citizens were suffering from want of the necessities of life.[153] For he thought they would then be forced by lack of food either to beg for peace of their own volition or, if they remained defiant, they would be more readily overcome if he attacked them repeatedly later, when, after a blockade, they must either starve or be forced to surrender.

xxxix. Therefore the emperor ordered that all their means of exit be carefully watched. He deprived them of traffic in grain and other provisions and issued an edict setting forth the penalty to be visited on transgressors and the reward to be given those who would betray any who sold these things. But the people of Milan, though they had an abundance of grain and all other supplies inside the city, were nevertheless very much tormented by fear of the coming siege, and as provisions were already being sold in small quantities, the fact that they could not eat what they pleased aroused in them the greater desire, and they suffered as though all supplies had already failed.[154] Sometimes, too, the emperor, accompanied by his warriors, advanced as far as the city, thinking they would take some chance in consequence of which he might either defeat them in a general engagement if they came out to meet him, or, if they attempted a sally, that they would still not remain unscathed by disaster. And so it happened. For as they rashly came forth to display their strength, he made an attack upon them, capturing and killing many.

xl (xxxiv). And when the emperor and his army had gone past Milan on this campaign, the Milanese with five hundred horsemen came in secret to New Lodi on the holy day of Whitsunday [May 31] and drove off cattle as booty. But Bishop Carsidonius of Mantua and Marchese Werner of Ancona followed them with adequate forces, and when the people of Milan heard the loud voices of the very few Ger-

---

[153] This, with the remainder of the present chapter and the first sentence of chapter xxxix, is taken from Josephus *Wars* III.vii.11–12, an account of Vespasian's siege of Jotapata.

[154] This lengthy sentence is largely copied from Josephus, *loc. cit.*, but slightly modified to make it apply to food, where Josephus spoke only of water. Rahewin's choice of a quotation here is unfortunate; Frederick did not besiege or blockade Milan at this time (late May, 1159), lacking sufficient troops for such an enterprise until his main German forces arrived in July.

mans, they were terrified and turned in flight; some were killed and sixteen of their better men taken prisoner.[155] Moreover, it was just that divine vengeance overtook them, so that those who had shown contempt for the reverence and honor due this most holy day were themselves obliged to return with loss and with disgrace.

xli. For forty days the land of the enemy was ravaged. Among other citadels, towers, and fortifications suitable for defense by art or nature, a certain stronghold which was called St. John's Mount, considered impregnable up to that time, was besieged and, within a short time, captured.[156] Thus gradually the various outposts of the rebellious city were reduced and of its many towns and forts scarcely two were still left.

xlii (xxxv). During these days the people of Brescia, who also were eager for rebellion, entered the region of Cremona to ravage and pillage it. For they were bound to the people of Milan by ties of friendship and alliance. But the people of Cremona, warned in advance by their scouts, were ready. Bursting forth from ambush they took the Brescians by surprise. After a short struggle the invaders were put to flight and their booty was recovered. Sixty-seven horsemen and about three hundred foot soldiers were killed or captured by the men of Cremona.

After devastating the enemies' land the emperor went on to Lodi [late June, 1159] and there dismissed his Italian troops, awaiting the forces expected from beyond the mountains.

xliii (xxxvi). And the plight of the Milanese grew worse every day, since they were more and more driven to crime by their adversities, and by now a severe famine had its grip on the people in the city. Most of them, indeed, were moved to greater resistance, not by hope of victory, but by despair.[157] Beholding their many miseries, they did not repent of their design, but were made blind and mad. They even formed a conspiracy against the person of the most Christian emperor,

[155] Otto Morena, a citizen of Lodi, mentions no Germans in this action, but takes full credit for the men of Lodi (pp. 65–67).

[156] The location of this fortress is not known.

[157] These two sentences come bodily from Josephus *Wars* VI.i.1. The assertions that the Milanese were suffering at this time are fundamentally implausible, and one is inclined to suspect Rahewin of yielding to the twin temptations of glorifying the emperor, and of using what seemed to him a good quotation. It is somewhat surprising to find Giesebrecht (V, 194) taking this description at its face value.

forgetting the legally established punishment for this deed: "He shall suffer the loss of his life and his memory shall be branded with infamy after his death." [158] They found a certain man, who pretended that he was foolish and demented, and sent him to Frederick's camp—he was then staying at Lodi—that he might somehow lay violent hands on the emperor. Now this man was so large physically, and so strong, that it seemed not without reason that he had formed so bold a plot. And so, inspired by much flattery and many promises, he prepared himself for this great and unheard-of crime. He went to Lodi, entered the camp, and, feigning stupidity or a fit of madness, like such men was made a subject of jest and sport instead of being barred. Now Frederick's tents at that time were pitched almost on the bank of the Adda. The nature and location of the place were such that if a man slipped he must inevitably be killed by a fall from the steep precipice or swallowed up in the whirling waters of the stream that flowed by at its foot.

Accordingly, the aforesaid man, choosing a day and hour suitable for effecting his intended crime, when he might find the emperor alone, beheld him leaving his sleeping tent at daybreak on a certain morning that (as was his custom) he might offer up his prayers to God before the relics of the saints. Thinking he had secured the desired opportunity, the man rushed up, laid his accursed hands upon the emperor, and —now dragging, now carrying him—began to make for the edge of the precipice. He might perhaps have accomplished his infamous purpose had not divine mercy extended a hand to defend the divine prince. For while both were struggling in this fashion with all their might, the one pulling, the other resisting, it happened that both became entangled in the ropes by which the tents were fastened, and fell to the ground. And by this time the sound of the emperor's shouts had been heard and had aroused his attendants. They rushed up, seized the wicked monster, and after beating him soundly cast him over the cliff at that very spot to drown. Such was the common belief about him at the time. However, we have heard that the man was really crazy, and lost his life in all innocence.[159]

xliv (xxxvii). The Milanese, lamenting the failure of this crime, now planned another. They hired eight of their number to burn Lodi.

---

[158] *Institutes* IV.xviii.3.

[159] These last two sentences are lacking in two manuscripts, and may have been added later. Cf. the opening sentence of the following chapter.

When one of them tried to fulfill his promise, late at night, and had set fire to some houses, the watchmen found him and caught him. In the morning, when he had confessed his purpose, they hung him on a gallows set up to face Milan. Another spy also, who pretended that he was a monk, being guilty of the same crimes, was killed in the same way.

xlv. Not long afterward, as we have been told, a letter was brought to the emperor by a certain divinely inspired seer, in which it was stated that a Spaniard or Arab or Saracen, an old man of grotesque face and cross-eyed, had come into Italy with about twenty followers or companions. It declared that he was far superior to his predecessors in accursed wiles and the poisoner's art, and that he despised death. He and his followers believed that they would acquire great gain and glory and win eternal fame by shedding the emperor's blood. He would bring precious objects as gifts—medicines, rings, gems, bridles, spurs—all smeared with a poisonous powder, and so violently and effectively virulent that the emperor could not escape death if he merely touched them with his bare hand. He carried a hidden dagger also, next to his thigh, so that if, through any interference, the attempted poisoning were to fail, he might use it to perpetrate his dastardly crime.

Upon receiving this information, the emperor, revealing his plan to only a few, ordered that the approaching magician be placed under observation. Accordingly, when he came, after the emperor had learned positively that what had been reported to him was true, he gave instructions that the man be arrested. The emperor inquired at whose instigation the magician had been beguiled into so great a crime, and promised that if he told the truth all punishment would be remitted, but if he chose to utter falsehoods his body would be subjected to torture. The magician mocked at both blows and torture, and besides threatened that if he suffered a mortal injury the emperor would undoubtedly die at once with him. But he was greatly mistaken. For the emperor, despising his threats, when unable to extort from him any evidence concerning his accomplices and the instigators of the crime,[160] gave up this dangerous person, the inventor of so great a crime, to crucifixion, as he deserved, and bestowed lavish thanks upon God, the preserver of his safety, because he had escaped the poisons and the wiles of so mighty a villain.

[160] Josephus *Wars* I.xxvi.4.

xlvi (xxxviii). Meanwhile, the Empress Beatrice, Duke Henry [the Lion] of Bavaria and Saxony, and Conrad, bishop of Augsburg, as had been decided,[161] gathered troops and speedily began the journey with provisions, money, arms, and other things needful.[162] Setting forth with a great army, they arrived in Italy within a few days [July 20, 1159], and by their coming brought joy to our men and inspired fear in the enemy. For this duke, as has been stated above,[163] was the son of Duke Henry [the Proud] and Gertrude, daughter of the Emperor Lothar. Bereft of his father and mother while still in the cradle,[164] when he grew to manhood he was endowed with physical strength and comely in appearance, but was especially notable for his great intelligence. He was not corrupted by luxury or idleness, but— as is the custom of the Saxons—he rode horseback, hurled the spear, vied with his companions in running, and although he surpassed all in fame yet he was dear to all. His aim (as is said of a certain man) was modesty, decorum, but above all austerity. He vied with the brave in valor, with the modest in humility, with the innocent in temperance. He preferred to be, rather than to seem, good. So the less he sought for glory, the more he attained it. In all famous undertakings, he did the most and spoke least concerning himself.

This man had, as has been said above,[165] received from the emperor the duchy of Bavaria. Learning the character and habits of its men, by his great vigilance and wisdom he soon achieved such fame that, after establishing peace throughout all Bavaria, he became exceedingly dear to the good and a source of great terror to the bad.[166] So, fearing him in his absence as though he were present, no one dared break the laws of peace which he had established upon pain of death. When he had united his troops with the royal army, in a short space of time new and old became one, and all became equally valorous.[167]

Then, not long afterward [late September, 1159], the emperor's uncle, Welf, prince of Sardinia, duke of Spoleto, and marchese of

---

[161] See above, IV.xxviii.   [162] Cf. Sallust *Jugurtha* xliii.3.

[163] See above, II.vii and see I.xix.

[164] From this point to the end of the present paragraph, Rahewin offers us a picture of Duke Henry the Lion drawn entirely from Sallust, composed in equal parts of that author's accounts of Jugurtha and of Cato (*Jugurtha* vi.1 and *Catiline* liv.5–6). Cato is the "certain man" mentioned below.   [165] See above, II.xliii, lv.

[166] Much of this sentence is drawn from Sallust *Jugurtha* vii.4.

[167] *Ibid.*, lxxxvii.3.

Tuscany,[168] also brought up a new army, arriving in great state, and by his coming gave to our men hope of victory and to our adversaries confidence that they might enter upon negotiations. So these two men, very closely related in blood, as one was the son of the other's brother, vied with each other in opposite virtues. Welf won his fame by giving, helping, pardoning; Duke Henry, by severity and the suppression of evildoers. The affability of the one and the firmness of the other were praised. Welf, intent on the affairs of his friends, would neglect his own, refusing nothing worth giving. He longed for great power and desired an army, a new war in which his valor might be conspicuous. Duke Henry, on the other hand, cultivated self-control and strove not with the rich for riches, nor with intriguers at intrigue, but— whether present or absent—for the pursuit of peace. So there lived, within our memory, these two men of great courage and divergent characters, Duke Henry and Duke Welf. Since the opportunity presented itself, it was not my intention to pass over them in silence, but rather to portray the nature and character of each, so far as I am qualified to do so. It is very pleasant that our times have found, in these two very famous men, their Cato and their Caesar.[169]

But I return to the point whence I digressed.

xlvii (xxxix). Cremona and Milan, ancient enemies, always hostile and jealous of each other, never thought of laying down their weapons until one should completely destroy the other or at least win a decisive victory. Cremona, therefore, taking advantage of the present opportunity, urged Frederick to destroy the city of Crema, promising him eleven thousand talents. It was from the following incident that the affair started. Although Crema is within the territory and diocese of Cremona and must be ruled by the decision of the latter's church in spiritual and secular matters, with self-willed audacity she had broken away from her head and impiously allied herself with her foes: though a daughter city, she had joined Milan against her mother. Being summoned to appear before the emperor for this defection, Crema could be forced neither by legal citation nor by the security which it had long

---

[168] Welf VI (see above, IV.xiii). He was a brother of Henry the Proud, uncle of Henry the Lion, and son of Henry the Black, whose sister Judith was Frederick's mother.

[169] This long comparison of Welf and Henry is largely drawn from Sallust's comparison of Caesar and Cato (*Catiline* liii.6, liv.3–6), with Welf as Caesar and Henry as Cato; in the final sentence Rahewin brings his models into the open,

ago posted to appear in court before her adversaries. Wherefore, because of her failure to appear and her obstinate absence, she received a severe sentence and was declared an enemy.

xlviii (xl). Therefore the emperor, assembling so strong a force that his army seemed superior to that which he had had at the siege of Milan, dispatched one part with the people of Cremona against Crema. He himself, with the remainder, again entered the territory of the people of Milan to ravage the lands of Liguria. He ranged across that entire hostile country with the soldiery of the Germans, and there was fulfilled that saying: "That which the palmerworm hath left hath the locust eaten; and that which the locust hath left hath the cankerworm eaten." [170] But the people of Cremona, coming with auxiliaries and great forces, eagerly invested Crema with siege and assailed it with all their might. The townsmen resisted bravely from the walls; and before the walls a battle was valiantly fought by horse and foot. There, of our men, Marchese Werner, of Ancona, having attained in that battle the glory of a brave man,[171] was slain. Very many others on both sides, were either killed or seriously wounded.

Now Crema was situated in a level, open plain, quite generously provided with defense by men and, through the kindness of nature, defended in part of its circumference by a swamp. Besides, in addition to the great deep moats filled with water, it was surrounded by a high double wall that could easily ward off all approach and attack. The citizens of the town were very bold warriors, and because they had experienced too great success in fighting with their allies (the people of Milan and of Brescia) they had become cruel, insolent, and arrogant. Therefore, after the city was surrounded by siegeworks, sallies of their foes were carefully guarded against, and machines and other equipment useful for a siege were diligently set up.

xlix (xli). While these things were going on at Crema, certain very noble Romans came to the court as envoys of the senate and the people of Rome, with assurances of loyalty and devotion. They asked that the emperor should not, by reason of the iniquity of a few commoners, seek to destroy the many good and noble men. It was through them that he had the good fortune to be named emperor of the City and of the world. Frederick, because he had dealt very severely with them on his former expedition, received their representatives graciously, gave

[170] Joel 1:4.   [171] Josephus *Wars* I.xvii.

them a friendly answer, and after remaining with them for several days, bestowed royal gifts upon them and dismissed them.[172] He sent with them the oft-mentioned Count Palatine Otto and Master Herbert, provost of Aachen, a prudent man with long experience in affairs of state, ordering them to deal with the Roman people for the strengthening of the senate and the admission of an [imperial] prefect, to reach a settlement with the Roman pontiff—if he were willing—on the points previously mentioned,[173] and to establish harmony.

l. Coming to the City, they were received with due honor both by the people and by the senate, and many messengers went to and fro as mediators between them and the supreme pontiff. Though the Romans, after their fashion, sought to maintain the ancient dignity of their city, the royal messengers suffered themselves to be found in no respect inferior; nay, they contrived to be waited upon more frequently than they waited upon the others.

li (xlii). Meanwhile Frederick, who remained in Liguria, strove to inflict some defeat upon the Milanese, who had all fled to the city and intrenched themselves within. Therefore he planned with the most warlike of the citizens of Pavia that they should make a raid near Milan and permit themselves to be put to flight by the enemy; but he himself would fall upon the pursuers from ambush. Nor was he far wrong in his expectation. For the Milanese, when they became aware of this attack—for the Pavians had already begun to make off with their booty—pursued them vigorously, and, despite their resistance, cut them down with great ardor. And now those who were to yield in pretended fear were not far from actual flight, for they had diverged a little from the place of ambush.

Then Frederick, encouraging his men, came up from the rear and unexpectedly attacked the now eager and almost victorious enemy. He brought welcome aid to his men upon learning of their imminent rout. The Milanese, after thinking they had all but won the victory, saw themselves surrounded by the royal horse and realized that no opportunity of escape was left. Being unprepared, they were cut down and taken captive; horses and men alike suffered. Then followed a hor-

---

[172] This embassy is mentioned above, IV.xxxiv, xxxvi. Frederick's cordiality may be ascribed to the diplomatic changes since his "severe" treatment in 1155 (see above, II.xxx–xxxiii); he was then an ally of the pope, while the Romans were negotiating with William of Sicily, but now he has parted from the papacy, and the pope has made terms with William.   [173] See above, IV.xxxiv, xxxvi.

rible spectacle on the open plains, since the enemy, cut off and able neither to fight nor to flee, were destroyed without mercy. Finally, everything in sight was strewn with missiles, arms, and the bodies of the dead and dying.[174] The number of those killed or captured in that battle the emperor himself states in his letter written to Albert, bishop of Freising. For he says, among other things:

"Moreover, we send you encouragement with regard to our present situation, having no doubt of your anxiety for the honor of the empire and our success. Among other matters, 'the Lord hath done great things for us, whereof we are glad'[175] and offer to Him the utmost thanks. For God has delivered into our hands so great a multitude of the people of Milan that on the Ides of July [July 15, 1159], the date on which the dispersion of the apostles is customarily observed, we led off in chains as captives six hundred of the boldest men of the city; about one hundred and fifty others were killed in the fields and on the roads. Those who were drowned and wounded are beyond measure or number. So we returned victorious to the city of New Lodi."

lii (xliii). At this time Pope Hadrian closed his days at Anagni on the Kalends of September [September 1, 1159], and on the second day before the Nones of September [September 4] he was buried in the church of blessed Peter with all due honor, in the presence of the clergy, the senate, and the Roman people, while the royal representatives were still there. After his death the cardinals, unable to agree, destroyed the unity of the Church by a double election. Some of them chose Octavian, cardinal priest of the title of St. Cecilia, to whom they gave the name Victor;[176] others selected Roland, cardinal priest of the title of St. Mark and chancellor of the Roman Church, on whom they bestowed the name Alexander. But that the account of this affair may proceed in continuous and unbroken course, we shall meanwhile discuss others matters a little, that at the proper time we may dwell upon it at greater length, as the importance of the matter demands.

---

[174] Rahewin's account of this engagement is based on Sallust *Jugurtha* ci (apparently a favorite passage, for he drew heavily from it above, III.xi).

[175] Psalms 126:3.

[176] Cardinal Octavian, now the anti-pope Victor IV (1159–64), was the leader of a small group of pro-imperial cardinals. Cardinal Roland, now Pope Alexander III (1159–81), had been Hadrian's chief adviser, and leader of the group opposing Frederick and leaning toward an alliance with William of Sicily. For this disputed election and the subsequent schism, see below, IV.lix–lxvi.

liii (xliv). The emperor made ready another expedition to ravage the territory of Milan. But when he had advanced some distance and his foragers could find in all that territory no fodder for the horses, he returned and with his entire army took up the siege of Crema [late July, 1159]. Then at last fear settled down upon a city destined to perish, and a great dejection possessed its inhabitants.[177] Inside and out, all was filled with tumult, and many engines of war were built by both sides. Each party had its daily occupations: the one made sallies; the other, assaults. The fighting went on with great fury every day.[178] At the various gates where each prince was in command, the struggle was the fiercest, and no one placed more confidence in another than in himself. The townsmen conducted themselves likewise, and prepared everything useful for the defense of the fortifications according to their several abilities, concealing their lack of confidence in the outcome. Sometimes their success, sometimes their distress, inspired courage for many deeds.[179]

liv (xlv). And one day, when it had been discovered that Frederick had left the camp to visit his consort the empress, who was staying in a neighboring stronghold named San Bassano, the people of Crema issued forth with about six hundred horsemen to attack the gate which the king's household troops were guarding. A great battle was begun.[180] For a long time both sides with equal fortune did nothing but kill. The ground ran with blood. Though our men resisted with all their might, as much for shame as for pride, they could not force the enemy to retreat. On that day they fought bitterly and valiantly. For—if we may believe the story—the brooks in the fields were stained and swollen with the blood of the slain and the wounded; they were filled with blood.[181] When it was dusk, both sides retired, one party to its fortified camp, the other to the safety of its walls.

lv. When Frederick upon his return learned of the obstinate audacity of the foe, he was moved both to indignation and to wrath that those who, in such dire straits, ought rather to have been humble and suppliant, actually took the offensive and, though besieged, still dared

---

[177] This and the following sentence are drawn from Josephus *Wars* II.xxii.1.

[178] This and the two following sentences come largely from Sallust *Jugurtha* lx.1, 5.

[179] Cf. Josephus *Wars* III.ii.2.

[180] The three following sentences are taken from Florus *Epitome* II.xiii.80–81.

[181] This sentence is based upon Jordanes *Getica* xl.208—a description of the battle of Châlons in the year 451.

attack the victors. For they had already, in their sallies, often attempted to burn the siege engines, to destroy the towers, and to kill our men. They neglected no type of daring or display, in their ignorance of what the future had in store. And now, when their pride should have been broken, they boasted insolently of their deeds. But it was a pitiful sight when those outside cut off the heads of the slain and played ball with them, tossing them from the right hand into the left, and used them in mocking display. But those in the town, thinking it shameful to dare less, afforded a heart-rending spectacle by tearing limb from limb upon their walls prisoners from our army, without mercy.

lvi (xlvi). This disaster for a little while caused Frederick sorrow and righteous indignation. As he could not restrain their insane fury, and respect for the emperor did not check their mad frenzy, he determined to administer a severe punishment upon his stubborn foes, that the penalty of certain death might subjugate them where patient leniency had failed. Therefore he ordered that the captives from their number should be hanged on gallows before their walls. But that contumacious people, not to be outdone, likewise gave over to death certain of our men, prisoners in chains, and hanged them.

Then Frederick cried:

"Has our very benevolence incited you, who are doomed to perish, against us? Have you nourished your insolence on our leniency? Hitherto we have spared you though you fought against us; we have had mercy on those of you whom we held prisoners (*vestros captivos*), we have kept faith with you when you offered pledges. We moved our siege engines up to your walls unwillingly. We have always restrained our soldiers when they were greedy for your blood. All this you count as naught, and with wicked temerity provoke us to destroy you, to the doom of your sons and your grandsons. Accordingly, I shall now employ the rights of war. I shall contend against your defiance, without the least pity on you who have been unwilling to spare yourselves." [182]

With these words, violently enraged because those who were in the category of captives placed themselves on a par with the victors, he ordered that announcement be made by the voice of a herald that they

---

[182] This address is taken entirely from one delivered at Jerusalem by Titus (Josephus *Wars* VI.vi.2). It seems rather out of place here—especially the reference to proper treatment of captives, following on the heels of Rahewin's account of their being hanged.

should flee to him no more for refuge nor hope for good faith: for none was to be spared. So let them fight with all their might, and take measures for their own safety as best they could. For now he would act in all things in accordance with the laws of war.[183]

Therefore he ordered their hostages, to the number of forty, to be brought out to be hanged. Meantime, certain Milanese nobles, six knights who had been taken prisoner on a treacherous mission to the people of Piacenza, were brought in (for, as has been said above,[184] even at that time Piacenza feigned devotion and obedience to the emperor). One of them, a nephew of the archbishop of Milan, was a rich man and powerful in the councils of the Ligurians. Disdainfully refusing the large sum offered for their ransom, the emperor ordered them also to be executed, and they perished as had those mentioned above.

lvii (xlvii). And now many engines of war were brought up to destroy the city; now towers were built and put into action. The enemy resisted with all their might and persistence, warded off the towers from the walls, and repelled our siege engines by hurling rocks from their machines. But the emperor, thinking that a check must be offered to their unbridled spirits, determined that their hostages should be tied to the siege engines and exposed to the fire of their machines, commonly called mangonels,[185] nine of which were in use within the city.

The rebels (though this is a thing unheard of even among barbarians, horrible to tell of, and incredible when heard), nevertheless, struck the towers with frequent blows. Neither the bond of kinship and common blood nor pity for youth could move them. And so several children died miserably, struck by the stones, while others though remaining alive, suffered yet more pitifully, hanging there and expecting a most cruel death and the horror of so dire a fate. O how criminal an act! You might there have seen children fastened to the machines beseeching their parents, reproaching them, by word or gesture, for cruelty and inhumanity. On the other hand, the unhappy parents lamented their luckless children, called themselves most wretched—yet did not cease from hurling the stones. Yet one of them consoled the children by saying to them:

"O happy are they whose fate it is to die well rather than to live

---

[183] This paragraph is drawn word for word from Josephus *loc. cit.*, sec. 3.
[184] IV.xi, xxxi.   [185] *Mangas;* see above, II.xxi.

wretchedly! Be not afraid to die, since by death you will escape great evils. If we, fighting for liberty, were brave men, we too would not delay or await advice. For death brings freedom to men's souls, and happy indeed are they who, having died for their country, already have received immortality. How many of our predecessors have died in this fashion and under such conditions—some under torture both by fire and the lash—others, after being partly eaten by wild beasts, were saved alive to serve as another meal. We who still live are more wretched than you; though we often wish for death, we do not receive it. Let each of us consider the cruelty of slavery, whether among barbarians or his own countrymen: one will see his wife led to shame; a father, with his hands tied behind his back, will hear the voice of a son, crying for aid; another will see unhappy old men sitting amid the ashes of their country. Can any one of us, I say, contemplating these things, endure to look upon the light of day, even if he himself could live free from danger? O, would that we had all died before we saw our city destroyed by the hands of the people of Cremona; before we beheld our sacred land utterly ravaged by the impious Pavians!"

While he was attempting to speak further, they all interrupted him, and were inspired by a kind of unrestrained frenzy to hurl their missiles, supposing this to be a proof of valor and sound reasoning, to stupefy the minds of the enemy and arouse admiration for their audacity. A few, to be sure, following the dictates of reason, had wished to show consideration for their sons, but others were swayed by a desire to kill the children, consoling themselves for the necessity of slaughtering them by taking thought of the miseries they must endure if they were made subject to the enemy.[186]

Thus was Crema at that time affected—or rather afflicted.

lviii (xlviii). But the Milanese, thinking that Frederick in his concern for the siege of Crema could not assist those in difficulties elsewhere, set out about twenty thousand strong and invested a certain

---

[186] This unseemly episode is recounted by Otto Morena (pp. 79–81), who says nine of the prisoners were killed, the *Gesta di Federico in Italia* (pp. 112–13), and the *Gesta Federici in Lombardia* (pp. 37–38), which says Frederick so used about twenty captives, of whom seven were killed. None of these accounts gives any hint that children were involved. Otto Morena names five of the Milanese, and four of them may be identified with prisoners taken in battle shortly before (p. 72). The tale of the children tied to the siege engines seems to rest upon the shaky testimony of Rahewin alone, who, for the address and the whole episode, leans heavily upon Josephus *Wars* VII.viii.6–ix.1.

town in the direction of Lake Como, *Manerbe* by name.[187] They threw up earthworks, brought up siege engines, and strove by all means to reduce that stronghold. But Count Gozwin, who was then by the emperor's command capably governing the county of Seprio and Martesana, sent messengers to the court to tell of the enemy's attempt and to ask for instructions. He said that he would assemble what troops he could, if some reinforcements were sent from the army. The emperor decided to send five hundred armed horsemen thither immediately. The count, collecting his own forces, assembled no small army. And now, when all was ready, he showed himself to the Milanese, threatening them.[188] He neither attacked nor left them unmolested, merely distracting the enemy from their plans and not giving battle until the soldiers expected from the camp should arrive. The Ligurians, thinking that the emperor must of necessity come to the aid of his distressed men and that there would undoubtedly be a battle, raised the siege and, taking to flight, made haste to escape to their city. When the count saw this he pursued them vigorously, pressing hard upon them, killing, capturing, and carrying off rich spoil. Those who escaped fled, losing everything, and—many of them wounded—with great difficulty returned to their city.

lix (xlix). Meanwhile, the people of Piacenza were by many proofs shown to be planning rebellion. They were holding frequent conferences with the Milanese, secretly providing them with grain and other necessities, and had even sent some of their men to the aid of Crema. The emperor, thinking it better to have known enemies than false friends, because, as the saying goes, "there is no deadlier curse than an enemy masquerading as a friend," [189] and regarding them as very unstable and without much trust in either side, pronounced them enemies by reason of their treachery.

But the account demands that our discussion return to the schism in the Roman Church, whence we digressed. We would again remind the reader that he should not judge the truth of this matter from what we say or write, but decide for himself, after comparing all that was written on both sides, which is the more reasonable or—so to speak—

---

[187] Probably Erba, just east of Como.

[188] Most of this and the two following sentences comes from Sallust *Jugurtha* lv.8 and lvi.

[189] Boethius *De consolatione* III. prose v.

"who bore arms with greater justice." [190] For if we were either to extoll or extenuate the case of either side, we would be departing from our purpose. And assuredly, the rest of our history would not be sound were we to show favor in this important part of it.

lx (1). When the cardinals, the clergy, and the Roman people were divided (as has been stated above) in the election of a Roman pontiff, since one man, that is, Octavian, had been consecrated as bishop by his adherents and followers on the first Sunday of October [October 4, 1159] and the other, that is, Roland, on the eighteenth day of September,[191] both of them sent letters all over the world to explain the matter. Their contents were as follows:

"Bishop Victor, the servant of the servants of God, to his venerable brothers, the patriarchs, archbishops, and bishops, and to his very dear sons, the abbots, dukes, margraves, counts, and other princes, and to the illustrious imperial household, all those at the very sacred court of our lord Frederick the most serene and invincible emperor of the Romans, greeting and apostolic benediction.

"We believe that Your Highnesses have not forgotten how earnestly and how much we have hitherto in all sincerity esteemed the beauty of the ecclesiastical estate, the honor of the Roman empire, and the excellence of all good men, and what marks of mutual affection we have frequently exchanged. But now we desire to show to you and to the empire proof of even greater affection, since we have, by God's will, attained to a higher dignity. Wherefore we earnestly and confidently entreat you all by your reverence for the blessed Peter, the prince of the apostles, and by that constant and inviolable love which has existed between us, that you ask and exhort our lord, the most invincible emperor, to watch over the empire, entrusted to him by divine clemency, and the Church of God, the bride of Jesus Christ, of which he has been divinely appointed guardian and defender. Let him not delay to come to her aid, lest amid so great discord the malice of her adversaries may impiously prevail, the little bark of the blessed Peter be shattered by storms and tempests [192] in his time, and the imperial honor be dimmed.

"Besides, we have thought it worth relating to all of you how, by God's favor, we have been called to the apostolic office. When our

---

[190] Lucan *Pharsalia* I.126.   [191] Rather, September 20, 1159.
[192] Cf. Luke 5:3; John 6:16–21.

predecessor, Pope Hadrian, of blessed memory, went the way of all flesh and was buried in the basilica of the blessed Peter, we all assembled for the election of a pope. After long consultation and deliberation, finally through divine inspiration, by the choice of our venerable brethren, the cardinal bishops and cardinal priests of the Holy Roman Church, and of the Roman clergy, at the petition of the people of Rome, with the assent of the senatorial order and of the honorable captains besides, by God's favor we were canonically elected and placed upon the apostolic throne.[193] Then on the first Sunday of October [October 4] we received consecration and the full powers of our office.

Wherefore, we humbly beseech you all to aid us by your prayers to Him from whom comes all power and the dignity that attaches to high office. But if letters come to you from the party of that Roland, the former chancellor (who is associated with William of Sicily in a conspiracy and plot against the Church of God and the empire, and who on the twelfth day after our election had himself installed—unheard-of since the world began [194]), spew them from you as full of lies and designed by a schismatic and a heretic, and by no means listen to them in any wise.

"Given at Segni, on the fifth day before the Kalends of November [October 28, 1159].

lxi (li). "Bishop Alexander,[195] the servant of the servants of God, to his venerable brother, Bishop Gerard, and to his beloved sons, the canons of the church of Bologna, and the doctors of law and the other masters residing in Bologna, greeting and apostolic benediction.

"The eternal and unchangeable providence of the Creator has willed that the Holy and Immaculate Church from the very inception of its founding should be so governed that there should be one pastor and teacher, to whom without contradiction all the prelates of the churches shall subject themselves, and that the members, clinging as it were to their head, should be united with him by a certain marvelous unity, and

---

[193] For a more detailed account of this election from Victor's side, see the letter of his cardinals, below, IV.lxii. For the other side of the election, see the letter of Pope Alexander, below, IV.lxi. The election took place September 7, 1159.

[194] Cf. John 9:32.

[195] This letter bears no date. It is, however, almost identical with that sent by Alexander to the archbishop of Genoa on September 26, 1159 (printed in Doeberl, IV, 137–43); it differs only in the final paragraph, where our copy speaks of Octavian's consecration in the past tense, thus showing it was written after October 4.

should by no means depart from him. But He who made a promise to His apostles, to strengthen their faith, saying: 'Lo, I am with you alway, even unto the end of the world,' [196] undoubtedly will by no means permit His Church, in which the apostles themselves assumed the ministry of teaching, to be deprived of the fulfillment of His promise, but will cause it to endure forever in its own status and order, although—like Peter's little boat—it may seem at times to be tossed about by the waves.[197] But now three false brethren,[198] who indeed 'went out from us, but were not of us,' [199] transforming themselves into angels of light although they are devils,[200] are striving to split and to tear Christ's seamless garment,[201], which He Himself, in the language of the Psalmist, seeks to save from the lions and from the sword and to deliver from the power of the dog.[202] Yet Christ, the founder and head of the Church,[203] protects and guides her, His only bride, and though the ship of the glorious fisherman may frequently be tossed about, He does not permit it to be wrecked by the waves.

"Now when our predecessor of blessed memory, Pope Hadrian, had paid the debt of nature on the Kalends of September, while we were at Anagni, and at God's call had journeyed from earth to heaven, from the depths to the heights, after his body had been taken to Rome and, on the second day before the Nones of September [September 4], had been buried in the church of the blessed Peter with due honor, in the presence of almost all the brethren [cardinals], then (as is customary) all the brethren and we ourselves with them began to give earnest heed to the selection of a pontiff in his stead. And when we had busied ourselves with the election for three days, finally everyone present except three, namely, Octavian, John of St. Martin,[204] and Guido of Crema [205]—God is our witness that we lie not but speak the absolute

---

[196] Matthew 28:20.

[197] Cf. Luke 5:3; John 6:16–21; above, preceding chapter.

[198] Cf. Galatians 2:4.   [199] I John 2:19.

[200] Cf. II Corinthians 11:14.

[201] John 19:23, also cited in the preceding letter.

[202] Psalms 22:20–21.   [203] Ephesians 5:23.

[204] Cardinal priest of Saints Silvester and Martin.

[205] Cardinal priest of St. Calixtus; see above, iv.iii. Though Pope Alexander insists that only these three cardinals opposed his election, it will be noted that five cardinals signed the letter against him printed in the following chapter. In this letter they claim that Alexander was elected by a vote of fourteen to nine. Each side is apparently guilty of some exaggeration.

truth, just as it is—agreed harmoniously and with one accord upon our person, insufficient for this burden and by no means suited for the eminence of so great an office. With the assent of the clergy and the people, they elected us pontiff of Rome. But two, the aforesaid John and Guido, nominating the third, Octavian, stubbornly supported his election. Hereupon Octavian himself was swept into such audacity and madness that—like a maniac—he violently tore from our neck with his own hands the mantle, with which—according to the custom of the Church—Odo, the first of the deacons,[206] had invested us (though struggling and resisting, because we saw our unworthiness), and bore it off amid a tumultuous uproar. But some of the senators had seen this monstrous act, and one of them, divinely inspired, snatched the mantle from the madman's hand. But he straightway turned his flaming eyes in a frenzy toward a certain chaplain of his, who had come instructed and prepared for this, crying out and signaling that he should quickly produce the mantle that he had craftily brought with him. He did so without delay, and that same Octavian— greedy for honor—taking off his cap and inclining his head, after all the brethren had either left or were present involuntarily, assumed the mantle, at the hands of that same chaplain and a certain clerk of his. He himself—for there was no other—assisted the chaplain and the clerk. And we believe that it was through divine judgment that the part of the mantle which should have covered him in front covered his back, as many looked on and laughed. And when he himself frantically strove to remedy this, because he could not find the head-piece of the mantle—being beside himself—he slung the fringes around his neck, so that at all events the mantle might seem to be attached to him somehow. And so it came to pass that, even as his mind was distorted and his purpose perverse, so his mantle was put on crooked and awry, in token of his damnation.

"When this had been done, the doors of the church, which had been closed, were opened, and armed men, whom he had manifestly hired for money, rushed in with drawn swords, with an immense din, and that deadly pest, because he had no cardinal bishops, was surrounded by a throng of armed men. But the brethren, unexpectedly beholding a deed so monstrous—one unheard of since the world began [207]—and

---

[206] Or Otto, cardinal deacon of St. George *ad Velum Aureum*.
[207] John 9:32.

fearing lest they be cut down by the hired soldiers, betook themselves, together with us, to the protection of the church. And there, with the aid of certain senators whom he had corrupted with money, he had us kept under armed guard with all diligence, day and night, for nine successive days lest we should go forth in freedom. To be sure, as the people raised a continuous, unceasing uproar and raged furiously against the senators for their great impiety, we were taken from that stronghold, but those same senators placed us in a more secure and safe place in Trastevere,[208] receiving money for doing so. When we had spent three full days there, and the entire populace would no longer endure such treachery and malice, the senators, coming with the nobles and the people, conducted us and our brethren through the City with pomp and respect. We were lauded and extolled, and bells were rung everywhere along our route. When we had finally been thus snatched from the violence of the persecutor and restored to liberty, on the following Sunday [September 20], in the presence of our venerable brothers, the cardinal bishops Gregory of Sabina, Hubald of Ostia, Bernard, Walter, Julius, and B.,[209] and of abbots, priors, judges, advocates, notaries of the papal court, the *primicerius*, and the school of cantors, the nobles, too, and some of the populace of the City, assembled at Nimfa, not far from Rome, we received the rite of consecration, as is customary in the Roman Church, and there with ceremonial and solemnity we received the pontifical crown.

But the aforesaid Octavian, though both while he was in the City and after secretly leaving it he had summoned many bishops for his consecration—or rather his execration—was able to secure only one, namely, the bishop of Ferentino, to endorse his temerity and madness. He sought to entice some bishops by imperial threats,[210] some by lay violence, some by money and flattery, but—as God opposed him—he accomplished nothing. Hence even to the present day he can find no

---

[208] Two miles south of St. Peter's.

[209] These are the cardinal bishops Gregory of Sabina, Hubald of Ostia, Bernard of Porto, Walter of Albano, and Julius of Palestrina. The sixth, "B.," is in error; the only other cardinal bishop was Imar of Tusculum, who took the opposite side in this controversy. The Genoese copy of this bull mentioned above gives him as Bernard, bishop of Terracina (who was not a cardinal). Kohl suggests, rather implausibly, Boso, cardinal deacon (not bishop) of Saints Cosmas and Damian.

[210] *Imperialibus minis*, i.e., threats of retribution at the hands of the emperor if they failed to support him.

one to lay the hands of execration [211] upon him and make himself responsible for such great presumption and impiety, though he is trying in every way. But the aforesaid [cardinals] John and Guido, wrapped in the dark night of blindness (as it is written: 'When the wicked cometh, then cometh also contempt' [212]) as yet do not repent of their damnable presumption, but still with stubborn perfidy worship that same Octavian, whom they have set up as an image [213] for themselves and, forsaking the unity of the Church, presume even until now to adore him like an idol or an effigy. But he, foreshadowing for us the times of Antichrist, is still so far exalted above himself that he even 'sitteth in the temple of God, shewing himself that he is God,' [214] and many have seen with their own eyes, not without shedding many tears, the abomination of desolation, standing in the holy place.[215]

"Knowing, in truth, our weakness and our dearth of virtues, we cast our thoughts on the Lord, hoping and fully trusting in Christ's mercy that He will cause His Holy Church—for which He Himself appeared in our mortal substance, that He might show it 'not having spot, or wrinkle' [216]—to rejoice in longed-for peace. Nothing can any longer withstand her, as soon as her only Bridegroom shall will to dispel all clouds and dangers, and the tempest has been allayed. Now, therefore, since we lack confidence in the quality of our merits, but have absolute faith in your honor and piety, we ask that our weakness be aided by your prayers and those of the Church universal, beseeching and earnestly imploring your charity by apostolic writings, that as Catholic men you interpose yourselves, like impregnable walls, in defense of the Lord's house,[217] and that you continue unmoved in your devotion and fidelity to your mother, the Holy Roman Church, and by no means depart from her unity. But if the aforesaid impious man shall chance to have sent into your parts some of his damnable writings, spurn them as they deserve, despise and reject them as vain and sacrilegious.

"Finally, Your Discretion should know that on the eighth day from our consecration [September 27]—for we set that as the limit for him to repent and return to the unity of our mother Church—with lighted

---

[211] That is, consecration; see above, in this paragraph. Octavian was consecrated as Victor IV on October 4, at Farfa, by the cardinal bishop Imar of Tusculum, assisted by the bishops of Melfi and Ferentino.

[212] Proverbs 18:3.   [213] Cf. Daniel 3:12, 18.   [214] II Thessalonians 2:4.
[215] Matthew 24:15.   [216] Ephesians 5:27.   [217] Cf. Ezekiel 13:5.

candles, with our clergy assembled in the church by the common will and counsel of our brother bishops and cardinals, we have fettered the aforesaid Octavian, the apostate and schismatic, with the bonds of anathema and excommunication, as disobedient and contumacious, together with those who presumed to lay upon him the hands, not of consecration, but of execration, and we have condemned them with their instigator, the devil."

lxii (lii). "To their venerable brethren in Christ, the patriarchs, archbishops, bishops, abbots, dukes, princes, provosts, priors, and other prelates of the churches to whom this letter shall come: Imar, [cardinal] bishop of Tusculum, first of the bishops; the cardinal priests John, of the church of Saints Silvester and Martin, and Guido of Crema, of the church of St. Calixtus, and Raymond, cardinal deacon of St. Mary *in Via Lata;* and Sy.[Simon, cardinal deacon] of St. Mary *in Dompnica* and abbot of Subiaco, perpetual greeting in the Lord.[218]

"From the time that friendship was established at Benevento between our lord Pope Hadrian and William of Sicily [1156], contrary to the honor of the Church of God and of the empire, no small dissension and discord have arisen not without cause between the cardinals of the Holy Roman Church. For we, who desired that the honor and dignity of the Holy Church of God should in no wise be diminished, by no means gave our assent to the friendship which had been established to the detriment of the Church and of the empire. But others, blinded by money and many promises, and held fast bound to the aforesaid Sicilian, wickedly defended this treaty, and won over very many to partake in their error, stubbornly resisting our efforts and desires with all their might.

"Then, in the course of time, as it was reported that the emperor had entered Italy and subjected the greater part of it to his power, the aforesaid brethren who were bound to the Sicilian began to importune

---

[218] *Reimundus diaconus cardinalis Sanctae Mariae in Via lata et Sy. Sanctae Mariae in Dompnica et Sublacus abbas;* Kohl takes the latter to be abbot of St. Mary *in Dompnica* and Subiaco; Simson, to be cardinal deacon of St. Mary *in Dompnica* and abbot of Subiaco. He was certainly abbot of Subiaco. St. Mary *in Dompnica* was a cardinal diaconate, but no Cardinal Simon is known. The inclusion of his name with the other four cardinals would seem to imply that he was of their number; possibly he was an appointee of the antipope. At any rate, this letter comes from the cardinals supporting Octavian. It is undated, but would seem to have been written shortly after his consecration, October 4, 1159.

the lord pope, and to deceive him very craftily so that upon some pretext or other the lord emperor and all his followers should be placed under excommunication, and that both we and they should bind ourselves by an oath to do this. But we, on the contrary, declared that the Sicilian—who had by violence robbed the Church of all her rights, spiritual as well as temporal—should be excommunicated rather than the emperor who was laboring faithfully to regain the rights of the Roman Church and of the empire, and to lead back the Church from slavery to liberty. Upon hearing this, the adherents of the Sicilian blushed and said no more of their aforementioned plan. So this plan had thus been brought to naught by our zeal and tireless vigilance. Then, while our venerable brother Octavian, then cardinal priest of the Holy Roman Church, now pontiff of the apostolic see, together with brother William, cardinal priest of St. Peter in Chains, was on a mission to the emperor,[219] the lord pope set forth from the City with those who agreed with him and the adherents of the aforesaid William, and came to Anagni. There at length all the adherents of the aforesaid William, in the presence of the lord pope, in open conspiracy, bound themselves by an oath that they would subject the emperor to excommunication and from that time forth would steadily oppose his honor and his will to the death, and, in the event of the lord pope's death, they would choose as pope no one except from the number of those who had sworn this oath. Moreover, they enjoined by oath the near-by bishops not to place their hands in consecration upon anyone who was elected without the assent of the Sicilian faction.

"Now after our father Hadrian—already mentioned so frequently—died at Anagni on the Kalends of September, we all assembled there, and a great contention arose concerning his body, whether it was to be buried there or brought to Rome. It was finally transported to Rome, after we had first unanimously and in all sincerity made and consigned to writing the following agreement:

" 'In the name of the Lord, Amen. The cardinal bishops, priests, and deacons of the Holy Roman Church have agreed and promised each other in all sincerity that in the election of the future pope they will act in accordance with the custom of that Church, namely, that certain of the brothers shall be set apart to hear the wish of each and to make careful inquiry and keep a faithful record; and if it be God's

[219] See above, IV.xxxiv.

will that they can harmoniously agree on some one of the same brothers, well and good. But if not, then let some outside person be discussed, and if we can agree in harmony, good. But if not, let no one proceed further without common consent; and let this agreement be observed without deceit or evil intent.'

"When this compact had been sincerely confirmed, after the burial of the body in the church of the blessed Peter, we convened to elect a pope and (in accordance with the aforesaid custom) set apart certain ones to make careful inquiry into the wishes of all, to listen, and to record. But when the election proceeded but slowly on account of the conspiracy of the opposing party, as the third day was drawing to a close it had finally come to this, that fourteen cardinals of the opposition, who were held bound by their oath, named Chancellor Roland. But we—nine in number—who had no part in the accursed oath, chose our venerable brother the cardinal priest Octavian, knowing him to be a thoroughly honorable and pious man, worthy and able to rule the apostolic see, and to restore and maintain the unity of peace and concord between the Church and the empire. As the matter was being conducted in this fashion, and we perceived that the opposing party wished completely to override the agreement which had in all sincerity been confirmed, we recalled the aforesaid pact to their minds, and strictly forbade them, in the name of Almighty God and all the saints and by virtue of our own authority, to place the mantle upon anyone without the common consent of all of us (as the agreement provided). And by the same authority, we absolutely forbade Chancellor Roland to accept it. They made light of our words and admonitions and hastened to invest him with the mantle. But before he was so invested we (desiring to oppose their wickedness rather than consent to it, and by no means acquiescing in their evil attempt), in response to a petition of the Roman people, upon election by all the clergy, and with the assent also of almost the entire senate and of all the captains, barons, and nobles, both those living within the City and those outside, invested our elected candidate with the mantle, enthroned him upon the seat of the blessed Peter, and led him thence with all due honor to St. Peter's palace, all the people shouting their acclaim, the clergy chanting a hymn to God, in all solemnity.

"But the cardinals of the opposing party withdrew, betook themselves to the stronghold of blessed Peter, and there remained shut up

for eight days or more. Being afterward led forth thence by the senators, they withdrew to a place outside the City and on the twelfth day
thereafter—unheard-of since the world began [220]—in a stronghold
named Cisterna, between Arricia and Terracina,[221] invested Chancellor Roland with the mantle, and on the following Sunday [September
20] execrated him,[222] and straightway sending messengers throughout
all Italy, they absolutely forbade the bishops to come to the consecration of our elected pope, threatening them with excommunication and
desposition from office forever. Nevertheless, he was consecrated with
all honor, in the name of God, on the first Sunday of October [October
4].

"We have told you, our brethren, the truth of this matter, adding
nothing to it, and calling Him to witness who cannot be deceived. And
'if an angel from heaven preach any other gospel unto you,' [223] it
would be completely false. But, nevertheless, we omit many things and
tell you even this as briefly as possible, lest we should burden your ears
by too prolix an account. Give heed, therefore, to these things. And we
earnestly beseech, adjure, and exhort you by all possible means, in the
name of the Lord, not to be moved from your opinion by word or by
letter, but to continue with us, fixed and immovable, in the truth."

lxiii (liii). "To Frederick,[224] by the grace of God the glorious, illustrious, magnificent, and sublime emperor of the Romans, the [car-
dinal] bishops Gregory of Sabina, Hubald of Ostia, Julius of Palestrina, Bernard of Porto, and Walter of Albano, and the [cardinal]
priests Ubertus, of the title of the Holy [Cross], A[staldo], of the
title of [St.] Prisca, John, of the title of Saints John and Paul, Henry,
of the title of Saints Nereus and Achilles, Ildebert, of the title of the
Basilica of the Twelve Apostles, John, of the title of St. Anastasia,
Bonadies, of the title of St. Chrysogonus, Albert, of the title of St.

---

[220] John 9:32, already quoted in the letters of both rival popes above.

[221] Cisterna is midway between Rome and Terracina, about twenty-five miles
southeast of the former city.

[222] That is, "execrated" in the sense in which this word was used by Pope Alexander
in the preceding letter. The similarities of phrase and allusion in the letters of these
rival factions are rather marked; it would seem that they read each other with some
care.   [223] Galatians 1:8.

[224] Having read the letters of the rival popes and of the Victorian cardinals, we
come now to the letter of the majority faction of the cardinals, supporting Alexander,
and signed by twenty-three cardinals. It is undated, but was written at about the time
of the other letters.

Lawrence *in Lucina*, and William, of the title of St. Peter in Chains, and the cardinal deacons Odo of St. George *ad Velum Aureum*, R[udolf] of St. Lucia *in Septasolis*, Hyacinth of St. Mary *in Cosmedin*, Odo of St. Nicholas *in Carcere Tullii*, Ardicio of St. Theodore, B[oso] of Saints Cosmas and Damian, C[inthius] of St. Hadrian, Peter of St. Eustace, and J[ohn of St. Mary *in Porticu*], being assembled voluntarily and by inspiration of the Lord, greeting and a glorious victory over your enemies.

"The greater the power conferred upon, and assigned to, Your Excellency by God, and the more sublime the station of honor among mortals that is yours to hold, so much the more does it become Your Imperial Majesty to honor the Very Holy Roman Church, your special and unique mother, and always to provide for her welfare and advantage, and particularly in her time of need.

"It is fitting—nay, most fitting—that we should inform Your Imperial Highness by letter of what has recently occurred in that same Roman Church, and of the incredible deed perpetrated by those regarded as her sons. For when, on the Kalends of September, our lord of blessed memory, Pope Hadrian, had paid the debt of nature at Anagni and had journeyed from earth to heaven, from the depths to the heights, at God's call, three false brothers, namely, Octavian and John of St. Martin and Guido of Crema, who indeed 'went out from us, but were not of us,' 'transforming themselves into angels of light although they are devils,' and so forth." [225]

And farther on:

"Further be it known to Your Sublime Grace that the Count Palatine Otto, supporting Octavian's presumption, has greatly persecuted our aforesaid lord [pope] and has without just cause sought to divide and throw into confusion the Church of God. For he has violently entered Campania and the patrimony of blessed Peter, with that intruder and apostate Octavian, and has endeavored by every possible means to subjugate that land. Therefore we—and the entire Church of God with us—as suppliants implore Your Majesty to take pains to learn the truth of this violent usurpation, and to ponder earnestly how you ought to proceed in so grave a matter for your soul's safety and the honor of the

---

[225] Here Rahewin seems to have realized that this last sentence has become a repetition of the letter of Pope Alexander (above, iv.lxi), and he therefore omits part of it.

empire. Consider and take heed how you should conduct yourself toward the Very Holy Roman Church and her only Bridegroom, our Lord Jesus Christ, without whom no one can obtain earthly rule or attain to the heavenly realm, and how, by virtue of your imperial office, you should in every way guard and protect her from her assailants and especially from schismatics and heretics. For we would honor you in every way as the special defender and patron of the Roman Church, and strive, with God's aid, by all possible means, for the increase of your glory. But we ask and very earnestly implore that you love and honor the Holy Roman Church as your mother and take thought for her peace and tranquillity, using such means as are consonant with the imperial majesty, and on no account foster the great iniquity of the aforesaid usurper and schismatic."

lxiv (liv). Frederick, moved by the perplexing evil of the new schism, upon the advice of the princes determined to take heed that the status of neither the Church nor the realm should receive any hurt from it.[226] Therefore, hearing that each of those who had been elected had been consecrated for the bishop's office, and that each had been condemned by sentence of excommunication, the one by the other, he thought that the controversy could be ended only by a judgment of the Church itself. Moreover, he thought that he had the authority to call a Church council, following the example of emperors of old (for instance, Justinian, Theodosius, and Charles), and considering that there could be no proper decision unless the opposing parties to the dispute were brought together, he sent the venerable and wise men bishops Daniel of Prague and Herman of Verden to summon both, with a letter of which the following is a copy: [227]

lxv (lv). "Frederick, by the grace of God emperor of the Romans and august forever, to Chancellor Roland and the other cardinals who elected him pontiff of Rome, greeting and every good wish. Since, by divine preordained favor, we have undertaken the governance of the Roman empire, we must in all our ways safeguard His law, by whose boon and of whose will we have attained the high pinnacle of our station. Therefore, with this most pious purpose, we must not only protect all the churches within our empire, but should also zealously provide for the Very Holy Church of Rome, whose care and defense are

[226] Cf. Sallust *Catiline* xxix.2.
[227] The following letter was written in late October, 1159.

believed to have been specially entrusted to us by Divine Providence. Therefore, we grieve greatly over the discord which has arisen among you in the selection of a bishop of Rome. For we fear lest, by reason of this schism, the Church that was redeemed by Christ's blood be torn asunder, and especially lest the strength of the Church abroad wane, since its unity is destroyed within. But that we may apply to this affliction a suitable remedy, and one pleasing to God, by the advice of men of religion, we have summoned a general court and council to be held at Pavia on the octave of Epiphany [January 13, 1160]. To it we have summoned the archbishops, bishops, abbots, and pious and God-fearing men of all our empire and of other realms—namely, England, France, Hungary, Denmark—in order that, setting aside all secular judgment, this extremely important matter may be settled by the decision of churchmen only, so that thereby due honor may be rendered to God and that the Roman Church may not be deprived by anyone of its integrity and justice, or the state of affairs in the City, the seat of our empire, be thrown into confusion. Accordingly, we commend the matter to Your Wisdom and bid you, in the name of Almighty God and the whole Catholic Church, come to that same court or council to hear and accept the verdict of the churchmen. For God is our witness [228] that in this court we seek nothing because of love or hatred of any person, but only the honor of God and the unity of His Church. And if you wish to come to this solemn council of the Church to consider the matter, the venerable fathers and bishops of the Catholic Church and our own very dear princes, Herman of Verden and Daniel of Prague, whom we have sent to you from our palace, together with the count palatine, our kinsman,[229] and our other legates, will guarantee you safe conduct. But if you are unwilling to accept God's justice and that of the Church in so solemn a council, may God see it and judge. But as for us, by the grace of Him who giveth salvation unto kings,[230] we shall honor God's justice, as beseems none more than the emperor of Rome."

lxvi (lvi). Furthermore, the following may suffice as an example of the letter whereby the bishops across the mountains were summoned to this meeting:

"Frederick, by the grace of God emperor of the Romans and august

---

[228] Romans 1:9.   [229] Otto of Wittelsbach.
[230] Psalms 144:10.

forever, to Hartmann, bishop of Brixen, greeting and every good wish.

"That at the time of His passion Christ was content to have two swords,[231] was, we believe, a marvelous revelation regarding the Roman Church and the Roman empire, since by these two institutions the whole world is directed in both divine and human matters. And although one God, one pope, one emperor, is sufficient, and there should be also but one Church of God, we now have—we cannot speak of it without sorrow—two popes in the Roman Church. For when Pope Hadrian died, on the Kalends of September, the cardinals (who seemed to be immovable pillars, upon whom the holy and universal Church might most firmly rest), seeking not the things which are God's, but their own,[232] and disrupting the unity of the Church, chose and consecrated two popes. By reason of so great and harmful a rift in the Church, the whole Italian Church is, truly, thrown into confusion. From the schism in the head, dissensions have now permeated the lower members and would have defiled the entire body of the Church, had we not, by the advice and assistance of pious men, led by the spirit of God, opposed to such shameless impiety the rigor of justice. Lest, therefore, the universal Church be imperiled by so disastrous a discord, the Roman empire, which by divine clemency is ready to heal so baneful a malady, should solicitously provide for the welfare of all, and—lest such evils pervade the Church of God—wisely prevent such things in the future. Therefore, we brought together all the bishops, both Italian and German, and all the other princes and devout men zealous for God and the Church, and carefully considered what should be done. We have found reliable evidence in the decretals of the Roman pontiffs and statutes of the Church that, when a schism arises in the Roman Church through strife between two popes, we should summon them both and decide the case in accordance with the judgment and advice of orthodox men. Therefore, by the advice of all the bishops and other princes present, we have proclaimed a solemn court and general council of all churchmen to be held on the octave of Epiphany, to which we have summoned the two who call themselves pontiffs of Rome, and all the bishops of our empire and of other realms, namely, France, England, Spain,[233] and Hungary, that in our presence it may

---

[231] See Luke 22:38.   [232] Philippians 2:21.

[233] On page 300 above Denmark appears in the list instead of Spain.

be determined upon due investigation which of them ought rightfully to rule the Universal Church. But inasmuch as your wisdom is greatly needed for the restoration of the unity of the Church, and we can by no means dispense with it, we most solicitously request and exhort Your Love that, putting aside all excuses, in loyalty to the Church and to the empire, you come to the aforesaid court, that by your coming the unity and peace and tranquillity of the Church may be restored. But meanwhile, refuse your adherence to either party in the aforesaid schism, and by no means accept either as just and reasonable.

"Given at Crema on the tenth day before the Kalends of November [October 23, 1159]."

lxvii (lvii). But we must return to what was done at Crema. The people of Crema, as has been said above,[234] had been visited with affliction in the case of both their hostages and captives. Now their sallies and their boldness abated somewhat, and they thought rather to outwit and destroy our men by shrewdness and cunning. For they made certain instruments very much like mousetraps but stronger, to match the strength of the human body, and set them up on the roads and about the moat, by which many straying unawares might easily be captured or killed. They also roofed over many ditches with frail coverings, and those who crashed through them were similarly captured or killed. As these and many other snares such as robbers use were continually being made by the besieged, both for plunder and to burn the siege engines, Frederick became more and more annoyed at their craftiness and their audacity. And because he had given up hope of capturing the city by starvation—for they had an abundance of grain—he again determined to have recourse to force of arms.[235] All the soldiers were very eager for this; disgusted by the length of the siege and wearied by their many exertions, they were becoming melancholy and wanted the war ended in any fashion. For it was now the sixth month of the siege and the rains and bitter cold had been greater than usual that winter.

lxviii (lviii). Therefore, bringing up all his machines, Frederick ordered the army to storm the city.[236] He raised aloft towers covered on all sides with iron and other material, so that they might be firm by

---

[234] See above, iv.lvi, lvii.

[235] This and the preceding sentence are drawn from Josephus *Wars* iii.vii.13.

[236] The remainder of this paragraph is largely borrowed from *ibid.*, secs. 24–30. We are now near the end of the siege of Crema, in January, 1160.

their weight and not easily burned. He placed them on mounds, and filled them with slingers and archers and the bravest of his warriors, who themselves could not be seen, but who could very easily see those standing on the walls or walking about in the city. The enemy could not readily avoid arrows that came from above, nor could they retaliate against men whom they could not see. As often as they assailed the machines with iron weights, red-hot and barbed to catch onto them, those on top rendered their efforts vain by extinguishing the fire with water and detaching the hooks and barbs of the iron with long poles and stakes. For they had attached blades to these, so that if any of the material fastened to the towers to lighten the blows from the war engines had caught fire, they might immediately cut it off.[237] And so the people of Crema offered much resistance, although many of them fell every day, and they could do but little damage to their foes.

lxix (lix). And since we are anxious to reach the end of this siege, to move on to other matters, we would like to touch upon the last and greatest combat, fiercely fought with shifting fortunes. The emperor, seeing that the townsmen had no mercy on themselves and would not spare the city, decided on a general attack. Therefore, selecting the bravest men from the several companies,[238] he stationed them at various places in the towers, some above, some lower, so that while those lower down attacked bridges in order to gain entrance to the city over the walls, those higher up might defend them with javelins and arrows against injury from the enemy. The towers themselves were of tremendous height, jutting up over a hundred feet and accommodating many men on each level. He distributed the remainder of the army around the walls, giving instructions that when the bridges were moved into position, they also would attempt either to surmount or to break through the wall at the point where they were stationed. Thus he disposed of both his detachments.[239]

Now the town was surrounded and everything was ablaze with arms,[240] with the trumpeters and standard-bearers of all the companies also assembled and awaiting the signal to attack on all sides. The

---

[237] The confusion here is Rahewin's; he has pieced together rather clumsily two separate passages in Josephus. In the first, the Romans are protecting their towers from the Jews; in the second, the Jews are protecting their walls from the Roman rams.

[238] This and the preceding sentence are drawn from Josephus *Wars* VI.ii.5.

[239] *Ibid.*   [240] Much of this sentence is from *ibid.*, III.vii.27.

besieged, seeing this, quickly made ready and boldly awaited the
assault on the walls and in those machines called "cats" [*gattas*],[241]
so that when the bridges were moved into position they might seize
them or throw them down, and hinder by various means those attempting to scale the walls. At that time they displayed deeds of great
daring lest, even in the face of utter disaster, they might appear inferior to our men. Now the bridges were with much difficulty put in
place, and the entire line set foot on the wall.[242] The people of Crema,
well protected inside their machines, gave the firstcomers, above and
below, a warm welcome with their spears, while those in the rear were
checked by missiles from their engines. The men before the walls were
scattered; those scaling the walls by ladders or other means were sent
tumbling to the ground. But our men did not lack courage in adversity, nor did the Cremans prove wanting in ferocity. Indeed, one of
our soldiers named Bertolf of Urach, who had reached the city
among the very first by leaping from a bridge, though surrounded
by the enemy, showed himself a most valiant fighter. Singlehanded,
he pursued many far into the city and was brought down by one of
them by a blow from a long axe, from behind; for all who were in
front avoided him, as he ran through their midst, both fearing and
admiring the man's audacity. Finally, when they had killed him, one
of them, cruelly venting his fury upon the dead, scalped him (it was
said) and, after first very carefully combing the hair, attached the
scalp to his helmet. He was a base fellow and utterly shameless,
neither moved by the man's courage nor pitying our human lot. Another, they permitted to crawl about the streets after cutting off his
hands and feet—a wanton jest. Furthermore, although those who attempted to scale the wall are individually worthy of remembrance,
yet Otto, count palatine of Bavaria, proved himself the bravest of
them all. Though repeatedly driven back from the wall and repeatedly returning before the others to the task he had begun, by virtue
of his courage he was an honor to the whole miserable affair.[243] Not
with impunity, however, nor for long did the Cremans have occasion
to rejoice over their good fortune. For so many of the townsmen were
killed or wounded that day by the various missiles sent by our men

---

[241] Employed usually in the sense of an enclosed and protected ram. Here, however,
it appears to be used as a protective machine.

[242] For the last three sentences cf. Josephus *Wars* III. vii.27.

[243] Much of these last two sentences is taken from Josephus *Wars* VI.iii.2.

from the height of the towers, that they were driven from the outer wall and took refuge within the inner fortifications connected with a second wall. Then for the first time they despaired of their cause.

lxx (lx). The emperor, seeing that the fall of Crema was near (for exertion, fear, and calamity had broken the strength and courage of the besieged),[244] postponed the council which was to have been held on the octave of Epiphany [January 13], and directed all his attention to the reduction of the city. For their valiant young men had by now fallen, and many succumbed every day to spears and arrows, and, as has been said, they could do our men no hurt in return.[245] In such straits, taking counsel of necessity, they sought a conference with Pilgrim, the patriarch of the church of Aquileia, and Henry [the Lion], duke of Bavaria and Saxony, and at their request a place and time were set for the wiser and more distinguished men of the city to present themselves before the aforesaid leaders. When morning came and both parties were present at the appointed place, the patriarch, a learned man endowed with many virtues who had, besides the authority of his office, the gift of great eloquence, is said to have begun by speaking to them as follows:

lxxi (lxi). "If I did not see that you are inclined to give thought to conditions of peace, and recognize in you the purer and most sincere part of the people of Crema, I should never have come out to you or ventured to confer with you. For (as a certain writer says), 'It is vain to speak of what is good if the unanimous attitude of all the inhabitants is directed toward what is bad.' But since youth made some of you unaware of the evils of war, while others were prompted by an ill-advised hope of freedom, and still others were inflamed by avarice, measures must be taken, upon the advice of the few who are good, to cure them of these errors. But if this has not been done since the war started, at least repentance now may minimize your transgression. While you were unwilling to avoid the storm by remaining in the harbor, you may still feel a timely concern for your shipwrecked bark in the midst of its blasts. Have compassion, if not on your city, which is already lost and on the verge of destruction, at least on your sons who still survive, and on your wives. Spare the remnant of your men, even though you were unwilling to spare the dear shrines within the walls of your country. Knowing now the ferocity of the Germans,

---

[244] *Ibid.* VI.viii.4.   [245] *Ibid.* III.vii.30.

their valor, and their great size, doubt not that their spirits are greater than their bodies, and that their souls hold death in contempt. I shall tell you briefly what I think. You must bow your necks to the victorious prince, and put your trust, not in arms, but in surrender. For if, despising peace, you persist in your revolt, undoubtedly you will be subjected to greater perils than those you have yet suffered." [246]

To these words they made reply, repressing a little the grief in their hearts, saying: they had taken up arms, not against the emperor, but against their own countrymen of Cremona.[247] Long ago they had determined that they wished to serve neither one party nor another, but only God and the emperor. They had shown in many ways that they preferred death to dishonorable slavery. They had made an alliance with the people of Milan and—while it had pleased God—had kept it inviolate. They were feeling God's anger because of their sins; the emperor's good fortune was superior. For though they had an abundance of arms and no lack of food supplies it was only too clear that God had taken from them the hope of victory. But they asked that they be obliged to pay the penalty not to their kinsmen and great enemies of Cremona, but only to the emperor. They desired to end the war: they could not escape the emperor's valor.

lxxii (lxii). When the princes previously named saw that the Cremans desired peace and were surfeited with war, they reported to the court what had been said. It was satisfactory; conditions of peace were discussed, drawn up, and accepted without objection by the townsmen. Now the terms were these: that the people of Crema were to surrender their city, and they themselves, being granted their lives, might go where they pleased with their wives and children, taking with them as much of their property as each could carry on his back at one time. But the Milanese and Brescians, who had come in to defend this city, leaving their weapons and all their possessions, were to consider it gain enough that their lives were spared. All these terms were finally fulfilled on the sixth day before the Kalends of February [January 27, 1160]. After about twenty thousand people of both sexes had left the town, it was given up to the flames and the soldiers were allowed

---

[246] This address comes bodily from a speech of King Agrippa, *ibid.* II.xvi. In it Rahewin inserts a vague reference to his source: "as a certain writer says."

[247] Thus far this paragraph is mostly copied from Josephus, *loc. cit.*—the reaction of the Jews to Agrippa's speech.

to loot it. After its destruction was complete, the divine Augustus, with all his jubilant army, departed for Pavia to celebrate the joyous victory.[248] When his approach was announced, the entire population of the city came forth into the roads and streets to meet him [February 3, 1160], with old men and young, with their wives and children, and wherever he halted on his march, with many cries they extolled the majesty and the mildness of his countenance, calling him a man worthy to triumph and their savior, the only person who deserved to be entitled Roman emperor. The entire city was adorned like a temple and was redolent throughout with various aromatic odors. But though he could scarcely reach the church through the crowd that surrounded it, before he went to the palace he paid his vows to Almighty God, "who giveth salvation unto kings," [249] offering thanks for the triumph he had been vouchsafed.

The council which he had planned to hold on the octave of Epiphany [January 13], he decided to convoke in that same city of Pavia on Candlemas Day.[250] Furthermore, an imperial letter was immediately sent all around the empire with regard to the subjection—or rather the destruction—of Crema. It read as follows:

lxxiii (lxiii). "Frederick, by the grace of God emperor of the Romans and august forever.

"Your Prudence is aware, we believe, that so great a gift of divine grace, so evidently accorded to our honor, to the praise and glory of Christ's name, cannot be concealed or hidden like a merely private matter. Therefore we make it known to Your Love and Devotion, that you, who are very dear and loyal to us, may share in our honor and our joys. For on the day following the conversion of St. Paul [January 26], God granted us complete victory over Crema, and thus we have triumphed gloriously over her, and yet we have granted the wretched folk that were in the city their lives. For both divine and human law demand that the utmost clemency should ever dwell in a prince."

lxxiv (lxiv). It was the time at which the council announced for

---

[248] The following account of Frederick's reception in Pavia, to the end of the present paragraph, is Josephus' description (*op. cit.* VII.iv) of Vespasian's arrival in Rome, save that Rahewin substitutes a church (with a Biblical quotation) for Vespasian's palace and household gods.

[249] Psalms 144:10.

[250] *In purificatione sanctae Mariae*—February 2. The council convened February 5, 1160.

Pavia was to be held, and the archbishops and bishops and other prelates of the churches assembled from all parts of the realm, on both sides of the Alps, awaited it eagerly. Then the emperor admonished all to commend the cause of the Catholic Church to God by fasting and prayers and, together with the priests and all the people, besought divine aid through the faithful intercession of the saints. Then he convoked the council [February 5, 1160] and when he had sat down he said to the bishops:

"Although I know that, by virtue of my office and the dignity of the empire, the authority to convoke councils (especially in such great perils of the Church) is vested in me—for it is recorded that the emperors Constantine and Theodosius and Justinian also, and in more recent times Charles the Great and Otto did so—yet I commit to your wisdom and your power the authority to reach a decision in this very great and important matter. For God has constituted you priests, and given you authority to judge us also. And because it is not our place to judge you in those matters which pertain to God, we charge you to be and to act in this case as though you expected judgment upon yourselves from God only."

When he had said this, Frederick withdrew from the council, entrusting the entire investigation to the Church and to the innumerable churchmen present. For there were about fifty archbishops and bishops, but it was impossible to estimate the abbots and provosts because of their multitude. There were present also representatives of various countries, who promised that whatever was decreed by the synod would certainly be accepted by their people.[251]

lxxv (lxv). And so the bishops and all the clergy sat for seven days while the case was heard. Finally, victory in the dispute fell to the lord Octavian, who had come personally with his supporters. The council gave a verdict for him, condemning Roland and reproving him because, though duly summoned, he was said to have stubbornly refused to present himself before the council.

But we would remind the reader repeatedly that in this matter he is not to consult our account in order to discover the truth of this

---

[251] Though Rahewin puts the best possible face upon this council, no church outside the empire was represented. As he says, some other governments sent observers; but it was a council of prelates faithful to Frederick, and he ran little risk by withdrawing from its meetings. There could be no doubt that it would decide for the antipope.

matter,[252] but to rely on the letters and documents which have come into our hands and have seemed to deserve inclusion in this work, subjecting them to his own judgment, since they seem to give a sufficiently faithful account of this controversy and the verdict of the council.[253]

lxxvi (lxvi). "Upon their most invincible and glorious lord Frederick, emperor of the Romans and august forever, and upon the venerable fathers assembled in Christ's name, the brethren who are at Rome, the canons of the basilica of the blessed Peter, prince of the apostles, [invoke] the presence of an angel mighty in counsel and the consoling grace of the Holy Spirit.

"Most holy fathers, whom God hath chosen to console the sorrowful and correct sinners, as the apostle says, 'warn the unruly,' 'comfort the feebleminded,' [254] give heed to our entreaties and stretch forth the hand of consolation to assuage our grief. For so great and so all-embracing is the occasion for our sorrow that we can only with difficulty decide at what point we ought to begin. But as it is an occasion for grief and sorrow, we have decided to begin with lamentation and sorrow. Therefore, 'behold, and see if there be any sorrow like unto our sorrow,' [255] when we see our mother, the Roman Church, once radiant with splendor, shamefully rent and mutilated by her own sons, nay, rather by outsiders, since those whom she nourished and raised up have become false, and have rebelled against her.[256] There she lies in the mire, and perceives not her shame and her loss. Hence we say with Jeremiah, lamenting the destruction of his Jerusalem: 'The kings of the earth, and all the inhabitants of the world, would not have believed that the adversary and the enemy should have entered into the gates of Jerusalem.' [257] Truly Jerusalem was our mother, the Roman Church, which gave peace to all who came to her and asked for it. But now we, too, say in our sorrow, as once she did: Our 'Jerusalem hath grievously sinned; therefore she is removed.' [258] Not undeservedly, 'for the sins of her prophets, and the iniquities of her priests; they have

---

[252] See above, iv.lxiv. Rahewin, though clearly leaning to the imperial side in this controversy, is careful to appear neutral. It is to be noted, however, that the documents which now follow are all statements of the case for Octavian.

[253] The long letter which follows bears no date, but was presumably written just before the council, in early February. It comes from the Roman clergy favorable to the antipope.   [254] I Thessalonians 5:14.

[255] Lamentations 1:12.   [256] Cf. Isaiah 1:2.

[257] Lamentations 4:12.   [258] Lamentations 1:8.

wandered as blind men in the streets; the anger of the Lord hath divided them.' [259] And truly. For 'the face of the Lord is against them that do evil, to cut off the remembrance of them from the earth.' [260] Hence are we covered with shame. Truly our present Jerusalem has grievously sinned through envy and hatred and many iniquities. Because it would take too long to relate them all, we shall describe the election of the Roman pontiff and make known the cause of the dissension.

"Accordingly, when Pope Hadrian, of blessed memory, went the way of all flesh in the first watch of the Kalends of September, immediately a very great throng assembled, in which senators, too, were present, and by their advice the body was transported to Rome. But although a disagreement arose among the cardinals, yet they finally agreed to return to Rome and to elect in harmony some one of themselves. If they could not do so, they would seek some outside person. If, however, they could not agree on one, they would postpone the election until they could find a suitable person whom they would elect harmoniously. And this was unanimously ratified. Now, after this they returned immediately to Rome. The lord Octavian and certain others came to pay the last rites to the dead. But certain others sent Boso,[261] that author of evil, that first-born of Satan, on ahead to occupy the castle of St. Peter, whose garrison had sworn fidelity to him while Pope Hadrian was still alive; and afterward they followed him to that same place. But the lord of Tusculum [262] went to the palace. The lord Octavian and the lord chancellor Roland, and certain others came to our houses.[263] But when summoned by those who were at the castle, they replied that they would never go there, for fear of Boso, lest—as had been told them—they be taken prisoner by Boso's confederates. And the lord chancellor said: 'I shall go and make them come down to you.' The deacon *de Carcere* [264] went with him, and they did not come back. And so for two days they could not agree on a place in which to

[259] Lamentations 4:13, 14, 16.   [260] Psalms 34:16.

[261] Boso, an English Benedictine monk of St. Alban's, and a nephew of Hadrian IV, was named cardinal deacon of Saints Cosmas and Damian by his uncle in 1155. He is the author of a series of lives of twelfth-century popes (very brief save for Hadrian IV and Alexander III) printed in *Liber pontificalis*, ed. L. Duchesne (Paris, 1886–92), II, 351–446.

[262] The senior cardinal bishop, Imar of Tusculum.

[263] That is, the houses of the canons of St. Peter's, who are writing this letter.

[264] Cardinal deacon Odo of St. Nicholas *in Carcere Tulliano*.

conduct the election. Finally, they came down from the castle on Saturday [September 5], and all began to discuss the election behind the altar of St. Peter. And as they could not agree, those who desired concord and peace in the Church said: 'Leave the election to us, and we will choose one of you, or do you conduct the election and choose of us whom you please.' And they would not. Finally, there arose, as though in anger, Odo, [cardinal] deacon of St. George, and Hildebrand Crassus, cardinal [priest] of the Holy Apostles, and John of Naples,[265] and, taking the mantle, wished to place it upon the lord chancellor Roland. But they could not, since the saner and better part [266] of the cardinals, in the name of Almighty God and the blessed princes of the apostles, Peter and Paul, and of the whole Church forbade it. Despite this prohibition, however, they made another attempt to robe him; but they could not, and did not even touch the chancellor with the mantle. Yet it was no fault of theirs that he was not invested with it. But the Roman clergy, who had assembled in the church of St. Peter for the election of the supreme pontiff, upon hearing the uproar, ran in. Surrounding Lord Odo,[267] who was with the cardinals near the altar of blessed Peter, they all cried out, saying: 'Choose Lord Octavian, through whom alone the Church can have peace!' Then at the request of the Roman people, and by the choice of all the clergy, the entire chapter of the basilica of St. Peter consenting and desiring it, the lord cardinal Octavian was elected by the saner part of the cardinals and invested with the mantle and placed upon the throne of St. Peter, without any objection, all jubilantly singing the *Te Deum laudamus*. Then, as is customary, the lord cardinals and all the Roman clergy who had been present throughout or who had come afterward, and the greater part of the Roman people, all kissed his feet. When they saw this, the lord chancellor Roland and those who (as was said) had been bound

---

[265] There were four cardinals named John at this time: John of Pisa, cardinal priest of Saints Silvester and Martin (and a supporter of Octavian); John of Sutri, cardinal priest of Saints John and Paul; John of Anagni, cardinal deacon of St. Mary *in Porticu*; and the cardinal priest of St. Anastasia, who thus must, by elimination, be identified with John of Naples.

[266] *Saniore et meliori parte;* Octavian's party here falls back on the doctrine that a correct minority is superior to an erring majority. This suggests the theory, developed in the following century, of the weight to be given to the *major et sanior pars* in episcopal elections. See Alan Gewirth, *Marsilius of Padua and Medieval Political Philosophy*, pp. 182–99, esp. 193–96, and the references there given.

[267] Giesebrecht (VI, 392–93) feels this should read "Octavian" rather than "Odo."

by the oath did not protest or object in any way, but with bowed heads turned back and returned to the castle like men disappointed in their hope. Then the lord cardinals, the clergy, the judges, the notaries, the senators, and the Roman people joyfully conducted their lord-elect to his palace, with banners and standards,[268] crying out in the Roman fashion: 'Pope Victor! St. Peter chooses him.'

"Now on the following day certain of the Roman clergy went up to the castle and, kissing the hand of the lord chancellor, began to ask him and those who were with him to take measures for the peace of the Church. But a certain deacon of the court answered them, as though indignant: 'Yesterday you kissed the feet of Octavian, who stripped his brother, the lord chancellor, of the mantle and put it upon himself, and do you now come to us?' And the lord chancellor said: 'Do not say what is not true, Lord Cardinal. The lord Octavian never stripped me of the mantle, because I never was robed in it.' And so, during a whole week, the lord chancellor and his followers remained in the church of St. Peter. On the ninth day they came down to Trastevere, remaining that day and the next. On the eleventh they came forth and reached Nero's cistern,[269] in which Nero hid from the Romans who were pursuing him. Most appropriately they came to a cistern, because 'they have forsaken the fountain of living waters and hewed them out cisterns, broken cisterns, that can hold no water.' [270] And there, on the following day (which was the twelfth from the election of Lord Victor), they invested the chancellor with the stole and pallium of error, to the destruction and confusion of the Church, and there first sang the *Te Deum laudamus.* Who of you, most holy fathers, has heard of such a thing? So far as was in their power, the Roman Church today has become two-headed.

"Now we must cease speaking, that Lord Otto, the count palatine, and Lord Guido, count of Biandrate, and Lord Provost Herbert,[271] very prudent men, legates of the imperial majesty, may have their turn, to report what they have discovered concerning the lord chancellor and his followers. While the lord bishops [272] have reported the

---

[268] *Signis bandonis,* which Giesebrecht (VI, 388) would correct to read *signis et bandonis;* cf. below, IV.lxxvii, lxxx.

[269] That is, Cisterna; see above, IV.lxii.

[270] Jeremiah 2:13.

[271] The imperial legates sent to Rome; see above, IV.xlix.

[272] Possibly a reference to the bishops in Rome with these legates; see below, IV.lxxx.

known facts, the lord legates of the emperor will be able to set forth in greater detail whatever instances of humility and of truth they have discovered. Since, we believe, they were present in the City when the Roman clergy assembled at the church of St. Peter, they themselves may report what they saw of that event. To confirm this, we are sending to Your Holiness two of our brethren, Peter Christian, deacon of our church, and the subdeacon, Peter Guido, chamberlain (*camerarius*) of the Holy Roman Church, that they may, by word of mouth, give you testimony of the truth of all these matters.

"At our Lord's last supper, whereat he performed the sacrament of human redemption, the apostles declared that they had two swords, which you also have. What you should do therein and thereby, no one of you fails to understand. There it was said by Christ: 'It is enough.' [273] And we, who ought to follow in Christ's footsteps, say unto you, our lords, as we set an end to this work, 'It is enough.' May the wisdom of the Omnipotent Father, who knows and can unite the prayers and the wishes of all, teach you all, and unite you to the destruction of Babylonish confusion, and the expulsion of simony from the Church, and the establishment of the peace desired by all the world!"

lxxvii (lxvii). It seems best to set down also the acts of the council, which were reduced to writing in simple language:

"These are the points which were canonically approved in the council of Pavia with reference to the election of the lord pope Victor. The lord Octavian and no one else was solemnly invested by the cardinals with the mantle at Rome, in the church of St. Peter, upon petition of the people and by the consent and desires of the clergy. In the presence of the chancellor, who offered no objection, he was installed on the throne of St. Peter, the *Te Deum laudamus* was solemnly chanted for him by the cardinals and the Roman clergy, and the name "Victor" was bestowed upon him. There a multitude of the clergy and the Roman people came to his feet. Then the notary, in accordance with an ancient custom of the Romans, mounting the platform, cried out in a loud voice, saying to the people: 'Hear ye citizens of Rome and assemblage of the republic! Our father Hadrian died on the second day of the week, and, on the Saturday next following, Lord Octavian, cardinal of St. Cecilia, was elected Roman pontiff and invested with the mantle and installed on the throne of St. Peter and named Pope

[273] Luke 22:38.

Victor.[274] Are you content?' The clergy and people replied in a loud voice: 'We are.' A second and a third time the people were asked if they were content and replied in a clear voice: 'We are.' Then with banners and other papal insignia the lord pope was escorted to the palace with songs of praise. Accordingly, when all this had been duly performed, the chapter of St. Peter came straightway to the feet of the same Pope Victor, offered obedience, and showed him due reverence. A great throng, clergy and people, similarly offered obedience.

"Now on the following day the rectors of the Roman clergy, approaching the lord chancellor and the cardinals who were with him, desired to know if he had been invested with the mantle, as some were saying. They found that he was not invested with the mantle nor distinguished by any sort of badge of office and, in the course of conversation with him and his cardinals, they learned from his lips and theirs that he never had been invested with the mantle and that that was falsely attributed to him. Upon hearing and learning this, the rectors came to the feet of Lord Pope Victor and rendered him obedience and reverence.

"Witnesses to all the aforesaid points were: Peter Christian, deacon of the basilica of St. Peter, and all his brethren, and two rectors of the Roman clergy, namely, the priests Blasius and Manerius, and seven archpriests of the city of Rome, and four others—deacons and subdeacons.

"Then the Prior of [St. John] Lateran and his canons gave obedience.

"The clergy of the patriarchal [275] church of St. Mary the Greater gave obedience.

"The abbot of the patriarchal church of St. Paul gave obedience through his representatives, and in token of obedience sent him some of the possessions of his church.

"The abbot of the patriarchal church of St. Lawrence, with his monks, gave obedience.

"The abbot of [St.] Cirengius gave obedience.

"The abbot of St. Silvester, with his monks, gave obedience.

[274] Hadrian died Tuesday, September 1; Octavian's "election" came on the following Monday, September 7.
[275] That is, one of the five Roman churches pertaining directly to the pope (St. John Lateran, St. Peter, St. Mary the Greater, St. Paul, and St. Lawrence.

"The abbot of St. Alexius on the Aventine Hill, with his monks, gave obedience.

"The abbot of St. Blasius, with his monks, gave obedience.

"The convent of St. Sabina gave obedience.

"The convent of St. Mary on the Capitol gave obedience.

"The convent of the monks of Saints Cosmas and Damian gave obedience.

"The abbot of St. Valentine gave obedience.

"The master of the brethren of the Temple of Jerusalem on the Aventine Hill, with his brethren, gave obedience.

"The titular church (*cardinalia*) of St. Marcellus gave obedience.

"The clergy of the titular church of the Holy Apostles gave obedience.

"The clergy of the titular church of St. Peter in Chains gave obedience.

"The clergy of the titular church of St. Silvester gave obedience.

"The clergy of the titular church of St. Sixtus gave obedience.

"The clergy of the titular church of St. Sabina gave obedience.

"The clergy of the titular church of St. Balbina gave obedience.

"The titular church of St. Cyriacus in the Baths of Diocletian gave obedience.

"The clergy of the titular church of St. Mary in Trastevere gave obedience.

"The clergy of the titular church of St. Mary *in Porticu* gave obedience.

"The clergy of the titular church of St. Nicholas *in Carcere* gave obedience.

"The monastery of St. Agatha gave obedience.

"The archpriest of St. Apollinaris gave obedience.

"The archpriest of St. Trypho gave obedience.

"The archpriest of St. Bartholomew gave obedience.

"The church of St. Celsus gave obedience.

"The church of St. Mary *in Monasterio* gave obedience.

"The church of St. Mary *in Palaria* gave obedience.

"The church of St. Salvator *de Curte* gave obedience.

"The archpriest of St. Vincent, with his clergy, gave obedience.

"The archpriest of St. Catherine, with his clergy, gave obedience.

"The archpriest of St. Thomas *de Parrione* gave obedience.

"The archpriest of St. Anastasia, with his clergy, gave obedience.

"The archpriest of St. Salvator *de Campo*, with his clergy, gave obedience.

"The archpriest of St. Mary *in Monte Celso*, with his clergy, gave obedience.

"And many other churches and monasteries, which we can scarcely enumerate, gave obedience.

"After the elevation of the lord Victor, the canons of St. Peter sent canons of their number to Chancellor Roland, to see if he had been invested with the mantle, as certain people believed, or in any way exalted. Twice investigators were sent, and twice they reported that he had not assumed the mantle or been in any way altered in rank. But on the following day, that all doubt might be dispelled, the canons sent certain of their number to visit the cardinals' table, which they maintained, and see if he occupied (at least at the table) a higher place than usual, or even whether he was the first in the blessing of the table or seemed in any way to be regarded as of higher rank among the cardinals in place or dignity or garb. In all these respects they found him in no wise exalted or changed; and after this fashion the canons scrutinized the chancellor's status for eight whole days in succession.

"Basso and John *de Romano* [276] declare: 'After the chancellor had returned to the castle, while our lord Victor sat on the papal throne, John *Phizutus*, a clerk, and John *de Bucca-Lata*, a layman, desired to invest the chancellor with the mantle. He scornfully repulsed them, saying: "Do not make me a laughingstock. There is the pope, go to him and obey him!" '

"The priests Blasius and Manerius, rectors of the Roman clergy, say that on the day following the exaltation of the lord Victor they, with three other rectors of the clergy, went to the chancellor and to all the cardinals who were with him, and did not see him wearing the mantle or in any way raised in rank, and before they left they twice heard from the lips of the chancellor that he was not and had not been invested with the mantle. Besides, Cardinal Odo *de Carcere* [277] testified, in the presence of those very rectors and eyewitnesses, that Lord

---

[276] These two persons are identified in the following paragraph, though the name "Basso" there becomes "Barro."

[277] Cardinal deacon of St. Nicholas *in Carcere Tulliano*.

Octavian had offered no violence or hurt to the chancellor. Odo said likewise: 'It is without truth that this offense is attributed to the lord chancellor; no one took the mantle away from him, because he never had it.' After all these things had been thus done and learned, those rectors went to Lord Victor and did him obeisance and instructed the clergy to do the same. And this was done.

"The priests Barro and John, chaplains of the titular church of the chancellor, said that on the day following the elevation of Lord Victor they went to the chancellor and spoke to him as follows: 'When we heard that you had been invested with the mantle, we rejoiced, and now that we see it is not so, we grieve.' He said to them: 'Do not rejoice or grieve for me, because I neither was nor am I now invested with the mantle. Go and obey him whom you see wearing the mantle.' That these words actually issued thus from the chancellor's lips the priests Barro and John confided to certain of our clergy who were present; they swore on their souls that it was true.

"The clergy of the titular church of St. Chrysogonus said that on the day following the elevation of Lord Victor they approached their cardinal,[278] who was with the chancellor, and asked him, saying: 'All the clergy are going to the feet of the lord pope, so what shall *we* do?' He replied: 'Go to him like the rest.'

"Many of our people say that the chancellor departed from the City on the eleventh day without the mantle, without the stole, without a white horse, and without any change of garb, and went to Cisterna clad in a black cloak trimmed with fur and with a black almuce.

"John *de Romano* says that he heard John of Naples and Bonadies and certain other cardinals saying, at Cisterna: 'Since we are now without a shepherd and without a head, let us make ourselves a lord,' and thereupon they invested him with the mantle and chanted for him the *Te Deum laudamus* at Cisterna.

"John of St. Stephen and Wolfram state that they heard Pope Hadrian say to them, as he was leaving the City: 'Octavian, whom I sent into Lombardy, would excommunicate the Milanese, but I have told them not to be concerned about him, and that both they themselves and the people of Brescia should conduct themselves valiantly against the emperor, and I have arranged with them that, by reason of their resistance, the emperor will not be able to come to Rome.' Like-

---

[278] The cardinal priest Bonadies, mentioned below.

wise: 'I have also arranged with my cardinals that Octavian shall not be pope after my death.'

"Gimund and Wolfram say that they heard from the lips of the bishop [Gregory] of Sabina that he would gladly return to Lord Victor, but that he was so fast bound by his oath as to be unable to do so without perjury.

"The bishop of Alatri said, in the presence of the lord cardinal Guido of Crema, Gimund, John of Gaeta, and many others: 'I cannot come to Lord Victor, because I gave such assurance to the chancellor and his followers at Anagni that I cannot come to them until the Kalends; but after the Kalends I will come. Meanwhile, however, I regard him as my lord and my shepherd.' Therefore, when the Kalends were past, since he was prevented by illness, he sent his allegiance to the lord Victor through a certain clerk whom we have present with us.

"Regarding all the above points, the aforesaid rectors of the Roman clergy and the seven archpriests previously mentioned gave testimony, as also many honorable and devout members of the Roman clergy, and Peter, the prefect of the City, and Stephen *de Tebaldo*, and Stephen the Norman, and John of St. Stephen, and John of Gaeta, and Wolfram *de Gidocicca*, and Gimund of the house of Pierleone, and many other illustrious and very noble Romans who were present at all these events, and saw and related them all."

lxxviii (lxviii). After Victor had been thus confirmed and accepted as pope, the verdict of the sacerdotal council was presented to the emperor. After it had been respectfully received and approved, Victor was summoned to the church and received with great ceremony by a large assemblage of clergy and people, and was acclaimed as the supreme pontiff and universal pope. The divine emperor also humbly showed him the customary reverence and the service as stirrup-holder before the doors of the church, as Constantine had done for the blessed Silvester, and taking him by the hand he led him to his seat and enthroned him. Concerning the other things that were done there, consult the copies of letters that follow:

lxxix (lxix). "Frederick, by the grace of God emperor of the Romans and august forever, to his most beloved Eberhard, the venerable archbishop of Salzburg and his suffragans, the bishops Albert of Freising, Hartmann of Brixen, and Romanus of Gurk, and the entire province of Salzburg, his love and all good wishes.

"If you had been present at the holy council held at Pavia, you could yourself have seen what was done there and in the Roman Church. However, lest the truth be obscured and Your Sincerity be drawn into opposition by those who have already bespattered almost the whole world with their false accusations and their lies, we have thought it proper to indicate to you, as briefly as we can, the course of the entire matter—the absolute truth, without any admixture of falsehood.

"It is established—clearer than light—that while Pope Hadrian was still alive Chancellor Roland and certain cardinals, not giving heed to the Lord's saying: 'Let your communication be, Yea, yea; Nay, nay,' [279] formed a conspiracy with William of Sicily (once excommunicated by them) and with other enemies of the empire—the people of Milan, of Brescia, and of Piacenza. Lest, perchance, at the death of Pope Hadrian so iniquitous a faction might disappear, they swore mutually that, when the pope died, they would choose no successor save one who had joined with them in that same conspiracy.

"On this account, on the twelfth day after the election of Lord Victor as pope, while he was sitting on the seat of St. Peter, the aforesaid conspirators, going forth from the City, betook themselves to Nero's Cistern [Cisterna], 'forsaking the fountain of living waters,' [280] and set up as their idol Chancellor Roland, saying that this was Simon Peter —a man who presumed to attain to the summit of apostolic dignity by so wicked a usurpation. That this conspiracy had been formed, and that the previously mentioned Roland thereby entered upon his office in this fashion, is not fictitious, but has been made known in wondrous fashion to devout men, by Him who maketh manifest the counsels of the hearts.[281]

"While these things were going on at Rome and we were consulting men of religion—that is, archbishops and bishops—as to what should be done regarding so great a schism, there appeared, as though sent by God, the archbishop of Moutiers-en-Tarentaise, the abbot of Clairvaux, the abbot of Morimund,[282] and other abbots to the number of ten, seeking peace for the people of Milan. Upon receiving our terms,

[279] Matthew 5:37.
[280] Jeremiah 17:13; Cf. IV.lxxvi., above (Jeremiah 2:13).
[281] I Corinthians 4:5.
[282] It is uncertain whether this is the Cistercian abbey of Morimund in Champagne, where Otto of Freising had become a monk and had died, or its daughter house, Morimondo, near Milan, founded in 1134.

they returned to Milan to discover the wishes of the Milanese, and received from them the following reply: 'Lord fathers, we are bound by an oath to the lord pope and the cardinals, that we are not to return to the emperor's favor without their consent. And they, on the other hand, can make no peace without ours.' The abbots replied to them: 'You are no longer bound to the lord pope, for he is dead.' And they straightway made rejoinder: 'If the pope is dead, we are not freed thereby, because we are none the less under obligation to the cardinals and they to us.' The aforesaid father abbots have testified before many pious men that this is the reply they received from the Milanese.

"Besides this, we have obtained from letters intercepted on the highways many proofs that a conspiracy had been formed, as the bearer of this has very clearly seen and heard. And so, upon the advice of orthodox men (as we recall having informed you on another occasion),[283] we convoked a general assembly of churchmen at Pavia. To it we summoned, through the venerable bishops of Verden and Prague, both men who claimed to be Roman pontiffs, not to secular judgment, as the mouths of liars declare, but to an investigation by the Church. Now one of the two, who had a clearer conscience—I mean Lord Victor—voluntarily presented himself for judgment by the Church. But the other, namely, Roland, stubbornly refused and said that whereas he himself must judge all, he would be judged by none. So when the reverend council convened (wherein the patriarch of Aquileia and many pious archbishops and bishops had assembled), for eight days in succession the question was discussed with the greatest seriousness and after the most careful investigation, no laymen at all being present, which of the two was rightfully entitled to the office of the supreme pontiff. And so, after long deliberation, because that most infamous conspiracy, odious alike to God and to the Church, was not merely proved by manifest evidence, but revealed before the very eyes of the whole Church there present; and because nothing blameworthy was found in Lord Victor (save that a minority of the cardinals—those who were entirely unassociated with that conspiracy—elected him to reestablish a blessed peace between the empire and the papacy); invoking the grace of the Holy Spirit, the Church of God condemned Chancellor Roland as a conspirator and a schismatic who preached that discord and strife and perjury are good, and confirmed Lord Pope

[283] See above, IV.lxvi.

Victor as spiritual father and universal pontiff. Following the lead of the Church, we have accorded him our recognition and declare that, by the aid of divine clemency, he shall be father and ruler (*rectorem*) of the universal Church. We ask and earnestly desire that this action, supported by divine protection and firmly founded in apostolic stability upon that Rock—to wit, Christ—be approved by Your Blessedness for the peace of the entire Church and the security of the empire, and that it be maintained and upheld by the entire church entrusted to Your Holiness.

"Given at Pavia on the fifteenth day before the Kalends of March [February 15, 1160]."

lxxx (lxx). The following is the general rescript sent out into all parts of the world by those who presided over the synod:

"Because the disturbance of the apostolic see has deeply wounded the hearts of Christians, we, who were assembled at Pavia to heal the schism and to reëstablish peace in the Church, have felt that the nature of the case, the method of procedure, and the decision of the holy council should be fully made known to all of you, that by the present writing (revealing the whole truth) the hearts of our hearers may vigorously reject the false views which they perhaps had conceived, and that henceforth they may not be led astray by schismatic writings.

"Accordingly, when the assemblage of the orthodox had convened at Pavia in the name of the Lord, the case was lawfully and canonically discussed and carefully investigated for seven days in succession, all secular judgment being barred. It was adequately and canonically proved in the sight of the council by proper witnesses that the lord Pope Victor and no other had been elected in the basilica of St. Peter by the saner part of the cardinals, at the request of the people and with the consent and desires of the clergy, and had been solemnly invested with the mantle; that he was seated upon the throne of St. Peter (Roland, the former chancellor, being present and offering no objection), and that the *Te Deum laudamus* was there gloriously chanted for him by the cardinals and the Roman clergy; that he was escorted thence to the palace with banners and other papal insignia; and that the clergy and people, being asked according to custom by the notary if they were content, three times replied in clear tones, 'We are content.' It was proved also that Roland, on the twelfth day after Lord Victor's elevation, departing from the City, was first invested with the mantle at the cistern in which the emperor Nero once lay hidden when a fugitive from the City. It was proved that, on the second day after the elevation of Lord Victor, Roland, being asked by the rectors of the Roman clergy and the clerics of his own titular church whether they should obey Lord Victor, expressly admitted that he had never been invested with the mantle, and unequivocally declared: 'Go and swear allegiance to him whom you see invested with the mantle.'

"Witnesses to all these points, and they who swore to them, wearing the stole and touching the Very Holy Gospels, were: Lord Peter Christian, deacon of the basilica of St. Peter, who took oath both for himself and for all his brethren; and the others, to wit, the priests Blasius and Manerius, venerable archpriests and rectors of the Roman clergy, the priest John, [the priest] Gentilis, the archpriest Aimeradus, the archpriest Berard, the archpriest John, the deacon Benedict, Master Tolomeus the archpriest, Master Gerard, Nicholas, and other honorable Roman clerics. Besides these, Peter, the illustrious prefect of the City, Stephen *de Tebaldo*, Stephen the Norman, Gimund of the house of Pierleone, John of [St.] Stephen, and other Roman princes and nobles who had come at the call of the most serene emperor, similarly gave testimony in the sight of the council covering the greater part of the aforesaid points, and were willing to swear. But because we had sufficient and most abundant testimony of many devout priests, we did not need the laymen for this. Then the venerable bishops Herman of Verden and Daniel of Prague and Otto, the count palatine, and Master Herbert, the provost, whom the lord emperor, upon the advice of twenty-two bishops and the abbots of Citeaux and of Clairvaux and other pious men present at that time, had sent to Rome to summon both factions to Pavia to appear before the council, gave testimony before the council that they had peremptorily and solemnly summoned Chancellor Roland and his party, by three edicts issued at intervals, before the council to be convoked at Pavia, with all secular judgment being barred, and that Chancellor Roland and his cardinals, by word of mouth and with their own lips, openly declared that they would not accept any decision or acquiesce in any investigation of the Church. We have seen also the letter of Cardinal Henry of Pisa,[284] directed to the lord emperor, in which the express statement was made that they would submit to no decision or investigation of the Church. Besides all this,

---

[284] Cardinal priest of Saints Nereus and Achilles.

that same Henry and Odo, cardinal [deacon] of St. Nicholas *de Carcere Tulliano*, who were at Genoa at the time of the council and before, and Cardinal John of Anagni [285] and John *Piozutus*,[286] subdeacons of the Holy Roman Church, who were then at Piacenza, were awaited by the entire council for eight days, were called by letters and messengers, and disdained to come.

"Being therefore sufficiently informed by all this, and the truth on both sides being fully revealed, the honorable council decided that the election of Lord Victor, who had come like a gentle and innocent lamb, humbly to accept the judgment of the Church, should be approved and confirmed, and the election of Roland declared utterly void. And so it was done. Accordingly, when the election of Lord Victor had been confirmed and accepted (all secular judgment being barred) upon invocation of the grace of the Holy Spirit, the most Christian emperor, after all the bishops and after all the clergy, last of all—upon the advice and request of the council—accepted and approved the election of Lord Victor. And after him all the princes and the innumerable throng of people who were present, being thrice asked if they were content, joyfully replied in a loud voice: 'We are content.'

"On the next day following, that is, the first Friday in Lent [February 12, 1160], Lord Victor was escorted in splendid procession from the church of St. Salvator outside the city [Pavia] in which he had been housed, to the cathedral church. There the most devout emperor received him before the doors of the church and humbly held his stirrup as he dismounted from his horse. Taking him by the hand, he led him up to the altar and kissed his feet, and we all—the patriarch, archbishops, bishops, and abbots, and all the princes, with the entire throng that was present—kissed the apostle's feet.

"But on the next day following, that is, on Saturday, in a general council that was held, the lord pope—and we with him—with lighted candles anathematized Chancellor Roland, the schismatic, and his principal followers, and handed him over to Satan for the destruction of the flesh, that his spirit may be saved in the day of the Lord.[287]

"This, too, we would not conceal from the wisdom of Your Discretion, that it was clearly shown that Chancellor Roland and his followers, certain cardinals, had sworn an oath while Pope Hadrian was still

[285] Cardinal deacon of St. Mary *in Porticu*.
[286] John *Phizutus;* see above, IV.lxxvii.   [287] I Corinthians 5:5.

alive. Now this was the tenor of that oath, that if Pope Hadrian happened to die in their lifetime, they would elect one of the cardinals who was bound by that same oath.

"As for the rest, in the name of Almighty God and the blessed apostles Peter and Paul, and all the saints, and orthodox men who by divine inspiration assembled to heal the schism, we humbly implore and admonish all of you in Christ that you hold as irrefutably fixed and established, beyond all doubt and ambiguity, that which the Church of God, assembled at Pavia, has faithfully ordained to the honor of the Creator and the peace of His Bride, our mother, the Very Holy Roman Church, and to the safety of all Christians.

"We pray that our Redeemer, Jesus Christ, may long preserve the universal pontiff, our Pope Victor, in whose holiness and piety we have absolute faith, and that He may afford him all manner of tranquillity and peace, so that through him Almighty God may be honored, and that the Roman Church and the entire Christian religion may achieve an eminence pleasing to God.

"Moreover, that all we have done may be the more manifest to those who read this, we have thought proper that the unanimity and the names of all of us be here subscribed:

"I, Pilgrim, patriarch of Aquileia, with my suffragans, was present and approved.

"I, Arnold, archbishop of Mainz, with fourteen suffragans, was present and approved.

"I, Hartwig, archbishop of Bremen, with my suffragans, approved.

"I, Hillin, archbishop of Trier, with my suffragans, approved.

"I, Rainald, archbishop of Cologne, with my suffragans, approved.

"I, Wichmann, archbishop of Magdeburg, with my suffragans, approved.

"The archbishop of Besançon approved through a legate and the bishop of Basel.

"The archbishop of Arles approved.

"The archbishop of Lyons, with his suffragans, approved.

"The archbishop of Vienne, with his suffragans, approved.

"Henry, king of England, by letter and by his legates, approved.

"The king of Hungary, by letter and by his legates, approved.

"The king of Bohemia approved.

"The king of Denmark approved.

"Guido, archbishop-elect of Ravenna,[288] approved.

"The bishop of Fermo approved.

"The bishop of Ferentino approved.

"The bishop of Mantua approved.

"The bishop of Bergamo approved.

"The bishop of Faenza approved.

"Moreover, a countless throng of abbots and archpriests of many kingdoms were present and approved.

"An immense number of Lombards were present and approved.

"Practically all the princes of the Roman empire, Germans as well as Italians, from the City and without it, were present and gave their approval with great enthusiasm."

lxxxi (lxxi). "To the most reverend father and lord Eberhard, archbishop of the church of Salzburg, Eberhard, by the grace of God bishop of Bamberg, however unworthy, offers devotion as loyal as it is due, together with his prayers.

"After about fifty bishops had assembled at Pavia and the question of the papacy had long been discussed, although at first almost all had favored a postponement to permit of fuller knowledge of the matter and another more general council, finally the party of Lord Victor prevailed, having in many ways obtained warrant for their victory from the other faction: because a conspiracy against the empire had preceded that act; because the investiture of Lord Victor had taken place earlier, the other later—whereby alone Innocent won the victory over Anacletus, although Anacletus had more electors, and men of greater wisdom and authority; [289] and finally because the opposing party had gone over to the enemies of the empire, being bound by oath to the Sicilian and to Milan, Brescia, and Piacenza, which seemed to be opposed to sound judgment. For such a bond both absolves subjects from their oaths of due loyalty and forbids those concerned to serve the emperor; and thus it prepares the way for division, the worst thing of all. This is clear from the situation itself and from the letters sent everywhere throughout Italy, both to cities and to bishops. As these bad be-

---

[288] See above, IV.xviii-xx.

[289] Octavian's supporters naturally emphasized this earlier precedent, the schism of Innocent II and Anacletus in 1130. Innocent was supported by only sixteen cardinals, his rival by twenty-seven; but Innocent was consecrated first, and eventually, with considerable assistance from St. Bernard of Clairvaux, and with the backing of Emperor Lothar, he was recognized as the true pope.

ginnings gave promise of a worse ending, namely, perpetual discord and division between the empire and the papacy, and since the one faction would not come, though assured escort with complete safety, or even send representatives in their stead to stand trial and receive the verdict, we accepted Lord Victor in the hope of peace and concord between the empire and the papacy. Yet a prolonged investigation preceded our decision: concerning the time and the order of his election; concerning those cardinals—nine in number—who first agreed on his election and afterward withdrew. Concerning all these matters the chapter of St. Peter and the Roman clergy offered testimony, in writing and by word of mouth from their messengers, under oath. The representative of the king of France promised for him that he would accept neither until he should receive ambassadors from the lord emperor. The messenger of the king of England declared that in these as in other matters he favored and opposed the same things [as the emperor]. The archbishops of Arles, Vienne, Lyons, and Besançon gave their approval by letters and agents. In our realm the archbishop of Trier is the only one of the number of archbishops on that side who did not give his approval;[290] however, all his suffragans approved. And so you are the only one still to be heard from. May an angel of great counsel direct thee according to his good pleasure, and keep thee in all thy ways.[291]

"Besides these matters the provost[292] will make known to you many things which it is not lawful for man to utter at present.[293] Rejoice with me that I have received permission to depart and am going home."

lxxxii (lxxii). "To his reverend lord in Christ, Eberhard, archbishop of Salzburg, brother Henry, called provost of Berchtesgaden, with pious prayers sends the assurance of due obedience.

"Were we to write all that we have heard and seen, we would seem to be writing not a letter but a book. But we briefly report to you, Father, the substance of what was done concerning the election of the two Roman pontiffs. The court which had been summoned to meet at Pavia

---

[290] The following chapter tells us that Archbishop Hillin of Trier was absent, pleading illness; but see above, IV.lxxx, where he is listed as approving the action of the council. He supported Octavian later, in any case.

[291] Cf. Psalms 91:11.

[292] Archbishop Eberhard's representative at the council, whose letter forms the following chapter.

[293] Cf. II Corinthians 12:4.

on the octave of Epiphany was postponed until the Friday before the beginning of Lent, because the lord emperor was detained by the destruction of Crema. At that gathering, in which were assembled the lord patriarch [of Aquileia], the archbishops, about fifty bishops from various lands, legates also of the king of France and of the archbishops (to wit, of Arles, Lyons, Vienne, Besançon, Trier, and the elect of Ravenna), the cardinals and clerics who were present on behalf of Victor stood forth and gave an account, point by point, of the election of each. But after this topic had been fully discussed by the bishops and other wise men for five days in succession, finally, on the sixth day, in an open session the points in the election were set forth anew, and details were confirmed by the canons of the church of St. Peter and the rectors of the Roman clergy, who took oath on the four gospels. But the other party neither came in person nor sent representatives to the gathering. We do not know why. Besides, very many letters were read, having the official seal, sent by Alexander [294] and the cardinals who are with him, and addressed to the bishops and cities of Lombardy, but intercepted by loyal adherents of the lord emperor. From their contents the machinations and plots of those people against the empire were clearly revealed. A postponement seemed to threaten no little danger both to the Church and to the empire, especially as there was no one present to contradict the aforesaid assertions and proofs, although, of course, both parties had been summoned for an examination, not before the court, but before the Church. Hence, the bishops gave their approval to Victor's party, which had proved (under oath, as has been said) that he had been invested with the mantle eleven days before Alexander was invested, and had been enthroned on the seat of St. Peter in the presence of the opposing faction and without any objection. They solemnly accepted the aforesaid Victor, as pope, in the Church, and rendered him the customary honors. These things were done, for the reasons stated above, with the support of the lord emperor and the subjects of the empire.[295] Wherefore he himself conferred the customary honor upon that same person—now established as pope—when he dismounted before the doors of the church.

[294] That is, Roland (Alexander III).

[295] *Domino imperatore et fidelibus imperii annitentibus;* this would seem to be a rather damaging admission, in view of the reiterated statements above to the effect that imperial pressure was not exerted in the council.

"Moreover, on the second day following, the oft-mentioned lord Victor solemnly held an official synod and, extinguishing the candles, fettered by the bonds of anathema the leader of the other party, together with certain of his adherents, namely, the bishops of Ostia and Porto [296] (because they had presumed to lay hands of consecration upon him), and the cardinals Henry of Pisa,[297] John of Naples,[298] and Hyacinth.[299] Now he excommunicated Henry of Pisa on this account: because at his command Master Raymond, the cardinal,[300] was robbed and foully beaten. He also included in the same sentence the provost of Piacenza, because he attacked the lord of Tusculum [301] with an armed band, robbed him, and inflicted many indignities upon him. Besides, he summoned William of Sicily and the people of Milan to render canonical satisfaction for their attacks on the churches and the empire.

"There were present at all these transactions the metropolitans (the lord patriarch of Aquileia, the archbishops of Mainz, Cologne, Magdeburg, and Bremen) with some of their suffragans, and the greater part of the bishops of Lombardy, most of whom bestowed ready and complete approval upon the aforesaid confirmation. But the lord patriarch and certain others gave their assent because of the exigencies of the empire that have been mentioned, subject to a later judgment by the Catholic Church. All the absent archbishops whom we have listed gave full approval (for themselves and their suffragans), except the archbishop of Trier who, being prevented by illness after he had set out on the journey, had sent merely a letter offering his excuses. But his suffragans, the bishops of Toul and Verdun, were present and, on behalf of themselves and their fellow suffragan of Metz, pledged themselves unreservedly. The lord bishops of Bamberg, Passau, and Regensburg followed the example of the patriarch. To obtain approval for all that had been done, legates were sent: the lord archbishop of Cologne to France, the bishop of Verden [302] to Spain, and the bishop of Prague to Hungary.

---

[296] The cardinal bishop Hubald of Ostia (later Pope Lucius III) and Bernard of Porto.   [297] Cardinal priest of Saints Nereus and Achilles.

[298] See above, IV.lxxvi and note 265.

[299] Cardinal deacon of St. Mary *in Cosmedin* and later Pope Celestine III.

[300] Cardinal deacon of St. Mary *in Via Lata*, an adherent of the antipope.

[301] Imar of Tusculum, the only cardinal bishop supporting Octavian.

[302] *Verdunensis*, but properly *Verdensis*, since Bishop Herman of Verden is meant.

"If in the meantime other writings, certain of which we have seen, not containing the absolute truth about these matters, should come to your hands, let Your Holiness know that, so far as we could do so, we have made known the unvarnished truth about these matters. We shall give you a fuller account when we come."

lxxxiii. This is the reason so many letters were sent to Eberhard, archbishop of Salzburg, about the proceedings of the council. After he had set forth for the council and had already reached the city of Vicenza, by way of Friuli and the march of Verona, being taken seriously ill he was forced to return home.

Now, since we have made mention of so great a man, we shall say something of his life and character. Although, like a candle put on a candlestick,[303] they will shine most brightly in the house of our province, yet envious fame will with more difficulty detract from his virtues among those who dwell far away, if his life is recorded in writing.

Now this venerable man was of mature years, notably conversant with Biblical literature, of remarkable faith and unusual piety. He was so marked in kindliness and affection that he might truthfully say: 'I am made all things to all men that I may benefit all.' [304] In benefactions he was generous, in almsgiving and in entertaining pilgrims so zealous that the amount expended every day for the support of the poor and the monasteries and pilgrims seemed burdensome not only to his household but even to the whole diocese.[305] Yet he himself was not at all troubled by a load of this kind, since he offset these inconveniences by the reward of a good reputation (which, however, he by no means sought) and an eternal recompense. He never shrank from the squalor of the poor. He permitted himself to be touched and handled by lepers; nay, he did not even fear to touch them himself occasionally, and to kiss their hands. Nor did he think it sufficient to make use of his servants in ministering to the poor, but he himself would sometimes set the food before them with his own hands, girding up his clothes. He would hand them a bowl and pour out the water for washing not only their hands but also their feet.

Thus he not only afforded them perfect doctrine by his words, but also gave them an example of perfect doctrine by his actions. It was

[303] Cf. Matthew 5:15.   [304] Cf. I Corinthians 9:22.

[305] This and the following sentence are in large part copied from Einhard *Vita Karoli* xxi.

deservedly said of him (as of old of one of the saints): "This is he whose life corresponds to his speech, and whose speech corresponds to his life, because he does what he teaches and teaches what he does."

By these and other virtues and gifts of divine grace he had won very many to imitate him, but the hearts of all to love him.

But enough of this.

lxxxiv (lxxiv). After the business of the council had thus been completed, and ambassadors sent (as has been said above) [306] to the kings of Spain, England, France, Denmark, Bohemia, and Hungary, [Frederick] sent ambassadors also to Manuel, the emperor of the Greeks: namely, Henry, duke of Carinthia, a valiant man, experienced in councils of war; Henry, notary of the sacred palace,[307] a man of great integrity and industry; and Neimerius, the son of Peter Polani, doge of Venice, who had previously been held in captivity [by Manuel], but was now free. They bore replies, it was said, to a request of the prince of Constantinople concerning the coasts of Pentapolis and Apulia [308] and certain more secret inquiries regarding opposition to William, the son of Roger of Sicily and his successor on the throne.

But seeing that all Lombardy had been severely ravaged by the uninterrupted campaigns of the past two years, since in its frequent expeditions and raids against the enemy the army had been unable to spare even its friends, the emperor decided that it was advantageous for that land to be quiet for a little while and to recover, until, brought back under cultivation, it could better support new adversities in the coming year, and receive and maintain a new army.

lxxxv (lxxv). And so,[309] being about to disband his army, Frederick called into his presence the officers and the best of the soldiers and told them that he was very grateful for the good will and loyalty which they had so consistently displayed toward him. He praised them individually for their good conduct and the courage that they had shown in fighting amid many great perils, that neither the multitude of their enemies nor the greatness of the cities and the reckless audacity and fierce cruelty of their adversaries had deterred them from displaying their customary valor. He said also that he would take great care to

---

[306] IV.lxxxii.   [307] See Book III, Prologue.

[308] See above, II.xlix and III.xx. Pentapolis was the coastal region north of Apulia, running from below Osimo to above Rimini.

[309] This paragraph comes largely from Josephus *Wars* VII.i.2–3.

reward with due favor and honors the merits of those who had been his companions in arms and that no one of those who had done more than the rest would fail to receive a just return. Those who had, to his knowledge, performed some brave and notable act in the war he commended, calling them individually by name. Then he distributed, lavishly and regally, gold and silver, vessels made of silver and of gold, and likewise costly garments, benefices in fief, and other gifts. But after all had been gladdened and rewarded in this way, according as each had shown himself worthy, and the entire army had expressed its thanks and gratitude with great applause, he let them all go whither they pleased. But he himself, with a few others, remained in Italy.

But as we do not propose to have the books of this work exceed the number of the evangels, before we bring this fourth volume to a close, we desire, after having briefly touched upon the deeds and the exploits of the most serene prince, to set forth in a few words his habits and other aspects of his life and his conduct of the administration of the realm.[310]

lxxxvi. Now divine, august Frederick is (as a certain writer says of Theodoric) [311] in character and appearance such a man that he deserves to be studied even by those not in close touch with him. The Lord God and the plan of nature have joined to bestow lavishly upon him the gift of perfect happiness. His character is such that not even those envious of his power can belittle its praise. His person is well proportioned. He is shorter than very tall men, but taller and more noble than men of medium height. His hair is golden, curling a little above his forehead. His ears are scarcely covered by the hair above them, as the barber (out of respect for the empire) keeps the hair on his head and cheeks short by constantly cutting it. His eyes are sharp and piercing, his nose well formed, his beard reddish,[312] his lips delicate and not distended by too long a mouth. His whole face is bright and cheerful.[313] His teeth are even and snow white in color. The skin of his throat and

---

[310] The last half of this sentence is drawn from Einhard, *op. cit.*, v.

[311] Apollinaris Sidonius *Epistles* I.ii, from which this paragraph (save where otherwise noted) is drawn. It is a description of Theodoric II of the Visigoths (453–66).

[312] *Barba subrufa;* this, with the color of the hair, and the cutting of the hair on the head (rather than only on the face) are the only respects in which this picture of Frederick has departed from that of Theodoric to this point.

[313] This sentence is copied from Einhard, *op. cit.*, xxii. The next sentence seems to be original with Rahewin.

neck (which is rather plump but not fat) is milk-white and often suffused with the ruddy glow of youth; modesty rather than anger causes him to blush frequently. His shoulders are rather broad, and he is strongly built. His thighs, supported by stout calves, are proper and sturdy.

His gait is firm and steady, his voice clear, and his entire bearing manly. Because of his figure, he has an air of dignity and authority, standing or sitting. His health is very good, except that sometimes he is subject to a day's fever.[314] He is a lover of warfare, but only that peace may be secured thereby. He is quick of hand, very wise in counsel, merciful to suppliants, kind to those taken under his protection.

If you ask about his daily routine when abroad, he attends matins at church and the services of his priests, either alone or with a very small following, and worships so earnestly [315] that he has set a pattern and an example to all the Italians of the honor and reverence that are to be paid to bishops and to the clergy. He shows so great respect to divine services that he honors with becoming silence every hour in which psalms are sung to God, nor does anyone venture meanwhile to trouble him about any business matter. His devotions ended and, after celebration of the Mass, having been blessed by the holy relics, he dedicates the rest of the morning to the task of governing his empire.[316] If he engages in the chase, he is second to none in training, judging, and making use of horses, dogs, and falcons and other such birds. In hunting he himself strings the bow, takes the arrows, sets and shoots them. You choose what he is to hit, he hits what you have chosen.

At meals there is both restraint and royal abundance; moderate rather than excessive drinking prevails, but the hungry cannot complain of frugality. When it is time for play, he lays aside for a little while his regal dignity, and is in such a humor that his condescension is not open to criticism, his severity is not bloodthirsty. Toward the members of his household he is not threatening in his manner of address, or contemptuous toward proffered counsel, or vindictive in spy-

---

[314] These last three sentences come bodily from Einhard *loc. cit.* (save that Charlemagne suffered from fever for four years). The remainder of the paragraph is largely taken from Jordanes *Getica* xxxv.182, also quoted (but correctly applied to Attila the Hun) in *Two Cities* iv.xxviii.

[315] Thus far, this sentence is from Sidonius, *loc. cit.*

[316] The end of this sentence comes from Sidonius *loc. cit.* The remainder of the paragraph is borrowed from the same work, i.ii and iv.ix.

ing out a fault.[317] He earnestly searches the Scriptures and the exploits of ancient kings. He generally distributes with his own hand alms to the poor and scrupulously divides a tenth of his income among churches and monasteries. He is very eloquent in his mother tongue, but can understand Latin more readily than he can speak it. He wears his native costume and is neither extravagant nor frivolous in dress—yet is not meanly clad. It pleases him to have his camp display the panoply of Mars rather than of Venus.

Although he is so conspicuous for the extension of his kingdom and the conquest of peoples, and is constantly engaged in such occupations, yet he has in various places started many public works for the beautification and convenience of the realm; some of them he has actually completed, and a great part of his substance he sets aside for pious honoring [of his ancestors].[318] For he has most fittingly restored the very beautiful palaces built long ago by Charles the Great at Nijmegen and near the village of Ingelheim, adorned with famous workmanship—structures very well built, but crumbling through neglect as well as age.[319] Hereby he gave signal evidence of his innate greatness of soul. At Kaiserslautern he built a royal palace of red stone on a lavish scale. For on one side he surrounded it by a strong wall; the other side was washed by a fish pond like a lake, supporting all kinds of fish and game birds, to feast the eye as well as the taste. It also has adjacent to it a park that affords pasture to a large herd of deer and wild goats. The royal splendor of all these things and their abundance (which precludes enumeration) are well worth the spectators' effort.

In Italy too he displayed such magnificent generosity in restoring palaces and churches at Monza, at Lodi, and in other places and cities that the entire empire will enjoy forever the munificence and the memory of so great an emperor. Although the kings of Spain, England,

---

[317] This much of the present paragraph is largely drawn from *ibid.*, I.ii and IV.ix. The remainder comes partly from Einhard, *op. cit.*, xxiii–xxvii, but the final sentence is taken from Sidonius *op. cit.*, IV.xx.

[318] All but the last clause of this sentence is copied directly from Einhard, *op. cit.*, xvii, who in turn borrowed from Suetonius *De vita Caesarum* II.xxix, xxx.

[319] These are the two palaces listed in Einhard *loc. cit.* It is impossible to tell from this passage whether Rahewin simply copied the names out of Einhard, or whether Frederick (who did take much interest in Charlemagne, and even had him canonized by his antipope Paschal III in 1166) actually did repair these structures. This sentence seems to be modeled upon Josephus *Wars* I.xxi (a discussion of Herod's building and restoration), from which the following sentence is taken.

France, Denmark, Bohemia, and Hungary always mistrusted his power, Frederick so bound them to himself through friendship and alliance that as often as they sent him letters or ambassadors, they proclaimed that they accorded him the right to command, while they did not lack the will to obey.[320] He prevailed upon Manuel, the emperor of Constantinople, who voluntarily sought friendship and alliance with him, to term himself emperor not of Rome, but of New Rome, whereas he had been—like his predecessors—calling himself the emperor of the Romans.

And, not to prolong the tale, he considered, throughout the entire period of his reign, that nothing was better, nothing more pleasing, than that the Roman empire should by his instrumentality and his efforts thrive and flourish with its ancient prestige.[321]

These are the exploits of the glorious emperor up to the present year, which is the one thousand, one hundred, and sixtieth from the incarnation of the Lord, which is reckoned the seventh [eighth] of his reign but the fifth of his rule as emperor. May he still successfully perform much in the government of the realm and at last, in the presence of the King of Kings, receive, with the most pious princes, the eternal reward of his merits.

These flowers, O best of the Augusti, your beloved uncle, Bishop Otto, as well as the diligence of my insignificant self, have culled from the widespreading meadows of your exploits that we might weave them into the wreath of this little work. We have left for more skilled writers and those more intimately associated with you the further deeds that are known and told of you.[322] If these seem to anyone invidious, or if men judge them trivial, yet we shall be consoled by the fruit of our obedience, because we obeyed your behest. As to the quality of the work, do you, my beloved masters,[323] see to that, since we have chosen you as critics and correctors of this work. For you must decide what to publish; you must determine what you think should be deleted.

[HERE ENDS THE FOURTH BOOK]

---

[320] This and the following sentence are based on Einhard, *op. cit.*, xvi.

[321] *Ibid.*, xxvii.

[322] The two preceding sentences come largely from Jordanes *Getica* lx.316. The remainder of the paragraph is closely modeled on Orosius VII.xliii.

[323] Ulrich and Henry; see above, III, Prologue.

APPENDIX

IN the year from the incarnation of the Lord 1160, a serious battle was fought by the emperor against the people of Milan at a town called Carcano,[1] and when he seemed already vanquished, and the Latins with him were fleeing, he won a gallant victory. About five hundred of the enemy were slain; of our men, only five. In that same year or the next [June 24, 1160], Arnold, a very old and wise man, archchancellor and archbishop of Mainz, being forced by an incendiary fire to come out from the church of St. James, was cruelly slain by his *ministeriales*.

In the year 1162 from the incarnation of the Lord, Milan was again besieged in a new way, with camps built around it in a circle.

In the year 1163, Milan was captured and utterly destroyed.[2] Géza, the king of Hungary, died [1161].

In the year 1164, when Géza's brothers and his little son quarreled, the boy won the support of the emperor by a gift of five thousand marks.[3] The people of Verona, Vicenza, Padua, and Treviso rebelled. Octavian died, and Guido was chosen in his stead.[4] Eberhard, the venerable archbishop of Salzburg, died; Conrad, bishop of Passau, was chosen in his stead; Robert followed Conrad, and Albo, canon of Freising, followed Robert.[5] Hartwig, the worthless bishop of Regensburg, and Hartmann of Brixen, a bishop worthy of God, died [1164].

In the year 1166 from the incarnation of the Lord, a court was held in Würzburg on Whitsunday [May 23, 1165]. There a sworn agreement was entered upon by the emperor and the princes who were pres-

[1] In the Brianza Valley, north of Monza. This engagement was fought August 9, 1160.

[2] This siege of Milan lasted from late May, 1161, to March, 1162 (not 1163).

[3] Géza II died in 1161; his brothers Ladislav and Stephen tried to seize the throne, but the latter was ousted in 1162 by Géza's son, Stephen III.

[4] Octavian (Victor IV) died in April, 1164; Cardinal Guido of Crema succeeded him as the antipope Paschal III.

[5] Eberhard died June 22, 1164; his successor, Bishop Conrad of Passau, was a brother of Otto of Freising. Robert (or Rupert) followed Conrad as bishop of Passau for a year, and was succeeded in turn by Albo in 1165.

ent, both secular and ecclesiastical, that Paschal should always be recognized as pope, and that upon his death no one not of his party should be elected; likewise, after the death of the emperor no one should succeed him without taking an oath that he would defend that same party. Only Albert of Freising was unwilling to swear at that time. For Conrad of Mainz had already been declared an enemy.[6] In that same year Albert of Freising, after prolonged opposition, was forced to swear to obey Paschal conscientiously as long as the empire supported his party and as long as he wished to retain his temporalities.

In that same year also the emperor, at about the time of the festival of St. Peter,[7] went down and forced the Hungarians (who had fraudulently withheld the greater part of the money previously promised) to swear a new oath. There the king of Bohemia brought into his presence one of the petty kings of the Russians and subjected him to Frederick's sway. Great famine in all the land.

1167 [1166]. The emperor entered Italy sometime in the autumn [October] and there, with the cooperation of his chancellor, Christian,[8] confirmed Paschal by repeated oaths. Upon the instigation of this same chancellor, it was further stipulated that no one of them should ever seek to be absolved from his oath and, if such absolution were offered, should never accept it.

In the same year H[enry Jasomirgott], duke of Austria, and the count palatine Otto the Elder, who had been sent to Greece, returned unsuccessful—except that they had received magnificent presents.[9] Duke Henry gave his daughter [Agnes] in marriage to the king of Hungary [Stephen III]. A serious war broke out between the Saxons and Duke H[enry the Lion] of Bavaria.

1168 [1167]. The emperor severely harassed the people of Ravenna, Faenza (Fagenses), and Bologna and forced them to surrender. Christian was substituted for Lord Conrad at Mainz. Salzburg,

---

[6] Conrad of Wittelsbach, elected archbishop of Mainz in 1160, had refused to accept the antipope and had gone into exile, first to France and then to Rome, where he was made cardinal bishop of Sabina in 1167. Though Frederick had been able to force the German bishops to accept the antipope Victor IV, there was considerable resistance to Paschal III.

[7] August 1, or possibly June 29 (festival of Saints Peter and Paul).

[8] Archbishop of Mainz after Conrad's exile; see the following paragraph.

[9] This is Rahewin's only hint of the difficulties that arose between the two emperors, Frederick and Manuel. The latter had opposed Frederick's candidate in Hungary, and was now intriguing with Pope Alexander and the kingdom of Sicily.

long ago proscribed by the emperor on Alexander's account, was burned; it is uncertain whether by instigation of the enemy or accidentally. Conrad, the emperor's brother, entered Italy to regain the imperial favor which he had some time before foolishly forfeited, but returned without success. Welf the Elder, Henry, the burgrave, and Frederick, count palatine, set out for Jerusalem.[10]

1168 [1167]. The Hungarian [Stephen III] with the aid of his father-in-law, Duke H[enry] of Austria, made war on the emperor of the Greeks [Manuel] because he had received and assisted his brother [Béla], who claimed the kingdom, and had bestowed his daughter upon him in marriage. In the same year the emperor besieged and captured Ancona. Meanwhile, he dispatched Rainald of Cologne and Christian of Mainz with troops to Rome. The Romans met them with an army between Tusculum and the City, gave battle, were defeated and exterminated [May 29]. About nine thousand of the Romans fell there, about three thousand were taken captive. The emperor followed them, burned the Leonine city and the porticos of the church of St. Peter. The church (transformed into a fortress by the Romans), he took and would have destroyed, had he not been moved by religious scruples to spare it.

After this he turned toward Lombardy. The people of Cremona, Brescia, and Milan having returned to their homes, and the inhabitants of Lodi, Bergamo, and Mantua having joined the enemies of the empire, they rebelled against it. At the same time a severe pestilence attacked the army and in large measure destroyed it.[11] There died at that time, of the princes, Archbishop Rainald of Cologne, the bishops Daniel of Prague, Eberhard of Regensburg, Conrad of Augsburg, Godfrey of Speyer, Herman of Verden, N. of Zeitz,[12] Frederick, the son of King Conrad,[13] Welf [VII] the Younger, Berengar of Sulz-

---

[10] Duke Welf VI, Burgrave Henry of Regensburg, and Frederick of Wittelsbach, a brother of the count palatine Otto.

[11] The plague struck Frederick's army at Rome in August, 1167, and its ravages were so great as to prevent his campaign against the kingdom of Sicily. This disaster marks the turning point of Frederick's fortunes in Italy. With his remaining forces, he withdrew northward to Pavia, one of the few Lombard towns still loyal. In Lombardy he suffered additional reverses, and only with great difficulty escaped into Burgundy with the small remnant of the great army he had led south the year before.

[12] No bishop of Zeitz died in this year; Bishop Alexander of Liége, who died at Rome August 9, 1167, may be intended here.

[13] Duke Frederick of Swabia, son of Conrad III, and first cousin of the emperor.

bach, and countless barons. The emperor announced the destruction of his men and the rebellion of the Italians in a letter sent throughout the entire extent of his kingdom. Conrad succeeded the bishop of Regensburg, Hartwig succeeded the bishop of Augsburg. But in the City that same pestilence raged undiminished, so that, the story goes, women bereft of their husbands were obliged to seek men in marriage from other cities.

1169. Roland, also called Alexander, again departed from the City.[14] For upon returning from France in that same year, relying upon certain of the Roman nobles and William of Sicily, he had occupied the patriarch's seat in the Lateran. The emperor returned from Italy [1168]—a perilous passage. Not long afterward Guido [Paschal III] was established at Rome by those faithful to the emperor [1167]. Conrad of Salzburg (who steadfastly supported Roland) died, and Albert, the son of the king of Bohemia, his sister's son,[15] was chosen in his stead [1168]. Meanwhile, the newly elected bishops were compelled by the emperor to receive their consecration from Christian of Mainz.

Guido, also known as Paschal, died and was buried in the basilica of St. Peter at Rome [1168]. By the Romans (except the Cencii), John, bishop of Albano,[16] was chosen as pope and named Calixtus III. King Louis of France and Henry of England waged war on each other. They were urged by the emperor to make peace; to the king of France he added threats for there was alliance and friendship between the emperor and the king of England: the latter had given his daughter [Matilda] as wife to Henry, duke of Bavaria and Saxony.

Hartwig, bishop of Augsburg, having been consecrated by Christian, held ordinations; Albert of Freising, now free, so to speak, and released from the schism by Guido's death, did likewise. In the same year the king of Jerusalem triumphed gloriously over the Saracens.[17]

[14] Alexander III had returned to Rome from France in 1165, but fled to Benevento (in the kingdom of Sicily) during Frederick's attack on Rome in the summer of 1167.

[15] Archbishop Conrad (brother of Otto of Freising) had been forced into exile for his support of Alexander III. His successor and nephew (the son of his sister Gertrude by Vladislav II of Bohemia), Adalbert, also recognized Alexander, and was removed from office, but restored to it in 1183.

[16] Abbot of Struma, and apparently created cardinal bishop of Albano by one of the antipopes.

[17] Amaury, king of Jerusalem (1162–74); the reference here is presumably to one of his four invasions of Egypt between 1163 and 1168.

1170 [1169]. The emperor spent Christmas in Alsace. At the time of Candlemas he held a diet at Nuremberg.[18] There he readily received back into favor the king of Bohemia, who had offended him.[19] Albo, the bishop-elect of Passau, who had been expelled from his see (*episcopio*) by his people, he restored to the bishopric in appearance only, by no means in reality; for he was incensed at him because he refused consecration at the hands of Christian. For the same reason he there dealt severely with Conrad, bishop-elect of Regensburg, and appointed a hearing for him on this point for the following Whitsunday [June 8] that he might either receive ordination from Christian or relinquish the bishopric.

At the beginning of Lent [March 4] the abbots of Citeaux and Clairvaux discussed the schism with the emperor and urged that he send Bishop [Eberhard] of Bamberg to Rome with them. And this was done. But on account of the insolence of the Lombards the commission itself failed of success; [20] for the bishop himself was sent back by them and forced to return home. At about the same time [March 15] Archbishop-elect [Adalbert] of Salzburg was consecrated by Ulrich, patriarch of Aquileia, contrary to the emperor's wishes. Easter was celebrated in Alsace [April 20, 1169].

[18] *Circa purificationem sanctae Mariae;* February 2, 1169. The diet was held in the middle of February.

[19] Frederick's very friendly relations with Vladislav II had cooled when the latter's son was removed as archbishop of Salzburg; see above, note 15.

[20] From this remark H. Böhmer (*Neues Archiv,* XXI [1895–96], 655, note 1) thinks we may conclude that this passage was written after the treaty of Venice in 1177—when Rahewin was already dead.

BIBLIOGRAPHY

This list is in no sense exhaustive. It includes only those works which were found useful in annotating the translation. For additional works on Otto of Freising, see the *Two Cities*, translated by Charles Christopher Mierow (New York, 1928) and published as No. 9 in the "Records of Civilization," pp. 81–84.

Editions of the GESTA FRIDERICI

Johannes Cuspinianus. Ottonis Phrisingensis episcopi . . . De gestis Friderici primi . . . libri duo: Radevici Phrisingensis ecclesiae canonici libri duo, prioribus additi. . . . Strasburg, 1515. Republished by Bertrand Tissier in "Bibliotheca patrum Cisterciensium," Vol. VIII, pp. 115–213, Paris, 1669.

Petrus Pithoeus. Ottonis, episcopi Frisingensis . . . de gestis Friderici I . . . libri duo: Radevici Frisingensis . . . de eiusdem Friderici gestis libri II. . . . Basel, 1569.

Christianus Urstisius (Christian Wurstisen). Ottonis Frisingensis episcopi, de gestis Friderici primi . . . libri duo . . . : Radevici ecclesiae Frisingensis canonici, de rebus gestis Friderici I . . . continuatae ad Ottonem historiae, libri duo. In "Germaniae historicorum illustrium tomus unus," pp. 401–563. Frankfort, 1585; reprinted 1670.

L. A. Muratori. Ottonis Frisingensis episcopi, eiusque continuatoris Radevici libri de gestis Friderici I . . . castigati. "Rerum Italicarum scriptores," Vol. VI, cols. 631–858. Milan, 1725.

Roger Wilmans. Gesta Friderici I imperatoris auctoribus Ottone episcopo et Ragewino praeposito Frisingensibus. "Mon. Germ. Hist.: Scriptores," Vol. XX, pp. 338–493. Hanover, 1868.

Georg Waitz. Ottonis et Rahewini Gesta Friderici I imperatoris. Hanover, 1884. "Scriptores rerum Germanicarum in usum scholarum . . ." Revised edition of the one by Wilmans.

B. de Simson. Ottonis et Rahewini Gesta Friderici I imperatoris. Hanover and Leipzig, 1912. "Scriptores rerum Germanicarum in usum scholarum. . . ." A revision of the previous edition by Waitz.

German Translations of the GESTA FRIDERICI

Friedrich Schiller. Denkwürdigkeiten aus dem Leben Kaiser Friedrichs des

Ersten. In Part I, Vol. II, pp. 113–416, of "Allgemeine Sammlung historischer Memoires." Jena, 1790.

Horst Kohl. Thaten Friedrichs von Bischof Otto von Freising (Leipzig, 1883) and Rahewins Fortsetzung der Thaten Friedrichs . . . (Leipzig, 1886). "Die Geschichtschreiber der deutschen Vorzeit. Zwölftes Jahrhundert." Vol. IX a, b.

Sources and Literature

Barraclough, Geoffrey. Origins of Modern Germany. Oxford, 1947. See pp. 167–92.

Below, Georg von. Die italienische Kaiserpolitik des deutschen Mittelalters, mit besonderem Hinblick auf die Politik Friedrich Barbarossas. Munich, 1927. *Historische Zeitschrift,* Beiheft 10.

Bernheim, Ernst. "Der Charakter Ottos von Freising und seiner Werke," *Mittheilungen des Instituts für österreichische Geschichtsforschung,* VI (1885), 1–51.

Böhm, Franz. Das Bild Friedrich Barbarossas und seines Kaisertums in den ausländischen Quellen seiner Zeit. Berlin, 1936. "Historische Studien," Heft 289.

Brezzi, Paolo. "Ottone di Frisinga," *Bollettino dell' istituto storico italiano per il medio evo,* LIV (1939), 129–328.

Bühler, Johannes. Die Hohenstaufen, nach zeitgenössischen Quellen. Leipzig, 1925.

Constitutiones = Constitutiones et acta publica imperatorum et regum. "Mon. Germ. Hist.: Leges." Sec. IV, Vol. I. Hanover, 1893.

Dittmar, Guilielmus. De fontibus nonnullis historiae Friderici I Barbarossae quaestionum specimen. Königsberg, 1864.

Doeberl, M. Monumenta Germaniae selecta ab anno 768 usque ad annum 1250. Munich, 1889–94. Vols. III, IV, V only were published.

Dollinger, Philippe. L'Evolution des classes rurales en Bavière depuis la fin de l'époque carolingienne jusqu'au milieu du XIIIᵉ siècle. Paris, 1949.

Engel, Johannes. Das Schisma Barbarossas im Bistum und Hochstift Freising, 1159–77. Munich, 1930.

Fellner, Felix. "The 'Two Cities' of Otto of Freising and Its Influence on the Catholic Philosophy of History," *Catholic Historical Review,* XX (1934–35), 154–74.

Flamm, Hermann. "Eine Miniatur aus dem Kreise der Herrad von Landsberg," *Repertorium für Kunstwissenschaft,* XXXVII (1915), 123–62.

Frings, Theodor. "Die Vorauer Handschrift und Otto von Freising," *Beiträge zur Geschichte der deutschen Sprache und Literatur,* LV (1931), 223–30.

Gesta Federici I. imperatoris in Lombardia. *See* Holder-Egger, Oswald.

Gewirth, Alan. Marsilius of Padua, the Defender of Peace. Vol. I: Marsilius of Padua and Medieval Political Philosophy. New York, 1951. "Records of Civilization," No. 46.

Giesebrecht, Wilhelm von. Geschichte der deutschen Kaiserzeit, 6 vols. in 8. Brunswick and Leipzig, 1875–95 (dates vary according to the edition). Vol. V, Part I (1880).

Grotefend, Hermann. Der Werth der Gesta Friderici imperatoris des Bischofs Otto von Freising für die Geschichte des Reichs unter Friedrich I. Hanover, 1870.

Gundlach, W. "Zu Rahewin," *Neues Archiv*, XI (1886), 569–70.

Güterbock, Ferdinand. Das Geschichtswerk des Otto Morena und seiner Fortsetzer über die Taten Friedrichs I in der Lombardei. Berlin, 1930. "Scriptores rerum Germanicarum," new series, VII.

Haid, Kassian. "Otto von Freising," *Cistercienser-Chronik*, Vols. XLIV–XLV (1932–33). Scattered through both volumes.

Hampe, Karl. Deutsche Kaisergeschichte in der Zeit der Salier und Staufer. Leipzig, 1912.

Hauck, Albert, *Kirchengeschichte Deutschlands*. 5 vols. Leipzig, 1887–1911. Vol. IV (5th ed. 1925).

Hegesippus. De bello Judaico et excidio urbis Hierosolymitanae. Ed. C. F. Weber and J. Caesar. Marburg, 1864. The work is based upon Josephus, De bello Judaico, and is, by some scholars, ascribed to St. Ambrose.

Hist. Trip. = M. Aurelii Cassiodori Historia ecclesiastica vocata tripartita . . . Ed. Migne, Pl., LXIX, cols. 879–1214.

Hofmeister, A. "Studien über Otto von Freising," *Neues Archiv*, XXXVII (1911–12), 99–161, 633–768.

Holder-Egger, Oswald, ed. Gesta Federici I. imperatoris in Lombardia auct. cive Mediolanensi. Hanover, 1892. "Scriptores rerum Germanicarum. . . ."

Hudson, John. Flavii Josephi Opera quae reperiri potuerunt omnia. . . . 2 vols., Oxford, 1720.

Jaffe, Philipp. Bibliotheca rerum Germanicarum. 6 vols., Berlin, 1844–73.

Jordan, Gustav. Ragewins Gesta Friderici imperatoris. Eine quellenkritische Untersuchung. Strassburg, 1881.

Jordanes = Jordanis Romana et Getica. Ed. Theodor Mommsen in "Mon. Germ. hist.: Scriptores." Auctores antiquissimi, Vol. V, Part I. Berlin, 1882.

Josephus, Flavius. De bello Judaico libri septem, interprete Rufino Aquileiensi . . . Ed. by Edward Cardwell. Oxford, 1837.

Josephus *Wars* = Flavius Josephus. De bello Judaico, tr. by William

Whiston and pub. in The Genuine Works of Josephus, 1737; many times reprinted.

Kauffmann, Heinz. Die italienische Politik Kaiser Friedrichs I nach dem Frieden von Constanz, 1183–89. Greifswald, 1933.

Kern, Fritz. Kingship and Law in the Middle Ages. Tr. by S. B. Crimes. Oxford, 1939. "Studies in Mediaeval History," ed. by Geoffrey Barraclough, Vol. IV.

Knapke, Paul. Frederick Barbarossa's Conflict with the Papacy. Washington, D.C., 1939.

Koeppler, H. "Frederick Barbarossa and the Schools of Bologna," *English Historical Review*, LIV (1939), 577–607.

Kohl, Horst. "Beiträge zur Kritik Rahewins," *Jahresbericht des königl. Gymnasium zu Chemnitz* (1890), pp. 1–24.

Kugler, B. Studien zur Geschichte des zweiten Kreuzzuges. Stuttgart, 1866. See pp. 7–10.

Leeper, A. W. A. History of Medieval Austria. London, 1941.

Levison, Wilhelm. "Otto von Freising und das Privileg Friedrichs I für das Herzogtum Österreich," *Neues Archiv*, XXXIV (1909), 210–15.

Lindt, K. Zur Kritik des zweiten Buches der Gesta Friderici des Ottos von Freising. Darmstadt, 1902.

Lloyd, Roger. "A Forgotten Historian," *Church Quarterly Review*, CXVI (1933), 66–74.

Lüdecke, W. Der historische Wert des ersten Buches von Ottos von Freising Gesta Friderici. Halle, 1884. Continued in *Stendaler Gymnasialprogramm* (1885), pp. 1–32.

Manitius, Max, Geschichte der lateinischen Literatur des Mittelalters. 3 vols. Munich, 1911–1931. Vol. III.

—— "Zu Rahewin, Ruotger und Lambert," *Neues Archiv*, XII (1887), 361–85.

Mansi = Sacrorum conciliorum nova et amplissima collectio. 31 vols., ed. by J. D. Mansi *et al.* Florence and Venice, 1759–98. New edition and continuation. Vols. XXXII– . Paris, 1901–

Marczali, H. Ungarns Geschichtsquellen im Zeitalter der Árpáden. Berlin, 1882. See pp. 150–52.

Martens, Carl. Ein Beitrag zur Kritik Ragewins. Greifswald, 1877.

Mayer, Theodor. "Die Ausbildung der Grundlagen des modernen deutschen Staates im hohen Mittelalter," *Historische Zeitschrift*, CLIX (1939), 457–87.

Meyer, Hans. Die Militärpolitik Friedrich Barbarossas im Zusammenhang mit seiner Italienpolitik. Berlin, 1930. "Historische Studien," Vol. 200.

Michael, Wolfgang. Die Formen des unmittelbaren Verkehrs zwischen den deutschen Kaisern und souveränen Fürsten vornehmlich im X. XI. und XII. Jahrhundert. Hamburg and Leipzig, 1888.

Mierow, Charles Christopher, "Bishop Otto of Freising, Historian and Man," *Proceedings of the American Philological Association*, LXXX (1949), 393–401.

—— "Otto of Freising: a Medieval Historian at Work," *Philological Quarterly*, XIV (1935), 344–62.

—— "Otto of Freising and His Two Cities Theory," *Philological Quarterly*, XXIV (1945), 97–105.

—— The Gothic History of Jordanes. Princeton, 1915.

Neues Archiv = Neues Archiv der Gesellschaft für ältere deutsche Geschichtskunde. Hanover, etc., 1876–1935.

Nörenberg, Helmut. Die Darstellung Friedrich Barbarossas in den Gesten Ottos von Freising mit Hinblick auf Ottos augustinische Geschichtsauffassung. Swinemünde, 1917.

Oman, Sir Charles W. C. A History of the Art of War in the Middle Ages. 2d. ed. rev., 2 vols., London [1924].

Ottmar, E. "Das Carmen de Friderico imperatore aus Bergamo und seine Beziehungen zu Otto-Rahewins Gesta Friderici, Gunthers Ligurinus, und Burchard von Ursbergs Chronik," *Neues Archiv*, XLVI (1925), 430–89.

Otto, Eberhard. "Otto von Freising und Friedrich Barbarossa," Historische Vierteljahrschrift, XXXI (1937–39), 27–56.

Otto Morena. Historia Frederici I. *See* Güterbock, Ferdinand.

PG = Patrologiae cursus completus. Series Graeca. Ed. J. P. Migne, 161 vols. in 165. Paris, 1857–86.

PL = Patrologiae cursus completus, Series Latina. Ed. J. P. Migne, 221 vols. Paris, 1844–65.

Plesner, Johan. L'Emigration de la campagne à la ville libre de Florence au XIIIe siècle. Copenhagen, 1934.

Pozor, Hans. Die politische Haltung Ottos von Freising. Halle, 1937.

Prutz, Hans. Radewins Fortsetzung der Gesta Friderici imperatoris des Otto von Freising, ihre Zusammensetzung und ihr Werth. Danzig, 1873.

Ribbeck, Walter. Kaiser Friedrich I und die römische Curie in den Jahren 1157–1159. Leipzig, 1881.

Riezler, Sigmund. "Namen und Vaterland des Geschichtschreibers Rachwin," *Forschungen zur deutschen Geschichte*, XVIII (1878), 539–40.

Savigny, Friedrich Carl von. Geschichte des römischen Rechts im Mittelalter, 6 vols., Heidelberg, 1815–31 [2d ed., 7 vols., Heidelberg, 1834–51).

Schmidlin, J. Die geschichtsphilosophische und kirchenpolitische Weltan-
schauung Ottos von Freising. Freiburg i.B., 1906.

Schramm, Percy Ernst. Kaiser, Rom und Renovatio. Leipzig-Berlin, 1929.

Schrörs, Heinrich. Untersuchungen zu dem Streite Kaiser Friedrichs I mit
Papst Hadrian IV, 1157–58. Bonn, [1915?]

Simonsfeld, Henry. "Bemerkungen zu Ragewin," *Neues Archiv*, IX
(1884), 203–8.

——— "Bemerkungen zu Rahewin," *Historische Aufsätze dem Andenken
an Georg Waitz gewidmet*. Hanover, 1886, pp. 204–27.

——— Jahrbücher des deutschen Reichs unter Friedrich I. Leipzig, 1908.
Vol. I, 1152–58; no more published.

Simson, B. von. "Ueber die verschiedenen Rezensionen von Ottos und
Rahewins Gesta Friderici I," *Neues Archiv*, XXXVI (1911), 681–716.

Spörl, Johannes. Grundformen hochmittelalterlicher Geschichtsanschauung:
Studien zum Weltbild der Geschichtsschreiber des 12. Jahrhunderts.
Munich, 1935. See pp. 32–50.

Stach, Walter. "Politische Dichtung im Zeitalter Friedrichs I. Der Ligurinus im Widerstreit mit Otto und Rahewin," *Neue Jahrbücher für
deutsche Wissenschaft*, XIII (1937), 385–410.

Testa, Giovanni. History of the War of Frederick I against the Communes
of Lombardy. London, 1877.

Vacandard, A. "Arnauld de Brescia," *Revue des questions historiques*,
XXXV (1884), 52–114.

Wagner, Paul. Eberhard II, Bischof von Bamberg. Halle, s.d. See
pp. 99–112.

Waitz, Georg. "Ueber die verschiedenen Recensionen von Ottos und Rahewins Gesta Friderici I," *Sitzungsberichte der königlich preussischen Aka-
demie der Wissenschaften zu Berlin* (Jahrgang 1884), pp. 331–42.

Wattenbach, Wilhelm. Deutschlands Geschichtsquellen im Mittelalter. 5th
ed. Berlin, 1885–86. See II, 241–56.

Wild. Radevicus und sein Verhältniss zu Otto von Freisingen. Görlitz, 1865.

INDEX

Aachen, crowning of Barbarossa at, 17, 116-17

Abelard, Peter, 4, 7, 143; silence imposed upon, by pope and bishops, 82; most controversial figure of twelfth century, 82*n*; education, intellect, character, 83; opinions and teachings: trial of, 83-88; books burned, 84, 85; apologetic by, 87; death, 88

Absolution for crusaders, 73

Acerbus Morena, 10

Adalbero, abp. of Trier, 64

Adalbert, abp. of Salzburg, 339

Adam, abbot of Ebrach, 75

Adam of Petit-Pont, 89

Adda, river, 207, 208, 227, 272*n*

Adelaide, daughter of Margrave Dietpold: separated from Barbarossa, 123

Adolph, count of Altena, son of, 108, 168, 169

Aegean (*erroneously* Tyrrhenian) Sea, 80*n*

Aemilia, province, 126, 127

Agnes, daughter of Frederick of Saarbrücken, marriage to Duke Frederick II, 53; son and daughter, 53

Agnes, daughter of Henry IV, 43; wife of Frederick I, duke of Swabia, 4, 41*n*; their sons, 41*n*, 43; marriage to Leopold, margrave of Austria, 41*n*, 43; their sons, 42*n*, 246

Agnes, sister of Otto of Freising and wife of Vladislav II of Poland, 64*n*, 76*n*, 175*n*, 246*n*

Agnes of Austria, marriage to Stephen III of Hungary, 336

Aimeradus, archpriest, 322

Alatri, bp. of, 318

Alberic, bp. of Lodi, 234

Alberic, bp. of Reggio, 234

Alberic, knight of Verona, 156, 158

Alberic of Rheims, 84

Albert, cardinal priest of the title of St. Lawrence *in Lucina,* 297

Albert I (the Elder), abp. of Mainz, 49; rebellions instigated by, 45, 46, 47; obtained regalia from Empress Matilda, 48; brother: death, 53

Albert II (the Younger), abp. of Mainz, 53

Albert, son of Vladislav of Bohemia, chosen abp. of Salzburg, 338

Albert, bp. of Freising, 263, 318; Otto's successor, 251; forced to swear obedience to Paschal (III, antipope), 336; released from schism by Guido's death, 338

Albert, bp. of Trent, 198

Albert, chaplain of Conrad III, 56, 59

Albert, count of Tyrol, 216

Albert of Meissen, 108

Albert the Bear, margrave of Saxony, 52, 160

Albo, bp.-elect of Passau, 339

Albo, canon of Freising, 335

Alboin, Scandinavian leader, 127

Aldericus, chancellor of Louis VII, 187

Alemannia, countries for which term used, 12, 42, 174*n*

Alexander III, Pope (Roland Bandinelli), 180*n*; chosen pope by anti-imperial cardinals, 282; had been Pope Hadrian IV's chief adviser: political leanings, 282, 319; when consecrated, 288, 292, 297; his letter explaining the election, 289 ff.; resulting schism in Church, 288-301, 307-29; letter from cardinals supporting, 297-99; accusations against, by pro-imperialist party, 319; anathematized by antipope, 323, 328; Emperor Manuel intriguing with, 336*n*; fled from Rome, 338; fate of two supporters, 338*n*

Alexander, bp. of Liége, 337*n*